PRAISE FOR
The Power of Ritual

A beautifully written, impressively researched, and intelligently structured book about the history and practice of ritual throughout the world, which expands our understanding of what ritual is and what it does in fascinating ways. A thorough and comprehensive analysis of this subject, it will be the definitive text in the field, of great value to the academic community as a teaching tool, and to professionals, clinicians, and practitioners as a seminal reference work.

—Altie Karper, Editorial Director, Schocken Books, Knopf Doubleday Publishing Group, Random House, Inc.

This is an exquisite and informative book of value to anyone confronting—and trying to understand—ritual processes. It has many potential readers: clergy, professors, students, and lay people interested in understanding, designing, and performing rituals. I found that virtually every page will motivate teachers to engage conversation among their students. I wish that this book had been available during my long teaching career—I would have used it in all my relevant courses!

—Claire R. Farrer PhD, author of *Living Life's Circle: Mescalero Apache Cosmovision* and *Thunder Rides a Black Horse*

This book was as much an eye-opener epiphany for me as Davis-Floyd's first book *Birth as an American Rite of Passage*. Before I read *The Power of Ritual*, I thought I knew what ritual was, yet now I know that it is so much more—it can be everything from a simple conversation-opener to a powerful healing process, from an individual's daily habits to full-scale ceremony. I have learned much from this book that I can apply to my own life to enable me to more consciously perform my daily, family, and professional rituals, much to my benefit and that of others.

—Debra Pascali-Bonaro LCCE, BDT/PDT(DONA), co-author of *Orgasmic Birth: Your Guide to a Safe, Satisfying and Pleasurable Birth Experience*

Disclaimer—I am not an anthropologist. But I loved this book. It reads like a Pulitzer Prize-winning novel. The writing is both scientific and personal, easily accessible to anthropologists and informed lay people. We travel with the authors across the globe, from the fishing villages of the Trobriand Islands to the obstetrical units of modern Western hospitals where we learn about the rituals practiced there. Yet to me, this book is much more than an in-depth exploration of the meaning and efficacy of rituals. It is a cornucopia of fresh and exciting insights into our culture, society and human nature. *The Power of Ritual* is a powerful and enjoyable book and I recommend it without reservation.

—Thomas R Verny MD, DHL, DPsych, FRCPC, FAPA, author of *The Secret Life of the Unborn Child*, Founder of the Association for Pre- and Perinatal Psychology and Health (APPPAH), Editor-in-chief, JOPPPAH.

Jointly authored by a cultural/medical anthropologist and one of the first neuroanthropologists, this book is the go-to resource for anyone seeking a holistic, modern understanding of the human phenomenon of ritual. It will have a wide audience, from the general public to college students in anthropology, sociology, and psychology, among others. Seasoned, professional authors at the pinnacles of their careers, Robbie Davis-Floyd and Charles Laughlin not only assemble information and insights from a panoply of anthropologically-known societies, but also enrich their discussion of ritual's power from their own personal life experiences. The results are exciting and potentially life-changing for anyone with an enquiring mind and heart.

Readers will find here a comprehensive and logical exploration of topics integral to the understanding of ritual, ranging from its use of symbolism, its cognitive matrix, and its relationship to myth and the process of "truing," to the mechanics of altered states of consciousness and the power of ritual performance in generating transformation. One of the centers of the book lies in its explanation of how the creation stories of subjugated peoples of the world contribute to their ongoing cultural resilience and ability to generate and maintain balanced personalities in the face of injustice and deprivation. This central insight can be used by all in the quest to achieve fair and meaningful lives in harmony with others on our planet through the power of ritual.

—Megan Biesele, author of *Women Like Meat: The Folklore and Foraging Ideology of the Kalahari Ju ʻhoansi*, coauthor of *Healing Makes Our Hearts Happy: Spirituality and Cultural Transformation among the Kalahari Ju ʻhoansi*

Ritual is indeed a powerful force at the core of what it is to be human. In this comprehensive survey, Davis-Floyd and Laughlin combine academic and experiential perspectives on something all of us share by virtue of being human. The capacity for ritual is hard-wired into our biogenetic program but takes different forms in different cultures. For most of our time on earth, humans have been hunters and gatherers living in small-scale societies. Our rituals then emphasized transformative experience through various means of achieving an altered state of consciousness: lucid dreaming, vision quests, music and dance, and psychoactive drugs. As these egalitarian societies evolved into hierarchical agricultural, herding, and industrial societies, rituals often served as mechanisms of state control. As the book's title suggests, ritual is a power that may be used for good or evil. The authors do explain the dark side of ritual, yet stress ritual's ability to carry humans through times of great stress and even to support a a worldview the authors call "global humanism." While the book is solidly grounded in anthropological and neurological evidence, it comes to life in the authors' stories of their own experiences. Above all, the authors write well and draw the reader into their stories.

—Robin Ridington, Professor Emeritus of Anthropology at the University of British Columbia, author of *Trail to Heaven: Knowledge and Narrative in a Northern Native Community,* and coauthor of *Where Happiness Dwells: A History of the Dane-zaa First Nations* and *Blessing for a Long Time: The Sacred Pole of the Omaha Tribe.*

The Power of Ritual

by

Robbie Davis-Floyd

and

Charles D. Laughlin

DAILY GRAIL PUBLISHING

The Power of Ritual
Copyright © Robbie Davis-Floyd and Charles D. Laughlin, 2016.

All rights reserved. No part of this book may be reproduced, stored, or transmitted in any form without permission in writing from the publisher, except by a reviewer who may quote brief passages for review purposes.

ISBN: 978-0-9874224-9-1

Daily Grail Publishing
Brisbane, Australia
publications@dailygrail.com
www.dailygrail.com

Robbie Davis-Floyd:

I dedicate this book to Ashley Lundgren Floyd, wife of my son and daughter of my heart, for walking the road with me.

Charles D. Laughlin:

I dedicate this book to my lovely daughter Kate and her magnificent Tim—may they live long and prosper.

Table of Contents

Foreword by Betty Sue Flowers, editor for Joseph Campbell's *The Power of Myth*	xvii
Acknowledgments	xix
Glossary of Technical Terms and Abbreviations	xxi
Preface: About the Authors and Their Academic and Personal Engagement with Ritual	xxxi
Chapter 1: What is Ritual? An Introduction to Thoughts, Theories and Definitions	1

Animal and Human Ritual as Behavioral Coordination and Communication

Why Ritual Matters: Its Effectiveness in the World

A Working Definition of Ritual

   Patterning, Repetition, and Symbolism: Coordination and Communication

   Rituals as Enactments of Beliefs and Values

Thoughts and Theories about Ritual

   Roy Rappaport: The Role of Ritual in Ecological Management

   Scott Atran: Ritual Involvement in Cooperation and Conflict

   Candace Aleorta and Richard Sosis: Ritual and Emotional Adaptation

   Caroline Humphrey and James Laidlaw: Ritual as Archetypal Action

   Pascal Boyer: A Cognitive Theory of Ritual

   Harvey Whitehouse: Modes of Religiosity

   Victor Turner, Richard Schechner, and Ronald Grimes: Ritual as Performance

The Characteristics of Ritual and the Contents of This Book

Chapter 2: Symbolism in Ritual	31

Symbols Are Brain Talk

The Core, Emotional, and Cortical Brains

    The Core Brain
    The Emotional Brain
    The Cortical Brain
    Integration of the Three Levels of the Brain
The Power of Symbols
    How Symbols Work
    Symbolic Penetration
    Socialization and Ritual Symbolic Penetration
Core Symbols
Interpreting Core Symbolism
    Labs as Rituals
    The So of East Africa, Their "Gray Goop," and Charlie's Efforts to Understand Its Symbolic Meaning
    Interpreting Symbolism in Unfamiliar Cultures: Experiential Knowledge vs. Rational Analysis
    Understanding and Acting on Core Symbolism: Michael Winkelman and the Messenger Mice
    Oral and Written Texts: The Changing Meanings of Core Symbols over Time
Examples of Symbolic Interpretation
    Confrontation with the Quintessence of Evil
    Naro's Unhappy Resting Place
    The Great Kettle Debate
Summary: The Power of Symbols

Chapter 3: The Cognitive Matrix of Ritual: Myths and Paradigms   69

The Cognitive Imperative and the Cycle of Meaning
    An Example of Mythic Interpretation: The Navajo Origin Myth
    Another Example of Mythic Interpretation: Dream Incubation
The Myth/Paradigm Ritual Complex
    Myths and Paradigms
    Indigenous Psychology and the Myth-Ritual Complex
    The Myth-Ritual Complex and Human Development
    Ritual as Mythic Enactment: The Navajo *Kinaalda* Ceremony
    Ritual as Paradigmatic Enactment
The Technocratic, Humanistic, and Holistic Paradigms of Birth and Health

Care and Their Enactments in Ritual
Summary: The Human Need to Understand

Chapter 4: Myths, Paradigms, Rituals, and the Process of Truing   99
Myth and the Process of Truing
    Truing and the Brain
    Truing, Intuition and Action in the World
    Truing and Culture: Sensate, Ideational and Idealistic Cultures
Myth, Truing, the Physics of the Vacuum, and the Origin of Our Universe
    Myth, Paradigms, Ritual Enactment, and Truing
    Mythic and Paradigmatic Matrices: Revitalization and Change
How the Cycle of Meaning Operates along the Twin Axes of Instantiation and Interpretation: The Sun Dance and the American Space Program
    Sun Dance: The Twin Axes in the Mythic Matrix
    NASA's Space Program and the Twin Axes in the Paradigmatic Matrix
Summary: The Human Need to Know

Chapter 5: Ritual Drivers: Generating and Controlling States of Consciousness   127
States and Warps of Consciousness
Mimesis and States of Consciousness
Types of Ritual Drivers and Examples of How They Work
    Ritual Drivers at Work: The Ancient !Kung Trance Dance and Contemporary Breath Therapy
    Percussion and Transition: One Student's Intentional Use of Ritual Drivers
    Electronic Fetal Monitoring as an Extrinsic Ritual Driver
Ritual and Warp Control
Monophasic and Polyphasic Cultures
Transferring Information across States of Consciousness
Ritual and the Control of States of Consciousness
Ritual Drivers and the Cycle of Meaning
Portals as Ritual Drivers into Multiple Realities
Why Are Ritual Drivers So Compelling?
Summary: SOCs, WOCs, and Ritual Drivers

Chapter 6: Ritual Techniques and Technologies   161

Ritual Technique and Technology: Divination and Intent
    Rituals of Divination: The Purloined Pots
What Is "Technology"?
    Internal and External Coordination
    Experiencing Technologically
    From Technique to Technology
Ritual Technique and Technology
    Ritual Reinforces an Instrumental Lifeworld
    Ritual and Prior Knowledge
    Ritual as Divine Inspiration
    Ritual as a Vehicle for Psychic Power
Instrumentality and Ritual
    Spooky Causation in Modern Science
    Robbie's Spooky Quantum Physics Story: Peyton, the DFW Airport, and a Spontaneous Ritual Performance
    The Implements of Ritual Practice
    Hi-Tech and Virtual Rituals
Summary: Ritual Technique and Technology

Chapter 7: Ritual Framing: Order, Formality, Inviolability   193

Physical and Non-Physical Frames
Ritual Frames: Energy and Power
The Meaning and Power of Shrines and Altars
Formality and Order in Ritual: Why They Matter
    The Trobriand Islanders: Fishing, Canoes, and Cranking Gears
    Bolivian Tin Miners: "The Devil is in the details"
    Contemporary Obstetricians, Ritual, and Danger: The Power Is in the Rituals
Inviolability and Inevitability: "The Ritual Train"
    A Wedding and a Cesarean Section: Riding the Ritual Train
Breaking Frame: Purposeful Disruption of Ritual
The Ludic Dimension of Ritual: Breaking the Frame to Enhance the Energy
Framing and Flow
Ritual Order: Enhancing Courage and Confidence

When Rituals Fail
Summary: Ritual Order and Ritual Failure

Chapter 8: Ritual as Performance: Generating Emotion, Belief and Transformation   225

Ritual, Belief, and Emotion
    Ritual Healing from Soul Loss through an Indigenous Shamanic Ceremony: Juan the Chamula
    Ritual Healing from "Soul Loss" through Contemporary Psychotherapy: Robbie the Anthropologist
    Robbie the Anthropologist and Juan the Chamula: Healing from Soul Loss across Time, Space, and Culture
    Western Medicine: A Differing Perspective
The Excitation and Relaxation Nervous Systems: Ritual, Flow, and Ecstasy
Ritual Mechanisms for Engendering Emotion and Belief
    Ritual Performance
    Masters of Ritual: Charisma and Ritual Command
    Ritual and Emotionally Charged Beliefs
    Ritual as a Generator of Collective Effervescence
    Raw Ritual Experience and Its Cultural Interpretation
    Beauty as a Ritual Mechanism
    Beauty and the Mandala of Perception
    Drama: Acting, Stylization, Staging, Intensification
Rites of Passage and Religious Conversions: Transformation through Ritual
Ritual and Cognitive Transformation
    Religious and Cult Conversions
    Robbie's Unwanted Conversion Experience
    Conversion Experiences and Ritual Socialization
Summary: Ritual, Emotion, and Belief

Chapter 9: Ritual and the Four Stages of Cognition   263

Cognitive Simplification: How Rituals Speak to the Masses
Concrete and Fluid Thinking: The Four Stages of Cognition
    Concrete Thinking: Stages 1 and 2
        Stage 1 Thinking: Naïve Realism, Fundamentalism, and Fanaticism
            Stage 1 Thinking: Maladaptive Manifestations

    Stage 2 Thinking: Ethnocentrism
        Stage 2 Thinking: Maladaptive Manifestations
  Fluid Thinking: Stages 3 and 4
    Stage 3 Thinking: Cultural Relativism
    Stage 4 Thinking: Global Humanism
Ritual and the 4 Stages of Cognition: Stage 1: Naïve Realism/Fundamentalism/Fanaticism, Stage 2: Ethnocentrism, Stage 3: Cultural Relativism, and Stage 4: Global Humanism
  Examples of Stage 4 Rituals: Midwives and Women
Ritual, Cognition, and Stress: Substage and Stabilization
  Cognitive Anchors: Earthquakes and House Fires
  Cognitive Anchors and Rituals of Stabilization
  Eustress and Distress
  Ritual and Stress Reduction
  Stress and the Myth/Ritual Complex
  Stress and the Modern Paradigm/Ritual Complex
Summary: Concrete and Fluid Thinking, The Four Stages of Cognition, Ritual, and Stress

Chapter 10: Ritual's Paradoxical Roles: Preserving the Status Quo and Effecting Social Change   295

Cognitive Simplification: How Rituals Speak to the Masses

Historical Relationships vs. Ecological Adaptation: The Consistent Human Choice to Preserve the Historical Status Quo through the Rituals That Enact It

  Cultural Conservatism and Cultural Change

Cultural Mnemonics, Cultural "Memories"

From Big-Men to Kings to Dictators: Changing and then Preserving the Cultural Status Quo through Ritual

Ritualized Control through Social Consensus–or Not!

Effecting Social Change through Ritual: Revitalization Movements

Revitalization Movements and Collective Rituals: Failure and Success in Effecting Social Change

Revitalization Movements among Traditional People

  Cargo Cults as Failed Revitalization Movements

  A Paiute Prophet: Wovoka and the Creation of the Ghost Dance Religion

  Charlie Yahey: A Dane-zaa Dreamer and His Invention of a Myth

Current Revitalization Movements

Ritual as Adaptive Technique

The Contemporary Invention of Ritual: Effecting Social Change

    The Paradigm Shift of Holistic Obstetricians: "The Good Guys and Girls" of Brazil

    Herb Kelleher and Southwest Airlines: The Intentional Creation of a Consciously Alternative Corporate Culture

Summary: Ritual, Cultural Preservation, and Social Change

Chapter 11: Designing Rituals   327

Jerusalem

Religious Syncretism as Adaptive Ritual Strategy

Implicit vs. Explicit Ideologies and Their Enactment in Ritual

    Quesalid and Implicit vs. Explicit Rituals

The Intentional Creation of Personal Rituals: Two Memorial Services, Two Weddings, and One Birthday Party

    Peyton's Memorial Service/Birthday Party: A Conscious Ritual Enactment of Personal Beliefs and Values That Worked

    Peyton's Second Memorial Service: A Ritual That Failed

    A Wedding That Worked: Chris and Lisa

    Weddings and Funerals: Lessons from Personal Rituals

    Rima's "Sensational at Sixty" Surprise Birthday Ritual

Ray Robertson Designs a Puberty Rite

Our Pink and Ruby Tents for Adolescent Girls *(written by Jeanna Lurie)*

Charlie's Personal Tantric Rituals

    An Aside: "Tantra" in the West

    Tantric Dreamwork

Prayer Practice among Evangelical Christians

Designing Personal Rituals: Healing and Danger

Summary: Designing Personal Rituals – Failure and Success

Chapter 12: Conclusion: The Power of Ritual   369

Chapter Summaries

Parting Remarks

Appendix: How to Create and Perform an Effective Stage 4 Ritual: Things to Remember and Include   381

Author Biographies	383
References	385
Index	401

Foreword

by Betty Sue Flowers, Editor of
Joseph Campbell and the Power of Myth

As series consultant for Bill Moyers' PBS program, *Joseph Campbell and the Power of Myth*, I was often asked what accounted for Campbell's amazing popularity. "It wasn't just his knowledge of mythology," I would answer, "but his great storytelling abilities, his capacity to personalize the study of myth so that he presented himself as a student, just like us, and his inclination, always, to relate myths to the concerns of everyday life."

In *The Power of Ritual*, Robbie Davis-Floyd and Charles D. Laughlin have done for ritual what Campbell did for myth—tell stories, personalize the study of ritual, and relate ritual to the concerns of everyday life.

In many ways, the power of ritual is greater than the power of myth in that ritual lasts longer. Christians, for example, decorate Easter eggs and Christmas trees every year—the origins of these rituals in pagan myth having been obscured for centuries. And early Christian missionaries, like the Romans before them, found that if they kept the *rituals* of the local gods they were replacing, the local *myths* would gradually morph into versions of the new story that was being imported. Perhaps, at some level, it is easier to change a belief than a habit, especially if that habit is designed to procure favor and protection.

As we know from the way that children often insist on a particular bedtime ritual before releasing themselves into sleep, it's the repetition, not the content, of the ritual that creates its power. For a brief moment, our vulnerability to the unknown is set aside because we know what will happen next. As with the principle of "three times" so often encountered in folk tales, we experience the first time something happens as an event; the second time establishes a pattern; but the third time is a qualitatively different experience because we *anticipate* it. Rather than fate happening to us, we dance with it by knowing the steps in advance.

Repetition itself is a human compulsion, as Freud so famously pointed out, and when members of a group perform a repetitive act together, the individual becomes part of a larger, synchronized whole, at least for that moment. The evolutionary advantage of a group that can synchronize its members to act together is powerful.

All these aspects of ritual and more are explored by two authors whose anthropological insight ranges from brain function to birth practices and from Brazilian doctors to Buddhist lamas. In *The Power of Ritual* they offer readers a personal journey through a universal landscape.

Reference

Campbell, Joseph, with Bill Moyers (1988) *The Power of Myth*, edited by Betty Sue Flowers. New York: Doubleday.

Acknowledgments

We wholeheartedly thank our reviewers Megan Biesele, Claire (Ginger) Farrer, Betty Sue Flowers, Henci Goer, Brigitte Jordan, Robin Ridington, Eugenia (Nia) Georges, Greg Taylor, Thomas Verny, Debra Pascali Bonaro, and Elizabeth Davis for their invaluable contributions to the improvement of this book.

Glossary of Terms Used

(The terms and abbreviations we commonly use in this book as we define them for our own purposes)

Affective semantics: Emotional meaning.

Altered states of consciousness (ASCs): States of consciousness (SOCs) other than normal waking consciousness, such as dreaming, trance, hypnosis, fugue state (reversible amnesia), and so forth.

Archetype: From the work of Carl G. Jung, who recognized that certain symbols seem to have universal occurrence and appeal. Their universality suggests that their meaning is "hard-wired" into the human brain. In Jung's sense, archetypes are encoded in the human brain as the result of thousands of generations of species-typical experience.

Archetypal cosmology: Applying a Jungian perspective, the universal aspects of cultural cosmologies.

BCE: Before the common era, now used as standard terminology to replace the Christian "BC"-"before Christ."

Brain structures:

- the *core brain*, which mediates somatic regulation, metabolism, physical and psychological arousal, etc.
- the *emotional brain*, which mediates emotional states
- the *cortical brain* which mediates imagination, thought, modulation of emotion, planning, etc.

Biogenetic structuralism: A school of thought and theory that integrates sociocultural anthropology and the neurosciences.

Cargo cults: Millenarian-type movements in which people believe that if they follow certain ritual practices, they will cause resources or wealth to appear by magic.

CE: Common Era, now standard terminology replacing the Christian "AD"—Anno Domini, "the year of the Lord," meaning the era after Christ.

Cognitive imperative: The human drive to order the world into significant elements and events and unify them into a systematic cognitive whole, aka a belief system or worldview.

Cognitive regression: Regressing from complex to simpler ways of thinking, usually under conditions of extreme stress.

Collective consciousness: What a people collectively experience and believe, including how they tend to think about the world they live in and its meaning.

Core symbols: Powerful cultural symbols that carry significant meaning for all or most members of a given society or culture because they represent its core values.

Cultural relativism: A way of thinking about and understanding cultures by comparing them to each other. The understanding that the meaning and value of a cultural trait (behavior, action, belief, practice) can only be evaluated from within a cultural frame of reference. Cultural relativists tend to refrain from assuming that any particular culture is superior to any other.

Cultural universal: A phenomenon—such as shelter, language, finding and preparing food, symbol, ritual, myth, etc.—found in every human society.

Cosmology: A people's/culture's systemic understanding of the universe, their place in it, and their relationship to it, always depicted and enacted in their body of myths, their rituals, and, more recently, in their paradigms.

Cycle of meaning: Each society tries to integrate its collective knowledge, or worldview, with the experiences of individual members. A worldview is expressed through the culture's myth/paradigm/ritual complex in such a way that it leads people to interpret their experiences in ways that bring alive and confirm that worldview. This tautology—you believe in something, then you interpret your experiences in ways that confirm your beliefs, so then you believe even more deeply—is what we mean by a culture's "cycle of meaning."

GLOSSARY OF TERMS USED

Decode: Figure out the meaning of.

Distress: "Bad stress" that can drive us to hyper-emotional, Substage thinking and reactions, and can lead to physical breakdown, heart attacks, cancer and other nasty diseases and mental problems.

Eidetic image: A clear, vivid, stable image of some object before the mind's eye, most useful in meditation.

Ethnocentrism: The tendency for people to experience, evaluate, interpret, and respond to events from their own limited cultural point of view, and to believe and affirm that *their way is best*.

Entrain: To link-up (or to synchronize) elements, organs and processes in the way that compartments are linked together to make a train. Also, to synchronize one's own bodily movements and feelings with those of others.

Exaptation: The facility by which physiological (even neurophysiological) structures either (1) proved adaptive long ago and later on prove adaptive in new ways; or (2) were not particularly adaptive before, but prove to be adaptive to new situations now.

Eustress: Good stress, in that it challenges us to peak cognition, positive feelings, and adaptive action.

Expressive culture: Forms and types of human cultural behavior that represent ideals and normative patterns of behavior, how humans are represented to each other, appropriate social behavior, and appropriate emotional reactions. (e.g., religion, folklore, stories, chants, drama, art, performance, literature, proverbs, poetry, music, ballads).

Fanatics: Individuals who believe so strongly that their way is the only right way that they want to make everyone else fit inside their box/belief system, or disappear.

Fixed action pattern: Animals, including humans, are genetically endowed with sequences of behavior that, once begun, tend to continue until they are completed.

Flow: A state of consciousness (SOC) in which there is no inhibition, repression, fear or hesitation. Flow is the experience of fully "letting go" into the action, which in turn results in creativity and happiness. Flow occurs when the central nervous system is totally involved in an act or course of action. There is no interference by alternative systems in the body. Metabolic, motor, emotional and cognitive-imaging systems are all entrained (synchronized) in a single, unitary and unfolding activity.

Fundamentalists: True believers of any religious persuasion or political ideology (Jehovah's Witnesses, Southern Baptists, Mormons, some Islamists, Orthodox Jews, etc.). Fundamentalists know that there are other belief systems and ways of thinking out there in the world, but deeply believe that *their worldview is the right one for everyone* and that those who do not adopt it are at best misguided and at worst, doomed.

Global humanism: The understanding that all people everywhere are interconnected, and should participate in a global democracy, recognize a set of universal human rights, and enter into a planet-wide social contract that guarantees basic human rights to all human beings.

Hazing: The imposition of physical and mental hardships during initiatory rites of passage, designed to break down participants' normal sense of self in order to rebuild it in conformity with the belief and value system of the group into which they are being initiated.

Idealistic and ideational cultures: Both adopt a more balanced view in which knowledge derived from the local mode becomes integrated with knowledge arising from development of archetypal structures. It is in the balanced idealistic cultures, as well as the more extreme ideational cultures, that a corpus of mythological tradition forms a living core of knowledge. From the point of view of people living in an extremely ideational culture, what we might consider "mystical" knowledge or experience is not mystical at all. It is simply "the way things are." In these cultures, all states of consciousness are of relevance to the people's understanding of themselves and their reality.

Invented tradition: New cultural "traditions" consciously created in stylistic similarity with older traditions, and often enacted in new rituals that also seem and feel traditional, thereby giving entirely new belief systems the feel and flavor of being strongly entrenched and sanctioned by ancient tradition even when they are not.

Indigenous psychologies: The cultural views, theories, conjectures, classifications, assumptions and metaphors—together with notions embedded in social institutions—held by indigenous peoples that have to do with psychological topics. These psychologies are indigenous theories about the nature of mind, the person and his/her relation to the world. They contain advice and injunctions about the way that people should act and feel, and how they can find happiness and success in life. An indigenous psychology embodies the culture's own perspectives on the nature of humans and their behaviors, values, and beliefs. Indigenous psychologies organize individual experience and collective social life and address a broad range of conceptions and issues, including consciousness, agency, social hierarchy, and the physical and supernatural worlds.

Initial structures: Rudimentary, genetically programmed circuits of neural cells, many of which are present in a baby before its birth, in which the neural structures that develop through childhood to eventually become the adult brain have their beginnings.

Intention movements: Incompletely performed actions that signal a readiness for certain activities (e.g., a set of movements that indicate that a bird is preparing for flight, or for mating).

Instantiate: To represent a (usually cultural) abstraction by a concrete instance, have it come alive in lived experience, as in "heroes instantiate ideals." To embody an idea in experience.

Just-so stories: Traditional cultural stories that explain naturally occurring phenomena to children in culturally meaningful, often humorous, ways.

Lifeworld: An individual or cultural world of life experience infused with cultural meaning.

Limen (from the Latin, meaning "threshold"): A cognitively experienced passageway or tunnel through which the consciousness of an individual or group may pass to an alternative state of consciousness (SOC), or to a new social identity.

Mimesis: The ability to mimic—a fundamental expressive capacity underlying human cognitive evolution, mythic thought, and ritual action.

Mimesis (Inter-state): in which activities in one SOC influence experiences had in another SOC. In order for this to happen, memory of the activities in one SOC (say, being "awake") are retained across the warp and thus can inform experiences had in another SOC (say a "dream").

Monophasic: Monophasic cultures are characterized by a marked concern for the world as presented to the senses and are all about material values, with relatively less concern for inner growth, spiritual development, and balance among states of consciousness.

Mnemonics: Cultural artifacts and institutions like art, monuments, writing, story-telling, architecture, folklore, etc. that can operate as *reminders* of information relevant to both the past and the future.

Myth: An origin story—a story that cultural members tell about where they came from, who they are, and what their existence means. Occasionally a myth, or system of myths (a *mythology*) will touch upon the future of things to come.

Multi-vocal: Expressing many meanings with one single voice—e.g., symbols are multi-vocal.

Neural networks: Complex brain circuits that mediate symbols and their meaning, as well as the moment-by-moment stream of consciousness.

Naïve realists: Individuals who believe that the world of their experience is the real extramental world. Individuals raised in one culture with one unified belief system who simply do not know that there is any other way to think about or experience the world, or have so little exposure to other ways of thinking that they discount them as irrelevant.

Paradigm: A cognitive model, or systemic way of thinking, that provides a template for individual and cultural perceptions and interpretations of reality, consisting of a set of cohesive and internally consistent principles, tenets, beliefs, propositions, or guidelines for action.

Penetration/Symbolic penetration: The ways in which something outside the body links up to a set of cultural meanings in our brains through a vast series of neural networks. *Expressive penetration* occurs when we act in a symbolic way in order to produce meaning in another person.

Polyphasic: We use this term to describe cultures that incorporate multiple states of consciousness into their worldview and self-identity.

Polysemic: Having multiple meanings simultaneously. A symbol may have a number of meanings, some of which are context-specific. A cross worn around a person's neck may mean something different than a cross tattooed on a person's bicep.

Plot: The elaboration of stories or situation of ritual elements in a meaningful sequence.

Portalling: Sometimes shamans will use meditation devices to aid them in moving from one metaphysical realm to another—a process of transforming SOCs called *portalling*. A meditation object used to alter the SOC of a shaman or practitioner is called a *portalling device*.

Praxis: Practice of any kind that is socially embedded and meaningful and can be interpreted as such by theorists and analysts.

Revitalization movement: A deliberate, organized, conscious effort by members of a society to construct a more satisfying culture through the creation of a social movement and its complement of rituals to revitalize that culture.

Rhythmo-affective semantics: A rhythm-centered system of meaning that expresses fundamental emotions.

Rite of passage: A series of rituals designed to conduct an individual (or group) from one social state or status to another, thereby effecting transformations both in society's perceptions of the individual and in the individual's perception of her- or himself.

Rite of reversal: A series of rituals that constitute the inverse, reverse, or the opposite of culturally normal behavior.

Ritual: A patterned, repetitive, and symbolic enactment of a cultural (or individual) belief or value.

Ritual driver: Any recurrent element in a ritual that has a predictable effect on the bodies and minds of participants. There are essentially two different kinds of ritual drivers: *extrinsic drivers* that depend upon stimuli outside a person's body (drumming, flickering flames, the use of an icon like a mandala, the electronic fetal monitor in childbirth), and *intrinsic drivers* that are initiated from within the person's body (fasting, breathing techniques, meditation).

Sensate cultures: Cultures that privilege local ways of knowing over knowing in the more archetypal cosmological mode. Sensate cultures, like that of the ancient Romans and our own contemporary technocracies, produce populations that are off-balance toward a materialistic, secular, empirical understanding of the world. One of the characteristics of a sensate culture is that its members will tend *not* to reverence a living mythology.

Shaman: A traditional spiritual practitioner usually focused on healing people through altering his or her own SOC. Shamans are also often experts in the use of local medicinal plants for healing, and are almost always experts in their cultural cosmological belief systems and in various psychotherapeutic techniques. So-called "flying shamans" may be specialists in leaving their body and traveling to the spirit world to communicate with ancestors, spirits and gods to attain information for, or carry messages from the people. He or she may retrieve lost souls or objects.

Stages of cognition: Various levels of complexity of thinking about the lifeworlds of individuals and cultures.

State of consciousness (SOC): A recurring and identifiable episode of experience which typically is recognized as distinct from other such episodes, and perhaps labeled: for example, we may say we are "awake," "stoned," "drunk," "depressed," "dreaming," "excited," "tired-out," "angry," "out-of-body," "playing," etc.

Strange-making: Making the commonplace strange by juxtaposing it with the unfamiliar, such as shaving the heads of military trainees so that they suddenly seem strange to themselves, as a way of breaking down their identity so that it can be reconstructed anew via an initiatory rite of passage.

Substage: A mental/neurological condition that occurs when an individual's cognitive system bottoms-out and is unable to deal with complexity, usually occurring under conditions of extreme distress and intense emotion.

Symbol: An object, idea or action that "stands for something else," providing a source of cultural meaning; e.g., the flag stands for the nation, the cross for a religion, a brand icon for a product or company.

Symbolic inversion: Metaphorically turning specific elements of the belief system upside-down or inside-out, so that the high is brought low, and the low is raised high, and the world in general is thrown into confusion—a common technique in rites of passage and annual cultural festivals in which the poor can pretend to be rich, for example.

Symbolic process: The process by which the brain makes sense of what it perceives via symbols.

Symbolizing: The process by which an object or event in the world is attributed meaning within our brains.

Symbolic pregnance: The meanings associated with a symbol can be vast; for instance, the feelings and beliefs that are associated with a nation's flag may be so great, we would say that the flag is "pregnant" with meaning.

Synaptic plasticity: The ability of the brain's system of synapses involved in memory storage to change, grow and become elaborated.

Syncretism, religious: Religious syncretism is the process by which people combine elements of differing religions, usually in an effort to preserve some parts of an indigenous religion while conforming sufficiently to the religion dominant in their region to appear to be practicing it.

Technology: Techniques for doing something that involve the use of artifacts. Technology is a special type of symbolic process involving both activity in the world and feedback about the effects of such activity upon the world—the "praxis" aspect of symbolic activity.

The technological imperative: "If you *can* do it with technology, you *must and will* do it with technology."

Technocracy: A contemporary society organized around an ideology of progress through the development and utilization of high technology and the global transmission of information and ideas. The prime value in a technocratic society is efficiency via the use of high technologies.

Thin description: A simple description of what took place, lacking any kind of interpretation.

Thick description: Interpretive description that layers in the meaning of the event.

True, or true-up: To make imagined/mythological/cosmological/paradigmatic reality match environmental reality well enough for people to survive and thrive in the world. When our experience is trued sufficiently, we believe that the world of our experience *is* reality, or at least act as if we do.

Truing: (see "true").

Trued knowledge: Knowledge rendered sufficiently accurate to enable humans to adapt to their environments well enough to be able to survive and thrive in them.

Warps of consciousness (WOCs or warps): The points of experiential and neurophysiological transition between states of consciousness.

Preface

About the Authors and Their Academic and Personal Engagement with Ritual

This book is written by two anthropologists—Robbie Elizabeth Davis-Floyd and Charles Dennis Laughlin—with different histories of engagement with the study and practice of ritual. (In keeping with the informal tone we wish to maintain, throughout the book we will refer to ourselves as "Robbie" and "Charlie" rather than "Davis-Floyd" and "Laughlin.") Most of the time we will speak with a unified voice, but in this Preface, we will speak individually in order to give our readers a feeling for why each of us is so interested in ritual, and why it is important to us to communicate what we have found out.

Robbie Davis-Floyd

This book grows out of my thirty years of research on ritual and technology in American childbirth, and in particular, out of a workshop I have often presented on "The Power of Ritual" to diverse groups around the country. Audiences for this workshop have included priests, psychotherapists, physicists, female professionals, social scientists, health care practitioners (nurses, midwives, physicians, childbirth educators), men's movement participants and workshop leaders, business managers, New Agers, university students, drug and alcohol addicts, members (or former members) of cults, and aerospace engineers. During the course of these workshops, I have often noted a high level of confusion among people who are designing and performing rituals on a regular basis as a part of, for example, religious or spiritual retreats, psychotherapy intensives, men's movement weekends-in-the-woods (popular in recent past decades), and self-help seminars. They tell me that they "intuit" what ritual is all about, but their sense of it is vague, unformed. They come to my workshops to find out what they themselves are actually up to! I am always delighted when such people show up in my audiences, as one of the major reasons why I started teaching these workshops was my concern about the uncritical use of ritual that has characterized the explosion of interest in the new spirituality, alternative healing, and self-help movements, to name only a few. Ritual is an extraordinarily powerful socializing tool that can be just as easily manipulated for ill as used for good. The naiveté of many contemporary ritual practitioners has worried me for a long time, and these workshops—and now this book—serve as my way of combating that naiveté. I often receive letters of thanks from such practitioners for "raising their consciousness" about precisely how ritual works, about its very real benefits, and about its equally real dangers. This information enables them to be more conscious and more responsible about the way they use the rituals they create.

My interest in ritual developed both from personal experience and from my anthropological studies of American childbirth, midwifery, and obstetrics. My childhood in Casper, Wyoming was punctuated with ritual events, many of which focused around the local rodeos that happened during the summers, and the seasonal celebrations of Easter, Thanksgiving, and Christmas. But my deepest ritual imprinting came from growing up in the Presbyterian Church. Although I moved away from that religion in later years, the hymns we sang in church every Sunday, the vivid memory of the light streaming through the stained glass window showing Jesus' ascension, the feeling of peace and completion that would descend over me as the minister raised his arms to give the final blessing—all these still resonate in my being and provide me with a sense of stability. In particular the words of the Doxology, which I must have sung at least 500 times during my childhood churchgoing years, still give me the goose bumps I used to get as I rose as one with the whole congregation, to sing joyously:

> *Glory be to the Father, and to the Son, and to the Holy Ghost*
> *As it was in the beginning, it is now and ever shall be*
> *World without end, Amen, Amen*

As I typed those words just now, singing as my fingers moved over the computer keys, that same uplifting feeling surged inside of me, goose bumps popped out on my arms once again, and I was right back in memory inside that beautiful church staring at the light shining through that stained glass window. Such is the power of ritual to affect our emotions, even decades after the fact.

But now as I reread the words of the Doxology, my critical faculties come into play: that song, which purports to be so timeless and so universal, does not encompass certain facts that I accept as reality. Things *are not* as they were in the beginning—in fact, change is the one constant of both human and universal experience. Our world is not "without end" —one day, billions of years from now, the Earth will be swallowed up in flames when its sun turns into a red giant. And there are no females and no "female principle" in that song, only a father, a son, and an androgynous spirit which is the closest the Presbyterianism of my youth could get to acknowledging that males are not the only gender. So I can't even find *myself* in its words—they do not charter my existence, like a good myth should. As an experiment, I sing the song once more and note that in spite of my intellectual objections, the goosebumps and uplifting sensation return. As we shall see throughout this book, *rituals primarily affect our emotions*—through triggering a powerful emotional response, ritual can get people to believe or at least resonate deeply with ideologies that they might intellectually reject (see Whitehouse 2005).

In my early years as an anthropology student during the 1970s, I studied shamanism and ritual healing in Mexico, and worked for a time with two Mexican shamans, one traditional and one thoroughly cosmopolitan. Those experiences, which involved both anthropological observation and personal participation in rituals of various sorts, taught me a great deal about ritual's flexibility as I saw it stretch to encompass the contrasting realities of the pre- and postmodern worlds. I watched with amazement as the people participating in the rituals that the traditional shaman had been performing for decades suddenly began to include American New Agers seeking connection with the earth and with traditional cultures—in Don Lucio, the traditional shaman I worked with, I guess these seekers found at least a facsimile of Castaneda's Don Juan. And I was equally fascinated by the postmodern shaman, Edgardo Vasquez Gomez. A wealthy upper class Mexican gentleman, he had studied traditional shamanic techniques all over Mexico, and was eclectically combining them with a European esoteric spiritual system based on the works of Gurdjieff, which invited individuals to "wake up" to a greater awareness of everyday life. His use of ritual to stimulate this kind of awareness in his followers was masterful; watching him manipulate people's states of consciousness was a lesson to me in the intentional use of ritual to achieve instrumental (practical) ends. (Both Don Lucio and Edgardo are now deceased.)

Perhaps my deepest engagements with ritual came during my participation, in later years, with a New Age healing group that evolved, over time, into a cult. I got involved in part because I wanted to do an anthropological study of that group. I watched and participated and took notes as their at-first tenuous belief system crystallized into an intensely tight and cohesive worldview. For the first two years, I didn't believe a word of it—it was just a story, albeit a fascinating one, and my anthropological detachment remained intact. But the ritual process, as we will demonstrate in this book, can be overwhelming. Embarrassing as it is to admit, against my will I eventually got fully converted to that worldview. The moment of conversion was a devastating experience (described later in this book). I knew it had happened and I was furious about it, but I could not change the fact that in an instant I had gone from not believing to fully believing their story about the nature of the world and the purpose of life. It took me six months to unconvert myself. Succeeding in that endeavor was a matter of personal self-esteem—I could not respect myself as long as I remained a true believer in a fantastical system that promised the power of Jesus-like ascension to anyone willing to work hard enough to "clear their issues" completely so that they could expand, in the flesh, into "full oneness with the universe"—and save humanity in the process!

Although I suffered greatly during that time, I also learned a tremendous amount, firsthand, about the power of ritual to engender belief and influence experience, and about the human capacity for free will and individual choice. We can be heavily influenced by ritual, but we can also make individual decisions about how we will respond to that influence. Since that time, my participation in religious ritual has been limited to expansive, humanistic rituals that enact belief systems I consciously choose to hold. Yet I still feel the seductive pull of that other path, one in which the meaning of every event could be forced to fit into a cohesive and intelligible cosmology, and my place and importance in the cosmological scheme were assured. Life seemed so much easier when all my questions got answered by Father André, a spiritual entity (channeled by the group leader Karen), who for a time served as my guide through life's bewildering maze. Father André's counsel seemed to remove the bewilderment and offer in its place the comfort of understanding—an understanding confirmed daily by the ritual experiences his followers constructed.

My personal experience of ritual took a new turn following the sudden death of my 20-year-old daughter Peyton in a car accident on September

12, 2000. The Memorial Service her father, her brother, and I designed for her in Austin, our home town, which was followed one week later by a second service designed by her many friends in New York, where she had been living, carried us through the initial, near-immobilizing shock, and allowed us to share with others the unspeakable grief we felt and will always feel. Those profoundly individualized services, which were not directed by ministers but were collectively performed by family and friends, enacted our understandings of who Peyton was and what her beliefs and values were, and concretized the multiple legacies she has left to the world (see Chapter 11 on "Designing Rituals," for a full description of Peyton's Memorial Service). Over time we have designed and performed many other rituals to help us grieve her death and celebrate her life. None of those many rituals we performed in her honor healed the pain that I thought would never end. Yet each one deepened my experience and understanding of the power of ritual to channel chaos and suffering into paths that lead to meaning and coherence, and thus to increase one's chances of surviving—and perhaps even integrating—the most devastating kinds of loss. Then finally, miracle of miracles, the last one we performed did just that!

Five of Peyton's best friends accompanied me to my ancestral home in Northern Louisiana with the explicit purpose of burying her ashes on the 10th anniversary of her death, in Peyton's and my ancestral cemetery—such a beautiful place, in the midst of the woods—many of our ancestors had been buried there from the early 1800s on. We spent the weekend reminiscing about her and celebrating her life. Then on September 12, 2010, precisely 10 years after she died, we collectively buried her ashes at the foot of my parents' graves, right in front of her gravestone. That gravestone took me months to design, as I wanted it to be a true reflection of who she was and the kind of life she lived. Here are the words carved into it on the front:

PEYTON ELIZABETH FLOYD
SEPT. 16, 1979—SEPT. 12, 2000
BELOVED DAUGHTER OF ROBERT NEWTON FLOYD
AND ROBBIE ELIZABETH DAVIS-FLOYD
ADORED SISTER OF JASON PHILLIP FLOYD
Dancer, diver, dolphin lover, healer,
gourmet cook, and friend
Life is all about "livin'—L-I-V-I-N!"

And on the back, a poem that I adapted from the words to a song that her close friend Abby Jones had written about Peyton:

PEYTON

She swam for seven summers straight with wild dolphins
She loved the oceans and the mountains and the streams
She danced with grace and grit and utter beauty
She lived her life full-on with total passion
To all her friends she was an inspiration
She would have dropped a falling star to catch a dream!

Well, I wanted everyone who stops by that gravestone to have a sense of who she was and how she chose to live, and knowing that those words will be there for hopefully centuries to come was one of my ways of ensuring her life legacy.

Our spontaneous ritual celebration on that sunny day in the Keatchie cemetery was a ritual that worked—a perfect rite of passage and celebration. I set the lovely Japanese urn containing her ashes, some locks of her hair, and her baby teeth (all of her remaining DNA, which I knew I had to let go of so that I could stop fantasizing about cloning her) into the hole in the ground that my dear friend Travis Whitfield had dug, and let go of it all in that single act. Her cherished friend Brian Hudson perched himself on her gravestone with his guitar, and commenced our spontaneous ceremony by singing "Oh, What a Beautiful Morning"—and indeed it was! And Brian also sang "Sweet Dreams"—a lovely lullaby he had written for Peyton before she died. Then her friend and mentor Jamison grabbed the guitar and sang (to the tune of "Me and Bobby McGee"), "Me and Peyton Floyd"—the lyrics were all about the long car trips he and Peyton had enjoyed together and their adventures along the way. Then each and every one present—Brian, Jamison, Corrie, Oliver, Adam, Travis, and Mary took turns speaking about what Peyton had meant and continues to mean in our lives. No planned order—we simply followed the flow, together creating in the moment a ritual of both celebration and completion. As a final touch, Adam laid a bouquet of flowers on her gravestone, and we walked away replete with love, awe, and a profound and lasting sense of shared caring—after which, I can say in all honesty, my pain over my daughter's death metamorphosed into a deep sense of acceptance and closure, bringing me, finally, peace. Such is the power of the rituals that we seek to celebrate, and to intellectually and critically analyze in the following pages.

In addition to these deeply personal experiences with ritual, I have explored ritual academically in various ways. For my first book, *Birth as an American Rite of Passage* (1992, 2004), I interviewed 100 women about their pregnancy and birth experiences. As I listened to woman after woman recount her birth story, I was increasingly struck by the standardized way in which this highly individual process was treated in the hospital. Most American women, for example, routinely receive intravenous injection (IV) for hydration during labor, even though there is no good scientific reason why they can't eat and drink to hydrate themselves. Many American women have their labors induced or augmented with the synthetic hormone Pitocin, even though Pitocin induction and augmentation have been shown scientifically to have negative side effects. And most American women are routinely hooked up to electronic fetal monitors for most of their labors, even though many studies have shown that walking around during labor has many benefits, including increasing blood and oxygen supply to the baby, while lying still attached to monitors reduces the baby's blood and oxygen supply and increases the likelihood of cesarean sections.

At first I was unable to explain how a medical specialty like obstetrics, which purports to be science-based, could routinely employ so many procedures that are unsupported by science. Eventually I realized that the "routine" was the key: these procedures were in fact rituals! Every human culture employs ritual to help its members face danger and uncertainty and to make transitions from one social state to another, so every culture ritualizes major life passages like birth and death. American culture could be no exception to this universal human fact; thus it should not have been surprising to me that hospital birth is so heavily ritualized. But in most cultures, rituals are recognized as such, whereas in the hospital, rituals are disguised as "necessary medical procedures."

What clued me in to the fact that "routine procedures" for labor and birth (such as electronic fetal monitoring and Pitocin augmentation) are rituals was the enormous discrepancy I uncovered between the findings of science, which support non-interventionist approaches to normal birth, and actual medical practice. Scientific evidence clearly shows that electronic fetal monitoring leads to many unnecessary cesareans, yet it continues to be routinely employed; scientific evidence also shows that upright positions are the most physiologically efficacious for birth, but most American women are asked to give birth flat on their backs with their feet up in stirrups, which science has shown to be the most physiologically dysfunctional birth position ever invented (it compresses the pelvis, making pushing more difficult and birth more dangerous).

Thus it became obvious to me that science is not the driver behind these routines; rather, tradition, custom, and cultural values constitute those drivers. Hooking women up to electronic fetal monitors enacts our cultural value on information and high technology and makes both women and physicians feel that they have some control over the chaotic natural process of birth. Placing women flat on their backs with their feet in stirrups makes it easier for the physician to see what is going on and to get in there to cut an episiotomy or apply the forceps or vacuum extractor. In 2015, U.S. cesarean rates stood at 33%, making the cesarean a ritualized procedure that gives the doctor a total and usually very welcome sense of control over the birth process. As I showed in that first book, through its rituals, modern obstetrics deconstructs the natural process of birth and reconstructs it as a technological process of production. In so doing, medical personnel enact the high cultural value we place on controlling and transcending nature through the use of ever-more-sophisticated high technologies.

One day early on in my research for *Birth as an American Rite of Passage*, I wandered through the book displays at the annual convention of the American Anthropological Association looking for books that might help me understand the rituals I was seeing everywhere in American hospitals. At the Columbia University Press booth, my eye fell on a black volume with a gold and very promising title, *The Spectrum of Ritual*. I picked up that book and was immediately entranced. Most anthropological works on ritual up to that point had concentrated on the effects of ritual in the social world, but *I wanted to know what ritual did to the human body and the human brain*. I knew that ritual's effects on human neurophysiology must be the primary source of its extraordinary power to shift human perception—to make someone who is afraid feel safe, for example, or someone who is in doubt to feel certain. *The Spectrum of Ritual* contained many of the answers for which I had been searching. A few years later, at another convention, I was fortunate enough to meet one of its authors, Charles Laughlin, a world authority on ritual. Our rich conversations and mutual passion for understanding ritual eventually led to our co-authorship of this book.

Charles D. Laughlin

Most of my anthropological work has revolved around a single question: While I intuit with absolute certainty that everything in the universe, me included, is part of a unified, organic whole (the *Thusness*), I routinely experience myself as separate from—and when I was younger, alienated from—the world. When I first became conscious (sometime in the early 1960s) of this dissonance in my being, I had no language to express that insight, nor even to talk about my dilemma with others. Then I discovered the writings of Alfred North Whitehead, particularly his magnum opus *Process and Reality*. This book allowed my rational mind to begin to catch up to that insight. *Process and Reality* became my bible—and still is, for that matter, especially the corrected edition. For some years I had no language of my own with which to describe my comprehension apart from that of Whitehead. He gave me the words to talk about the Thusness and my existence as a part of it, but couldn't explain to my satisfaction why I continued to experience myself as alienated from it. Whitehead had little to say about the brain structures that might underlie my experience. That came later. I recall trying to work all this out while staying at the Makerere University guest house in Kampala, Uganda, in 1969, waiting to get everything my wife, my three kids and I needed to go into the field among the So (aka Tepes, Tepeth) people in Karamoja District, Uganda.

Later on, with the aid of judicious doses of LSD-25 (about 5 or 6 "trips" between 1966 and 1969, all but one well-planned à la Tim Leary's pithy instructions), I came to realize that one could experience harmony with the Thusness through a unitive intuition that effected perception and feeling. I learned that I was capable of numerous states of mind, and that my usual state of mind had a lot to do with my inability to experience connection with the world. I gradually learned that I am actually never separate from the Thusness and that the world is continuously feeding me and I am feeding it. The boundaries of "me" are very permeable, and where "I" begin and leave off is a matter of taste and convention.

I was a philosophy major then (what else?!). But those were the days of avid Kantian transcendentalism, and when I got a B- for an 85-page paper on Gandhi's philosophy of *satyagraha* (non-violence), I became disenchanted with academic philosophy altogether. Then one day a poet friend of mine, Julia Kookin, gave me Colin Turnbull's wonderful book *The Forest People* (1962). That book changed my life. A popular and well-written account of the author's sojourn among the Mbuti Pygmies of the (formerly) Belgian

Congo, it was for me proof positive that there are human beings on the planet who routinely experience unitive states of mind. Here were genuinely non-alienated human beings! When they felt things were falling apart, they interpreted this as a sign that "the forest had fallen asleep," and held a *molimo* ceremony "to wake the forest up." That was that! I immediately changed my major and completed a B.A. in anthropology (1966) in just over a year.

At some point around 1969, I figured out that my mind states were how my brain experiences itself and its environment. I also became aware that people are walking around unaware that they are bodies capable of consciousness by grace of their nervous systems. It is such a curious form of self-ignorance, when you think about it. It still puzzles me today. People have no trouble with the notion that they digest hamburgers with their stomachs, or that they pump blood with their hearts, or that they grasp their beer bottle with their hand, but they seem to have trouble getting their minds around the idea that they think, feel, dream, imagine, experience, intend, act, etc., with their brains. They somehow experience their "minds" as distinct from (apart from, separate from—yes, *alienated from*) their bodies.

I sensed early on that somehow or other there was a mind-body schism at work. Eureka! I began to understand how I, myself, had come to experience myself as alienated from the Thusness. The problem of alienation shifted for me from a philosophical one to a neurological one, and moreover a problem that seems to begin with early conditioning—the early pre- and perinatal alienation of the mind from the body—an easy matter to accomplish given our (Euroamerican cultural) obstetrical and parenting patterns.

I got sidetracked doing a PhD at the University of Oregon (1972), and by the time I was ready to go into the field, the political climate in the Congo (then called Zaire) was such that doing work with the Pygmies was out of the question. Colin Turnbull (with whom I had corresponded since reading his book) suggested a number of possibilities and I chose to do ethnographic fieldwork among the So of northeastern Uganda. Nothing much was known about the So, so I ended up doing fundamental ethnographic research when I got there. One of the first experiences I had with the So was participating in one of their health-related exorcism rituals – which we will describe later on.

A crucial juncture in my work occurred when I met the late Eugene G. d'Aquili at a conference in 1972. Gene was a neurologically-trained psychiatrist and anthropologist; we immediately realized that we had a common interest in the relationship between brain and culture. We collaborated on writing our first book, *Biogenetic Structuralism* (1974), which takes the view that the structures producing universal patterns in cognitions, beliefs, behaviors, techniques, images, thoughts, feelings, perceptions, experiences, and so on, are in fact the brain structures that are common to people everywhere.

After meeting Gene and working on *Biogenetic Structuralism* together, I realized that I needed to seek some training in the neurosciences, so I applied for a postdoc with the National Science Foundation. I was awarded the position, and so became a Fellow of the Institute of Neurological Sciences at the University of Pennsylvania under Drs. Richard Sprague and William Chambers. It was in Philadelphia (Gene d'Aquili's home town) that I met John McManus. John, trained as a social psychologist at Syracuse University in New York, was an expert on the work of Jean Piaget. John's critique of biogenetic structuralism quickly forced Gene and me to become more developmental in our view of how the brain works.

We decided that we needed to do a major study of a single "universal" cultural institution as a practical example of how our approach could be applied. In 1975, the year after the publication of our first book, Gene and I teamed up with John and several other specialists in various fields to produce a book-length application of the theory of biogenetic structuralism to an account of ceremonial ritual, which eventually became the book *The Spectrum of Ritual* (1979)—that Robbie discovered by chance (or by fate) and found so illuminating.

As it turned out, the application of biogenetic structuralism to ritual led us to better understand science itself and its profound limitations relative to the study of consciousness and culture. As a consequence, our approach became steadily more experiential, especially relative to the study of ritual and religion. In the process of understanding human rituals, such as ceremonial rituals like the Catholic Mass and the Pygmys' *molimo* ceremony, we came to appreciate how important *symbolism* is to the functioning of ritual. This understanding led eventually to our most ambitious project together, the book *Brain, Symbol and Experience* (1990). In this work, John, Gene and I examined the relations between the brain, the brain's inherent symbolic function, and the phenomenology of experience in the study of consciousness. We argued for combining anthropology, the neurosciences, and contemplation as the most productive way to explore and explain consciousness.

I became convinced in the late 1970s that the most direct access to consciousness we have is the study of our own minds. After all, my consciousness is the only consciousness I can know from direct experience. Consequently, I got involved in various systems of meditation, including the esoteric Tarot, Christian prayer, Husserlian phenomenology, Hindu yoga, and Buddhist meditation. I got especially interested in the type of Buddhist meditation practiced by Tibetan Tantric Buddhists because of their heavy reliance on techniques that involve intense concentration upon complex symbols. So in good anthropological fashion, I became a monk (or lama) for seven years and spent a lot of time in Tibetan and other Buddhist monasteries in Nepal, India, Southeast Asia and elsewhere (never alas in Tibet), learning to calm my mind and concentrate on the mental properties that produce consciousness.

As anyone knows who has done the work, the course of meditative practice and resulting series of intuitive realizations is hard to describe to others. It is literally ineffable—a process so internal, one that transforms one's view of self and world in such profound and subtle ways—that to describe the process in detail for people who have not followed at least some spiritual path is virtually impossible. Beyond any doubt, these experiences affected my understanding of biogenetic structuralism. For instance, at some point along the contemplative path one comes to fully realize that there is no permanent substance to anything one can put one's mind to, including the self. The illusory conception of a permanent ego utterly fails in the face of direct experience to the contrary, and falls away. One consequence of this letting go of ego is that one no longer expends energy looking for the little mental "me," the homunculus in the brain, the "ghost in the machine."

My meditative work was carried out during lengthy retreats in my home, or in retreat centers or monasteries in such places as Lumbini, Nepal, Samye Ling in Scotland, the Benedictine priory in Montreal (under the late Dom John Main), a cabin on the banks of a lake near Whitehorse, Yukon, and the like. As a consequence of all this self-study, I came to realize many lessons that have fed my writings, including what the full-on experience of loving kindness is like, what Jesus meant by the koan "*before Abraham was, I am,*" what "bardo" experiences are like, that all sensory experience is constituted by granules (particles, or "dots"), that the overall organization of every moment of consciousness is largely due to intentionality, that time consciousness is a cognitive binding together of epochs of sensory experience, that *archetypes* (universal forms) are alive in the being and tend to become active and to perfect and simplify themselves in visions, fantasies and projections when the ego-will is not functioning, and so on. In due course I came to experience and understand what Buddhists call *Nirvana*, or *sunyata* – the essence of mind. All of these experiences and more were suggested and evoked by ritual activities that I was taught along the way, or constructed for myself. My appreciation for the great power of ritual to evoke often profound spiritual experiences grew immeasurably over this period.

A curious thing happened during a planned trip to Mexico and Central America in the early 1990s to test out some hypotheses I had about the role of shamanism and kingship among the ancient Maya. I had become interested in the Navajo concept of *hozho,* or "beauty" (the Navajo are a nation of indigenous people living in the American Southwest). It seemed to me from reading the literature that ritual is used by the Navajo to return someone to a state of "beauty" and "harmony" only when someone loses that state of mind. Having spent the previous decade learning all sorts of ritual practices geared toward producing a unified mind state, I found it curious that the Navajo seemed to do it "backwards," and I could not imagine why. I took a "side trip" to Navajo to find out more about ritual and *hozho,* and ended up staying in Navajo for the entire trip. (A couple of years later I did go to Mexico and Central America to research the Maya shaman-king matter.) As a consequence of this trip, I shifted my ethnographic interest from Tibetan Buddhism and monastic culture to the philosophy and religion of the Navajo people. In a roundabout way, it was ritual that led to my interest in Navajo thought and experience. I was interested, you see, in getting at the experiences behind the concept of *hozho.* What were people experiencing that they called *hozho,* and how did they know when they were losing this state? And how did ritual assure a return to that state once it was lost?

Of course I have continued my interest in the total range of human experience, including transpersonal experiences such as I have had during lucid dreaming, meditation, drug trips, initiation rituals, etc., as evidence of the full range of possibilities of which the human brain is capable (see my latest book, *Communing with the Gods: Consciousness, Culture, and the Dreaming Brain* (2011) for an account of cross-cultural dreaming).

As I mentioned, I did follow up on my interest in the role of alternative mind states and ancient Maya kingship. I discovered, as others before me have, that the Maya king or *Ahau* was perceived to be a shaman who had the skill to intercede with the forces of the underworld and to evoke their power for the benefit of his society. Thus in a real sense, the Maya king was a specialist who used rituals to transform spiritual power into political power at the level of the ancient state. He presided over highly elaborate public rituals that involved many of the elements and properties we will talk about in this book (see also Holmberg 2000 on ritual and political power in Tamang communities of Nepal).

At some point in the late 1970s, I discovered that there were other anthropologists who were interested in both ritual and alternative states of consciousness. We came together under the banner of "transpersonal anthropology," held meetings, and published a journal. Through a long and eventful history, these early pioneers of transpersonal anthropology formed what is today called the Society for the Anthropology of Consciousness (SAC for short), a section of the American Anthropological Association.

In a way, this book marks for me a return full circle to the roots of biogenetic structural thinking. As I have grown older and (hopefully) wiser, my respect for the power of ritual has grown along with the extraordinary experiences I have encountered exploring the rituals of other cultures. Rituals are not only meaningful to people, they are profoundly efficacious, and for many they have utility beyond what most Euroamericans would assume. Indeed, from a very real perspective, rituals are at the very root of what it means to be human. Humans seek knowledge, and frequently attain knowledge by participating in rituals. Rituals are at the same time dramatic, meaningful, instructive, socially integrative, and useful. And as we shall show throughout this book, everybody on the planet has experiences of rituals, from Christenings to Bar and Bat Mitzvahs, from football and other games to military boot-camp maneuvers, from parades to prayer services in a mosque, temple, or church, and so many more. Considering the fact that everybody sooner or later participates in rituals, a book that addresses how rituals work is more than appropriate and informative—it is downright necessary.

Suggested Reading

Davis-Floyd, Robbie (2004[1992]) *Birth as an American Rite of Passage*. Berkeley: University of California Press.

Finkler, Kaja (1985) *Spiritualist Healers in Mexico: Successes and Failures of Alternative Therapeutics*. South Hadley, MA: Bergin & Garvey Publishers.

Laughlin, Charles D. (2011) *Communing with the Gods: Consciousness, Culture and the Dreaming Brain*. Brisbane: Daily Grail.

Laughlin, Charles D., John McManus and Eugene G. d'Aquili (1990) *Brain, Symbol and Experience: Toward a Neurophenomenology of Consciousness*. New York: Columbia University Press.

Turnbull, Colin M. (1962) *The Forest People. A Study of the Pygmies of the Congo*. New York: Simon and Schuster.

Chapter 1

WHAT IS RITUAL?
AN INTRODUCTION TO THOUGHTS, THEORIES AND DEFINITIONS

Animal and Human Ritual as Behavioral Coordination and Communication. Why Ritual Matters: Its Effectiveness in the World. A Working Definition of Ritual. Thoughts and Theories about Ritual. The Characteristics of Ritual and the Contents of This Book.

> As Glenna began the opening conjuration of the ritual, a silence fell over the circle. Through the castings and chargings of the circle, through the invocation of the Goddess, it grew, and as Albion and Loik and Joaquin Murietta hammered out a dancing rhythm on their drums, as we whirled in a double sunwise ring, that silence swelled into waves of unseen lightness, flooding our circle, washing about our shoulders, breaking over our heads. Afterwards we wandered about the gardens, laughing and clowning, drunk on the very air itself, babbling to each other: it worked!
>
> — Margot Adler, *Drawing Down the Moon*

A common misconception in the industrialized world holds ritual to be something that goes on in more primitive societies, while we, in our scientific enlightenment, lead rational, non-ritualistic lives. But the facts are otherwise. All human cultures, including our own, use ritual as the physical and metaphysical means for dealing with everyday life and the mystery and unpredictability of the natural, psychological, social, and cosmic realms. Ritual plays significant roles in the social behaviors of most animal species—its pervasiveness in human life reflects ancient biological programming that allows members of a species to communicate and coordinate their lives through behavioral symbols.

What is ritual? What does it do and how does it work? What do animal and human rituals share in common? Why does human ritual often produce an experience of the sacred, spiritual and supernatural? And why does it just as often work toward secular, practical ends? Why does ritual constitute what anthropologists call a *cultural universal* (meaning that it is found in every culture and society)? Where does its power come from, and how can societies and individuals tap that power?

We will address these questions from an anthropological point of view that integrates biological, psychological, spiritual, and sociocultural perspectives on ritual. Anthropology is the study of humans in their myriad manifestations. It includes comparisons of human and animal behaviors, and studies ranging from the fossilized bones and habitats of our ancestors that provide clues about human evolution (called physical anthropology), to the ruins of ancient societies (archaeology), to the development of languages across cultures (linguistic anthropology), to the complexities of historical or contemporary cultures (cultural anthropology). For the past century and a half, cultural anthropologists have left the familiar surroundings of their own homelands to study other cultures and to try to make sense of them in terms that non-members can understand. In every culture they have studied, anthropologists have encountered rituals. These range from the ritualized daily behaviors of an individual to the group dynamics of a crowd, from the simple prayers of a family sitting down to eat to lavish large-scale ceremonies like feasts and seasonal holidays. And today we can speak even of global rituals in which billions of people across the planet participate in the same experience at the same time, including for examples the celebrations marking the dawning of the Third Millennium, the funeral of Princess Diana, the wedding of Kate Middleton to Prince William, Queen Elizabeth's Diamond Jubilee celebration of 60 years of her rule, the Olympic Games and football's (soccer's) World Cup, and, very specific to the United States, the large-scale rituals performed to honor the dead of 9/11 and to commemorate the deeply felt national experience of being attacked on homeland soil (for the first time since the British attack in 1812).

Many of the individual elements of these rituals seem incomprehensible at first glance. Why, for example, do the So people of Uganda have a ritual in which they smear themselves with gray clay and march around in formation waving their walking sticks in the air? Why does a Catholic priest wear long white robes? Why do shamans dance ecstatically for hours to "heal their community," and why are their practices remarkably similar around the world? Why have some of the ancient spiritual healing rituals of shamans been adopted by modern educated professionals? Why do contemporary sports fans paint their bodies in the colors of their chosen team? Why do actors, before performing a play, gather together in a circle and chant?

Often it is only after years of fieldwork that the anthropologist manages to figure out the meaning of such practices. Yet anthropologists have found that this effort to "decode" the rituals of other cultures—and their own—is always worth the struggle, for such rituals often embody the most essential elements of the culture. Rituals are performances in which cultures—and individuals—describe and display the most important and basic aspects of their personalities and express their deepest values and beliefs. Performing these rituals is a part of human nature and biology that is deeply embedded in genetic evolution.

During the 20th and early 21st centuries, anthropologists have made enormous strides in understanding ritual, and ethologists (scientists who study animal behavior) have expanded our knowledge about the broad evolutionary basis of ritual through studies of other species of social animals. Yet much of what these scholars have written about ritual is highly technical and its implications inaccessible to the general public. This book synthesizes a myriad of anthropological and ethological discoveries about ritual in what we hope is a straightforward and useful format. Its purpose is to explain ritual to people who use it, to people who are interested in it, and to students engaged in its study. In order to communicate the flavor of how anthropologists think about ritual, we will summarize a number of recent theories of ritual, while at the same time pointing to those aspects of theory that bolster our performance approach. This book is not about theory per se, but about ritual itself—what it is, how it works, what makes it powerful, what makes it dangerous, and most of all, what makes it useful to contemporary humans. When we do bring up theoretical debates and perspectives, we will do so in order to address the central focus of the book, the *power* of ritual.

We intend this book to serve students of various social sciences—especially anthropology, sociology, comparative religion, religious studies, political science, and others—as a comprehensive textbook, a single source that can complement and draw together the myriad of articles and bewildering tomes professors presently use to teach about ritual. For the general public, our principal purposes in writing this book are to: (1) help our readers to understand why so many people feel the need for rituals and what exactly they are doing when they create or participate in rituals (we include an Appendix on "How to Create and Perform an Effective Ritual"); (2) explain why, when people try to change ritualized behaviors (their own or those of others), they may discover that it is harder to accomplish than they imagined; and (3) draw public attention to ritual's power and potential to be used both for good and for ill—what William Sax (2010) calls the "efficacy of ritual." Public awareness of ritual tends to focus on its positive aspects, but the shadow side of ritual is as powerful as the light. Ritual may be used for the good of individuals, communities, and even corporations, as well as manipulated by politicians, religious and cult leaders, and others to sway people's perceptions, emotions and behaviors.

ANIMAL AND HUMAN RITUAL AS BEHAVIORAL COORDINATION AND COMMUNICATION

> What ritual does for me is to link me back into my body and ancient heritage as an animal. For me ritual is a language of the whole person, one that speaks from and to our evolutionary ancient heritage. But this connection with the past is not merely a vestige of earlier capabilities. Ritual is a vital part of contemporary human existence, a part of our evolved psychology that is still as relevant to human health as our need to breath, eat, and reproduce.
>
> — Michael Winkelman, personal communication, 2011

We recognize when an animal is on alert by its taut body posture because when we are on alert, ours is in much the same state. The lizard scurries away from danger, the hunted prey screams when caught, the bonobo chimp smiles when feeling pleasure—we do the same. An elephant troop forms a protective circle around a female giving birth, just as do medical or midwifery teams and family and friends. Baby bears mimic the battles of their elders in play just as human children do. The alpha gorilla beats his chest, the male stag vies for a female's attention by stomping on the ground to challenge his rival, the guy in the bar flashes his cash when paying the bill while glaring at his potential rival. Similar behaviors in other animals shed light on the underlying causes and functions of human ritual, helping us to see how those behaviors are linked to basic brain functions.

Ritual addresses an adaptive problem encountered by all species: how to coordinate the action of individuals into collective, socially coherent and coordinated patterns. Virtually all large brained social animals exhibit ritualized behaviors (Schechner 1995:229). Studies have shown that both the social play of animals and human rituals are formats for instilling and developing altruism—a requisite for cementing social bonds (Chick 2008). All social animals have spacing techniques through which they can create "personal space" even in the midst of a crowd. Yet these separations among members of a group must be superseded in order for group activities to be coordinated. This coordination requires controlling the information transmitted between members of the same species, and the meaning of that information. Studies of ritualistic behaviors in non-human animals indicate their fundamental importance in communication— these ritualistic display signals were selected through evolution to enable members of animal groups to provide information to each other. Animals and birds use often complex rituals in order to prepare themselves to mate—rituals we call "foreplay" when humans are concerned (see Léveillé 2007 for birds; Spomer 1996 for North American herd animals).

Animal rituals are techniques both for communicating and coordinating behavior. Ethologists like Nobel Prize winners Konrad Lorenz and Nikolaas Tinbergen have called these animal rituals *fixed action patterns*, because they are basically instinctual and once begun, are usually carried out to completion. Animal ritual displays are a type of fixed action pattern known as "intention movements"—in this case, actions that signal a readiness for certain activities (e.g., a set of movements preparing a bird for flight, or for mating). These stereotyped bodily movements or sounds communicate basic messages and constitute repetitive patterns that coordinate perceptions, emotions, cognitive processes and motor behaviors, synchronizing these processes across individual participants to coordinate the behavior of the group (d'Aquili, Laughlin and McManus 1979:156; Salzen 2010; Smith 1979, 1990).

Humans also manifest fixed action patterns—like sucking, grasping, crawling, and walking—that are genetically "wired-in" to our body's organization. However, we, like other big-brained animals, also have the ability to establish recurring behavioral sequences that work well, and that we do not have to recall every time we want to do something. These sequences may or may not incorporate fixed action patterns. For instance, we are born with the inherent ability to walk, but we may adapt this ability to riding a bicycle. We are born with the ability to suck, but we can incorporate that ability in a behavioral sequence to syphon gas from a tank. In other words, animals and humans alike have the capacity to *ritualize* behaviors—to learn to sequence one behavior after another to get something done—like finding, putting on, and tying our shoes, chopping our vegetables and meat in a particular way, cooking our food, cleaning our kitchens, rinsing recyclable materials, putting them into the recycling bin, and taking it out on the street on Thursdays, and so forth (see d'Aquili, Laughlin and McManus 1979:28-41; Bell 1997: 80-81).

As among animals, ritual in humans serves a primary biological function in facilitating coordinated group action. For example, the formalized displays of animals are continued in the nonverbal communication—body language (Rowlands 2006)—of humans, such as behaviors for greeting and challenging others. Animal uses of ritual to establish, maintain, and recognize differences in social status—like that of the alpha female or male—also remain prevalent in humans, who find ritual essential to asserting and maintaining social roles or "face" (see Goffman and Best 2005). Such social roles are constantly shifting in response to changes in circumstance, like the birth of a new family member or the maturation of a child. Members of social groups need to maintain the coordination of the group in spite of such changes in membership. The social adaptations such changes require are often achieved through rituals that minimize the conflicts that can occur during or as a result of the transitions. Since participation in ritual requires coordination of individual processes with group patterns, *ritual serves biologically as a mechanism for socialization*: "Ritual, inclusive of ceremonial ritual, is an evolutionary, ancient channel of communication that operates by virtue of homologous biological functions (i.e., synchronization, integration, tuning, etc.) in man and other vertebrates" (Laughlin, McManus & d'Aquili 1979:40-41). Ceremonial rituals found in all human societies are analogous to certain animal behaviors and displays, from gatherings of wolf packs to the seasonal migratory patterns of birds. The human ritual forms that have the greatest continuity with animal rituals largely operate outside of awareness because they are based in inherent brain processes that are non-linguistic. To be explicit, contrary to those scholars who consider ritual as an invention of humanity, perhaps analogous to the invention of language, we suggest that ritual is fundamental to the adaptation of all big-brained social animals, and that we humans inherited our ritual proclivities from our pre-human animal past. Indeed, ritual is so integral to human social and cognitive evolution that, as Tom Driver (1991:10) wrote, "to study humanity is to study ritual."

WHY RITUAL MATTERS: ITS EFFECTIVENESS IN THE WORLD

> Ritual is one of the oldest human activities—often considered as important as eating, sex, and shelter. Why has it persisted so long? Why does every attempt to suppress it result in creating it anew? What makes ritual seems at once so foundational that even the animals do it and so superfluous that Protestants once imagined they could dispense with it altogether?
>
> — Ronald Grimes, Introduction to *Readings in Ritual Studies* (1996a)

We turn now to a look at why ritual matters—at the instrumental roles it plays in the human world. We emphasize a perspective on ritual that is counter to many "commonsense" notions about ritual. Popular conceptions generally characterize rituals as repetitive behaviors that are ineffective, having no technical basis to achieve the intended effects—as just "habits," "customs," or "traditions." Yet to the contrary, rituals can be instrumental, producing effects at physical, emotional, personal, interpersonal, social, and cognitive levels. Rituals often incorporate physical activities and plant (and other) medicines that have psycho-physiological effects, including healing and altered states of consciousness. Rituals can affect personal expectations, producing emotional, psychological, and spiritual change. The charismatic dynamics of ritual can alter social relations, changing individual and collective psychodynamics and transforming identity. Ritual's effects on human physiology, psychology, emotions, spirituality, and culture constitute recurring themes in this book.

The communicative and expressive aspects of ritual are exemplified in its display of values, cosmology, spirituality, and appropriate social relations. Rituals communicate worldviews, rules for social behavior, and interpretive systems that order experience and behavior. Rituals embed guidelines for social behavior and self in symbols, artifacts, myths and psycho-dramatic activities, affecting all levels of human experience and functioning.

Rituals mediate psychosocial processes, re-establishing group cohesion by resolving conflicts, re-establishing group continuity in the face of loss and adversity, and modifying individual and group behavior to create social cohesion and harmony. Disruptions of social cohesion are often mediated through legal rituals that channel the social treatment of violators in culturally consensual ways such as undergoing ordeals, physical punishment, restitution, court trials, and so on. Rituals affect general health: they can enhance a sense of social solidarity and integration, raising an individual's endorphin levels and positively stimulating the immune system, often facilitating cures for all types of illness (Aizenstat and Bosnak 2009). Rituals can also reduce risk behaviors (unhealthy dietary intake, destructive activity, unwholesome relationships, excessive grieving, etc.) that may provoke further health problems.

Healing rituals work therapeutically at social, psychological, and physiological levels, typically requiring participation of a group of significant others, sometimes the entire community or extended family. These practices often explicitly recognize the source or cause of illness as stemming from within the group, and provide relief by re-establishing harmonious social relations. Rituals mediate relationships between the ill person and others in society, mandating certain care for and protection of the ill person, or conversely protecting the healthy from contact with the diseased. Rituals of purification often provide cleansing, sterilization, and changes in diet. Ritual's therapeutic effects often begin with diagnosis, which places illness conditions within conceptual frameworks that make them seem intelligible and controllable. Religious rituals (the most commonly recognized as rituals) connect the individual physically and emotionally with his or her (sub)culture's religion or spiritual path.

Rituals of social transition (called rites of passage) that mark and often effect, or at least facilitate, transitions between culturally recognized stages of life assist the individual and social group in adjusting to an individual's new status and its implications for behavior and social relations (Turnbull 1983). Transition rituals reduce the ambiguity associated with change, protecting individual psyches during the vulnerable period by reducing uncertainty and stress. Transition rituals are often directed towards the relationships between social conditions and physiological conditions (e.g., birth, puberty, marriage, pregnancy, menopause, death), demarcating certain points of the life cycle as especially significant. Ritual association of symbols and physiological processes provides a means of shaping and controlling human emotions and biological drives and then explaining them within wider cosmological frameworks.

To recap, rituals cannot be dismissed as ineffective meaningless actions or as merely symbolic statements that produce no results in the world. Understanding ritual requires perspectives that address the multiple instrumental dimensions of its effects.

A WORKING DEFINITION OF RITUAL

As you can imagine, there are many, many definitions of ritual from which one may choose (see Bell 1992; Grimes 1990: Appendix 16, 2014: 193-194). There are also many views on the nature, functions, meaning and efficacy of ritual in anthropology (see Handelman 1998:10-11; Snoek 2006), some of which we will discuss in the following section. Most anthropologists concentrate upon the role of ritual in religion (e.g., Stewart and Strathern 2014). This is quite natural, for most of the rituals we anthropologists encounter have something to do with magic and the "supernatural" (spirits, gods, ancestors, ghosts, etc.). But in this book we intend to broaden our coverage of ritual to include the secular, non-religious use of ritual.

We will use a working definition that Robbie developed in *Birth as an American Rite of Passage* (2004 [1992]:8): "*a ritual is a patterned, repetitive, and symbolic enactment of a cultural (or individual) belief or value.*" This definition is not intended to negate the importance of understanding the evolutionary origins of this very human phenomenon—precursors that include inherited intentional and pragmatic behavioral sequences. We recognize full well that there is an evolutionary continuum of complexity between simple fixed action patterns, simple ritualized behaviors, and ritual in the full-blown ceremonial sense (d'Aquili, Laughlin and McManus 1979; Grimes 2014:193). Ours is a working definition that we feel fits well with the way we will be presenting ritual practice in this book.

Since Robbie's formulation is a foundational concept for our book, let us take time to consider each of its components.

Patterning, Repetition, and Symbolism: Coordination and Communication

A quick run-through of events that have long been called rituals in both the scholarly and popular lexicons immediately makes obvious the reasons why we say that patterning and repetition (or "restoration"; see Schechner 2011) are two of the definitive characteristics of ritual. Events consensually labeled rituals include, among many others: church services, parades and processions, greetings and farewells, prayer, folk dances, pilgrimages, certain types of healing, bar and bat mitzvahs, graduations, initiation ceremonies, and presidential inaugurations. We think the reader will grant us that everything on this list is immediately recognizable as ritual and also as highly structured behavior that entails a distinct pattern. One recognizes a parade as different from normal traffic on the street because of the distinctive pattern of the parade—a pattern that repeats itself over and over in the various groupings that constitute the parade, from the bands that march by to the clowns and the floats.

Normal traffic on the street is also patterned and repetitive of course—most of cultural life is (see Schechner 1995:Chap. 3). This is where the third adjective in the definition comes in: ritual is patterned, repetitive, and *symbolic* behavior. This notion of "symbolic" emphasizes that ritual is a form of communication (Rothenbuhler 2006; Senft and Basso 2009). Normal traffic on the street doesn't symbolize or communicate anything in particular. People on the road generally aren't trying to make a statement by driving—they just want to get where they're going. The instrumental goal—getting there—is the most important reason for driving. A parade, on the other hand, is intentionally designed to be symbolic. Through parades, communities enact and display their values and celebrate their unity and diversity. Thus, parades are rituals: patterned, repetitive, and symbolic enactments that communicate cultural beliefs and values.

But wait, you say! When people drive, they are not just driving, they are also making symbolic statements. The kind of car they drive, the way they drive, the hand or electric signals they use—all these convey messages to others about the kind of people they are, how much money they have, and so forth. And the endless flow of traffic on city streets is powerfully symbolic of the "rat race" of technocratic life. So right away, as we try to define ritual, we are confronted with a problem that has plagued all those who have tried to write about and explain ritual: *it is extremely hard to separate out ritual from everyday life.*

Clearly a church (or mosque or temple) service is a ritual—it is patterned, repetitive, and highly symbolic—but in some ways so is an ordinary conversation. Conversations generally observe rules for turn-taking, employ repetitive elements, begin with greeting formulas and close with farewell formulas, stipulate appropriate social space, and can symbolize many things (Tannen 2005). Everyday acts like doing the laundry, cooking a meal, and getting dressed in the morning can also be patterned, repetitive, and symbolic. This fact reflects the deeply embedded nature of ritual within human behavior. Human behavior is ritualized at many different levels, some of which are shared with other animals, like grooming and greeting rituals and the sequencing of everyday activities. Complex human social activities, such as those exemplified in crowd behaviors, also reflect a ritual coordination of activities found in other animals. But humans have ritual behaviors that are unique to humans, and reflect the different adaptive needs of human communities. Consequently, understanding ritual requires that we distinguish among different forms of ritual behavior.

We suggest that ritual should not be thought of as something fixed, concrete, and discrete, but rather can most usefully be understood as existing on a *spectrum* from highly patterned and densely symbolic at one end (like a Catholic mass) to more loosely patterned and thinly symbolic at the other (like conversation). This range in the manifestation of ritual is precisely why Charlie and his co-authors Eugene d'Aquili and John McManus titled their book *The Spectrum of Ritual* (1979). Human greetings ("Hi, hello, how are you?" "I'm fine, how are you?") and conversations are ritualized in mundane forms similar to those seen in other animals, while we also engage in behavioral routines that are organized into very complex fixed patterns such as the Mass, which uses formal ritual to evoke a human relationship with the cosmos. Conversations, routines, and the Mass are all ritualistic and can be productively analyzed as ritual. But to understand why the Catholic Mass is more of a ritual than a conversation is, we must recognize the bases underlying the spectrum of ritual behaviors.

To recap, *ritual can usefully be thought of as existing on a spectrum that ranges from simple patterned and repetitive behavior, like habitually getting dressed the same way every morning, to complex patterned and repetitive behaviors, like participation in a Mass. The symbolic meanings attached to and conveyed by the ritual increase toward the complex end of the scale.* In other words, there is probably some but not much meaning in getting dressed the same way every day. But there is a great deal of meaning in the Catholic Mass that has taken many pages of written text to fully describe (e.g. Murphy 1979). To understand what both simple and complex rituals share in common, as well as what distinguishes them, requires that human ritual behavior be placed in comparative perspective, related to the behaviors of other animals (as we have seen above and will see in future chapters).

Rituals as Enactments of Beliefs and Values

As we stated above, *a ritual is a patterned, repetitive, and symbolic enactment of a cultural (or individual) belief or value.* We place "individual" in parentheses to indicate that most rituals are developed at the level of social groups, but it is also quite common for families and individuals to develop idiosyncratic and personal rituals that have meaning to them, like making an annual pilgrimage, saying daily prayers before a meal or at an altar, or taking your child for a walk by the river every day, complete with peanut butter and jelly sandwiches (thereby enacting the high value you place on the parent-child relationship). (See Sherman and Sherman 1990:95-100 regarding ritual and kinship beliefs.) Personal rituals may even be constructed as part of the process of developing one's own "personal mythology" (Feinstein and Krippner, 2009[1988]). Yet on the whole, and to put it most simply, *rituals often enact cultural beliefs and values,* establishing linkages among beliefs, values, and behaviors (see Handelman 1998:Chap. 2). Anthropologists figured out this relationship of ritual to values a long time ago, and for a century now have been using ritual to gain insights into understanding a given culture—this, despite contemporary attempts to distance ritual from meaning. If you study its rituals in a search for their meaning, you will arrive at the most important and deeply held beliefs and values of that culture, however diverse or standardized those beliefs may be.

In most cases, cultural rituals are inherently conservative—in other words, because rituals enact and display a culture's most basic beliefs and values, they also serve as mechanisms for transmitting and thus reinforcing and preserving those beliefs and values. Thus rituals usually work to enhance social cohesion, as their primary purpose in most cases is to align the behavior, values and belief system of the individual with those of the group. *The more a belief system is enacted through ritual, the stronger it is. The less it is enacted, the weaker it becomes.* That's why your minister (if you have one) so often exhorts you to come to church every Sunday—and prayer group every Wednesday night. If you stop going—if you cease to enact the rituals of your religion—over time your religion will have less and less meaning and significant attachments for you. That is one of the many reasons why traditional cultures all over the world are vanishing—as they cease to consistently enact their belief systems through ritual, those belief systems cease to affect behavior; eventually, the belief system itself may cease to exist.

THOUGHTS AND THEORIES ABOUT RITUAL

A "luxuriant jungle of theories about ritual has grown up" (Humphrey and Laidlaw 1998:64) in anthropology, especially over the last three decades. In their many attempts to understand and explain ritual, anthropologists have come up with dozens of theories about, and definitions of ritual—perhaps the best summaries of these may be found in Ron Grimes' book, *Readings in Ritual Studies* (1996c), Catherine Bell's book, *Ritual: Perspectives and Dimensions* (1997:Chap. 2), in David Hick's reader, *Ritual and Belief* (2010), and in Jens Kreinath, Jan Snoek and Michael Strausberg's huge tome, *Theorizing Rituals: Issues, Topics, Approaches, Concepts* (2008). Understanding human ritual is complicated by several factors: (1) the reluctance or inability of some theorists to connect ritual among animals and rituals among humans; (2) the range of complexity of ritual behaviors from bathroom body rituals like brushing teeth to full-blown ceremonies like a presidential inauguration, Catholic Mass or Super Bowl game; (3) the myriad intentions to which rituals may be directed (control of political perceptions, magical control of the weather, etc.); and (4) the embedding of ritual behaviors in many other social contexts, including mythological and paradigmatic belief systems. These associations have led to definitions that often restrict ritual to humans and their unique linguistic, ceremonial, and social behaviors. These often fail to acknowledge, for instance, the importance of the evolution of mimetics (i.e. imitation—"monkey see, monkey do") among primates and early hominins (species of primates leading to humans). Psychologist Susan Blackmore (2003) has suggested that the role of imitation in adaptation increased in both importance and complexity over the course of the evolution of the hominin brain. In fact, this process of increased complexity and importance explains for Blackmore the rapid increase in the size of the human brain.

Anthropologists do commonly focus upon certain crucial aspects of ritual. Some emphasize, for example, the ways in which ritual organizes humans' ecological strategies—how they work to live in balance with their environment (see Rappaport 1984; Grimes 2003a) and their economic systems of barter and exchange (Iteanu 2004). Others focus on ritual's role in maintaining or overthrowing political institutions and structures (de Lomnitz, Elena and Adler 2010). Anthropologists and practitioners primarily interested in religion tend to define ritual in terms of mystical beings or powers (Alcorta and Sosis 2005; Barrett and Lawson 2001; Stewart and Strathern 2014)—for example, a mechanism for "calling the spirits" or controlling the unseen forces behind events. Defining ritual in terms of economic systems or supernatural beliefs has obscured the relationships of human ritual to similar behaviors in other animals, and consequently has encouraged scholars to see ritual as occurring "out there" in the social field rather than recognizing ritual as also being "in here," both inside the human body/brain and inside as individual and shared experience.

We have already presented you with our own working definition of ritual. Here we will contextualize that definition in terms of several of the more important contemporary theories and definitions of ritual we will be discussing during the course of the book. This will give you a taste of the kinds of things anthropologists like to think about. But you should notice that most anthropological theories of ritual (cf. Handelman 1998 on "public events") have to do with religious ceremonies, and often the secular side of ritual, and the evolutionary emergence of complex rituals, are given short shrift.

Roy Rappaport: The Role of Ritual in Ecological Management

Roy Rappaport was one of those anthropologists who consider the essential structure of ritual to be universal (1999). He recognized that ritual is a form of communication, and may contain any number of local symbolic elements, yet nonetheless there is a universal structure to ritual that makes it uniquely efficacious.

> It seems apparent, and few students writing today would disagree, that ritual is not simply an alternative way to express any manner of thing, but that certain meanings and effects can

best, or even *only*, be expressed or achieved in ritual. Inasmuch as the substance of rituals is infinitely various, this must mean that these meanings and effects follow from ritual's universal form. (Rappaport 1999:30).

Let us take for instance one type of ritual, the theatrical play (like Shakespeare's *Macbeth* or Andrew Lloyd Webber's musical, *The Phantom of the Opera*). In Rappaport's terms, the symbolic content of the play contained within the original story or script remains the same through time. However, the symbolic content will vary from play to play as directors and actors impress their own personalities on the productions. Although the play may vary from performance to performance, it is structured by the universal features of ritual such that we can always recognize a play from other events in everyday life. For instance, everyday life is full of superfluous objects and happenings, but in a play there are no superfluous objects. As Anton Chekhov once said: "One must never place a loaded rifle on the stage if it isn't going to go off. It's wrong to make promises you don't mean to keep" (letter to Aleksandr Semenovich Lazarev, 1 November 1889).

Keeping in mind that all Western theater originated in Ancient Greek mystery plays, there is the sacred space (the stage, or as actors will often say, "treading the boards"; see Grimes 2007) and the sacred time (the duration of the play). The "acts and utterances" (Rappaport's terms) of performers are determined by others (playwright, director, coach, etc.); there is a "formality" to the performances (that is, acts and utterances are repetitive), the acts and utterances are invariant (the ritual has to be "done right" to be effective), and they constitute an enactment of the symbolic material (that is, the play is far more than a mere script—reading *Macbeth* and watching it performed are two very different types of communication). All of these features, and perhaps more, come together to distinguish ritual as a mode of communication distinctly different than any other mode (1999:Chap. 2).

We will return to Rappaport's thinking in Chapter 10 when we discuss the role of rituals in both maintaining culture and facilitating change.

Scott Atran: Ritual Involvement in Cooperation and Conflict

Following on from Rappaport's contention that ritual is uniquely efficacious as a mode of communication, Scott Atran (2002; Atran and Henrich 2010) has focused on the cognitive aspects that contribute to what he calls the "prosocial" effect of religious ritual. Certain of these cognitive processes are universal and operate within ritual contexts to reinforce prosocial religious beliefs:

According to Atran, in every society there are:

1. Widespread counterfactual and counterintuitive beliefs in supernatural agents (gods, ghosts, goblins, etc.);
2. Hard-to-fake public expressions of costly material commitments to supernatural agents, that is, offering and sacrifice (offerings of goods, property, time, life);
3. Mastering by supernatural agents of people's existential anxieties (death, deception, disease, catastrophe, pain, loneliness, injustice, want, loss);
4. Ritualized, rhythmic sensory coordination of (1), (2), and (3)—in other words, *communion* (congregation, intimate fellowship, etc.) (Atran and Norenzayan 2004:1).

Following in the footsteps of Mel Spiro (1953), Atran holds that religious rituals are performed in order to "...invoke supernatural agents to deal with emotionally eruptive existential anxieties, such as loneliness, calamity, and death" (ibid:16). Rituals evoke experiences that counter disbelief in supernatural aspects of the society's worldview, and as such are mechanisms of what A. F. C. Wallace (1966) called "revitalization" (see Chapter 4).

Considering that religions are rife with illogical, counterintuitive and non-empirical beliefs, the principle operators in ritual practice are those of memory, especially emotionally charged memory. Atran (2002:173) notes:

> Religion arises when (1) [genuine] emotions (2) ally with thought content whose truth implications are logically and factually impossible to evaluate (3) but that together convincingly evoke commitment to cultural mores. Religious beliefs and experiences cannot be consistently validated by social consensus either through deductive or inductive inference. Validation occurs only by satisfying the very emotions that motivate religious beliefs and experiences.

Many rituals arise within the context of religion, and as we shall see within secular culture as well, as a kind of narrative that strings together thoughts and emotions in a socially consistent manner. Recurring enactment of this behavioral narrative satisfies the original anxieties that give rise to religious belief in the first place. "Rituals intensify these natural movements to emotionally validate, and sanctify, any number of different cultural sets of moral sentiments" (ibid:173).

Candace Aleorta and Richard Sosis: Ritual and Emotional Adaptation

Candace Aleorta and Richard Sosis (2005:339) have written along similar lines as Atran, emphasizing that in many cases religious rituals evoke powerful, and often negative experiences that bring group members together as a tightly organized community: "These highly charged negative ritual experiences not only bond initiates, they also motivate intense cooperation and obedience under conditions of high individual risk and low central authority. The less powerful in such societies bear a larger share of the fitness costs of such subordination, but they may still gain greater benefits as members of a successful cooperative group than they would otherwise realize." As with many contemporary theorists (see also Barrett and Lawson 2001), Alcorta and Sosis are arguing from a cognitive science and evolutionary psychological perspective, both of which allow the discussion of the evolution of the brain's cognitive faculties in a way that older and more traditional anthropology disallowed. These approaches also bolster findings based upon experimental research, as well as ethnographic fieldwork.

Caroline Humphrey and James Laidlaw: Ritual as Archetypal Action

Equating ritual with religion the way many anthropologists do creates numerous conceptual and methodological problems, not the least of which is recognizing the efficacy of both secular rituals and rituals bereft of their original ideological frame (see Chapter 7). In their book, *The Archetypal Actions of Ritual*, Caroline Humphrey and James Laidlaw (1994) have examined this issue in depth and applied their analysis to the use of the *puja* (a ritual in which a deity or other religious symbol is worshiped; see Chapter 11 for the Tibetan Buddhist use of the *puja*) among Jain practitioners.

When one participates in a ritual performance, one accepts the pattern of activity designed by others. How one performs the ritual does not depend upon the actor's personal intentions. Rituals are, in other words, the products of culture—social acts that have been inculcated by the individual during the course of their enculturation. A crucial distinction must be made between the ritual action and its interpretation—a distinction not easily made, for it entails accepting the view that the ritual action itself is meaningless.

> [R]itual action appears to have an independent objective existence. Not only is this how the ritual practitioner sees his or her own action, but for similar reasons a ritual act appears to the outside observer, like a text, or a painting, or an artifact, *to invite interpretation.* And it is still more encouraging when the performers themselves can proffer interpretations of their own. (ibid:262).

The usual procedure used by ethnographers for studying a ritual is to observe it and then ask people what it "means"—to pick a ritual apart into its constituent elements and see how this action and that symbol combine to produce a narrative, a single holistic story. In reality, Humphrey and Laidlaw reason, it is the actors themselves, as individuals, that bring the meaning into the ritual actions, a process they call *ritual commitment,* a particular cognitive, emotional, interpretive point of view about one's own actions (ibid:88-89). Different participants may have different intentions while performing the same ritual. Some actors may be neophytes just practicing their moves (like a beginner learning the different movements in *tai chi*), while others may just be "going through the motions" concerned only with "getting it right." Yet another actor may be a master who carries into the action a wealth of past experience in memory. The error is in thinking that the ritual has one inherent meaning, perhaps the one we elicit from the master, while ignoring or rejecting the meaning—the *attitudes*—that other participants bring to, or generate during their actions. Rituals do not exist because they are meaningful; rather, they exist as culturally received and somewhat objective, even "archetypal" (see Chapter 2) actions. Rituals are thus bouts of socially "stipulated" and rule-driven actions accepted by the actors, and in so doing the actors give up their autonomy as the authors of their own activities (ibid:97-98).

A good example of how rituals may be embraced as rituals without the participants also embracing a monolithic meaning can be found in Phil Zuckerman's (2008) study of religion in Denmark and Sweden. In his fascinating book, *Society without God,* Zuckerman interviews many citizens of those countries—considered to be the least religious countries in the world—who continue to be baptized, confirmed, be married in the church and so forth, yet not believe in Jesus, God or any of the common supernatural attributions usually assumed for Christians. Rather, when asked why they do these rituals, their answers are often of the "that's the way we do things" variety. Participation in such "religious" rituals verges on the purely civic and secular, as we shall see in Chapter 4.

Pascal Boyer: A Cognitive Theory of Ritual

As did Charlie and his colleagues some years back (Laughlin and d'Aquili 1974; Laughlin, McManus and d'Aquili 1990, D'Aquili and Newberg 1998), anthropologist Pascal Boyer has suggested that certain universal ideas and acts derive from inherent cognitive structures in the brain. In his book, *The Naturalness of Religious Ideas* (1994) he argued that the human brain is predisposed to know in very human ways—ways that come quite naturally for people all over the globe—because the neurocognitive structures of the brain develop in childhood in similar ways across all cultures (Boyer 1996a). Some ideas and activities are easy to learn, others difficult or impossible because the brain is not "wired" that way (this is the same argument proposed years before Boyer by psychologists Martin Seligman and J. Hager in their book, *Biological Boundaries of Learning* 1972). Boyer's view is that the similarities among religious ideas and actions across cultures are explained by these limitations on knowing.

What makes Boyer's thinking useful to us is that he connects the very visible, very public actions of ritual with these natural, but invisible cognitions in the brain. Many aspects of human rituals are "probably fossilized versions of animal displays" (1994:222). The various elements that make up rituals may be isolated and studied with reference to the cognitive system that produces the elements. Among other things, Boyer's view eliminates the mind-body problem (treating mind as something distinct from body), for he considers both mental activity and ritual action to be bodily functions (see also Bell 2008). Moreover, rituals are recognized as such by people because of certain assumptions and intentions they have in their minds. In addition, the circumstances have to be just right—the right time of year (harvest time), the right place (temple, sacred space), the right persons performing the acts (chief, shaman, priest), the right sequence of actions (this is done before that can be done), and so forth. Like Humphrey and Laidlaw above, Boyer points out the fact that rarely is there a single all-pervasive interpretation of a ritual in the minds of its participants, but rather a myriad of intentions and interpretations. "[Even when people do have access to theological explanations for ritual sequences, they do not seem to make systematic usage of these resources" (1994:221). The emphasis in Boyer's view is that rituals are recognized as such as a category of event, and one to which each participant brings their own representations.

As we shall see in Chapter 3, Boyer pinpoints an aspect of the experience of ritual within the frame of reference we will address as the "cycle of meaning."

Harvey Whitehouse: Modes of Religiosity

You may have noticed by now that contemporary thinking about ritual often involves applying insights from *cognitive science*—an interdisciplinary study of the mind and how the mind comes to know what it knows and applies that knowing to problem solving (see Andresen 2001; Boyer 1993; Miller 2003). Harvey Whitehouse, perhaps more than any other anthropologist, has embraced a cognitive science approach to making sense of ritual (Whitehouse 2001, 2004, 2005, 2008a, 2008b). While the details and meanings associated with ritual appear to be endless across cultures, closer analysis shows that there exist clearly defined cognitive constraints upon activities considered by people to be a proper ritual (Barrett 2000; Whitehouse 2001). The most basic types of representations peppered throughout rituals derive from a preparedness to conceive of things and remember them in a similar way. "In short, ritual actions and ritual meanings are not as plastic as they might seem. They are directly constrained and shaped by universal properties of human cognition, derived from evolved neural architecture" (Whitehouse 2001:172).

Whitehouse's views on religion are influenced by his theory of *modes of religiosity* (2004, 2007; Atkinson and Whitehouse 2011). Pointing out that many anthropologists before him have recognized two basic forms of religion, he suggests those two types can be construed as an *imagistic mode* and a *doctrinal mode* of religiosity. These modes are polar opposites of each other, and require different faculties of memory for their transmission. The imagistic ritual—the use of emotionally-charged and evocative symbols—is the most ancient form. It occurs "infrequently" among small-scale societies; participants get highly aroused during the process (Whitehouse 2005). The pairing of infrequent calendrical repetition and high arousal leads to intense memories of these highly emotional events that can then sometimes lead to the concretizing/routinizing of ritual and the formation of new doctrine for the rituals to enact. An example might be an individual initiation rite. The doctrinal ritual, on the other hand, "...tends to be highly routinized, facilitating the storage of elaborate and conceptually complex religious teachings in semantic [e.g., textual meaning] memory, but also activating implicit [unconscious] memory in the performance of most ritual procedures" (Whitehouse 2004:63-64; see also Whitehouse 2000:1). An example would be the annual Fourth of July celebrations in the United States. These events are often marked by a town parade, popping off fireworks, and waving of flags. The feelings arising are generally excitement and pleasure. The symbols (flag, Uncle Sam, etc.) are doctrinally rich, evoking stories of the founding of the republic.

As we shall see later on, we share Maurice Bloch's (2004) reservations about Whitehouse's "ideal type" distinction between imagistic and doctrinal rituals, for there are numerous cases that can fit in with both types (for example, Tantric rituals that are repeated daily, but may lead to ecstatic experience; see Chapter 4).

Victor Turner, Richard Schechner, and Ronald Grimes: Ritual as Performance

As we will spell out in great depth as this book unfolds, we are inclined to emphasize a performance view of ritual (e.g., Tambiah 1979). Ronald Grimes, one of the premier performance theorists in ritual studies, writes that:

> Every religion depends on performativity generally, perhaps even on what we in the West call "the performative arts" more specifically. Although practitioners may not label what they do as either art or performance, they attend to the how, the art or technique, of their activities. Wherever ritual leaders gather, there is talk about matters of form and effectiveness. How did you do

that? Where did you learn that? Why didn't that work? (Grimes 2008:379; see also Grimes 2003b, 2014)

Grimes is using the term *performance* in its more dramaturgical sense, meaning a formal enactment that is repetitive, and which requires stipulated roles, techniques and planning. Regarding the historical connection between ritual and theater, anthropologist Victor Turner (1974, 1979, 1982) likewise emphasized reliance upon the performative aspects of ritual. For Turner, human beings are natural dramaturges—as the Bard would say, "All the world's a stage, and all the men and women merely players. They have their exits and their entrances, and one man in his time plays many parts..." (*As You Like It*, Act II, Scene VII). Peoples develop their rituals from repeated performances ("social dramas") and eventually ritual leads to true theatrical performances, frequently taking the form of religious mystery plays. Whether ritual or theatrical, the performance in certain circumstances has a transformative power, facilitating the passage of individuals from one phase of life to the next. An intermediary phase —the "betwixt and between" segment— Turner (1987) called the *liminal* phase (using the metaphor of a door's *limen*, or between space, in neither one room nor the other). We will return to Turner's thinking in Chapters 7 and 8 when we return to the transformative power of ritual performances.

Turner's interest in theater came to him easily, for his mother was an actress, and this interest led to his collaboration with drama theorist and director Richard Schechner (1986, 1993, 2011; Turner and Schechner 1988). Schechner, perhaps because of his direct experience of performance, comes closer than other theorists to appreciating the experiential dimensions of ritual. In his experimental work with actors, he has shown that body actions incorporated into a play "penetrate" to autonomic and other neural systems mediating emotion. In other words, not only can our emotions cause physical expressions, but also mimicking expressions can cause the emotions to arise. More than that, rituals can "drive" (generate) altered states of consciousness, a factor that is routinely missed in much of anthropological ritual theory. As we shall see in Chapter 3, this reciprocality between inner experience and ritual action is fundamental to the power of ritual across cultures.

Whitehouse (2004:3) notes that we recognize a ritual, as opposed to a ritualized pattern of behavior, by elements "...that lack any adequate technical relevance." Suppose that we get into a car with Charlie and he pulls out his key ring, selects a key, sticks it into the ignition and starts the car. Charlie is just repeating a ritualized procedure he has used thousands of times before. We take no notice of his actions because they all make perfect sense technically—that is, a series of causal acts required to start many cars. But suppose that Charlie were to pull out his key ring, select a key, stick it into the ignition, snap his fingers three times and then start the car. All of a sudden Charlie's actions would become more interesting to us, because we see him doing something that seems to have no technical relevance: snapping his fingers three times. No doubt this superfluous activity means something to Charlie, but we have no way of knowing what it means without asking him. In Whitehouse's terms (2004:4), the snapping of fingers "invites exegesis" (invites interpretation) because the ritual action has no intrinsic meaning of its own. This is a major difference between a technique and a ritual. While techniques may be ritualized—that is, made routine, like starting a car—they need not be rituals. On the other hand, rituals can be techniques when they are both carried out for a purpose (to "get something done"), and include elements that signal meaning and invite interpretation. For instance, Charlie may snap his fingers as a ritualized way of clearing his head in preparation for driving.

As we will show, grounding ritual in universal cognitive processes à la Pascal, Whitehouse and the others is a giant step in the right direction. However, contrary to Frits Staal's (1989) contention that rituals amount to "rules without meaning," we contend that rituals are the coalescence of both ritualization and significance. The notion that ritual is "meaningless" derives from an over-emphasis upon the cognitive processes of the most recently evolved cortical brain, as we have seen in the ideas of Atran, Boyer and others. In fact, the human body operates as a totality, and states of consciousness involve far more than cognitive acts. States of consciousness are mediated by many parallel and well "blended" physiological systems in the body (Fauconnier and Turner 2002)—all of which mediate meaning within the context of ritual action.

In this section, in order to provide some background and context for our own definition of ritual above, we have summarized several of the more important contemporary theories and definitions of ritual we will be discussing during the course of the book. Now we will move on to the specific characteristics that make ritual what it is and provide it with its performative power.

THE CHARACTERISTICS OF RITUAL AND THE CONTENTS OF THIS BOOK

In this book, we present and examine nine major characteristics of ritual that are integral to its myriad roles in human cultural life and central to the way it wields its power. These characteristics constitute what we call an *anatomy of ritual* (see also Grimes 2014). They include:

1. the neurobiological basis of ritual behaviors as coordination and communication systems that first developed in animals;
2. the use of symbols to convey a ritual's messages;
3. a cognitive matrix belief system) from which ritual emerges;
4. rhythm, repetition and redundancy: ritual drivers;
5. the use of tools, techniques, and technologies to accomplish ritual's multiple goals;
6. the framing of ritual performances;
7. the order and formality that separates ritual from everyday life, identifying it as ritual;
8. the sense of inviolability and inevitability that rituals can generate;
9. the acting, stylization, and staging that often give ritual its elements of high drama, the fact that it is performed and that it often intensifies toward a climax.

Not all rituals exhibit each of these characteristics; however, they are all salient features of ritual in general, all part of the anatomy of ritual and its capacity as a powerful communicative form. Understanding these characteristics of ritual—in other words, deconstructing its anatomy—is essential to understanding how it accomplishes its work in the world. So the early chapters of this book address these nine characteristics and how they work inside the human brain.

Chapter 2, "Symbolism in Ritual," is not so much about the meaning or interpretation of symbols, but rather describes the organization of the human brain, and shows how the symbols through which ritual works "penetrate" to different areas of the brain, accomplishing their work by entraining physical sensation, emotion, meaning and intellect. This is precisely the information about symbols and symbolism that is usually missed in anthropological accounts. We also describe "core symbols" and how to interpret them, and give some entertaining and illustrative examples of symbolic interpretation, including Darth Vader, an indigenous ancestor named Naro, and a contemporary debate among midwives over a kettle and what it signified for them.

Chapter 3, "The Cognitive Matrix of Ritual," describes the nature and roles of myths and paradigms—the cognitive matrices/belief systems that rituals enact, display and transmit to their participants. We use as examples the Navajo origin myth of Changing Woman, dream incubation, and what Robbie calls "the technocratic, humanistic, and holistic paradigms of medicine." We describe the human *cognitive imperative* to know and understand the world we live in, the *cycle of meaning* that cultures develop to meet that cognitive imperative, and the ways in which rituals make that cycle of meaning come alive—seem real—for its participants.

Chapter 4, "Myths, Paradigms, Rituals, and the Process of Truing," focuses on the relationship of myths and paradigms to reality and truth, explaining that these belief systems, while only partial pictures of larger realities, serve to "true" those pictures—to make them reflect enough of reality to ensure that the cultures that create and live through them will be able to function effectively in the world. We describe the differences among "sensate," "idealistic," and "ideational" cultures and how these different cultural types enact their beliefs and values through ritual, as well as how they manipulate myths and paradigms, and the rituals that enact them, to accommodate themselves to cultural and environmental change. The Native American Sun Dance and the American space program provide examples here of how the human cognitive imperative—the human "need to know" —can employ myth, paradigm, and ritual to fulfill that need.

Chapter 5, "Ritual Drivers and Their Effects on States of Consciousness," points out the wide range of rhythmic and repetitive stimuli through which rituals act on the human body and consciousness, and analyzes their neurological effects. We describe states and "warps" of consciousness and how information is transferred between them, "monophasic" and "polyphasic" cultures (can you already guess what we mean by these terms?), and how ritual can "drive," or control, states of consciousness among its participants. We look at "portals" as doorways to alternative states of consciousness (ASCs), and ask and answer the question, *"Why are ritual drivers so compelling?"*

Chapter 6, "Ritual Techniques and Technologies," describes the many tools and technologies used in ritual performances that enable ritual to do its work in the world and in the human brain and body. We ask: What is technology, how do technologies serve as implements of ritual practice, and how on earth did the ritual diviner find the purloined pots? What is "spooky causation," and how can ritual serve as a vehicle for "divine inspiration" and "psychic power"? And how, and in what ways, can the ancient technique called "ritual" manifest itself in the contemporary high-tech and virtual worlds?

Chapter 7, "Ritual Framing: Order, Formality, Inviolability," illustrates the ways in which ritual is framed—set apart from ordinary life, the order and formality that characterize ritual performances, and the sense of inviolability and inevitability they work to establish. We describe physical and non-physical ritual frames in terms of energy and power, and the meaning and power of shrines and altars of all types and kinds. Questions of why order and formality matter so much to the anatomy and effectiveness of ritual are answered through examples from the Trobriand Islands, the experiences of Bolivian tin miners (which will resonate for miners and factory workers of all types and in all countries), and contemporary obstetricians, who use ritual in entirely predictable and formalized ways to control the process of birth. And we ask, how can the "ritual train" lead a young woman who really doesn't want to get married to go through the ceremony anyway? What happens when someone chooses to "break the ritual frame," purposefully disrupting the ritual? And how does the "ludic" dimension of ritual—play and laughter—manage not to break the ritual frame, but only enhance it, thus making it more powerful?

In this chapter, we also describe the altered state of consciousness called "flow," making it clear that flow most often happens inside of a clearly delineated ritual frame—*the stronger the ritual, the deeper the sense of flow*—an experience so powerful that some people change their lives in an effort to achieve more of that experience. This chapter also describes how rituals enhance courage, enabling humans to do what they could not do without the sense that the rituals they perform will somehow see them successfully through the dangers they face. Finally, this chapter acknowledges that while rituals do have some degree of power (when believed in by the participants and performed correctly according to the participants), they are not all-powerful and they sometimes—or often—don't work, meaning that they do not accomplish the symbolic or instrumental work in the world that they were intended by their participants to do. So, we ask in this chapter, *what happens when rituals fail?*

In subsequent chapters, we focus on the effects that ritual can have on its participants, and the multiple roles ritual plays in social and individual life. These include: facilitating daily living, transmitting knowledge, acquiring information, transforming individual consciousness, engendering and concretizing belief, maintaining religious vitality, enhancing courage, effecting healing, cohering communities, initiating individuals into new social groups or new ways of being, preserving the status quo in a given society, and, paradoxically, effecting social change. These uses of ritual are evident in many domains of social life in the United States and many other countries. Particularly emphasized in this book are the roles of ritual in the domains of community, business, sports, religion, the military, spirituality movements, cult conversion, techno-medicine, and holistic healing. We have filled each chapter with examples of our points from both traditional and modern societies and from countries all over the world.

In Chapter 8, entitled "Ritual as Performance: Generating Emotion, Belief, and Transformation," we integrate our earlier descriptions of the anatomy of ritual in a focus on how ritual is performed—the acting, stylization, and staging that characterize ritual performances, their climactic nature, and the roles that charismatic ritual leaders, from cult leaders to priests to politicians, play in making these performances effective through generating emotional buildup and catharsis and achieving psychological transformation in their participants. No matter what the end goal is, very similar rituals are used to achieve that goal.

In Chapter 9, "Ritual and the Four Stages of Cognition," we make a clear distinction between rigid and fluid ways of thinking, delineate four stages of cognition, and more or less equate them with their anthropological equivalents. Stage 1 (rigid, concrete) thinking incorporates what anthropologists call *naïve realism* (our way is the only way because we know no other way), *fundamentalism* (our way is the only right way), and *fanaticism* (our way is so right that those who do not adhere to it should be either converted or exterminated). Stage 2 thinking, in anthropological terms, is called *ethnocentrism* (we know there are other ways, and that's OK for others, but our way is better!). We equate Stage 3 thinking to *cultural relativism*—a very fluid way of thinking (all ways are equal in relative value and no way is better than any other). And we identify Stage 4 fluid thinking as *global humanism* (we have to find a set of better ways that works for all). We explain each of these stages of cognition in relation to each other, and demonstrate how ritual can be employed to reinforce each way of thinking, and to reduce many kinds of stress by solidly grounding individuals in their belief system and worldview, giving them a sense of safety and stability in an uncertain world.

In Chapter 10, we confront ritual's paradoxical roles: ritual can work both to preserve the status quo and to effect social change. We provide multiple examples of ritual failure and ritual success in both endeavors, from the early Norse settlers in Greenland (whose ritual practices at first worked to preserve their cultural status quo in their new environment, yet eventually failed them by impeding their ability to adapt to environmental change), through various cultural revitalization movements (some of which failed to achieve social change, and some of which succeeded), to the contemporary invention of ritual by holistic obstetricians in Brazil and by Herb Kelleher, the founder of Southwest Airlines, who intentionally created a consciously alternative corporate culture that has long been hailed as an exemplar of how to run a successful business.

In Chapter 11, "Designing Rituals," we describe what it is like to design and carry out your own ceremonial rituals, and give examples of how such contrived affairs either work well, or don't, including examples that range from memorial ceremonies to weddings to puberty rites and "dream incubation."

And in our Conclusion (Chapter 12), we sum up our findings and leave you with room for further thinking about ritual, how it can work in the world and in your brain/body, and how you might use it for the most positive possible effects in your own life.

In the pages that follow we will stick mostly to standard English, but will ask our readers to bear with us as we introduce (as we have already started doing above) a few anthropological terms, perspectives and concepts that we find particularly useful for talking about and understanding ritual—what it is and how it works. For our readers' convenience, we include a Glossary at the beginning of the book that defines terms and abbreviations we use. In addition, we wish to note to our readers that some of you may find sections of some chapters, especially the earlier ones, rather heavy going. We have tried to make complex information and theories as clear and understandable as we could. We ask you to hang in there as you read—the earlier chapters are necessary background to the easier-reading ones that follow. We trust you will find that the book gets more engaging and exciting as the chapters progress!

Ritual is a complex subject—the anthropological writings on it could fill a library. And as we have seen, its cultural uses are myriad. Ritual is a powerful didactic and socializing tool, but often its power and influence go unrecognized because most people are not generally aware of its inner workings. To grasp these inner workings is to have a choice in our response to the rituals that permeate our daily lives.

Suggested Reading

Adler, Margot (1988) *Drawing Down the Moon: Witches, Druids, Goddess-Worshippers, and Other Pagans in America Today* (2nd edition.). Boston: Beacon Press.

Bell, Catherine (1997) *Ritual: Perspectives and Dimensions*. Oxford: Oxford University Press

Turnbull, Colin M. (1983) *The Human Cycle*. New York: Simon and Schuster.

Chapter 2

SYMBOLISM IN RITUAL

Symbols Are Brain Talk. The Core, Emotional, and Cortical Brains. The Power of Symbols. Core Symbols. Interpreting Core Symbolism. Examples of Symbolic Interpretation. Summary: The Power of Symbols.

Ritual's primary characteristic is that it has effects on individuals by sending messages through symbols. (Please note that symbols don't actually "send" messages—rather, people perceive meaning in symbols, in ways that may be similar or may differ individually, culturally, historically, etc. Saying that "symbols send messages" is a convenient shorthand we will use throughout this book.) A *symbol* is an object, form, idea or action that "stands for something else," providing a source of cultural meaning. Non-human animals also communicate with symbols—facial expressions, vocal calls, body posture, etc. —but they do not have the elaborate symbolic systems (including language) that we humans enjoy. Some authorities make a distinction between "symbol" (something that represents something else it is *not* connected to—e.g. white lilies associated with death) and "sign" (something that *is* connected to something else—e.g., ringing signals a telephone call). In this book we will not use this distinction, for as we shall see, both symbol and sign operate on the same basic symbolic process.

Symbols are *multi-vocal*—that is, many meanings can be combined and expressed in a single symbol (Deacon 1997; Donald 2001). For example, think about how many different things are symbolized by a cross. This one simple object can connote Christ's death, an action that itself conveys the central message of Christianity: the potential redemption and salvation of humankind. A cross can also connote a person's identification with the Christian community, while its style and design can indicate one specific Christian sect or group. A cross placed on the wall in someone's home indicates that this is a Christian household; a cross placed in a public space can be a political statement; a burning cross in someone's yard may send a hate message. These are only a few of the multiple messages this one symbol can send. It sends other messages in other cultures: in various shamanic traditions, the cross as *axis mundi* is a conceptualization of the source of the world—a symbol of connection and transition where two dimensions meet at the axis, which constitutes a symbolic threshold of transition—a portal—between those two dimensions.

Symbols serve, as expressed by anthropologist Clifford Geertz (1973), as "vehicles for conception." Claude Levi-Strauss (1996) has said that symbols are "goods to think with." Another useful way of thinking about symbols is as *vehicles for communication*. All symbols carry messages that can be received by the interpretive frameworks of the perceivers. The ease with which symbols evoke broad interpretive processes is what makes them so effective in communication and so essential to the processes and power of ritual. Contemporary cognitive linguistics is increasingly taking the position that an entire package of communicative modes evolved together (e.g., Levinson and Enfield 2006; Levinson and Holler 2014). It is no longer tenable to think in terms of language evolving alone, separate from other symbolic media, especially ritual.

SYMBOLS ARE BRAIN TALK

Symbols are the elements of what we call the *symbolic process*, the process by which the brain makes sense of what it perceives. The symbolic process is shorthand for how the cells of our nervous system interact in such an automatic and rapid way that we are barely aware of the difference between seeing something like the squiggly lines on this page and the meaning we attach to the lines as words, concepts, images, and thoughts. The reason why this linking of image and meaning is so rapid and natural is that symbolic interpretation is an innate human potential that unfolds naturally through environmental exposure and socialization. We have inherited this facility not just as humans, but more generally as a consequence of being animals with brains. All animals with brains operate similarly. Honeybees and dogs and chimpanzees all have this in common—their brains make sense of the world by way of the symbolic process.

You may well ask then, if all animals with brains operate via the symbolic process, does that mean all animals with brains have culture? If this question did occur to you, then welcome to anthropology!

Authorities have been arguing over this issue for decades. The answer of course depends on how you define culture. If you define it broadly enough, you will likely acknowledge that some of the big-brained social animals, like arctic wolves, African elephants, bottlenose dolphins, and chimpanzees have rudimentary culture. May we suggest that you read Frans de Waal and Frans Lantings' wonderful book, *Bonobo: The Forgotten Ape* (1997) and decide for yourself about the Bonobo chimpanzee, one of our closest biological relatives among surviving apes. What we can say for sure is that many other animals have rituals (d'Aquili, Laughlin and McManus 1979) —patterned, repetitive and symbolic performances that communicate important messages to others.

The outcome of symbolic processing is relatively stable and recurring across time, especially in adult humans and other animals. Similar stimuli evoke the same symbolic interpretation time after time. (For example, consider the effect that the Nazi swastika has on Jews, and many others, still today.) The neural structures that mediate symbols and meanings—that mediate each and every moment of experience for that matter—are linked across our billions of brain cells and their trillions of interconnections. These structures are made up of what we call *circuits*, an organization of cells that work together to do something very specific, and which come together to form a *neural network*—in this case, the network mediating symbols and their meaning. Neural networks are *componential* in their structure, the product of many neurophysiological circuits that combine (and recombine) in a distinct, recurring, and hierarchical network comprising each meaning field. At the same time, the neural networks mediating the whole field of perception alter the meaning field of any particular symbol in accordance with environmental context (is the cross on top of a church or burning in someone's front yard?).

Thus, different parts of our brain interpret different dimensions of symbols. As you may know, the cortex of the brain is divided into two hemispheres, the left and the right, that talk to each other across major neural tracts such as the corpus callosum. Straightforward verbal messages (like "pigs are pink") are decoded and analyzed in the left hemisphere of the brain, so we can choose whether or not to believe them ("I know better; pigs can be dark or light brown, black and white, black, or white—they are certainly not all pink!"). In contrast, non-verbal symbols are received by the right hemisphere of the brain, where they are interpreted as a *gestalt* (a whole) (see Table 2.1). In other words, instead of being intellectually analyzed, *a symbol's message will be felt in its totality through the body, the emotions and the intuitive faculty of the mind.* For example, when a Marine basic trainee is required to sleep with his rifle, he *in-corporates* its symbolic meanings—literally taking them into his psyche through the physical senses of his body. Of course, the whole brain takes part in all brain functions—it is important to keep in mind that the division between the functions of the hemisphere is not absolute but a matter of degree and complementarity of function, or of relative dominance.

Visual imagery is one of the most important and powerful symbolic tools found in ritual among humans and other primates. Visual imagery seems to involve many of the same systems that are involved in visual perception. Yet what is called the *primary visual cortex* is involved in producing images while awake with the eyes closed, but not when the images are dreamed (Kosslyn 1994:19-20). Also, it was once thought that the right hemisphere of the brain mediated all dream imagery, but we now know that it's not that simple. Experiments with patients who

Left hemisphere functions	Right hemisphere functions
analytic—dissects, segregates, categorizes, evaluates	synthetic— receives the gestalt, the whole
either/or logic, linear thinking	poetic, metaphoric, analogic
emphasizes differences, discontinuities	stresses similarities, relationships
works things through	creates A-HA! experiences
verbal	musical, pictorial, general semantics
speech	gestures, tone of voice
temporal (watches clock)	spatial
linear	holistic
intellectual, rational	emotional
individual more likely to be conscious of its functions	individual less likely to be conscious of its functions

Table 2.1. The Two Sides of the Human Brain (Frontal Cortex)

(Please note: This Table is oversimplified, because the whole brain operates in all brain functions, yet it is still generally useful in terms of brain hemispheric predominance)

have undergone right hemispherectomies (the right cortical hemisphere is surgically cut out) have shown that they dream in the same way as people with intact brains. Neuroscientists have concluded that under specific circumstances, both the right and left hemispheres participate in the generation of images.

Whereas we once thought that language functions were lodged solely in the left hemisphere for most people, we now know that the extent of hemispheric dominance depends on which language function is being addressed. "The left hemisphere seems dominant for producing overt speech, phonetic decoding, using syntax, and certain (but not all) semantic processes. The right hemisphere seems dominant for using the pragmatic aspects of language, integrating information across sentences, and using context" (Hellige 1993:110). Language processing thus requires mediation by many areas of cortex distributed over both hemispheres.

The fact that symbolic messages are generally physically and emotionally experienced, rather than being intellectually analyzed, means that *ritual participants are often unconscious of the powerful symbolic messages they are receiving.* We all have some idea of what it means to be unconscious of something. The something happens, but outside of our awareness. Some of these happenings are only unconscious because we are not paying attention to them at the moment—like driving a car while thinking about something else. We can become conscious of our driving in an instant if need be. (There are other things that happen at an unconscious level that are not so easy to become aware of—like what our liver is doing at the moment or how our skin is processing vitamin D when we are sun-bathing.) The brain often processes symbols at deeper levels of the unconscious, as when we may find ourselves profoundly moved by watching a flag flying high without even thinking about the fact that the flag is a symbol or knowing why it is affecting us in that way. Many people watching Princess Diana's funeral—or the wedding of her son William to Kate Middleton—were uncertain as to why they were so profoundly moved by the death—or marriage—of people they had never met. This is symbolic processing at its most powerful and unconscious level. It is safe to say that almost all of the symbolism affecting us is operating in part at an unconscious level.

For a more detailed example, consider a woman in early labor walking into a typical hospital and being asked to sit in a wheelchair for transport to the labor ward. She knows that she is quite capable of walking there by herself, and may understand that the purpose of the wheelchair is simply to protect the hospital from liability should she fall, and that it is used in this way for all women in labor so has nothing in particular to do with her as an individual. Nevertheless, a wheelchair is a powerful symbol of disability. To sit down and be wheeled is to convey the impression that one is disabled and weak. The laboring woman may know intellectually that she is not disabled, but she will be emotionally sensing the impression of disability simply through sitting in the chair. And when others—the nurses, the partner and family or friends who accompany her—look at her, they will see not an autonomous woman walking unsupported, but a woman in a wheelchair who looks disabled—a perception that may soon translate into subtle changes in the way they talk to and treat her (Davis-Floyd 2004:77-78).

And there is a further layer of symbolic meaning that accompanies sitting in a wheelchair instead of walking upright—in Western cultures' metaphorical systems, *up is good* and *down is bad*. To be "up" means to be on top of things, in control; to be "down" means to be subordinate to, not in control, lower on the totem pole. Interactionally, everyone else is now "up," and the laboring woman is "down" —a double whammy.

Significantly, no one stops to consider the fact that they are all receiving powerful symbolic messages that the woman in labor is disabled, not in control, and lower down on the interactional hierarchy than everyone else. These symbolic messages are received unconsciously: they are not thought about, they are simply experienced. Thus their effect is all the more powerful because the participants do not have a choice about what they feel. They don't stop to warn themselves not to treat the woman differently just because she is in a wheelchair; rather, they may start treating her differently without realizing it. If she goes from the wheelchair to the hospital bed, these impressions of disability will be intensified, for once she is wearing a hospital gown and lying in a hospital bed, she will look like any other hospital patient. Since most patients are sick, weak, and unable to care for themselves, she will appear to be the same. These symbolic impressions of illness and weakness will influence the way this laboring woman is viewed and thus treated by her caregivers and friends from the very first moments of her hospital stay.

Robbie experienced another dramatic example of how powerful a symbol of illness the hospital gown and plastic bracelet can be when a friend of hers was suddenly discharged from the hospital two days after an appendectomy. He had thought he would be spending another day, when the doctor suddenly decided that he was fine and could go home. One moment, sitting in his hospital bed, wearing a hospital gown, he appeared, felt, and acted weak and ill. But as he shed the gown, cut off the bracelet, took a shower, and put on his street clothes (which of course symbolize normality in relation to the abnormality of the hospital gown), he started to appear normal and act normal. By the time they left, he was feeling normal as well, and could hardly believe that only an hour before he had felt and acted weak and ill.

THE CORE, EMOTIONAL, AND CORTICAL BRAINS

Understanding how the brain works is fundamental—indeed, essential—to understanding the power of ritual. So it makes sense for us to spend some time developing a better understanding of our brain. The human brain and its symbol-making capacity are characterized by both the complementary right and left hemisphere processes introduced above, and by a hierarchy of other information processing capacities that emerged, complexified, and reorganized over the course of evolution. The human capacity to have experiences, be conscious, process information and meaning, and know the world is based on different brain strata. For the sake of convenience, we will talk about how the brain functions at three levels of structure:

- the *core brain*, which mediates somatic regulation, metabolism, physical and psychological arousal, etc.
- the *emotional brain*, which mediates emotional states
- the *cortical brain* which mediates imagination, thought, modulation of emotion, planning, etc.

To some extent, we humans share the lower levels of neural structure with other animals; their functions underlie the similarities in patterns of human behavior with those found in other vertebrates, including reptiles, birds and mammals. These older levels of brain structure are reflected in human behavior, particularly in forms of nonverbal communication. These lower brain systems were reworked and elaborated in the human brain over the course of our evolution, yet their propensity for the ritualization of behavior has remained. These three brain strata have their roles to play in different kinds of experience and information processing that can be both elicited and mediated through ritual processes.

The Core Brain

The core brain is responsible for the wake/sleep cycle and, in association with the endocrine system (the glands), regulates bodily functions (e.g., metabolism, digestion and respiration). The core brain can activate (as in wakefulness) and paralyze (as during sleep) the motor cortex, and plays a fundamental role in the regulation of the organism's daily behavior patterns and social interaction rituals. This core system mediates the integration of somatic and autonomic components used in non-verbal social communication, coordinating various levels and conflicting types of information and mechanisms for overall integration of behavior. The core brain plays a significant role in the ritualization of behavior, the regular sequencing of everyday behavior routines (e.g., getting up, shutting off the alarm clock, going to the kitchen and starting the coffee, stepping outside to get the newspaper, going to your favorite chair to read the paper and drink coffee, shaving and showering, taking the same route to work, etc.). While the core brain has "a mind of its own," it does not have the ability to learn how to cope with new situations, nor does it have knowledge of the subjective self or of symbols.

The Emotional Brain

One of the fundamental aspects of ritual is its power to evoke, manipulate, moderate and focus emotion, both within the individual and among social groups. The limbic system (emotional brain) is sandwiched between the core brain and the overlying cortex. It plays a fundamental role in generating emotions and integrating them with behavior. These structures of the "emotional brain" mediate sex, eating and drinking, fighting/self-defense, emotions, social relations, bonding and attachment, and sense of self.

For instance, it is known that large-brained animals like dolphins and elephants enter a phase of ritual interaction with potential mates before they copulate. We humans call this "foreplay." "Flirting" and foreplay are processes of ritual communication that function to reduce the social distance between two potential mates so that intimacy can occur, by reducing aggressive tendencies and allowing the desire to couple to increase. This layer of the brain serves as a two-way processing area between sensory input and motor output, connecting the primitive core brain with the frontal cortex, and integrating emotion and memory into behavior. Activities of these areas provide a basis for maternal care and bonding, which for humans laid the foundation for the family and society. The subjective and affective (emotional) experiences mediated by these areas also play a role in higher cognitive functions. They generate basic social personality and the sense of authenticity and feelings of conviction that humans use to substantiate mental ideas, concepts, beliefs, and theories, creating the feelings that the experiences we have of the world are valid. Central aspects of consciousness—our sense of self, the feeling of certainty in our knowledge, and our inclusion of others as reference points in our thinking—are all products of the emotional brain. Its capacity to modulate affect (emotion, feeling) in order to guide behavior is generally not deliberate, but neither is it unconscious. Rather this modulation manifests in intuitions and feelings that fall outside of the direct control of the intellect.

The Cortical Brain

The newest and most complex part of our brain is what we call the *neocortex*—the sheet of neural tissue that is layered over evolutionarily older systems—like a pancake covering a sausage in a pig-in-a-blanket. The neocortex is all crinkled up, forming ridges (one ridge called a *gyrus*) and valleys (one valley called a *sulcus*) giving the surface of our brain the look of a really big walnut. Under one square millimeter (or less than $2/100^{th}$ of a square inch) of cortex that is perhaps 4-6 millimeters (or 0.16 - 0.24 inches) thick, there will be approximately 100,000 neurons, and many times that many "support" cells. And all those cells are exquisitely organized, communicate with each other, consume energy, and have their distinct functions.

The neocortex is structurally divided into the two hemispheres we describe above—right and left. Communication between these two hemispheres is primarily by way of the *corpus callosum,* a bridge of neural tracts that lies between them—something like a ribbon of wires. The part of the corpus callosum that is related to language and emotional functions tends to be thinner in men (fewer connecting circuits) and thicker in women (more connecting circuits), which may explain to some extent why women are often viewed as "more emotional" than men: their thicker corpus callosum allows women to respond more easily to stimuli with their whole brains, rather than one hemisphere or the other as men tend to do. Women tend to empathize and communicate feelings more easily than men, while men are more naturally able to compartmentalize between the intellect and the emotions. Of course, men and women can develop the same capacities, and often do. Poets and writers, artists and engineers, may be male or female, but the developmental course they each go through may be different.

The neocortex is the level of brain organization where much of our perceptual and cognitive experience is produced and where the meaning of symbols and events is generated. The neocortex is divided into functional areas. The areas that input sensory information from the environment are generally located toward the back of the brain in each hemisphere, while the areas that control our body motions and activities are located toward the front of the brain in the *frontal cortex*. At the very front of the brain is located the *prefrontal cortex* (or PFC)—that part of the frontal cortex that causes us humans to have large foreheads in comparison to apes and chimps. (In addition, the human PFC exhibits more interconnections when compared with ape brains, both within the lobe and between the lobe and other areas of the brain.)

The PFC is perhaps the most important part of our frontal cortex from the perspective of the anthropology of ritual, for as we shall see: (1) the extent of PFC involvement in mediating our concerted activity over time makes an enormous difference in the intentionality of our experiences; (2) the extent of involvement of the medial part of the PFC determines the social quality of experiences; and (3) the evolution of the PFC among hominins (our direct ancestors) is the single most important reason why we developed the higher cortical functions that we humans enjoy today. The PFC is the evolutionarily youngest part of our brain, and is the seat of our executive cognitive functions. These include the mediation of intelligence and working memory, the modulation and suppression of emotion, the planning of activities and structuring goal-directed activities over lengthy periods of time, the *plotting* (putting symbolic elements in strategic places inside of rituals so that they form a kind of narrative) of symbolic action, and so forth. If we wish to carry out a complex, purposeful activity over a lengthy duration of time, simulate an ideal solution to a problem, or delay motor responses until the situation is fully understood, the involvement of the PFC as a component of our neural activity is essential, as it is for all primates.

Integration of the Three Levels of the Brain

These three levels of brain activity—the core brain, the emotional brain, and the cortical brain—are not stacked up like three pancakes (as brain scientists used to think when they formerly called them the reptilian, paleomammalian, and neomammalian brains). While it is true that the bottom layer—the core brain—is evolutionarily older than the layers above it, none of the layers has remained unchanged over the course of brain evolution. Far from it, for all the layers of the brain are interconnected with each other, and have resulted over evolutionary time in a gradual reorganization.

Connections between different areas and levels of the brain are reciprocal—information is exchanged in various directions. The different areas and levels of the brain talk to each other in the service of a holistic and effective response to the environment. If one area of the brain is destroyed by disease, injury, or surgery, the entire brain tries to reorganize itself to take over the functions of the damaged tissues. In the healthy brain, the PFC will often inhibit our emotional brain so that we don't fly off the handle in a confrontation. The core brain will modulate our arousal and awareness relative to possible dangers or opportunities perceived in the environment. Each area performs its function in relation to the other areas of the brain that, operating together, can all be involved in problem-solving, planning, imagining, conversing, and so forth. Aspects of our subjective minds are derived from these levels of brain function in ways that are crucial for learning, the transmission of culture, and problem-solving. A central aspect of this expressive and communication system is manifested in visual symbolism. Rituals, through their manipulation of symbols, play a fundamental role in manipulating and managing these expressive processes. *The great power of ritual stems in part from its ability to engage all levels of the brain, and thus control—or at least maximally mediate—the experiences of its participants.*

The core brain is primarily responsible for managing drives, impulses, compulsions and obsessions, and regulating them in our daily behavioral routines, basic forms of survival behavior, and social cooperation and integration. The emotional brain in its turn generates emotions and influences behavior with subjective information and feelings. Its emotional intelligence gives rise to the basic dynamics that underlie everyday social behavior and the tone of social interactions. These lower brain centers provide forms of expression that are often referred to as *non-verbal communication*—body language, facial expressions, posture, and gestures. Meanwhile, language and culture that derive from the neocortex dominate our attention, distracting us from the more basic brain processes and their roles in human consciousness, social identity, and behavior. Non-verbal awareness and emotional dynamics are generally unconscious, cut off from conscious awareness because of the domination of the left-hemisphere and language-based cultural rules of the neocortex. In other words, our thought and behavior, as well as our sense of well-being, require the coordination of many different kinds of competing information and motivations, processed in a simultaneous and parallel fashion all over the brain.

Again, most of us are unaware of this brain-wide integration of functions because conscious awareness is typically focused on the activities of the left hemisphere. Nevertheless, the intuitions, emotions, and unconscious decision-making processes of the right hemisphere, and those arising from the lower brain systems, contribute fundamental operations linked to the neocortex's higher cognitive processes. The lower brain processes provide our sense of self, the emotional dynamics of our relationships with others, the felt meanings we associate with self and others, and our convictions of certainty about feeling and beliefs. These lower brain dynamics can also produce emotional conflicts that we may repress to facilitate social adaptation. (Sometimes these repressed conflicts express themselves physiologically as various types of illness or pain—for example, a sore throat can result from not expressing emotional pain, a skin rash from repressed anger.)

One of the functions of ritual (and of the altered states of consciousness rituals can produce) is to integrate processes normally managed by the lower brain centers with the analytical power of the neocortex. Through the power of symbols that "penetrate" all levels of the brain (see below), ritual can tap into the lower brain systems, integrating their physiological and emotional subjectivity with the abstract systems of the neocortex. In other words, ritual can be used to bring unconscious processes that have been repressed and automatized (e.g., unconscious destructive habits or feelings) into consciousness.

Many psychotherapists, for example, use ritualized techniques to facilitate this kind of integration such as guided visualization—a process in which the therapist has a client imagine a series of events, often in the form of a story. (For Robbie's integrative experience of highly ritualized EMDR therapy, see Chapter 8.) For another example, some psychiatrists working with substance abuse among Native Americans have prescribed participation in sweat lodge rituals, Native American Church peyote rituals, and the Sun Dance ritual, and have found all of these ritual treatments to be sound and effective with certain individuals because of the emotional release and psychological catharsis they can generate.

It is important to note that the power of ritual to affect the human brain can also be employed in extremely negative and destructive ways that include hazing, brainwashing, torture, and the mistreatment of inmates in prisons and concentration camps, to name only a few (see Smith 1993). The cultures of prisons and other total institutions (such as hospitals, asylums, nursing homes; see Goffman 1961) may be built around a series of ritualized ways in which the authorities regularly abuse the inmates without feeling guilty about it, because "that's the way it's done around here." This is what we call the "shadow side" of ritual—it can be manipulated just as effectively for ill as for good.

THE POWER OF SYMBOLS

The power of ritual depends in large part upon the power of symbols. The brain is in a sense an organ of symbolism, for it operates in virtually every moment of consciousness to wed images with meanings in the manner described above. In the context of a social narrative—like story-telling—symbols are employed in narrative plots over time in a meaningful sequence. In both traditional and contemporary societies for instance, myths and folktales are often told to young children as a series of short "just-so" stories—how the rabbit lost its tail, how coyote tricked his way out of a crisis (see Kipling 2009)—because the ability of children to combine symbols is limited to short durations. As people mature, the mythology becomes more and more complex in *plot*—in the elaboration of the stories it tells—as their consciousness develops (as we will explain further in later chapters). How then do symbolic integration and mythological plot affect ritual activities in such an efficacious way?

How Symbols Work

The power of symbols derives from their operation on the whole body to bring about transformations in perception and experience. The first thing we have to do to understand symbols is to simply accept the fact that our on-going, moment-by-moment experience is heavily influenced by activities of our nervous system. Earlier on, we defined a symbol as an object, idea or action that "stands for something else," providing a source of multiple meanings. But it is more precise to say that the term "symbolizing" *refers to the process by which an object or an event out in the world is attributed meaning within our brains.* Our bodies (which, of course, contain our brains) are actively involved in producing the meaning of various things and happenings in our experience. If something is a symbol to us, it is because a whole network of associations becomes attached to that something. It might help us here if the reader will imagine that a symbol and its meaning(s) are much like a child's toy magnet under a piece of paper upon which we have scattered iron filings. When we move the magnet under the paper, the iron filings take on a distinct pattern that changes as we move the magnet. The magnet represents the symbol and the patterns formed by the iron filings represent meaning. In much this way, key symbols incorporated into a ritual will evoke a pattern of associations that are manipulated within our psyche in response to the plotting and placement of the symbols.

The cultural world is full of powerful symbols—flags display love of country, a Rolls Royce or Jaguar displays the wealth of its owner, a cross on top of a building clearly tells us that it is a church. Even our perception of a simple chair is loaded with symbolism. We know (if we are from a culture that utilizes chairs) that the object is fundamentally something to be sat upon. But there are chairs and there are chairs. The chair's shape and materials convey messages about the wealth and status of its owner or the place where it should be used, etc. It may be a movie theater seat or a royal throne, a cheap Wal-Mart camp chair or a valuable 18th century Chippendale. The sensory object we take to be a chair is the "symbol" and the cognitive associations we attribute to that object—"chair-ness", "wheelchair-ness", "antique-ness," and so forth—are the "meaning" of the symbol for us. The cognitive associations we make with the object function to extend and elaborate its meaning for us—like adding iron filings to the pattern on top of the paper.

Symbolic Penetration

The way that something outside of our body—a wheelchair, a bar/bat mitzvah, a photo, a song—links up to a set of meanings inside our body is called *penetration* by Charlie and his fellow biogenetic

Figure 2.1. An astronaut planting the American flag on the moon—an act with little instrumental value but laden with powerful symbolic meaning. What does this image symbolize for you?

structuralists. Insofar as we understand how things can "penetrate" us as symbols, the more fully we will come to understand why rituals are so powerful. ("Symbolic penetration" is a term that has nothing to do with sexual penetration, so please don't think of it that way!) The term actually refers to the way cells and organs interact within our body. When we eat one of our favorite dishes, we experience pleasure. But the organ that interprets the food in a pleasurable way is not the same organ that digests the food—so we can have a great time eating pizza and then wake up in the middle of the night with heartburn. The taste of the food reaches the body's various pleasure centers in the brain by way of a complex series of cellular interactions, and we experience the food as flavorful and satisfying. We would say that the wedge of pizza has "penetrated" to the pleasure centers. In the same way, the sight of the wheelchair penetrates to associations in our memory having to do with disability, injury, and lack of mobility, and the sight of a snake may in some people penetrate to the fear centers and produce terror. Similarly, the association of friends and eating pizza can link the idea of pizza to pleasure and social rewards—in spite of its potential to disturb our gastrointestinal systems.

"Penetration" actually involves cells "talking to each other" from organ to organ within our body. Penetration means that the stimulus physically causes network A to excite network B and so forth, until the target network that mediates the meaning is excited/stimulated. As we mentioned above, it is a significant fact that connections between organs, and between networks of cells within organs, are reciprocal—every connection between one organ or cell network and a target organ or cell network is matched by a complementary connection running in the other direction. Thus we can see that "penetration" often goes in both directions. We can desire the pleasure of the pizza experience and order out for pizza, or we can eat a bite of pizza and feel pleasure. In the first case the desired pizza evokes anticipated pleasure through penetration to the pleasure centers of our brain, and in the second case actually eating the newly delivered pizza fulfills our desire. In other words, a symbol may in one case *evoke meaning,* or in another case may be the *fulfillment of meaning,* depending upon which arose first, the meaning or the symbol.

A special kind of evoking and fulfilling penetration occurs when we communicate with other people. For instance, we may feel a lot of love for someone and send them a card on Valentine's Day. The card is a symbol expressing our loving feelings toward that person, and we hope that he or she will "get the message" when they receive the card—"getting the message" of course requires the kind of penetration we desire. For us the card expresses our inner feelings, which we hope will penetrate the consciousness of the recipient and evoke loving feelings in return. For many Americans, Christmas activities revolve around the ritual exchange of gifts that may have profound significance for both the giver and receiver. Gifts in such circumstances are powerful symbols of the kind of relationship that obtains between the parties to the exchange. The gifts may penetrate us deeply, and reinforce or even enhance the sense of bonding between relatives and other loved ones. Or the opposite may occur—an inappropriate gift may penetrate us with the message "This person does not understand me at all!"

The most common form of symbolic communication among humans is spoken and written language. When we communicate with other people through speaking or writing, we are expressing what we mean to say through arbitrary sounds and squiggles that the other person interprets, hopefully in the way we intend. But we all know that we can intend to say one thing and the other person can hear something quite different. *We are only able to exchange symbols, not the meaning itself.* So we have only limited control over what meaning the other person will attach to the sounds and squiggles we choose (a phenomenon often experienced in the attempt to interpret poetry, for instance). Language is thus a symbolic process that involves expressive penetration on the part of the speaker or writer, and evocative penetration on the part of the hearer or reader. (The symbol penetrates from the outside reality, through sensory detection, pattern recognition, association with context, and then into cognitive structures.)

Expressive penetration occurs when we act in a symbolic way in order to produce meaning in others. If we get angry at others, we expect our histrionics to "get inside" and "push their buttons" to emotionally affect them. We want them to understand and perhaps feel what we are feeling, so we speak loudly, make angry sounds, and manipulate our body language in order to "get through" (penetrate). The language that is used as part of a ritual—for example, the recitations, hymns, incantations, and sermons that are part of the Catholic Mass—is a significant part of the symbolism that enriches the ritual, and is likely to have more evocative power within the ritual than outside the ritual.

Whether the object or event is external to our body, as in the case of the wheelchair, or internal, as in the imagery of a dream, hallucination, or fantasy, the image becomes a symbol when it connects to its meaning from our memory and within our experience. The symbol is "re-cognized"—known again, or re-membered—literally "put together again." It really is magical how our mind is able to do this trick. We may never have seen a particular wheelchair before in our lives, and yet we know it for what it is—a wheelchair, with all that "wheelchair-ness" implies for us. The symbol "out there" has penetrated to and evoked its meaning inside our mind and body. As previously mentioned, Charlie lived for a time with a tribe of East African people called the So. The So of that time were terrified of hospitals, because the hospital was "the place where people go to die." Why? It turned out that hospital staff, insensitive to local cultural norms, required women to remove their neck rings when they were admitted into a ward. But in the So culture of that era, the only time a woman's neck rings were taken off was when she died—hence the automatic So association of hospital admission and death.

Socialization and Ritual Symbolic Penetration

The power of symbolic penetration is also based in processes of socialization that link cultural symbols with individual physiological responses.

Learning is an individual and neurophysiological process, but it can be influenced, conditioned, and manipulated by social processes. We learn the language(s) we hear spoken when we are children, and much of that learning involves associating arbitrary symbols (words and phrases) with their meanings. As a consequence of this social conditioning, all English speakers know the meaning of the word "water." But if we said to you, "*Misa kwe?*," the meaning would be lost to you because you were not raised in Uganda and had not learned the language of the So people (it means "give me water"). In the same way, the meaning of ritual symbols is laid down in the memory of each brain so that their penetration evokes similar meanings in all the participants. Social rituals depend for their efficacy on this social dimension of symbolic penetration. Ritual uses these previously established associations of symbols with physiological processes to manipulate the neural networks that can control the associated physiological processes. Through linking up (or entraining) multiple neural structures by means of symbols, ritual can elicit early associational learning (learning laid down while we are still babies and young children) and raise these associations into adult consciousness. In this way, ritual is able under certain circumstances to reveal previously repressed psychodynamics, and channel emotions of fear and anxiety, happiness and contentment, in socially useful ways.

Human development involves the entrainment of neurons into circuits and networks that mediate experiences, and can be elicited by symbolic stimuli. Socialization results in making physiological responses to symbols automatic and habitual (an adult frowns; recognizing the meaning of this symbol, the child's skin prickles, she feels a flash of fear, and to alleviate that fear, she alters her behavior). These mental effects upon physiology are an inherent aspect of development, as symbolic meanings increasingly elicit physiological responses in a child over time. In other words, the child's initial innate organization of neural networks is re-configured over time by learning to understand symbolic processes and their associated cultural patterns of interpretation and response. Socialization links the autonomic processes of the lower and largely unconscious brain centers with the symbolic structures of the neocortical brain. These learned linkages of experiences with physiological responses permit reciprocal effects, in which the ritual manipulation of symbolic structures can produce physiological responses.

Symbolic processes are obviously fundamental to the development of experience; they "tune" the central nervous system, enhancing the relationship between action, emotion, and cognition. Human perception is in its most fundamental form a symbolic process that allows us to interpret present stimuli in terms of our previous experiences. (In order for a single frown to immediately cause a child to alter her behavior, she must have previously experienced overt negative sanctions that were preceded by frowns; thus she learns to associate the frown with the sanctions that will result if she does not respond to the frown.) Experience, development, and socialization involve *entrainment*—the linking of neurons into circuits, and circuits into networks—through adaptation to the environment, including the family and cultural environment.

During a child's development, neurophysiological circuits form in response to repetitive social stimuli. So that we are on the same page here, let us look at how neurons work. We have elsewhere described the brain as a "community of cells" (Laughlin, McManus and d'Aquili 1990:34), by which we mean that our brain is like a vast human community in which the neurons and "support" cells are living organisms that organize themselves at both local (circuits, networks) and higher, more complex levels (interactions across hemispheres, and up and down the neural hierarchy), and that communicate among themselves. Neural cells have the capacity of *synaptic plasticity*—that is, the ability of the global system of synapses involved in memory storage to change and grow. Neurons are very special cells that communicate by "reaching out" and touching each other (neurons that touch other neurons are called *interneurons*) and other tissue cells, like those that make up muscles and other organs. This "reaching out" develops over time into more and more complex neural structures. It is also exquisitely selective and changeable. The point at which one neuron touches another in a circuit is called a *synapse*—a point of connection between nerve cells where one cell can influence the activity of another cell (see Figure 2.2). Synapses can exist between the tip of a cell's *axon* (an appendage reaching off the body of a nerve cell like a thread-like tentacle of a squid) and a *dendrite* (a smaller appendage like hair growing out of the body of the nerve cell). The axon communicates with the dendrite by releasing tiny bubbles of a chemical messenger (called a *neurotransmitter*) across a tiny gap (the *synaptic junction*) between the transmitting cell and the receiving cell. Synaptic plasticity is the ability of the cell to change the quality and properties of this biochemical communication.

It might help a bit to realize that there exist more synapses in your brain than there are stars in all the galaxies in the known universe! This multiplicity of synapses is the secret to the brain's profound complexity.

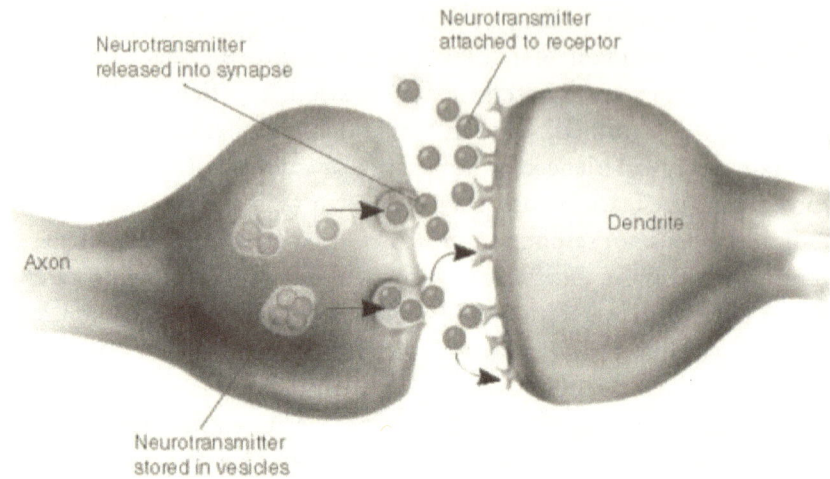

Figure 2.2. Neurotransmitters

Within the dynamic, ever-changing structure of all these synapses are stored all our memories (both personal and inherited). In light of our later discussion of the importance of sleep and dreaming for the efficacy of certain rituals (see also Richard Schechner (1982, 2011) on "restored behavior" or behavior that follows a cultural script stored in memory) we note here the important role sleep plays in potentiating, storing, associating, changing and developing the synaptic organizations that mediate our memories.

Communication between symbolic stimuli coming in through the senses and the deep structures of memory and affective/physiological association—*symbolic penetration*—occurs by way of cells influencing each other synaptically through a series of circuits that carry and alter information from the periphery of the body into the central nervous system and its networks, and then perhaps outward again, conducting commands from these deep structures to the muscles and organs that mediate behavior and metabolism. Thus ritual can influence biological processes by the manipulation and placement of symbols. Through symbols and the systems of meaning (like myths) that underlie them, *ritual bridges levels of the brain, linking various neurocognitive structures through the associative linkages symbols provide.*

The ritual process integrates the neural networks of the conscious mind with those of the lower brain structures, which are not normally accessible to consciousness. Integration of this previously unconscious material into consciousness via ritual performance can result in profound changes in the individual's experience of self and world, including alteration of behavior, personality, self-understanding, and autonomic balance. (We will provide many examples in the following chapters.) In other words, the ritual use of symbolic associations entrains physiological processes involved in basic emotions, social attachments, needs of the self, and senses of comfort, security, and certainty, providing catharses for fears, anxieties and other psychodynamic processes by altering those psychological processes mediated by lower and older brain centers. For instance, smells may operate to evoke strong memories that are normally outside the normal everyday round of associations. Thus, in many cultures, olfactory stimuli (such as incense) are specifically used in rituals to evoke such memories and integrate them with the conscious experiences people have during ritual participation.

Symbolic penetration via ritual performance can in fact evoke healing processes within our bodies because it operates on these brain structures, mediating and transforming them, often outside of awareness. Symbolic healing processes can in effect de-structure the ego, evoking latent aspects of the self, transforming emotions, and transforming and integrating the information stored in latent or suppressed neural networks. Symbols can reorder these structures to produce healing through integration of this previously unconscious material. For instance, it has been shown experimentally that if a patient visualizes his or her injury as the site of a battle between opponents (say, a pack of white dogs against dark demons) in which the "good guys" eventually defeat the "bad guys," there is a corresponding increase in the population of lymphocytes and macrophages (immune system cells) at the actual site of the injury (see Weil and Rossman 2006). As we shall see in Chapter 8, this use of visualization—or "guided imagery"—for the purpose of healing is fundamental to shamanic healing systems all over the globe.

The power of particular symbols and messages to penetrate differs widely. Abstract cognitive symbols that are easily recognized and understood by the prefrontal cortex (PFC) may seem the most powerful, but they do not necessarily penetrate to the lower brain systems that drive emotions, metabolism, or behavior. For instance, we may receive lots of symbolic messages about what to do to maximize health (e.g., "smoking is dangerous," "wear your seatbelts"), and we may agree with and accept those messages at the cognitive level. But then there is the issue of acting on those messages. As much as we intellectually accept the message, it may not penetrate to the lower brain systems. Conversely, these lower brain systems can send messages that penetrate "up" to the various cortical systems and have profound effects upon our behavior and emotions, even if the neocortex doesn't rationally accept them.

For example, we might continue to smoke because our lower brain system desires pleasure, stress release, or the security of fitting into a peer group, or we are subject to a chemically based nicotine addiction. Or we might carry into adulthood an irrational fear of white furry objects stemming from a childhood trauma with a white rabbit—a trauma deeply embedded in the limbic system that continues to affect our emotional responses and behaviors. The objects of our desire or our trauma (a cigarette, a white fur coat), or photographs of those objects (as in advertisements) work as symbols that immediately penetrate to those lower brain levels, evoking the desire to smoke or the fear we felt as a child. Because the wiring of the brain is mostly bottom-up (from the lower, more primitive areas to the neocortex), rather than top-down, the messages evoked from the lower emotional or behavioral levels of the brain can be very compelling. Our best intentions (like stopping smoking) may go unfulfilled because the higher brain can't easily force its message on the lower brain systems. Similarly, irrational fears may persist in spite of the person knowing that they are irrational because the powerful ascending messages from the lower brain easily overwhelm the rational cortical messages.

Ritual is a technique that helps humans reinforce the penetration of messages from deep in the brain. Messages that begin in the neocortex may be more easily ignored by the emotional brain than are the powerful survival-oriented messages ascending from the lower brain centers. Rituals engage and manipulate these older systems in order to enhance the upwards penetration of the symbolic messages they send. Thus rituals help humans to overcome our instinctive fight-or-flight responses to danger, and to engage instead in cooperative behaviors that enhance the wellbeing of the group.

Soldiers, for example, are put through complex ritual programs—called "basic training"—full of all sorts of physically strenuous ordeals that alter the natural human tendency to avoid life-threatening situations, replacing it instead with feelings of social cohesion and the ability to engage head-on in battle (see Chapter 8 on rites of passage). Police trainees go through similar programs, as do fire-fighters, emergency medical technicians, airline pilots, and members of other professions who often have to face dangerous situations that might cause them to flee if they were not ritually socialized to fight.

The point we wish to emphasize here is that individuals can consciously use symbols to affect their own lower brain centers (for instance, in healing themselves), and societies can use collective rituals, which link symbols and patterned behavior, to affect the lower parts of the brains of multiple individuals. Individuals may discover the power of symbolic healing by themselves, or under the influence of a modern physician or therapist. But for a group to routinely apply this kind of collective, ritualized healing requires socialization, usually from a very early age (see e.g. Benedetti 2008 on the cultural aspects of the "placebo" effect in healing).

CORE SYMBOLS

At the very center of the symbolism through which rituals work lie what may be called a society's *core symbols*. Whereas most of the symbols used in people's everyday interaction and communication are not really recognized as symbols per se, a society's core symbols are perceived as such by most people in that society. A national flag, the Presidential Seal, the Statue of Liberty, the Christian cross, the Jewish Star of David, a corporation's logo—all of these are core symbols that incorporate a great deal of meaning and significance for the people who value them, as well as for people outside the society who see the core symbol as representing the nation, religion, or corporate group. The American flag may be reverenced by Americans and Kuwaitis and vilified by Iranians, Palestinians, and the Taliban. The core symbol and the people that symbol evokes often become cognitively equated. Thus the core symbol may be the focus of devotion, identification, and activity for a given group. Among the Navajo of the American Southwest, the corn plant is at the same time a major staple crop and a powerful symbol of the people's worldview. The corn stalk is for the Navajo what the "World Tree" or "Vision Serpent" was for the Ancient Maya and the Tree of Life is for practitioners of Kabbalah. Within the core symbol of the corn plant, one may read the relations between the levels of reality—the underworld, this world, and the sky—as well as the four sacred directions and all the sacred things that are reverenced by the people.

Likewise, high technology is a core symbol of the American technocracy. Like corn for the Navajo, in a technocracy, high technology is simultaneously a major economic driver, an essential element of daily life, and a powerful symbol of the technocratic worldview, which centers around an ideology of progress through the development of high technologies and the control over nature and daily life these technologies provide (Davis-Floyd 1994, 2004). High technology represents the ongoing fulfillment of that ideological mandate, and thus its pervasive presence is a constant reassurance that we are achieving our cultural goals.

We can better understand the role of core symbols in ritual by looking at some of the properties of core symbols:

1. **Core symbols are pervasive.** These symbols pervade most domains of life, involving both the sacred and the everyday. Just as corn is the most common food resource of the Navajo, so too does the corn plant remind people of the major elements of their religious life. Just as high-tech products are pervasive in American life, so too do they remind people of their overall faith in the benefits and goals promised by technology.

2. **Core symbols may be archetypal in origin.** Symbols may derive from and represent the deep levels of the human psyche. The term "archetype" comes from the work of Carl G. Jung (1964) who recognized that certain symbols seem to have universal occurrence and appeal. Their universality suggests that their meaning is "hard-wired" into the human brain by way of genetic inheritance. In Jung's sense, archetypes are encoded in the human brain as the result of hundreds of generations of species-typical experience. Hence, symbols like the Goddess, the Trickster, the Underworld are considered by many students of mythology to be images generated by the human mind to reflect its own essential nature—a nature that gets projected out onto the world in mythical stories, artifacts, sacred landscapes, and ritual performances. Such archetypes still exist and play significant roles in the modern technocracy—for example, we exhibit an archetypal fascination with the "upper world" long recognized by traditional shamans as we reach toward "the heavens" by exploring outer space.

3. **Core symbols often link individual identity with that of "others" in one's social group.** People often display their group membership, and represent themselves to themselves, through their group's core symbols. Doctors may wear a white coat and sling a stethoscope around their necks even if they are not planning to see patients. A student from Canada might stitch a maple leaf to his or her backpack to identify with being Canadian. In Israel, the kind of yarmulke (*kippah*) men wear can signify their membership in a particular religious sect or that they are non-religious, secular Jews. When young people from certain North American Plains Indian cultures reach puberty, they go on a vision quest during which one

of the culture's repertoire of sacred beings may appear to them and give them instructions and perhaps signal their life's career. Thereafter, they identify themselves with that sacred entity and thus with the mythology that is associated with the entity.

4. **Core symbols lie at the very center of nationalism and work to bind the homeland together.** Patriotism and cultural identity are really a set of emotionally charged beliefs organized around a set of core symbols that, for the people involved, signify their group identity. Often this feeling of membership is linked to the land itself by way of defined and meaningful boundaries and landmarks. As Paul Devereux has shown in his books *Symbolic Landscapes* and *Re-Visioning the Earth,* people for many thousands of years have been projecting their cultural identity upon nature so as to produce "sacred landscapes." Everyone knows of the famous Stonehenge on the Salisbury Plain in England, which dates back to around 4000 BCE. But few realize that this great structure was made from stones weighing 5 tons or more each that were quarried and transported from as far as 130 miles away by sea shore rafts and rollers, forming part of a gigantic structure of earthworks found over much of Neolithic England. One authority estimates that Stonehenge alone took roughly 1.5 million man-days of work to complete. Obviously its Neolithic constructors considered it tremendously important to modify their natural environment in these meaningful ways. (The problem there is that today we no longer know just what that meaning was to those ancient people. When the once-living belief-and-meaning system of a given society is completely lost to time, it is very difficult, often impossible, to reconstruct it.) Within these symbolically pregnant landscapes, ritual performances have been played out in which the mythological events that were the people's origins are enacted. From the beginnings of human prehistory, people have bound themselves together by linking core symbols, landscape, and ritual in a deeply emotional package of significance.

5. **Core symbols reveal the hidden forces operating in the world.** Core symbols often operate to evoke an epiphany—that is, the realization of normally hidden forces or the existence of sacred beings. The Catholic priest performing a Mass will wear raiment that is essentially designed after the street clothes of Romans living at the time of Christ. The raiment is worn over the priest's everyday street clothes, thus symbolically binding the time of Christ with our own time and expressing the timelessness of Christ's message of love and salvation to the congregation. The Iroquois people in the Northeastern United States carry out healing ceremonies in which the spirit that causes the disease is invoked to cure the disease. The

spirit is revealed by way of healers wearing grotesque masks representing the normally invisible face of the disease-causing spirit. Likewise, high-tech diagnostic machines like CAT scanners, ultrasound, and x-ray machines can peer deep into the human body, making the hidden manifest. Symbolically speaking, there is little difference between the hidden spirit embodied in the mask and the hidden tumor revealed on the radiographic film—both facilitate decision-making and action in the world by revealing the operation of mysterious forces.

6. **Core symbols are "pregnant with meaning."** As we have seen, symbols are rich in cognitive and emotional associations that are readily accessed in the presence of the symbols—this is the power of symbolic penetration. Often the field of meaning and the emotional loading of a set of symbols grows ever greater during the course of one's life, as a result of repeated participation in rituals in which the symbolism is presented, renewed, and reinforced. When we speak of *symbolic pregnance* (as philosopher Ernst Cassirer (1957) called it), we are referring to the fact that symbols and their meanings are much like that toy magnet linked to a pile of iron filings on a piece of paper. Again, if we drag the magnet under the paper, the iron filings take on a distinct pattern which changes as we move the magnet. In the same way, core symbols incorporated into a ritual will evoke a pattern of associations that are manipulated within our psyche in response to the movement of the symbols.

For many people, the sight of McDonald's "golden arches" is sufficient to evoke hunger and memories of tasty meals while traveling down the nation's highways, and to cause them to take the exit and pull up to the order stand. What is interesting here is that the "golden arches" are not really golden, they are yellow. McDonald's, in a brilliant advertising moment, chose to label them "golden," a term which of course symbolizes so much more that is appealing to hungry people than "yellow" ever could—"golden arches" symbolize both great value and an invitation into heaven itself. In a sense, all of one's memory associations of McDonald's, whether they be positive or negative, are linked to and evoked by the symbol of the golden arches. Far beyond a mere desire to eat a Big Mac, the arches may penetrate to exciting and happy memories of childhood, parents, and special outings for some, while evoking negative associations with junk fast food and America's obesity problem for others.

In the same way, a prayer rug can both evoke memory associations of Islam and remind a Muslim to lay it out on the floor facing Mecca and kneel to pray, or can evoke fear of Muslim jihadists in others, just as a burka can evoke a sense of safety and protection in the Muslim women who wear it, yet for Westerners can symbolize women's oppression by the Muslim patriarchy.

7. **Core symbols are multi-vocal.** Symbols used in rituals often penetrate to many layers of meaning, depending upon how well-developed the individual participant is within the culture of the ritual. So much more than a piece of cloth, a flag speaks with many voices, evoking homeland, patriotism, the history of the nation it represents, the values of its people, and on and on. An electronic fetal monitoring machine, which Robbie has interpreted as the primary symbol of hospital birth (Davis-Floyd 2004), also speaks with many voices, promising to provide full information on the strength of the laboring mother's contractions and the condition of the fetal heart rate, representing the vast corporation that created it and all of the technological know-how that went into making it, and giving women a sense of psychological and emotional trust in the information it provides. (For more on the electronic fetal monitor and its ritual functions, see Chapters 5 and 7). Levels of symbolic meaning range from the most primitive emotional reactions to highly elaborate intellectual understandings of the symbols and their interrelations. Much of the power of symbols derives from the simultaneous evocation and interaction of meaning at all these various levels of association, from immediate visceral arousal and emotional evocation through memories layered over years of experience and philosophical self-reflections on meaning.

INTERPRETING CORE SYMBOLISM

Perhaps by now you can see why anthropologists find it a challenge to interpret the meaning of ritual performances: full understanding of the multiple layers of meaning enacted in rituals often requires years of participant observation, and sometimes official training in those rituals, to appreciate their nuances.

Labs as Rituals

Take for example the "labs" that high school and university students are familiar with through their chemistry, biology, or physics courses. These "labs" are not in fact laboratories for discovering something new, but are rather training exercises designed to condition the neophyte's mind to see the world in the way that a fully trained scientist does. The labs are actually rituals that produce experiences for the student that "bring reality" (which we will later call both "truing" and "instantiation") to the material being taught in the textbook and by the teacher in lectures. The words in the textbook take on many levels of meaning as the student gains direct experience with the physical world during well-established ritual procedures (called "experiments"). In a very real sense, you can't know what the symbolism in scientific writings means until you have the experiences upon which the writings are based.

The So of East Africa, Their "Gray Goop," and Charlie's Efforts to Understand Its Symbolic Meaning

This necessity of experience is why anthropologists studying various cultures depend so heavily both on participating in rituals as much as they can, and on talking to people who understand and can communicate the meaning of the ritual. During Charlie's ethnographic field experience among the East African So people, he experienced the difficulty of understanding the deep associations evoked by rituals. One morning early in his stay in So Land he awoke upon hearing a loud commotion down the hill from where he had pitched his tent. He bounded out of his sleeping bag, jumped in his clothes, and ran down the hill to see what was happening—just in time to see a large group of tribesmen and women lining up in front of a fellow who was slapping some gray goop across each person's chest in turn. Charlie joined the line and in turn received a swatch of gray goop across his chest. When everybody had been marked with the gray goop, they all lined up in military fashion and began to march back and forth. At the end of each march people would stop and raise their sticks up in the air and yell something unintelligible (to Charlie) to the sky. They did this about three times and then suddenly the event was finished, the company disbanded, and everyone went their own way.

Charlie was thrilled of course! He knew that he had just participated in his first So ceremony. (Anthropologists simply love such stuff.) He sat right down and recorded what he had experienced and observed in meticulous detail. But after he had simmered down, it dawned on him that he had no idea whatever as to what purpose or meaning to attach to the ritual he had just undergone. (What Charlie wrote down was what anthropologist Clifford Geertz (1973) called a "thin description"—a simple description of what took place, lacking any kind of interpretation.) It took nine months of further research before he could safely say that he understood what the people were up to on that sunny day—an activity that had taken less than thirty minutes to complete. What he eventually learned (here comes what Geertz called a "thick description"—one that layers in the meaning of the event) was that the gray goop was clay from a sacred place in the local creek that was believed to protect each participant from evil. The march was a procedure prescribed by the shamans to exorcise the evil spirits that were causing the people an inordinate incidence of disease. (The So were experiencing the second year of what would eventually prove to be a devastating ten-year drought period in that part of Africa.)

Charlie's research challenge was to learn enough about the language and lore of the So people to comprehend the meaning associated with disease, walking sticks, gray clay, the sky, the earth, the cardinal directions—in fact the entire cosmology of a people who had lived in that area of the world for countless generations. His learning process involved questioning people who were very shy about talking to outsiders about their religious beliefs. The So had experienced several generations of Christian and Muslim missionaries who had been telling them that they were pagans and that their beliefs and practices were wrong-headed. Even when Charlie had hung around long enough to make friends, it was difficult for him to get his mind around a

Figure 2.3. The So People of East Africa. Photo by Charles Laughlin.

worldview that put the mountain homelands of the So at the center of reality, and to think in terms of dead ancestors as mediators between God and the earth. And of course there are aspects of the So comprehension of reality and disease that Charlie never came to understand. Thus his interpretations of that ritual and other aspects of the So way of life have to be considered as partial at best. In other words, Charlie's understanding of So core symbolism is incomplete, as it must be for any outsider to a full-blown ritual tradition.

Interpreting Symbolism in Unfamiliar Cultures: Experiential Knowledge vs. Rational Analysis

The problem of just how to interpret symbolism in unfamiliar cultures has engaged students of ritual for a long time. Wilhelm Dilthey (1977), who wrote in the later part of the nineteenth century, observed that social science is the study of human minds by other human minds—hence social science is a thoroughly subjective enterprise. The task is to interpret the mind state of the people under study into another language and another way of thinking, and thereby to find out how subjective understanding influences people's activity in the world. Dilthey taught that this task is best accomplished by seeking an understanding that is both intuitive and intersubjectively valid. That is, one comes to know about things first by doing them, rather than by way of rational analysis, and then by comparing one's experiential knowledge with that of other people who have been doing the same thing. Such an understanding for most people is determined by their culture's worldview as it influences people's lived experience. Thus people come to know what their society's rituals are all about by participating in them and gradually accruing the meaning of activities along the way (the intuitive element). And much of this meaning will be influenced by the natural process of sharing of experiences among participants (the intersubjective validity element).

Understanding and Acting on Core Symbolism: Michael Winkelman and the Messenger Mice

Our colleague Michael Winkelman, a pre-eminent anthropologist of shamanism, adds to our understanding of core symbolism through the following report (personal communication 2011). Although Michael intellectually recognized the importance of participating in rituals in order to understand the relevance and application of ritual elements, at first he did not understand that the *practical aspects* (as opposed to the intellectual aspects) of this participation could only be known through participating. For example, from almost 20 years of studying shamanic ritual, he understood that animals were fundamental to shamanic ideology, practice, and behaviors. But reading about the importance of animal relationships and identity provided little insight into how animals actually come to play a role in shamanic practice. In the process of participating in shamanic activities and the associated animal world, Michael came to a very different appreciation of the role of the animal world in guiding behavior. Most people think very little of the actual animals (or their representations) that intersect our daily lives, and few people look for significance in those encounters. But, says Michael, once the shamanic path opens an awareness of the importance of animal powers, an awareness of their presence in everyday life expands. This awareness then allows the understanding that animals can act as messengers and guides for behavior.

For example, on two occasions when Michael was thinking that he would "speak his mind" by telling others what he thought on an important issue, mice unexpectedly showed up at his feet in unlikely places (on a path outside of a conference meeting room, and outside of a phone booth on a crowded street). These mice were behaving unusually—not scurrying off and hiding but standing squarely in his path, undeterred by his presence in spite of him nearly stepping on them! Without his experientially-based shamanic training and perspective, Michael would most likely have seen no meaning at all in the presence of these tiny creatures. Yet because of that perspective, he interpreted these mice as "messengers" encouraging timidity rather than a forceful outspokenness. This interpretation affected his behavior—he refrained from speaking and thereby, as it turned out, saved himself a great deal of trouble that probably would have descended upon him if he had.

In the terms we have been using in this chapter, the mouse-as-symbolic-messenger penetrated all three levels of Michael's brain in complex ways that produced certain responses. In his neocortex, his previous cultural learning and experiences had led to certain associations/meanings about mice and what they represent in their demeanor and behavior. Furthermore, his understanding of shamanic beliefs regarding the significance of animals appearing unexpectedly had long existed because of his years of studying and analyzing shamanism in various cultures.

His years of experiential participation in shamanic activities had evoked many emotional responses about the importance of animals as bearers of significant personal messages, and these experiential memories were triggered by the unexpected appearance of the mice and their unusual behavior. At the deeper levels of his brain, his participation in shamanic rituals and altered states of consciousness (ASCs) had entrained shamanic practices with sensations of peace and security—and special significance. The appearance of the mice penetrated through all brain strata to produce a profound difference in his behavior: he physically sensed, emotionally felt, and intellectually understood the importance and significance of the symbolic message conveyed by the presence of the mice in such unlikely places, and acted accordingly, to apparent great benefit.

Oral and Written Texts: The Changing Meanings of Core Symbols over Time

Philosopher and theologian Paul Ricoeur built upon the intuitive/intersubjective aspect of interpretation to emphasize the importance of interpreting texts in this symbolic way. "Texts" can be written (like the book you are reading, or the Dead Sea Scrolls) or oral, as with stories told around the campfire at night. Ricoeur showed that the meaning intended by the author of the "text" becomes less important over time than how the text is used and interpreted by people under its influence. The meaning of the text changes with every passing generation (as is clearly evident in Christianity regarding the evolving perceptions of the meaning of the chapters in the Bible over time, or even the physical attributes of Jesus in various ages). The same is true for other aspects of culture, including the meanings of core symbolism and ritual, because rituals in traditional societies are frequently intimately interconnected with cultural texts, such as myths and healing lore. In a very real sense, ritual of this sort is an enactment of a text (oral or written)—it is part of the process of interpreting the text for those who participate in the culture.

For example, before an initiate goes on a vision quest, he or she may have heard many stories over many years that pertain to the adventures and visions the initiate may experience during the quest. These stories lay down a template in the initiate's mind for what he or she is expected to accomplish during the vision quest. So the quest, if successful, becomes an individual enactment—a personal vivification—of these stories.

Ricoeur showed that in order to come to understand texts of this kind as an outsider to the culture, it is necessary first to study the fundamental meaning of the words in the stories behind the ritual, then second to participate as fully as possible in the stories by way of the rituals, and third to reflect upon the experiences we have as a consequence of this participation. Only by going through this three-stage process are we as outsiders able to approximate the real meaning inherent in the ritual. Take for example the traditional preparation of young Catholics to participate in the Mass. First they go through a period of indoctrination into the scriptures and other texts that inform the Mass, and only after passing their "catechism" will they be allowed to fully participate in the Eucharist. In fact there was a time when young people and all uninitiated persons were excluded from the Eucharist section of the Mass.

The renowned anthropologist Clifford Geertz (1983) applied this kind of interpretation to relate ritual procedures and core symbolism to the "local knowledge" found in communities of people. How do the concepts in peoples' heads motivate their activity? In particular, how do religious ideas influence social institutions and social history? Geertz was very cautious in his approach, for he denied that one can actually reconstruct the exact mind state of other people, insisting that we can only come to understand what their symbols mean in an approximate way. In contrast, the equally renowned anthropologist Victor Turner has shown that one may use interpretive methods to explore the unconscious mental processes of ritual and other symbolic media. Unlike Geertz, Turner came to realize that one can come to an intuitive grasp of the meaning of ritual symbolism by fully participating in rituals and other symbolic processes. People can and do communicate experience intersubjectively via symbols. Our task as students of ritual is actually more than merely coming to understand cultural meanings—it is the task of coming to share experience by way of symbolic penetration to the mental processes we all share as human beings.

EXAMPLES OF SYMBOLIC INTERPRETATION

In order to better appreciate the importance of lived experience in the process of interpreting ritual symbolism, we offer below a few examples in which both intuition and intersubjective validation were operating.

Confrontation with the Quintessence of Evil

Some years ago, one of Charlie's students, Ray Robertson, studied the phenomenon of the science fiction (SF) convention from the perspective of the anthropology of religion. An avid science fiction reader, he quickly immersed himself in the culture of SF "fandom" and attended many SF conventions ("cons" as they are called) to see what they were all about. He found that the SF fans who attend these cons are typically members of a community of SF aficionados who share a culture of understanding pertaining to the world around them, including personal identity, sexual mores, political values, attitudes about various scientific theories and enterprises, and so on.

For fandom, the SF con is essentially a complex ritual during which many of these values and attitudes are acted out in the form of role playing games and costumed pageantry. Many SF fans come to the cons dressed as characters from various SF novels, movies, and TV series. For example, *Star Trek* devotees (known as Trekkies or Trekkers) attend Trekkie cons dressed as their favorite *Star Trek* characters. There are contests for the best costumes, and there is much role-playing. A great deal of revelry takes place during the cons, especially during the nighttime. And there is sufficient "suspension of disbelief" about the role-playing that one can easily lose track of the normal world outside the hotel or conference center.

Well into the research, Robertson invited Charlie to a local SF con being held in a major hotel. During the evening the two friends were wandering down a corridor, deep in conversation about some arcane theoretical issue and oblivious of their surroundings. They turned the corner in the corridor and suddenly came face-to-face with a huge six-and-a-half-foot Darth Vader striding down the hall toward them. Dressed all in black with flowing robes and black plastic mask and helmet, the apparition seemed to have stepped right off the silver screen and into their lives. Both Robertson and Charlie independently had the same experience. They stopped abruptly and froze where they stood, and for a moment normal everyday reality was suspended. They were suddenly part of the *Star Wars* mythos and were facing the very quintessence of evil himself—the actual living, breathing Darth Vader. The next moment, the fan wearing the costume passed them and said, "Good day!" —and the spell was broken. But the experience left both anthropologists speechless and then intensely awestruck at the power of the SF con ritual environment to so alter their perception that the fictional Darth Vader had become totally real to them, if only for a moment. Moreover, for both of them, the experience became part of the meaning of the Darth Vader character ever after. In other words, in our terms in this chapter, their experience of the symbol powerfully, if temporarily, altered their perceptions of reality.

Naro's Unhappy Resting Place

When Charlie and his family moved into their more permanent location on the lovely green slopes of Mount Moroto among the So people of Karamoja District, Uganda, little did they know that just outside the thorn fence that demarcated their compound, a drama of significance was unfolding in the earth. Old grandmother Naro was becoming restive and was posing a serious threat to her lineage—a hole was opening in the earth where Naro had been buried some years before. People passing by were becoming increasingly concerned about the fact that the hole seemed to be expanding almost daily. There was much discussion about this phenomenon.

Among the So, when young men, women, and children die, they are taken into the bush where they are left in a sitting position under a tree. But when an important elder man or woman dies, a crypt is dug in the ground, topped with a log cover and buried under earth and stones. A great deal of ceremony attends the burying of important dead, for their patronage is desired in the afterworld. Moreover, the living are concerned that the person's ghost not come back to disturb them. Old Naro was one such important elder, and it was increasingly clear to her fellow tribesmen from the gradually widening hole in the top of her gravesite that she was displeased in some way. People became very anxious that the old woman might be signaling that she was dissatisfied and unhappy. And if things were to go on unchecked, Naro might claim the life of someone else in her lineage. She might be lonely and want someone from her family to join her.

It was finally decided that something had to be done about the situation. Preparations were made, resources were gathered, and important people were called together. On the appointed day, the elders gathered at the site of the grave and began a lengthy ceremony during which they carefully cleaned out the top of the grave, ritually slaughtered a goat, cooked food (including the goat) for everyone to eat, offered libations of beer and tobacco to Naro, and then filled in the opening with stones until a cairn was formed over the grave. Much relieved, the people from her lineage then settled down to consume the goat meat and other foods and to chat about everyday matters.

For Charlie, it was truly remarkable to perceive the effect the ritual had upon Naro's lineage mates—the alleviation of their anxiety was palpable. The rite seemed to stand as a kind of buffer between the living and their anxiety about death and the potentially dangerous intentions of the departed. (You will find more about ritual's "buffering" effect in Chapter 9.) And by being a part of the process, Charlie became very aware of the power of ritual to alleviate fear and suffering by removing a perceived deadly threat. Seeing that effect led to conversations with his So friends that further confirmed the meaning of the ritual to the people who had enacted it and to others who had simply observed, or made note of, that enactment.

The Great Kettle Debate

After over a decade of studying American midwives during the 1990s and early 2000s, Robbie became involved in an interesting group discussion about the symbolic meaning of a particular gift. The midwifery group leaders wanted to honor one of their members, the world-famous midwife Ina May Gaskin, and were debating what kind of gift would be most appropriate. They were thinking about giving her a big black kettle—a powerful cultural symbol not only of hearth and home in pioneer days, but also, for these particular midwives, of their desire to harken back to and reinterpret the cultural meanings attached to the European "witches" of the medieval and Renaissance periods. Their re-interpretation (which stemmed in part from a highly influential booklet written by Barbara Ehrenreich and Deirdre English in 1973 entitled *Witches, Midwives, and Nurses*) was that these witches were really wise women and healers who traced their roots to Druidic and other pagan traditions. Such women were often intentionally misrepresented by Inquisitors and others as devil-worshippers, and thus were heavily and unjustly persecuted during the European witch hunts of the Renaissance period. Black iron kettles, or cauldrons, have for hundreds of years been symbols of witches stirring up their brews, but have more recently become, for many women, symbols of female healers, good "witches" (wise women) who used such kettles to brew herbs and healing remedies, and who discovered many of the medicines we still use today, from chamomile tea for stomach pains to foxglove (its active ingredient is digitalis) to regulate the heart. Many of the midwives in the group thought a kettle would make an ideal gift, as the honoree was an herbalist herself. But a problem arose. There were a number of Christians in this midwifery group who were deeply offended by the symbolic association of kettle >> cauldron >> witch, and adamantly opposed such a gift. So in the end, the group decided to gift their honoree with a pressure cooker, which still evokes hearth and home but is far more symbolically neutral—in other words, far less culturally loaded—than a black kettle could ever be. (Ina May was very happy with the pressure cooker, and still uses it to this day.)

SUMMARY: THE POWER OF SYMBOLS

The primary characteristic of ritual is that it works through symbols that are situated or placed in serial relationships through time (like the multiple plots in a complex story) throughout the ritual performance—symbols are, in other words, the mechanisms, or building blocks, of ritual. Symbols convey complex multivocal cultural meanings. They operate both consciously and unconsciously because they can penetrate the levels or strata of the brain (core, emotional, and cortical), and consequently work to integrate instinctive, emotional, imaginative, and intellectual responses with the cultural messages they send. Part of the power of symbols derives from the fact that we can experience their messages with our bodies and emotions; we may or may not be intellectually aware of their penetration but may simply feel their effects. The above three examples illustrate the expressive and evocative power of symbols, their multivocality, and the importance of lived experience in symbolic interpretation. A regular guy dressed up as Darth Vader can express the individual's identification with *Star Wars* and can evoke in total strangers the experience of actually encountering this embodiment of evil. This is not merely an intellectual or cognitive, but a *felt* experience involving psychological, emotional, and physiological reactions. A collapsing grave can evoke pereceptions of a dead ancestor's displeasure, strike fear into a whole social group, and cause that group to enact a ritual to express their concern for that ancestor and fulfill their need to restore the cosmic order. For some women, a black kettle can evoke centuries of stereotyping and persecution and the need to reinterpret their conceptual heritage, while at the same time conveying the powers of evil witches and the devil for others. Each of these symbols is capable of penetrating individual consciousness and evoking strong emotional reactions in accordance with the system of beliefs it expresses. Core cultural symbols like a national flag or the Christian cross encapsulate essential elements of a culture, link individual identity with that of a group, and manifest hidden elements of the natural and cultural worlds. In the following chapter, we will more closely examine the role of symbols in the myths and paradigms that rituals enact.

Suggested Reading

Bell, Catherine (1997) *Ritual: Perspectives and Dimensions.* Oxford: Oxford University Press.

Damasio, Antonio (1999) *The Feeling of What Happens: Body and Emotion in the Making of Consciousness.* New York: Harcourt.

Devereux, Paul (1992) *Symbolic Landscapes.* Somerset, England: Gothic Image Publications.

Grimes, Ronald L. (1996) "Introduction." In Ronald L. Grimes (Ed.), *Readings in Ritual Studies.* Upper Saddle River NJ: Prentice Hall, pp. xiii-xvi.

Weil, Andrew and Martin Rossman (2006) *Self-Healing with Guided Imagery.* New York: Sounds True.

Chapter 3

THE COGNITIVE MATRIX OF RITUAL: MYTHS AND PARADIGMS

The Cognitive Imperative and the Cycle of Meaning. The Myth/Paradigm-Ritual Complex. The Technocratic, Humanistic, and Holistic Paradigms of Medicine. The Medical Spectrum. Summary: The Human Need to Understand.

A matrix (from the Latin *mater*, "mother"), like a womb, is something from within which something else emerges. Rituals are never arbitrary; they emerge from within the belief system of a group or individual, and their primary purpose, generally speaking, is to enact and transmit that belief system into the psyches of their participants, aligning their individual beliefs and values with those of the group. Each symbolic message contained within a given ritual often manifests one or more underlying cultural beliefs or values (Handelman 1998). Sometimes these beliefs are explicitly held, as is generally the case with religion: devout members of most religions know what they believe and can articulate those beliefs more or less clearly. But often the beliefs and values that ritual enacts are unconsciously held. In other words, people can ritually enact beliefs and values that they may not consciously know they hold, or can be socialized through ritual into accepting beliefs and values they may not even wish to hold (see McCauley and Lawson 2002).

There is of course no necessary link between myth and ritual—they are not two sides of the same coin. We have to emphasize this point, for there was a very influential group of theorists in the early days of anthropology who viewed myth and ritual as inextricably bound, and argued about whether myths beget rituals or vice versa—the so-called Cambridge *myth and ritual school* (Ackerman 2002; Bell 1992:14-15, 1997:5-8). It is very true that myth and ritual are commonly found to be entangled, but yet it is possible to have myth without ritual, and vice versa.

It is obvious that a myth is a narrative and any narrative may be enacted. *Because the belief system of a culture may be enacted through ritual, analysis of ritual can lead directly to a profound understanding of that belief system.* For this reason, anthropologists studying cultures other than their own have often focused on interpreting the rituals of that culture as a primary "way in" to understanding the culture. For example, Roy Warner's analysis of Memorial Day (which he calls "An American Sacred Ceremony") as a means of celebrating the unity of the nation in the face of its ethnic diversity provides important insights into American life. For another example, Peter Metcalf and Richard Huntington (1991) showed that a close understanding of a people's handling of death and performance of mortuary rituals can tell us a lot about the people's values, moral beliefs and worldview. As the great anthropologist A.M. Hocart (1883-1939) argued a century ago, myths and rituals express what people want most—namely "the good life." By that he meant that everyone on the planet desires longevity, vitality, good health, prosperity, and contentment (Hocart 1916). Thus in a sense all mythically rich rituals reveal the innermost collective desires of a people—goals they may not actually measure up to in everyday life, but often get closer to the more often the rituals are performed.

This chapter examines the cognitive matrix within which ritual produces its extraordinary power over human consciousness. We look at the relationship of ritual to myth in traditional societies, and to myths and paradigms in modern societies. Just as one can say that ritual enacts cultural beliefs and values, so also can one say that *ritual enacts myths,* or that *ritual enacts paradigms*—myths and paradigms are both *systems of meaning*. A *paradigm* is a model that provides a template for reality, consisting of a set of cohesive and internally consistent principles, beliefs, tenets, or guidelines for action. As do myths, paradigms integrate different levels of experience, meaning and explanation. We sum up this relationship as the *myth-ritual* (or *paradigm-ritual*) *complex*.

A word about language here: as we discuss the myth/paradigm-ritual complex, we will often use the labels "traditional" and "contemporary" to refer to the differences between small-scale societies with long histories and well-elaborated mythologies, as opposed to the larger and more diffuse national, regional, and ethnic groups that constitute contemporary society in its rich diversity. This traditional/contemporary dichotomy is not rigid. Today's traditional or indigenous societies are as "contemporary" as are the planet's nation-states. Traditional groups of people are still in touch with their cultural heritage—a heritage that may span tens and even hundreds of generations. In later chapters we will show how thousands of traditional societies that continue to exist creatively manipulate myth and ritual to eclectically combine the traditional and the modern, in ways that preserve their cultural integrity while enabling them to move more or less fluidly in the contemporary world. Contemporary societies also encompass many entirely new groups, from cults to gangs to "urban tribes," that quickly generate and adopt specific cosmologies with attendant myths, paradigms, rituals, and other "invented traditions." Today's traditional societies are increasingly embedded in many aspects of the globalized, modern world, and what we say about "traditional societies" often applies just as strongly to many recently formed contemporary groups.

THE COGNITIVE IMPERATIVE AND THE CYCLE OF MEANING

Humans have a drive to understand—a *cognitive imperative*—the drive to order the world into significant elements and events and unify them into a systematic cognitive whole. (Human cognitive understandings share processes with the information systems of other animals that provide implicit non-verbal understanding.) Myth and ritual play fundamental roles in the cognitive imperative, defining boundaries, revealing and imputing causes, and organizing humans' experience of their environment in order to remove uncertainty (Rappaport 1991:21) and buffer against existential anxieties (Atran 2002). This cognitive imperative for understanding the world is often achieved through the use of ritual to assimilate the novelty and variety presented to the human organism within a familiar cognitive structure. Ritual provides *meaningful* explanations by limiting relevant information, reducing uncertainty by linking the neural, emotional, social, and cognitive levels within each brain and across individuals. Using biologically grounded behaviors, rituals link innate structures of knowledge and experience with socially and culturally relevant meanings and associations. Ceremonial rituals are a special and more dramatic type of human ritual embedded in a cognitive matrix of meanings often associated with myth. Myth plays a vital role in providing conceptual integration, particularly for those events that humans find to be unpredictable and unexplained by any other means.

Members of traditional societies tend to ground their understanding of the world and themselves in a specific mythic cosmology, the elements of which have been passed down from generation to generation. Many subcultural groups within contemporary societies, from religious sects to various virtual communities, do the same, although there may be less time depth to their cultural heritage. By *cosmology*, we mean that people conceive of the world as:

1. a totality, which is
2. made up of everything in existence as parts of that totality, and
3. all the parts are causally entangled and interact in a systemic way, such that
4. the existence of the totality depends upon all the parts interacting and mutually influencing each other and the totality.
5. Much or most of the totality, as well as essential aspects and causal interactions of all the parts, is hidden to normal sensory perception.

We must emphasize here that there is a distinct difference between a worldview and a cosmology. Everyone has a *worldview*, by which we mean a person or group's collective conception or philosophy of the world they live in. While it is true that modern scientists use the term "cosmology" to refer to the systemic properties of our universe, from an anthropological point of view they are actually describing a kind of quasi-cosmology or simply a worldview that applies strictly to science, not the true *cosmology* of a people who go about their daily lives with an intimate understanding of and participation in the world-as-cosmos (an understanding that many of us living in contemporary societies do not have). In order to be a true cosmology in the anthropological sense, a people's worldview must be understood intuitively as a living system within the context of the people's everyday *lifeworld*—that is, within their everyday lived experience.

The Huichol people of northern Mexico say, "to be Huichol is to be sacred," thereby expressing their sense of their lifeworld as intimately bound up with their cosmology (Myerhoff 1974). Their cosmological understanding is not merely intellectual, *it is lived*—in other words, their cosmology is *instantiated* ("instantiate" means to represent an abstraction by a concrete instance, as in "heroes instantiate ideals") in their everyday experience of life.

Those of us living in modern technocratic societies also have that same intuition, but in a different way—we get that what we do in our daily lives impacts what we call "the planet" and/or "the ecology." Ever since the famous 1969 Apollo 11 "earthrise" photograph began to percolate throughout our collective consciousness, we have understood how very fragile our "life layer" is and how easily we can damage it. This understanding accelerated efforts to protect the environment and to stop the vast levels of pollution our industries have been producing for decades. It is no coincidence that the United States Environmental Protection Agency was proposed in the wake of that photo by President Richard Nixon and came into existence on December 2, 1970. We now watch our energy consumption, seek new and renewable energy resources, recycle basic materials, clean up messes, spills, and waterways, and penalize those who continue to foul our life layer. Debates about the extent to which human activities endanger the planet are always in the news these days. Discussions, points of view, and policy debates about industrial influences on climate change are embedded in contemporary consciousness. What is not open to debate is the use and efficacy of ritual applied by a growing number of "green" groups—groups of environmentalists concerned with stopping the destruction of the planet's ecosystem (see Grimes 2013).

Thus all peoples, whether traditional or modern/technocratic, intuitively grasp that what they do in their daily lives impacts upon the totality of existence, and that what happens in the world as a whole impinges on their daily lives. In the modern world of technocracy with its materialistic world view, the understanding of human-environment interaction tends to be a secular one. In more traditional societies where there is no separation of church and state, of religion and daily reality, *people tell a consistent story about the nature of reality, and they experience reality through that story, in a feedback loop that we call the "cycle of meaning."*

As Figure 3.1 illustrates, traditional cosmologies are expressed through a society's symbolic system, which includes myth, ritual, art and architecture, drama, performance, certain features of the landscape, games—and the beliefs and worldviews expressed in all of these and more. All these different media are interconnected within a culture's cognitive matrix—they are variant expressions of reality as understood by the people. Yet while the symbolic world and the world of direct, personal experience do overlap, they are not precisely the same. As John Cove, an anthropologist and student of mythology, noted: "…the relationship between mythological and lived-in realms is never a simple mirror image of each other. Each is more or less than the other. If the first [the mythological realm] has particular significance, it is in giving a foundation for meaning in the second [everyday lived experience]" (1987:28).

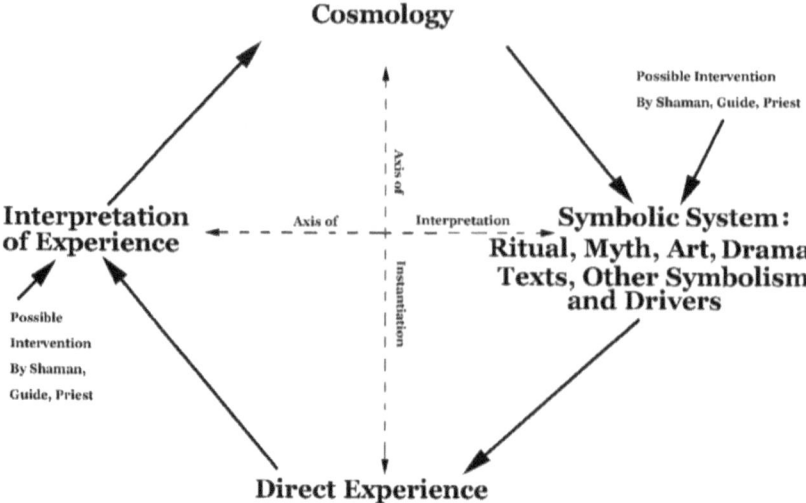

Figure 3.1. **The Cycle of Meaning.** The society's cosmology is expressed symbolically in its myth-ritual complex. Symbolic expression leads to direct experiences that are interpreted in such a way that the cosmology is brought alive and confirmed. Shamans and others, such as political leaders, may influence the process by controlling symbolic expression and again by helping to interpret experience.

An Example of Mythic Interpretation: The Navajo Origin Myth

Charlie has spent many years studying the Navajo people of the American Southwest who live in a land they conceive to be sacred. Navajoland (or as the Navajo themselves say, *Diné Bikéyah*, "*the land of the People*") is demarcated by four sacred mountains and a central "place of emergence." The people know about the origin of this sacred land and its People by way of stories that are passed down from generation to generation—stories that anthropologists call "myths" or "origin stories." These stories paint various pictures of the origin of the present world, just as the different gospels of the New Testament tell the stories of Jesus from different points of view. According to these Navajo origin stories, there existed several past worlds beginning with the darkest and then proceeding through various colors until the contemporary world—some of Charlie's Navajo friends call our present world the "Glitter World" because of all the colors in it. Each subsequent world evolved out of the previous world in a state of disastrous chaos. Various mythological beings climbed out of the last world into this world at the "place of emergence" and commenced creating all the beings that inhabit the present Glitter World. But this process was neither straightforward nor easy, for various factors, including sexual conflict, produced all sorts of aberrations in the form of monsters and other disruptions of the beautiful and harmonious relations among beings.

Seeing this reawakening of chaos, the Holy People (spirit beings) decided to take a hand and placed the baby Changing Woman, wrapped in a cradle, on the top of one of the central mountains, there to be discovered by Talking God (a male), who then turned the infant over to First Man and First Woman (both being primary gods) to raise. The First Couple did such a miraculous job of raising Changing Woman that she reached puberty in just twelve days. With her first menstruation, harmonious fertility was renewed in the world. The central ceremonial ritual of the Navajo, called the Blessing Way, became a celebration of Changing Woman's renewal of the earth, and of her subsequent mating with the Sun, which produced the hero twins, Monster Slayer and Born for Water, who went on many adventures and ended up killing most of the monsters that were infesting the earth. Once the earth was safe, Changing Woman created human beings, who then took over the world while the Holy People chose to retire to being the invisible essences of things in the Glitter World. Changing Woman herself became the cycle of existence, the climatological seasons, the phases of life, the cycle of day and night. She is for the Navajo the Earth Mother, the quintessence of fertility, the source of natural laws and movement, the perfect coordination of the male and female principles in the cosmos and here on earth.

From this story[1] we can see that the cosmology of the Navajo, and thus their whole mythopoeic symbolic system, are part of a living system of meaning for people born under the influence of this intact traditional culture. The story tells of the origins of the present world and portrays the

---

1. There are many versions of the Navajo myth of origin. The one we present here is a simplified and distilled version. For further information, see Maureen Trudelle Schwarz (1997) *Molded in the Image of Changing Woman*. Tucson, AZ: The University of Arizona Press; James K. McNeley (1981) *Holy Wind in Navajo Philosophy*. Tucson, AZ: University of Arizona Press; J.R. Farella (1984) *The Main Stalk: A Synthesis of Navajo Philosophy*. Tucson, AZ: University of Arizona Press.

two sides of the coin of change—on the one side harmony and beauty, on the other disharmony and ugliness. It also tells us that most of the really important dynamics of origin are invisible to normal perception. The Holy People are real to the Navajo, but have faded into the background of essential forces behind events. As well, the story reinforces the understanding that the life cycle of people and other beings is natural and lawful, that we are born, mature, age, and die. For the Navajo, this life cycle is as true for people as it is for whole worlds.

Now, how does the anthropologist as outsider come to understand how many Navajo people interpret the significance of this myth/origin story for their daily lives? The answer is simple—by living with the people, as Charlie has done, and listening to how they use the stories in their everyday lives. When we experience how a people utilize the stories, where and when and under what conditions the stories are unpacked and remembered, told, or referred to, then we begin to intuit the range of contexts within which people are informed by the stories. And as we will see below, one of the most common contexts within which myths like Changing Woman become real for people is ritual enactment.

Suffice it to say that the cosmology and its symbolic representations as depicted in a myth like the one about Changing Woman are part of a people's lifeworld, and in living in accordance with its meanings and the memory of its motifs, relations, and events, the cosmology is animated and reinforced within each person's consciousness. The fundamental assumptions of traditional cosmologies are rarely fully articulated by the members of that society. Rather, most people unselfconsciously and uncritically accept and participate in the worldview they inherit from their culture, interpreting their real life experiences in terms of that worldview, again, in a feedback loop that instantiates the cosmology in individual experience and thus appears to confirm its truth. For instance, Charlie found that the So people he lived with in Uganda would not enter a deep pool of water to either swim or wash themselves. They believed that pools are infested with a spirit called a *tegwech* that can attack a person and cause them to sicken and die. Children are taught from a young age to be afraid of these pools. They do not think about the *tegwech*, they just take their existence for granted. And as it turns out, the pools in question were in fact infested with *bilharzia*, the "liver fluke," which causes schistosomiasis, a disease with precisely the same symptoms as a *tegwech* attack.

Another Example of Mythic Interpretation: Dream Incubation

To take another example, consider the not uncommon phenomenon of "dream incubation" as discussed in Charlie's book *Communing with the Gods: Consciousness, Culture and the Dreaming Brain* (2011). A culture (such as the Australian Aborigines or the Papago Indians in the American Southwest) may believe that while one is asleep, one's soul can depart from the body and fly around and learn much. So a member of such a culture, who might want to discover something important, might use ritual to induce lucid dreams and actually experience himself as a consciousness flying free of his body and having spiritually significant adventures. For that individual, this experience both *instantiates* the belief system (makes it "come alive" in his personal experience) and appears to confirm its truth. (For the moment we will beg the question of whether or not the information people are able to attain in this way has any basis in reality—we will take this question up again in Chapter 8 when we discuss ritual and transpersonal experiences.)

Traditional cosmologies tend to be conservative and enduring. They resist radical changes in knowledge, for the principal functions of a traditional society's worldview are to organize their experiences of the world and to assure a complementarity of experience for the society's members. In contrast to science, which (ideally) seeks to discover the truth about the world, *the cycle of meaning* in traditional societies—and in many contemporary religious groups—*reflects the desire to imbue ordinary experience with meaning*. That is, the cognitive processes of the human brain usually work to associate what people perceive at the moment with patterns of meaning stored in their memories, rather than to either acquire new information about the world, or empirically test theories of the world.

A society's mythic system is ultimately the product of the creative imagination of its people. By "creative imagination," we do not mean mundane fantasy or fiction (i.e., imagined *un*-reality), but rather the ability to envision the essentially invisible aspects of reality (such as the spirit world of Holy People in the Navajo case, or the realm of the dead, or a God that is omnipresent in human affairs). Henry Corbin (1969) termed this ability the *imaginatio*. As Corbin noted, modern Euroamerican culture is marked by a vast chasm between the "reality" described by science and unreal fantasy: "In short," says Corbin, "there has ceased to be an intermediate level between empirically verifiable reality and unreality pure and simple." Science describes reality; all else is unreal. But traditional societies and contemporary religions maintain this intermediate level within the activities of the myth-ritual complex.

We are reminded of the story that anthropologist Marcel Griaule (1965) told on himself while he was doing fieldwork among the Dogon in Mali, West Africa. After years of visiting the Dogon, Griaule welcomed the decision the elders finally made to assign one of their number to instruct him on the "real truth" of things. They appointed the blind shaman Ogotemmeli to teach him about Dogon cosmology and myth. Ogotemmeli upended a grain basket, stuck an arrow in the bottom, and used the stair-stepped form of the basket to organize all the various animals and plants according to native categories. All of the leopards were on this step and all the elephants on that step, and so on. At one point, quite confused, Griaule asked Ogotemmeli how it was possible to put so many animals on a step. Thinking his student quite dense, the old shaman replied that didn't Griaule understand that these were all *symbols* and that you could put an endless number of symbols on a step? The Dogon, as well as other traditional peoples, understand the role of symbols in revealing and representing the elements and relations operating in the world around them.

THE MYTH/PARADIGM RITUAL COMPLEX

Myths and Paradigms

At the very center of a traditional society's symbolic system may be found a complex of myth and ritual from which other media (art, drama, games) derive their primary inspiration. Myth has long been defined in anthropology as the body of sacred stories that comprise a highly symbolic and coherent description of a people's origin, as well as the origin of significant aspects of the environment (animals, food, plants, changes in the weather, calamities, social roles, institutions, etc.). But because in this book we want to encompass the roles myth and ritual play in both traditional and contemporary societies, our definition is broader: as Betty Sue Flowers (personal communication 2011) points out, *"a myth is a story that organizes experience through telling something explicitly about meaning—where we're going, where we came from, or who we are."* Myths in all societies are primarily concerned with (1) making sense of the world and giving it meaning; and (2) transmitting knowledge about the primal relations in the cosmos upon which the existence and well-being of the people depend. Myths form the primary warp and weave in the fabric of a people's collective meaning, in which each of life's significant experiences finds a location, much like a patch (metaphorically speaking) finds its appropriate place in a quilt.

Myths do many things for people, from inspiring to severely limiting imagination and possibility. Myths charter the cultural world, laying out the blueprints for many of society's most basic categories and institutions. Consider the myth of Genesis, which charters at least four of the world's major religions (Judaism, Christianity, Islam, and Ba'hai) and has been formative in the development of many cultures, either generically or from the proselytizing efforts of missionaries. The early part of the Genesis story lays out a series of basic binary oppositions in terms of which people in many cultures still organize their experience: God created the world, dividing the heavens from the earth, day from night, dark from light, the waters from the land. Later on in (one telling of) the story God creates man, and then woman, who violates His orders and eats from the tree of knowledge, bringing God's wrath upon them both and causing them to be cast out of the Garden. That part of the story has served in countless cultures as a charter for and justification of patriarchy and the exploitation and domination of women by men.

And here we can see clearly the partial relationship between myth and historical reality. From an anthropological viewpoint, *the story of Adam and Eve being cast out of the Garden is a metaphorical way of addressing the transition from hunting and gathering to agriculture.* Hunting-gathering was the subsistence strategy that sustained the human species for over 150,000 years; agriculture only arose around 10,000 years ago. As anthropologists who have worked with the few remaining hunter-gatherer societies discovered, even in harsh environments like the Kalahari Desert of Southern Africa, getting enough food through gathering plants and hunting animals only took an average of around 3-5 hours a day, leaving plenty of time for other activities like games, storytelling, and dancing. But agriculture was extremely labor-intensive, requiring 8-10 hours per day of hard labor. So the transition from living off the bounty of the land through hunting and gathering, to working the fields by the "sweat of one's brow," was in overall effect getting "cast out of the Garden."

This encapsulation of historical events into one story is a characteristic feature of myths: they often collapse thousands of years of history into one story that sums up, or encapsulates, major lifestyle transitions. Today most anthropologists conclude that agriculture was a consequence of a rise in the population of various hunting-gathering groups at the end of the last Ice Age 12,000 years ago, leading to a depletion in natural resources and forcing people to move into less bountiful areas, making intentional food production a necessary adaptation. We suggest that this environmentally forced adaptation was encoded and encapsulated in the myth (origin story) of Genesis, which provided a divine explanation for the forced transition. Unfortunately for women, the story was told, and eventually written down around the 7th or 6th century BCE, by men in a form that blamed women for getting us "cast out of the Garden," setting in place thousands of years of patriarchal blame of women for the problems that actually faced human societies in general. (We should note here that Genesis as a creation narrative also worked toward the Jewish goal of establishing only one true God. Judaism was a monotheistic religion that opposed the polytheistic creation stories of Babylon, Israel's historic enemy, and other surrounding societies.)

A much more recent example of this forced transition from hunting-gathering to agriculture comes from the Huichol Indians, who were hunter-gatherers until the Spanish conquest of Mexico pushed them out of their desert home around San Luis Potosi and into the Sierra Madre mountain range of northern Mexico, where they had to grow maize to survive. This transition took over a century to complete. As Barbara Myerhoff showed in *Peyote Hunt* (1974), the Huichol, who had always gathered peyote (an hallucinogenic plant) in the desert for their religious ceremonies and had hunted deer, created new myths over time that wove the deer, the maize, and the peyote into a rich symbolic system that gave meaning to their new agricultural life by linking past and present into one cohesive picture (managing not to blame anyone in the process!).

We can contrast this successful transition made by the Huichol, who again had 100 years to accommodate their myths and rituals to their new agricultural reality, with the much less successful transition of a Ugandan tribal people known as the Ik. When the government of Uganda arbitrarily decided to turn the forested region in which they had hunted, gathered, and possibly also farmed for centuries into a game and hunting preserve for European tourists, the Ik were forcibly and suddenly relocated to another region in which farming was their only subsistence option. Given this massive and rapid change in their lifeworld, the Ik had no time to gradually develop a new cycle of meaning integrating their old and new realities as the Huichol had done. With the traditional myths and rituals that had made their previous existence now rendered meaningless, the Ik experienced a tragic cultural disintegration. Children were turned out of the family home at very young ages and had to group themselves in "age-bands" with no adult supervision (Tainter 2006; Turnbull 1972, 1978). Many children and elderly simply starved, as the food distributed by the government was generally confiscated by the strongest young men. While Turnbull's conclusions about the Ik and their implications for "human nature" have been critiqued by other scholars (Beidelman 1973; Heine 1985), they remain a compelling example of the need for a strong enough match between a people's lifeworld and their cycle of meaning to enable, beyond mere survival, a culturally ordered and satisfying life.

In addition to encapsulating history and generating meaning, myths can also create a moral order to situations faced by people in their daily lives, like the story of Moses and the Ten Commandments. Myths can also offer explanations for various phenomena and catastrophes that help people make sense of nonsensical events, and operate as a storage bank for culturally important information. Among New Guinea and other seafaring peoples of the Pacific, myths tell the story of epic sea voyages which, when they are enacted by modern seamen, prove to be templates for carrying out safe and successful ventures. Likewise, the myths of the Karuk Indians of California tell of spirit beings who joined and remained with human beings long enough to teach them the proper way to hunt and fish, and the proper use of medicines. In such cases, people do not merely recall the stories so much as act them out, identifying with the protagonists of the sagas.

Indigenous Psychology and the Myth-Ritual Complex

A people's understanding of themselves as persons is derived in part from their society's cosmology and its myth-ritual complex. These understandings include mental, emotional, behavioral and social capacities, as well as beliefs regarding individuals' dispositions and drives, and normal perceptual and cognitive capacities. Personality involves *cultural* concepts of the nature of the internal organization and dynamics of the person, and thus differs somewhat from culture to culture. Consequently, all cultures' conceptions of what it means to be a person constitute what we call an *indigenous psychology*. These indigenous models of personhood—as guides for people to identify and conduct themselves—are often embedded in, and reinforced by, the myth-ritual complex.

It is well to remember that the cognitive imperative applies as much to a people's understanding of themselves as it does to understanding objects and happenings "out there" in the world. As Paul Heelas and Andrew Lock (1981:3-18) note,

> Indigenous psychologies...are the cultural views, theories, conjectures, classifications, assumptions and metaphors—together with notions embedded in social institutions—which bear on psychological topics. These psychologies are statements about the nature of the person and his relation to the world. They contain advice and injunctions about the way that people should act, should feel, and how they can find happiness and success in life.

An indigenous psychology embodies the culture's own perspectives on the nature of humans and their behaviors, values, and beliefs. Indigenous psychologies organize individual experience and collective social life, and address a broad range of conceptions and issues, including consciousness, agency, social hierarchy and the physical and supernatural worlds.

Myth-telling, ritual, and other forms of expressive culture (e.g., religious liturgy, folklore, stories, chants, drama, art, performance, literature, proverbs, poetry, music, ballads) provide templates for indigenous personality. *Expressive culture* represents ideals and normative patterns of behavior, how humans are represented to each other, appropriate social behavior, and appropriate emotional reactions. Expressive culture's content depicts the group's understanding of personality dynamics. It provides information guiding socialization and the development of personality through models, ideals, and scenarios for behavior—all of which are typically grounded in myth and ritual. Expressive culture serves socialization functions by depicting appropriate expression of feelings, accentuating culturally important meanings, revealing social sentiment, prescribing proper means for fulfilling psychological needs, modeling ideal social behavior and social structure, and illustrating moral and ethical problems and ideal solutions.

The Myth-Ritual Complex and Human Development

There are two other important functions of myth we need to address here, for we are not just interested in myth as a repository or template for culture, but rather in how myth is acted out—enacted—in ritual. Those two functions are (1) transmitting socially important vicarious experience; and (2) aligning individual conceptual systems with socially valued experience (Faiola 2002; Sias, Lambie, and Foster 2006). In other words, myth is a primary mechanism for developing and maintaining what the great sociologist Emile Durkheim (1995 [1912]) called the "collective consciousness" fundamental to a people's religion and cosmology. Important domains of social experience are recorded in stories containing vivid imagery, so that the listener can imagine and internalize, say, the adventures of a hero or sacred being as if s/he were living in the present. (For example, Robbie's grandson Jax believes more firmly in his ability to climb the playground bars when he is wearing his Spiderman t-shirt and cap!) Moreover, the didactic quality of myth—the fact that mythological stories are told over and over to all members of the group with the explicit intent of teaching a group's cosmology or religion—assures that everyone shares the same body of core symbols and the sacred context in which the symbols apply. For instance, it is impossible to be a Christian without knowing the stories of Jesus' miraculous birth and of how He died on the cross to redeem the sins of humankind.

As Durkheim emphasized, the reality expressed in myth is not merely the figment of somebody's imagination, *but is reality itself imagined*. In other words, *through their myths, people collectively imagine reality, and then they live in the collective reality they have imagined*. For example, thousands of years ago the Australian aborigines imagined that when their bodies die, their spirits go to live in the Dreamtime, an alternate reality that surrounds and sometimes links with ordinary reality. Since that time, they have lived in the reality they imagined—their experience of life is permeated with experiences of entering Dreamtime in dreaming and in trance. And the landscape they traverse is dotted with sacred sites that serve as portals between this reality and Dreamtime, where for example the souls of the ancestors are known to be able to cross over and enter the body of a woman, making her pregnant. Cosmology is manifested in experience, and experience both confirms and further elaborates cosmology in an ongoing cycle of meaning.

In his book *The Inner Reaches of Outer Space: Metaphor as Myth and as Religion* (1986:xxiii), Joseph Campbell recognized myth's role in ensuring that the development of each member's consciousness proceeds in a way that maintains a collective understanding of reality:

> Thus a mythology is a control system, on the one hand framing its community to accord with an intuited order of nature and, on the

> other hand, by means of its symbolic pedagogic rites, conducting individuals through the ineluctable psychophysiological stages of transformation of a human lifetime—birth, childhood and adolescence, age, old age, and the release of death—in unbroken accord simultaneously with the requirements of this world and the rapture of participation in a manner of being beyond time... Their effect, therefore, is to wake the intellect to realizations equivalent to those of the insights that produce them.

Campbell further suggested that universal mythic themes may operate as innate triggers for cognitive structures in the depths of the human psyche. Mythic images, operating as metaphors, may be more effective than naturally occurring phenomena for triggering the growth of neurocognitive structures in the brain. For instance, hero myths can operate as *initiators*—that is, they may provide role models (patterns, templates) for enacting certain events, which in turn leads to development along certain lines (hunter, mother, farmer, wise leader, healer, playground bar-climber, etc.). The imagery in the myth may penetrate to the depths of the psyche and activate and potentiate the development of qualities and abilities (such as ambition or courage, aggression or empathy) appropriate to particular roles and valued by the society. By manipulating the motifs and elements of myth, a society can orchestrate certain specific kinds of psychic development in some or all of its members. These kinds of neurocognitive development become part of the collective consciousness of a people, a collective representation keyed to both the local and the universal realities within which people live their lives.

Take for example the attitude and practices pertaining to the Navajo role of warrior. The normal healthy human being lives in an on-going balance between "male" and "female" properties, according to Navajo indigenous psychology. But in the development of a warrior, who must face combat and come into intimate contact with the dead and dying, the "male" principle is accentuated during training—as indeed it is in modern military training (remember the soldier sleeping with his rifle). But unlike Western military culture, the Navajo consider the off-balance nature of warriorhood, though useful when needed, to be disharmonious, dangerous, and unhealthy. When warriors returned from battle, they were (and sometimes still are—the Navajo still have warriors who fight in the U.S. Armed Services) put through rituals designed to re-establish the balance between "male" and "female" psychological properties before they were allowed to fully return into the bosom of the family and community. We cannot help suggesting here that if all contemporary soldiers were put through this sort of ritual re-integration, their incidence of post-traumatic stress disorder (PTSD) might be much lower and their re-assimilation into society would likely be much smoother.

Humans do seem to have an innate need to link their potential as persons to their culture's ideal view of psychosocial dynamics, often patterning themselves after significant others who act as models. Establishing these relations of the individual self to the collective is a fundamental role of the myth-ritual complex. Cultural rituals are primary mechanisms for making these social connections, molding a universal template of neurocognitive operators (often represented in the concept of archetypes, especially the archetypal self) to the culture's specific social dynamics. Ritual is a mechanism through which human neural structures are given a content appropriate for their cultural context. As Scott Atran has noted, such universal neurocognitive operators would seem to be behind cross-culturally common ethnobiological categories and classification systems (Atran 1990; see also Berlin 1992).

While it is easiest to see and to analyze these primary roles of myth in small-scale traditional societies, it is important to understand that myths also play a similar critical role in today's modern world, not only in the highly specific cosmologies of small religious groups, but also in the more diffuse cosmologies of larger cultures and nation-states. Part of the capacity for mythic thinking is hard-wired into the human brain. There is no human culture without myth—we have long known that myth is a cultural universal (Hocart 1915)—and the societies of the contemporary world are no exception. Myths (origin stories) still form the basis of all religions and are foundational for many nations, cultures, and ethnic groups. (Consider for example the 1999 war in Kosovo, which had much to do with the mythological importance of that region for the Serbs.) And many archetypal and ancient myths, like the hero's journey or the apocalypse, still provide the basis for contemporary expressive forms, including painting, literature, movies, and even computer games.

Yet some of our most important cultural myths are unarticulated. For example, Robbie has written elsewhere about a central organizing myth of American society which she calls the *myth of technological transcendence*—the notion that through technology, we will ultimately transcend the limitations of nature. This myth enables us to face the problems presented by our untrammeled technological development with relative equanimity, even when the dangers presented are grave. Global warming due to over-pollution, resulting in rising sea levels, the deaths of many living organisms in the oceans, massive climate change in many areas, and regional water shortages due to the vanishing of polar and mountain icecaps? While we admit to possible short-term problems, ultimately we believe, because we have to in order to sleep at night, that the problems we have generated with technology will not lead to doom for humanity, but *will be solved with more technology*. This "myth of technological transcendence" is recounted in multiple forms in numerous futuristic movies, from *Star Wars* to *The Matrix* to the Pixar film *Wall-e* (which depicts a future in which the Earth becomes so polluted that its remaining humans flee the planet in a giant spaceship, returning many generations later when the Earth has regenerated and is capable of growing things once again).

Our faith in this myth of technological transcendence is extreme, and we enact that faith daily through advertisements touting the promise of new technologies, through the development of biotechnologies and research into the human genome, and through the billions of dollars we pour into high-tech development of cancer treatments and research even as we continue to pollute our environment and our food and get cancer as a result! Here we can see clearly another of the primary functions of myth, which is to enable a people to replace the conceptual fuzziness of an uncertain future with the hope and certainty that humanity (in the future, through technology), will prevail. Such certainty (at that time, through the belief that they were God's chosen people) got the ancient Hebrews through their period of wandering in the desert (the myth/origin story has this wandering lasting some four decades), and lets us contemporary citizens sleep at night instead of lying awake wondering what "on earth" might happen if too many glaciers melt and there are no longer enough fish in the rising, polluted seas.

Ritual as Mythic Enactment: The Navajo *Kinaalda* Ceremony

Myth works its way in the world through people's cognition and action. Myth has real effects in people's lives and, through human technological activities, on the environment as well. Many of the most specific of these effects are achieved through ritual. As Anthony F.C. Wallace (1966) liked to say, *ritual is the "work" of religion*, the place where myth takes form and shape. Rituals may enact myths in the form of an actual performance, like the Passion Play, in which aspects of mythology are brought alive through a society's particular style of dramaturgy. Or the society may sponsor individual or group pilgrimages during which mythic events are enacted upon the much grander stage of the sacred landscape. Through participation in ritual, people often attain mythologically rich experiences and insights; it is the mythical activity of ritual that contributes most dramatically to a traditional society's cycle of meaning.

Durkheim's realization that "myth is reality imagined" is an important one, for it separates our discussion from the naive views of modern people who think that mythic stories are just primitive nonsense. Indeed, anthropologists have shown that people's symbolic systems are very often grounded in reality, for the events described in myth, as we have seen with Genesis, often encapsulate historical events they have experienced and codify adaptive knowledge they have gained over generations, and perhaps centuries or millenia. In addition, myths provide a way of making visible what is hidden in the world.

The Navajo, as we have seen above, hold that all perceivable things in the world have invisible aspects that are imagined as "Holy People." For example, there are the Mountain People, the Star People, the River People, the Rain People, the Corn People, etc. For sophisticated Navajo thinkers, the Holy People are anthropomorphized symbols that stand for the invisible and vital element within all things, and which traditional Navajo philosophy equates with "Wind" (*nilch'I*). As James McNeley has shown in his book *Holy Wind in Navajo Philosophy* (1981), individuals also have such a hidden dimension, called "the Wind within one" (*nilch'I hwii"siziinii*). All these Winds are really part of the one and all-encompassing Holy Wind. Winds are never distinct unattached entities, and energy always flows in and out of even the most enduring objects. (Wind comes and goes from the human body through the breath, cowlicks in the hair, finger and toe tip swirls, the belly button, etc.) The coming and going of wind accounts for the tapestry of reciprocal causation that typifies the Navajo understanding of the cosmos. The choice of "wind" as the central metaphor is an explicit recognition, common to many cultures on the planet, that there are forces that, just like moving air, normally cannot be observed save by inference from their effects. We see again the powerful role of symbolism in putting a face upon the invisible but efficacious forces that play out in human affairs.

In order to see how myth can be enacted in ritual, let us return to the Navajo origin myth briefly described above, which tells the story of the birth and development of Changing Woman. In that story we mentioned that Changing Woman grew into womanhood and had her first menstruation. The Holy People wanted to mark the importance of her fertility, and to that end, created a puberty ceremony for Changing Woman which they called *Kinaalda* (taken from the verb which means "to menstruate for the first time"). All the Holy People showed up to celebrate Changing Woman's *Kinaalda* and sang songs and created ritual acts so that the offspring that she brought into the world would be beautiful and wholesome. During the ceremony, Salt Woman painted Changing Woman the color of white shell and gave her another name, White Shell Woman. The people gathered around and combed Changing Woman's hair and molded her body so that she would grow into a fine form. Then at dawn one morning she raced towards the sun and back again where she ground corn and did other things, like cooking and distributing corn pollen, that mature women have to do. During the process of the ceremony, Changing Woman not only went through the motions of enacting *Kinaalda*, she literally became *Kinaalda*. In other words, the ceremonial activities evoked the maturation potential within Changing Woman and set the course of her future development so that she became the quintessence of womanhood. Only then was she prepared to bear healthy, wholesome children.

Ever since, all Navajo women are strongly encouraged go through *Kinaalda* at the time of their first menses. As young girls they become prepared by their mothers and other women for their great day. They are taught that they will attain important powers when they come of age, and must comply with certain restrictions in order to protect others from those powers. When the joyous day arrives, the girls follow in the footsteps of Changing Woman, and repeat all of the ritual acts that the myth records for Changing Woman's *Kinaalda*. Many people significant to the young girl participate in the four-day ceremony. Her family members have their responsibilities—many of them will take part in activities like the race towards the sun that the girl must undergo. As a consequence, the pubescent girl is taught to identify with Changing Woman within a thoroughly social and thoroughly embodied context.

The essential point to emphasize here is the process of instantiation (embodiment of an idea in experience). The enactment of this most central myth of Navajo cosmology sets up young women to actually experience themselves as *Kinaalda*, as Changing Woman. Thus through myth and its concomitant rituals, an experience of significant growth and change lived by the individual is designed to become cognitively and experientially linked to the most important elements of the Navajo worldview. The naïve outside observer might call it "a set-up," for it is doubtful that all young girls in fact experience this identification with Changing Woman, and through Changing Woman to the vital processes operating in the cosmology.[2] But a sufficient number of girls do still experience this connection, particularly when they have been adequately prepared for years in advance. In all likelihood, a higher proportion of girls had this experience in olden times than at present, when there has been a significant drop in active participation in the traditional religious system—indicating its eventual end, for as we have previously noted, when members of a culture or religious group cease to enact its essential rituals on a regular basis, those rituals and their symbolic expressions of cultural belief will cease to carry meaning.

And yet, we note here with a certain irony that this "race toward the sun" lives on in its fairly recent and very postmodern incorporation into contemporary Wiccan puberty rituals for girls. At the end of their puberty festival, organized by their parents, young girls raised as Wiccans will race with their mothers down the beach toward the sun. At some point, the exhausted mother will stop, while the young girl races on—a lovely symbolic expression of her youth and its accompanying athletic prowess, and of her own "moving on" process as she develops into adolescence and later adulthood (see Hill 1998).

One aspect of the power of the Navajo *Kinaalda* ritual is that it incorporates many of the core symbols of Navajo cosmology. In Chapter 1, we mentioned that a major function of core cultural symbols is to reveal the hidden dimensions of the world. Myth encapsulates core symbols and weaves them into stories that further explicate these hidden dimensions. For instance, the *Kinaalda* draws upon the mythic recognition that hidden forces can produce both beautiful and constructive, as well as ugly and destructive, things to happen in the world. By identifying with Changing Woman, a young girl sees the positive, beautiful and productive aspects of her role as woman, and also becomes more aware of the polarized opposites of these aspects. These hidden energies, which constitute the essence of the world, are thus given a "face"—a form that may be contemplated, that is "pleasing to the mind," that may be painted on canvas or woven in cloth or enacted in ritual, and that may be imagined in daily life as the efficient cause of significant phenomena and events. For those members who are well versed in their society's symbolic system, the core myths and their various symbolic expressions are all of a piece. They form a single, ramified cognitive map within the context of which events—even events in the modern world of global politics and economics—make sense and are easily connected both

---

2. We wish to thank Charlie's friend and colleague, Tracey Prentice, for her input here. Interested readers may wish to also consult Schwarz op cit., and James Farella op cit. on the details of the *Kinaalda* ceremony.

to other contemporary events and to archetypal events that unfold in that timeless era of mythological mysteries.

Ritual as Paradigmatic Enactment

Unlike the myth of technological transcendence so prevalent in contemporary technocratic societies, myths in traditional societies are *stories*—they have characters, a plot, and a beginning, a middle, and end (thoroughly analyzed in the writings of the famous anthropologist Claude Levi-Strauss (see Deliège 2004 and Wilcken 2010)). In today's world, where mythological stories have ceased to have meaning for many people, *paradigms* have come to provide the structures within which people think and take action. Like myths, paradigms provide order and cohesiveness to the lifeworld, but they are not explicitly formulated into stories. For example, there has been discussion for well over three decades of a "paradigm shift" in business, from the old industrial paradigm to the new paradigm of the information society. The old and the new paradigms are not expressed as stories; rather, they are best described as a list of tenets—principles and guidelines:

Old paradigm of business:	New paradigm of business:
hierarchical, linear, top-down	lateral, webbed, networking
"my way or the highway"	input from each individual valued
fixed, rigid, compartmentalized	flexible, responsive
each player sees and takes responsibility only for parts	each player sees and takes responsibility for the systemic whole
aggressive, competitive (win/lose)	cooperative, partnership-oriented (win-win)
product-oriented, process irrelevant	the process is the product
short-term gain	long range view
manipulation and domination of nature	symbiosis with nature, stewardship
closed system (*tries to make reality conform to its dictates*)	open system (*responds to what is*)

Like the mythological systems of traditional societies, paradigms play a central role in the cycle of meaning for many individuals and groups in technocratic societies; they serve as the interpretive screen through which people who espouse a given paradigm will filter their perceptions of reality. In *The Structure of Scientific Revolutions* (2012), philosopher Thomas Kuhn famously demonstrated the profound effect paradigms have on scientific research—each time a scientific paradigm shifts, new possibilities are opened up while others close down. Just as a fish cannot see outside of the water it swims in, so an individual operating within a paradigm is subject to the illusion that the paradigm represents the whole of reality. But no paradigm actually does. All models of reality, no matter how complex, are bound to leave out some aspects of the "reality" they are attempting to model—we can say *that reality is always transcendental relative to either myths or paradigms.* Many paradigms come to constitute relatively closed conceptual systems that discount, explain away, or exclude incompatible information, regardless of its potential validity within another paradigm. Because paradigms create the parameters of thought, individuals who cannot "think beyond" the bounds of a given paradigm are often trapped within the limitations that all paradigms exhibit. For Kuhn showed that, far from being an accurate model of reality, *the most a paradigm can be is a set of beliefs about the nature of an ultimately unknowable, transcendental universe.*

The limitations of paradigms are counterbalanced by their advantages: like myths, paradigms provide clear conceptual models that facilitate one's movement in the world. In acting not only as models of, but also as templates for, "reality," paradigms enable us to behave in organized ways, to take actions that make sense under a given set of principles. "To paradigm," if you will, is to create the world through the picture we paint of it. We then can live as cultural beings in the organized and coherent paradigmatic world we have created. And one primary way in which we accomplish that is by enacting our paradigms in ritual.

The corporate world, for example, was and still is full of rituals that enact and thus reinforce the old paradigm of business, including rigidly followed behavioral pre- and proscriptions (what clothes to wear, whom you can talk to, and where and when), assembly lines designed for efficiency that do not take the experience of the worker into account, and hierarchical meetings in which the chain of command is overtly or subtly reinforced (the old "keys to the executive washroom" thinking). Those who seek to accomplish a "paradigm shift" within a given company fail if their retooling does not address the rituals, visible and invisible, that keep the old paradigm in effect. For, as we will discuss in detail in Chapter 10, *if you want to change the paradigm, you must change the rituals first.*

THE TECHNOCRATIC, HUMANISTIC, AND HOLISTIC PARADIGMS OF BIRTH AND HEALTH CARE AND THEIR ENACTMENTS IN RITUAL

Again, myths are explicit stories, whereas paradigms are implicit sets of principles and beliefs—in other words, while myths are spelled out in actual stories, paradigms are simply cohesive sets of beliefs that are not explicitly spelled out in stories. Thus it is easier to see how rituals enact myths than it is to see how rituals enact paradigms. To illustrate the latter, we will take three contrasting paradigms of health care and describe the differences in the rituals that enact each one. Our examples here come from what Robbie and her coauthor Gloria St. John described in *From Doctor to Healer: The Transformative Journey* (1998) as the *technocratic, humanistic,* and *holistic paradigms of medicine.* The technocratic paradigm defines the body as a machine, postulates the separation of mind and body, views the patient as an object, and charters an alienated, depersonalized physician-patient relationship (i.e., referring to a patient as "the gall bladder in Room 212" or "the cesarean in 313"). The humanistic paradigm defines the body as an organism, notes the connection of mind and body, views the patient as a subject, and stresses the importance of a personalized relationship between patient and practitioner. The holistic model of medicine defines the body as an energy field, insists that body, mind, and spirit are one, and views the patient and practitioner as part of one unified energy field so that each can affect the other for better or for worse.

The Technocratic, Humanistic, and Holistic Paradigms of Medicine

Excerpted from From Doctor to Healer: The Transformative Journey, Robbie Davis-Floyd and Gloria St. John. Rutgers University Press 1998.

The Technocratic Model of Medicine

1. Mind/body separation
2. The body as machine
3. The patient as object
4. Alienation of practitioner from patient
5. Diagnosis and treatment from the outside in (curing disease, repairing dysfunction)

6. Hierarchical organization and standardization of care
7. Authority and responsibility inherent in practitioner, not patient
8. Supervaluation of science and technology
9. Aggressive intervention with emphasis on short-term results
10. Death as defeat
11. Insistence on the superiority of technomedicine and intolerance of other modalities
12. A profit-driven system

Basic underlying principle: Separation
Type of thinking: Uni-modal, left-brained, linear

The Humanistic (Bio-Psycho-Social) Model of Medicine

1. Mind-body connection
2. The body as an organism
3. The patient as relational subject
4. Connection and mutual respect between practitioner and patient
5. Diagnosis and healing from the outside in and from the inside out
6. Balance between the needs of the institution and the individual
7. Information, decision-making, and responsibility shared between patient and practitioner
8. Science and technology counterbalanced with humanism
9. Focus on disease prevention
10. Death as an acceptable outcome
11. Technomedicine as the baseline, with open-mindedness toward other modalities
12. Compassion-driven care

Basic underlying principles: Balance and connection
Type of thinking: Bi-modal

The Holistic Model of Medicine

1. Oneness of body-mind-spirit
2. The body as an energy system interlinked with other energy systems
3. Healing the whole person in whole-life context

4. Essential unity of practitioner and client
5. Diagnosis and healing from the inside out
6. Individualization of care and lateral, webbed organizational structure
7. Authority and responsibility inherent in each individual
8. Science and technology placed at the service of the individual
9. A long-term focus on creating and maintaining health and well-being
10. Death as a step in a process
11. Healing as the focus
12. Embrace of multiple healing modalities

Basic underlying principles: Connection and integration
Type of thinking: Fluid, multimodal, right-brained

The Medical Spectrum

Technocratic Model >>><<< Humanistic Model >>><<< Holistic Model

The technocratic paradigm of medicine is hegemonic in most American hospitals—in fact, in most hospitals in most countries—and is daily enacted through numerous ritualized techniques and rituals that are usually viewed not as rituals, but as "necessary" procedures of traditional medical care—"necessary" because, for example, this technocratic paradigm defines birth as an inherently dysfunctional process that is likely to go wrong at any instant if an insistent series of technological interventions are not applied. We illustrate our point about how rituals enact paradigms through one small but revealing example. Imagine a woman going into a doctor's office for a pelvic exam. In a technocratic practice, she is ushered into a usually cold room, told to take off her clothes and put on a paper gown (a symbol, need we say of what?), and asked to lie down on a high table with her bare feet up in cold metal stirrups. The doctor enters, accompanied by the nurse, walks to the end of the table, and greets her while looking down at her genitals. With few words of preparation or explanation, he inserts his gloved hand into her vagina to examine her. If she tightens up in alarm or fear, he orders her to relax and if she doesn't, he forces his way in until he obtains the information he seeks.

In a humanistic practice, the doctor enters the room to chat with the patient while she is still in her street clothes (a symbol, so obviously, of her status as an autonomous individual). He/she asks the patient about her concerns around this visit and anything else that may be on her mind. After this conversation, he asks her to undress as he leaves the room. The cold metal stirrups are covered with socks or pads. During the exam the doctor explains what he is doing and checks with the woman to make sure she is feeling OK. If she tightens her muscles in alarm, he immediately withdraws his hand and talks to her about what is causing her to close up. If she is truly distressed, he helps her sit up, speaks reassuring words, and promises not to continue with the exam until she is ready. He talks with her about her past—was she sexually abused at some point? —and will recommend counseling or perhaps a support group.

In the first scenario, the doctor is enacting the beliefs and values of the technocratic paradigm of medicine—the body is a machine, time is of the essence, information is important, his status is higher than hers, the coldness of the metal on her feet is irrelevant, as are her experience of the exam and their relationship. In the second scenario, the doctor is enacting the values of humanism: status is not relevant, relationship is; body and mind are connected; if her muscles tense in fear, there is a good reason, most likely having to do with past sexual abuse, or simple, momentary fear that can easily be addressed. Obtaining needed information from a pelvic exam is not as immediately important as addressing her emotional state and not repeating or adding to past abuses.

In each case, the procedures are ritualistic: they are patterned and repetitive (being ushered into the examining room, being told to put on the gown, lying down on the table with legs spread, etc.). They are also symbolic: in the technocratic case, the white coat of the doctor contrasts with the naked genitals of the patient, and he is "up" and she is "down," both literally and interactionally. In the humanistic case, the white coat of the doctor is paralleled to some degree by the clothing of the patient during their first conversation, which takes place eye to eye, on a much more equal level. The pad over the stirrup sends the symbolic message that her experience matters, a message that is heavily reinforced if the doctor stops the exam to accommodate the woman's needs. There is no explicit myth being told here, but there are two implicit stories being acted out. The technocratic practitioner may not think much about what he is doing—he may simply be enacting the beliefs and values he was taught in medical school and residency, without awareness of the paradigm underlying them. The humanistic practitioner, in contrast, will very likely be aware that he is "doing it differently"—his choice to enact the values of humanism in his medical practice will usually be a very conscious one because it is alternative to the norm. In both cases, it is through ritual that each practitioner enacts and displays—and thus reinforces—the values that he or she holds.

In contrast, in a fully holistic practice, a homebirth midwife (see Cheyney 2011) would be performing any necessary vaginal exams in the mother's home, both dressed in regular clothes, on the mother's own bed. The mother and the midwife would likely spend an hour or so talking about any concerns the mother has, reinforcing their pre-existing relationship. The midwife would proceed with the exam ever-so-gently and immediately share with the mother any information she is obtaining as she is feeling it with her fingers. The midwife would be sensitive to the mother's energy and to the energy field established between them, and would be quick to address the mother's reactions and feelings, as the mother would also be sensitive to the midwife and trust in both her expertise and their relationship. The midwife would also encourage the mother to be sensitive to her baby's energy, to talk to her baby, touch her belly a lot, and send love to that baby all during pregnancy and during the labor and birth process. In this situation, we find less actual ritual and more actual, interactive communication between client and practitioner, because (in contrast to the technocratic and humanistic models), this holistic belief system is explicitly spelled out and enacted in explicit conversations between midwife and mother. (See Davis-Floyd 2001 for a full description of the technocratic, humanistic, and holistic models of birth, and Chapter 11 for a discussion of the differences between explicit and implicit belief systems and the differences in the rituals that enact them.)

SUMMARY: THE HUMAN NEED TO UNDERSTAND

Human beings universally seek to understand local events by referencing a more global worldview. This quest for meaning is met in part by the myth/paradigm ritual complex and the integration of individual processes within biologically-based patterns of knowing. Myths and paradigms can provide a conceptual system that links the archetypal features of human nature and capacities for knowing with culturally and personally specific systems of development and expression. These mythological or paradigmatic systems provide socially shared representations of personal and external realities. Ritual integrates archetypal psychology and cultural influences within a single frame of action. This interaction between the universal and the personal has the very great advantage of patterning personal knowledge and behavior to the immediate circumstances of the environment, while retaining a cosmic outlook within which individual and social responses may remain "real." The tension between archetypal and local ways of knowing can be resolved, at least to some extent, by the concerted, meaningful activity of ritual performance.

Suggested Reading

Davis-Floyd, Robbie and Gloria St. John (1998) *From Doctor to Healer: The Transformative Journey.* New Brunswick, NJ: Rutgers University Press.

Davis-Floyd, Robbie (2001) "The Technocratic, Humanistic, and Holistic Paradigms of Birth." *International Journal of Gynecology & Obstetrics* 75, Supplement No. 1, pp. S5-S23 (freely available at www.davis-floyd.com).

Deacon, Terrence W. (1997) *The Symbolic Species: The Co-Evolution of Language and the Brain.* New York: W.W. Norton.

Eliade, Mircea (1963) *Myth and Reality.* New York: Harper and Row.

Chapter 4

MYTHS, PARADIGMS, RITUALS, AND THE PROCESS OF TRUING

Myth and the Process of Truing. Myth, Truing, the Physics of the Vacuum, and the Origin of Our Universe. How the Cycle of Meaning Operates: The Sun Dance and the American Space Program. Summary: The Human Need to Know.

MYTH AND THE PROCESS OF TRUING

The myth/paradigm-ritual complex is grounded to reality in at least three important ways: (1) through the direct intuitive grasp of the order of reality; (2) through regulating the development of individual consciousness along socially collective paths; (3) through enactments in the world that have real effects and consequences. Let us now bear down a bit more on this question of "reality-grounding." Earlier we made the distinction between the quest for meaning typical of traditional cycles of meaning, and the quest for truth. We did not mean to imply that the system of meaning that people strive to bring alive in everyday experience is untrue in any fundamental way. Far from it! As Scott Atran (2002) has argued in his book, *In Gods We Trust,* religious beliefs and doctrines are rarely the product of logical thought or strictly empirical generalization. Yet the creative imagination represented in a living symbolic system nonetheless operates to "true-up" the collective consciousness of a people in such a way that remembered experiences are integrated within a culturally consensual story that assuages intense emotional vulnerabilities. In other words, the imagery in the stories often keeps the interpretation of experience closer to the actual nature of reality than rational thought alone is able to do.

Rational thought can take the form of logical chains that lead one further and further away from reality—we all know how easy it is to "rationalize" something that is untrue. While the rational faculties can easily lead us astray from the essential nature of things, genuine myth rarely does, because the symbols and metaphors encapsulated in myth usually derive from an individual or group's intuitive grasp of some essential aspect of the cosmos. As a consequence of this intuitive grasp, myths may under some circumstances be more "real" than are purely rational accounts of reality. What we want to do now is to develop a better understanding of how this relative accuracy of myth is achieved and how it works its way through ritual performance.

According to the dictionary, the word "true" means that one's statement is consistent with the facts, is in agreement with reality, represents things as they really are, or matches the cultural description of the way things are. The root of "true" means "telling the truth" in both the sense that what one says is without intentional deceit, and is consistent with reality as the culture (or individual) understands it. The root also refers to agreement about an act or statement with some standard, rule, or pattern. The connotation is that the statement is as it should be—it is "correct." Used as a verb, instead of as a noun or adjective, the word "true" implies a physical activity. When a carpenter refers to "truing a wall," it means that the wall is accurate as measured relative to a plan, a plumb line, or a level—the connotation here is that of an activity that makes something "true." And when a bicycle mechanic fixes a warped wheel, it is known as "truing the wheel." One may "true" something by adjusting or shaping it into accurate conformation with a pattern or plan. To "prove something true" is to verify it in relation to something else. And once upon a time, a tool that was used to true something was called a "truer."

Myth operates as a *truer of cognition,* in much the sense suggested by Joseph Campbell (1986, 1988). From now on we want to use the terms "truing" and "truer" in this very special sense. That is, *"truing" refers specifically to the inherent ability of the brain to produce an experiential world that conforms to the reality of the environment well enough to enable survival and adequate functioning.* The role of *truing* in adaptation is obvious. During the countless generations of the human brain's evolution, failure to model the world accurately enough to successfully move around in it resulted in death and a continuous selection against distortions of experienced reality. In the process of coming to know the world, intuition and imagination are at least as important as rationality in forming an accurate experiential picture of reality.

Some of the most complex and important cognition that goes on in our brains is of the intuitive and imagining kind. Indeed, were all of our cognition to be carried out within our conscious, rational minds, our consciousness would be quickly overwhelmed with information. This potential information overload is why most of the associations we make are handled by our mental depths—that is, within our unconscious faculties. Intuition and imagination develop early in childhood, *before* linguistically organized conceptual facilities. The production of lateral, metaphorical associations, so fundamental to the structure of mythology, is present in and typical of the thought of very young children. For example, contemporary children might associate Mommy with the family car because the car is blue and Mom is wearing a blue dress. Or they might associate Daddy with the game of checkers because he wears checkered tweed jackets (as Robbie's father often did). This process is fundamental to totemic thinking—one clan associates itself with an eagle because its members saw an eagle flying during an important clan ceremony, while another associates itself with a wombat—much as sports teams in many countries adopt totems relevant in their locations. Think about the sports teams in your locale—what totems have they adopted, and why?

Truing and the Brain

The human brain does not begin its life by experiencing a "blooming, buzzing chaos" or a "blank slate." On the contrary, the neural structures that develop through childhood to eventually become the adult brain have their beginning in rudimentary, genetically programmed circuits of neural cells, many of which are present in a baby before its birth. For purposes of our present discussion, we will call these early organizations of neural cells *initial structures*.[3] These initial structures of the brain produce the highly organized world of experience of the late-term fetus and infant. And they lay the foundation for human perception, emotion, cognition, and the other universal elements of human experience, including the eventual comprehension of myth and paradigm and the ritual behavior that stems from and expresses this comprehension.

The exact nature of the initial structural makeup of each individual person varies, as do the specifics of the individuals' development over his or her lifetime. Likewise, the expression and developmental course

---

3. The technical term for "initial structures" in biogenetic structuralism is *neurognosis* (neuronal knowing).

of the initial structures of each person's brain vary depending upon the history, environment, and social dynamics of the group's culture and the individual's (culturally rooted) personality. But these are based in the underlying initial structural origin of the imagery, organization, and thematic motifs that are definitive of myth, and that we recognize to be cross-culturally similar, even when festooned with culturally distinct surface material. For instance, the "changeling" in myths from various cultures may feature a human character becoming variously a tiger, hyena, wolf, bat, or killer whale, depending upon the local fauna and the values of a people. Yet the structure of the changeling remains the same—the notion that a human being can mysteriously change into an animal or other sort of creature, usually a carnivore of some kind. American pop culture, now gone global, is full of such stories—vampires, witches, daemons, werewolves, and cyborg transformers abound in comic books and novels, TV series, and movies. Creative contemporary authors of fiction know full well how to tap into the long-standing mythologies regarding human changelings, which both challenge and reinforce our understandings of what it means to be human—or not—and raise questions such as: what exactly is the relationship of humans to other species? And are we limited to our humanity, or can we become more than human?

Mythological stories are the expression of both (1) the fundamental structure of the human brain, because the fundamental organizations of neural cells are much the same for all humans everywhere at birth; they mediate species-typical (archetypal) knowledge about the self and world in much the same ways for every human); and (2) the varying environmental and cultural conditions characteristic of a particular society. The archetypal structure of myth comprises what we might call the *archetypal cosmology* upon which virtually all traditional worldviews are based. This archetypal cosmology assures the truing of all cultures' knowledge to reality (again, in enough ways to ensure that culture's survival). In common parlance, we are "wired" to know reality from a very human, species-typical point of view. But the entire "wired" complement of archetypal structures is never found active in any single individual. Rather, the field of archetypal structures and the archetypal cosmology they produce within each culture provide the human species with an organ of what Stephen J. Gould has called "exaptation"—the facility by which physiological structures either (1) proved adaptive long ago and later on prove adaptive in new ways; or (2) were not particularly adaptive before, but prove to be adaptive to new situations now.

The brain, with its vast store of archetypal structures, is our *organ of exaptation* par excellence. We do not have to do things in the same old way, driven by any "hard-wired" programming. We have flexible brains that can re-order themselves when we confront new challenges. Our brains are capable of coming up with wonderfully new ways of doing old things, and of inventing new processes and techniques that allow us to extend our bodies (and the thoughts that emanate from them) outward into the environment. We are able to learn and to express to others what we have learned. Yet what we learn and what we invent is always grounded upon the archetypal structure of our nervous system. Our brains are plastic (fluid) and able to mold themselves into new configurations in response to the world. Nevertheless, our brains' archetypal /species-typical structure is never left behind, for just as the structure of the oak tree is inherent in the acorn, so too are the possible configurations of the adult brain inherent in its archetypal structures.

The archetypal cosmology upon which the world's mythologies are grounded is thus produced by an organization of neurocognitive cells that represents—in its production of knowledge and experience—both the nature of reality and the body's own internal nature as part of that reality. The archetypal cosmology is constructed by the activity of living cells in our body. These cells grow in such a way that they reiterate an ancient ("archetypal") system of knowing with each passing generation. That is, the cells of each of our brains initially connect up according to instructions given in our body's DNA into an organization that has been reproduced over and over, generation after generation, for over 100,000 years with very little change. This archetypal structure is established in each of us while we are growing in the womb, and awaits activation after we are born. One of the mechanisms by which this system becomes activated is via its expression in a culture's corpus of myth. Returning once again to the cycle of meaning model, we can see that there is for babies a nascent cycle of meaning that ensures that the truing of the developing system of knowledge does not veer too far from environmental reality.

Keeping in mind that the human brain's complement of archetypal structures remains only potential until these structures are activated during development, the archetypal cosmology is expressed within the society's distinct style, embedded as it were like the 3-D figures in one of those stereographic pictures that you have to look at in just the right way in order to see the hidden image. The elements of the society's cosmology (images, relations, time, causation, etc.) *penetrate* into the depths of the brain where they are "recognized" by the target constellation of archetypal structures.

For example, we are born with the facility to recognize faces. The first faces we encounter (ideally, the mother's or father's) are sought out and recognized as faces, as objects of special interest to our newborn selves. The mother's face penetrates into the structures that mediate faces, and begins the development of our knowledge about faces and the people behind the faces, which will continue throughout life. The target archetypes become *potentiated* for development (à la Joseph Campbell's "innate releasing mechanisms") in just the right combination to true-up knowledge about reality and at the same time to give knowledge that distinctly cultural flavor characteristic of the society's "local knowledge" (to use Clifford Geertz's apt phrase) as it matures.

For instance, many cultures use masks in their rituals to represent spirit beings. A mask elaborates the normal human face in important and symbolic ways, but is still processed by the archetypal structures we are born with, which mediate faces in general (Young-Laughlin and Laughlin 1988). The archetypes in each individual brain that recognize the universal structure of the cosmology expressed by myth may also be part of the neural system that is generating experience, so that the archetypal cosmology is not only reiterated in each developing brain, but also the individual may experience the "archetypal" elements and relations directly.

Charlie noticed that when Tibetan Buddhist lamas first encountered Navajo shamans back in the 1970s, they found that they were kindred spirits, for they shared much of the same spiritual knowledge—including elements of archetypal cosmology such as unitary being (a sense of totality, or entanglement/oneness of everything with everything else), the illusory nature of the physical body, the relations between wholeness and health, so on. As is the case with the culture's cycle of meaning, the experiences arising relative to the archetypal cosmology act to both confirm the "truth" of the cosmology and bring it alive.

One of the most common reactions people have to the intuition of truth is that it seems as if they knew it already. In a very real sense we do know "the truth" before we hear it—when the embedded archetypal structures of myth penetrate to the archetypal structures of the developing brain that are ready for potentiation and development, the experience may be one of recognition —literally of "*re*-cognizing" or "*re*-calling" what our species has known throughout the ages of evolution of its collective unconscious. For instance, when we read the myths surrounding the legend of King Arthur and his quest for the Holy Grail, it is easy for many of us to identify with the knight on a quest and with his adventures while negotiating the dark forest with its terrifying monsters and challenges. The Quest myth encodes for many humans, male and female both, a developmentally important message—that each of us must confront our own unconscious if we are to grow—if we are to access the great wisdom that is symbolized by "the Grail."

For this reason, a society's mythology may be *multi-developmental*. The mythology may be so organized that it can effectively potentiate differing neurocognitive structures at different stages of maturation. Once an individual's complement of archetypal structures is on the path to maturation, the symbolic system may re-potentiate the developing structures at later junctures—may even participate in initiating the next stage of development. This possible re-potentiation of archetypal structures is why stories such as that of the Grail Quest—or Harry Potter—speak so richly to young, mid-life, and older people alike. For the very young, what most appeals may be doing battle with wizards or dragons and other beasties, while for young adults the relations between the knight and his lover (or Ron and Hermione) might matter most. For elders, the quest for the Grail itself—for the wisdom (or whatever) it represents—might be the most important. It was Indiana Jones' father, not Indiana himself, who spent years searching for the Holy Grail, and who, upon drinking from it, received "illumination." The hallmark of powerfully potentiating myths is their endurance over many generations and efficacy over the course of life. They are in a sense timeless, for they express the archetypal structure of our consciousness anew with each generation, and each generation finds its voice for expressing the ancient wisdom of the myth.

Some mythologies are actually arranged in multiple layers of narrative and interpretation, each subsequent and more complex layer given to the initiate when they are considered to be developmentally ready to receive that new layer. The Navajo explicitly recognize multiple levels of understanding of their mythic traditions—levels that range from the earliest childhood "just-so" stories to the understandings of the most advanced shamans. Another example is offered by anthropologist Dan Jorgensen (1980) from the Telefolmin people of the South Pacific. The Telefolmin have a system of myth that is structured into at least ten layers. The first layer is that told to young children in the form of many short "just so" stories about things like how the pig got its curly tail. As the children grow, they are initiated into more advanced versions of the stories. These stories are fewer in number and longer. By the time an adult is receiving initiation, the cycle of myths takes on the form of a single saga that takes days to tell. Moreover, the messages encoded in the myths become more and more advanced with each ascending level of initiation. This advancing over time has been the strategy of many Western mystery schools—simply google "Western mystery schools" for information about their many, varied, and often fascinating programs of initiation and spiritual development (see also Snoek 2014 on Masonic initiations).

Truing, Intuition and Action in the World

Knowledge is "trued" (rendered sufficiently accurate to enable humans to adapt to their environments well enough to be able to survive and thrive in them) in conformation with human archetypal cosmology. This coherence and integration of experience produced through truing generally occurs in two ways: through *intuitive understanding* and through *action in the world*. Intuitive truing brings knowledge into conformity with the general cosmological nature of reality, while action in the world tends to true knowledge to the individual's or group's local environment. We are born knowing in both senses, and mythology will often reflect both the global and local perspectives.

Take a simple example: The nature of time is the same for all people on the planet, because the brain produces the sense of time consciousness in the same way for everybody. (It was long thought, erroneously as it turns out, that traditional peoples might perceive time cyclically and not lineally—so-called "clock time"—as we do. We now know that all peoples perceive time as both lineal and cyclical (TenHouten 2005; Laughlin and Throop 2008).) But if you live in New York City, clock time is going to be different than if you live in New Delhi. Modern technocratic societies tend to emphasize linear time, while others, like the ancient Maya, emphasize cycles of time. Both kinds of societies will apply both linear and cyclical time to their local conditions in different ways (Laughlin and Throop 2008).

When we intuitively grasp our culture's cosmology, our knowledge tends to be holistic in its characteristics—that is, the world is seen as a totality in which everything is embedded/implicated in everything else ("a butterfly flaps its wings in Alaska and a hurricane happens in Chile" kind of intuition). But when we know things by virtue of our own activity in the world, as in weeding the garden, that knowledge tends to discriminate—to emphasize distinctions among local things immediately around us and our responses to them. In both of these processes ("everything is part of one vast undifferentiated Thusness" and "this is different from that"), we bring the knowing capacities of the lower brain systems into the grasp of the abstract cultural categories managed by the neocortex. Such experiences are the source of intuition, when the unformulated but experienced truth is expressed in the formal language systems of the conscious mind, thus connecting the preverbal and verbal minds.

Intuition typically labels a type of experience in which the answer to a question, the solution to a problem, guidance in following some goal, a creative impulse resulting in the emergence of some image, idea or pattern, springs into consciousness whole-cloth—seemingly out of nowhere. Adelbert Ames, the remarkable perceptual physiologist and philosopher, is said to have

> ...had the habit of putting a problem to himself in the evening just before he went to bed. Then he "forgot" it. The problem never seemed to disturb his sleep. But he often "found" the next morning on awakening that he had made progress on the problem. And as soon as he got to his office he would pick up his pencil and pad of paper and begin to write. He always said he didn't know just "what would come out..." (Cantril 1960:viii)

We have all had some experience of "seeing" through to the solution to some problem in this way. The "seeing" is an apprehension through sudden awareness of an activity that has always been operating and there to "see." This implicit sort of knowing is fundamental to the functioning of awareness and occurs in all of us from time to time. It is the kind of knowing upon which apprehension of myth (at whatever level of cognitive maturation) depends. There is a general appeal about the wisdom of myth that invites instantiation in the lived moment. The event happening before us reminds us of the general pattern of relations encountered ever so metaphorically in myth.

Take for example the (now widely spread around the globe) myth of Santa Claus. Children whose parents socialize them into that myth and its ensuing rituals of gift-giving and receiving tend to believe it until they reach a certain age when, due to their peers or to their own understanding of "reality," they cease to believe yet continue to engage in the fantasy, because they know their parents want them to and because believing in Santa Claus is fun (and enables them to write that letter to Santa, now intended for their parents). Such children have matured beyond literal belief in the myth of Santa Claus, yet they "see" that their pretended continuation of belief "invites instantiation in the lived moment" of Christmas morning, when their presents will "magically" (and ritually) appear. And parents who continue to live inside that myth with their children find an almost magical re-instantiation of their own childhood Christmas rituals, even when that re-instantiation involves putting together toys and other gifts that need assembly until the wee hours of Christmas morning! Such parents know the value of magic and belief enacted in ritual, and work hard to give that gift to their children, because they know deep-down that both magic and gift-giving are intrinsically good. A sense of the magical works to enhance children's imaginative abilities, and gift-giving works to enhance relationships. (Okay, we know that a huge consumer industry has evolved from all this ritualized gift-giving—and we applaud that industry for the massive ritual benefits it facilitates.)

Knowing through action in the world is much more locality-specific—coming to know in the classic Piagetian sense, in which the internal structures of our brain and body interact with our environment through the production of activity and resulting sensory feedback about the efficacy of that activity. Organisms like honey bees and dogs and human beings actually "feed forward" into the world. We act toward the world *as if* the knowledge we have is accurate. Our activity then operates as a reality check on the truth of that knowledge. The brain structures of children alternatively assimilate the world and accommodate themselves to feedback about the world. This process of assimilation and feedback is how the individual brain develops an experienced reality that is so rich with local detail, nuance, and proficiency. We grow into our local space, however small or large that space may be, and develop not only a repertoire of adaptive knowledge about that space, but also to some extent an identity conditioned by the physical and social particularities of that space.

Truing and Culture: Sensate, Ideational and Idealistic Cultures

Cultures privilege knowledge in different ways. Some cultures emphasize knowing in the archetypal way, while others emphasize knowing in the local, empirical sense—a phenomenon particularly evident in the way societies orchestrate the style of learning in their children. Pitirim Sorokin (1957, 1962) has suggested that societies tend to change back and forth over time, much like the swinging of a pendulum, moving from being *sensate cultures* at one point in time to being *ideational cultures* at another point in time, with the middle of the swing being a kind of impermanent "golden mean" between the extremes, which he called *idealistic cultures.*

Sensate cultures are those that privilege local ways of knowing over knowing in the more archetypal cosmological mode. Sensate cultures, like that of the ancient Romans and our own contemporary technocracies, produce populations that are off-balance toward a materialistic, secular, empirical understanding of the world. The problem, of course, is that cultures never stand still, and the balance struck in one generation between local and universal ways of knowing may be lost to subsequent generations in the continued swing of the culture toward the opposite pole—*ideational culture.*

Because they are way off balance, sensate cultures will over the course of generations tend to compensate by swinging back toward a more balanced view in which knowledge derived from the local mode becomes integrated with knowledge arising from development of archetypal structures (again, Sorokin called these more balanced systems *idealistic cultures*). This pendulum swing back to a more idealistic balance seems to be happening in Euroamerican culture at the present time, which has long been sensate but seems to be developing an increasing tolerance for mysticism, given the hundreds of thousands of "New-Agers" fascinated by "past lives," not to mention the also hundreds of thousands of fundamentalist Christians seeking mystical experiences of God and Jesus—for just a couple of examples. Our Foreword author Betty Sue Flowers noted in her review of this book, "Some would argue that Americans were much more tolerant of non-material realities when they were more religious and that we are decreasing rather than increasing our spiritual sensibilities." In response, we point to the proliferation of New Age ideas and ideals regarding non-religious "spirituality" that, in our experience, have come to permeate the emergent self-constructed cosmologies of cosmopolitan middle- and upper-classes around the world.

It is in the balanced idealistic cultures, as well as the more extreme ideational cultures, that a corpus of mythological tradition forms a living core of knowledge. It is fair to say that most of the several thousand cultures (some of which consist of only a few thousand people) currently co-existing on the planet lie along the scale from the middle (idealistic) to the ideational extreme.

From the point of view of people living in an extremely ideational culture, what we might consider "mystical" knowledge or experience is not mystical at all. It is simply "the way things are." After all, the word "occult" in English simply means "hidden" or "hard to see." When we finally experience and comprehend "the mysteries"—the archetypal structures from the depths of our unconscious—they are no longer hidden, and hence no longer "occult." The human brain is structurally prepared to apprehend the mysteries of archetypal cosmology, but to the extent that we have been conditioned by our (sensate cultural) upbringing not to do so is perhaps the extent to which we must apply effort and exotic techniques to produce mystical experiences.

One of the characteristics of a sensate culture is that it will tend *not* to reverence a living mythology, while a society way out on the ideational pole will relate everything of importance back to the culture's core mythology. A member of an ideational culture will be conditioned to evaluate and interpret events in terms of its archetypal cosmology, experienced through the medium of the sacred stories and performances of the group, and will live their lives in intimate accord with the mysteries of the hidden. Examples include traditional Australian Aboriginal societies, whose members relate features and events in their modern homeland back to *Tjukuba,* or the "Dreamtime"— the period before the human age when gigantic mythological characters like Python and Poisonous Snake left indelible marks on the sacred landscape. Other examples include the previously mentioned New Agers, many of whom live their contemporary lives in that same intimate accord with the mysteries of the hidden, relating many of their experiences to past lives, present dreams, and/or meditative experiences of the mystical, including communing with spirits and angels. In the midst of the contemporary technocracy, thousands if not hundreds of thousands choose to live in the midst of the mystical—Charlie and (sometimes) Robbie among them.

Our brains are born with the potential of knowing the world in both the holistic, archetypal style and in the culture-specific style of local adaptation. During their maturation, our brains will strive to establish a balance between the tensions produced by these two styles of knowing. But the brain is a living system of cells, and if the pressure of environmental and social conditions results in an over-emphasis upon the development of localized empirical knowledge— which is a condition typical of sensate cultures like our own—the inherent processes of integration will tend to reassert their activities wherever possible. Such compensatory processes may be experienced by the individual as "mystical" dreams, spontaneous visions, spirit or entity channeling and other phenomena—perhaps, as Carl Jung taught, calling us to a much greater personal involvement in the inner, unconscious workings of the psyche. In the absence of a corpus of sacred stories (as is the case for those of us living in contemporary technocracies), these experiences may produce confusion and uncertainty for the individual having them. A society that is characterized by a sensate culture that has lost touch with mythological tradition is not well positioned to guide its people to a way of life accommodated to the more holistic/archetypal aspects of reality. Rituals provide fundamental means for linking our current experience of the world with the fundamental mechanisms for knowing reality holistically, a truing that can give one a sense of coherence, meaning and personal integration.

Thus it is no accident that in our intensely sensate contemporary technocracy, we are experiencing a dramatic resurgence of charismatic religious groups and of holistic, spiritually oriented forms of healing and health care. By 1993, one-third of all Americans used some form of holistic or alternative health care (Eisenberg et al. 1993); today, far more than half do. Holistic, energy-based modalities like homeopathy, Reiki, acupuncture and acupressure, reflexology, Shiatsu, breath therapy, and many others are increasingly utilized by an American public disillusioned with the limitations of the sensate mechanistic medical approach. Their rapid growth, like the growth of charismatic religious groups, demonstrates the pendulum swing American society is undergoing as we seek to counterbalance the imbalance of our sensate lives by moving back toward more idealistic, and perhaps eventually more ideational, cultural forms.

MYTH, TRUING, THE PHYSICS OF THE VACUUM, AND THE ORIGIN OF OUR UNIVERSE

We have explained how myth operates to provide a sense of coherence, to true individual conceptual systems and experience to the world. Truing our mental models of reality occurs in both the holistic (e.g., the intuitive grasp of the holistic and systemic properties upon which the universe operates) and discriminating (empirical adaptation to things and events in the local environment) styles. Truing is accomplished in part through familiarization with sacred stories and through their enactment in ritual, both of which are directed at revealing the often hidden, but nonetheless real, nature of the cosmology in which people are embedded and entangled. And, just as with the Navajo notion of Holy Wind, most traditional cosmologies account for the energetic and causative aspects of the cosmos.

In our own cultural history, science has gone a long way in supplanting the truing function of the traditional myth-ritual complex. For a couple of centuries or more, the picture science has painted of the universe has been mechanical and related primarily to the experiences of a small number of people who were carrying out esoteric experiments and naturalistic observations in exotic places. However, with the advent of quantum physics, science has begun to portray the universe in ways that look more and more like that of a traditional holistic and archetypal cosmology. Scientists are coming to understand the universe as a vast sea of energy in which everything is awash. To take a prominent example, in his book *Wholeness and the Implicate Order,* physicist David Bohm sees the universe as simultaneously an "implicate order" and an "explicate order," with the explicate order of material things emerging and then dissolving back into a hidden and holistic sea of (implicate) energy.

Interesting for our purposes here is some of the work on the physics of the vacuum. Physicist Harold Puthoff (1976, 1990) has an interesting (and highly controversial) take on this subject. We see Puthoff's picture of reality as a scientific myth—an origin story, as so many myths are. For Puthoff, the universe is really an ocean of energy of various, random densities and frequencies. There exists a structure of underlying "zero-point" energy that permeates the universe—a *quantum sea* as it were. As Puthoff describes it, the vacuum of space (or the "ether" as it was once called) is really a plenum void—a "void" that is actually chock-full of energy. In the vacuum, so-called "virtual" particles are being created and annihilated, and the frequencies of electromagnetic flux are totally random. This sea of energy encompasses everything in the universe—we are bathed in it, it permeates everything and everyone, and is the medium through which everything is entangled in a vast, perhaps infinite totality. The common view is that this sea of energy, while intellectually and perhaps spiritually fascinating, is technologically unimportant—more a background than anything useful. Yet Puthoff thinks it might be possible to tap into the quantum sea directly to produce energies to power machines.

Again, this work is highly controversial in physics, yet useful for our purposes here because it is an explanatory framework developed by a scientist that has fascinating parallels in other cultures. For example,

Puthoff's account of the universe looks a lot like the Navajo notion of Holy Wind, which is for the Navajo the essential energy foundation and hidden inner nature of all things, be they local and small, or be they cosmic and very large. Indeed, this notion of a sea of energy is a motif repeated in many of the world's cosmologies. Anthropologist Carol Laderman (1991) found similar wind-related cosmological views among the traditional Malay of rural Malaysia, as did Barbara Tedlock (2005) in her study of female shamans in various countries, who are much more likely to use "wind" and "breath" for healing than the hallucinogens favored by their male counterparts. Also, in some schools of Buddhism the domain of ultimate transcendence and causation is the *alaya-vijnana* or "store-consciousness." The *alaya* is a domain of pure, non-dual awareness beyond all distinctions. (From Charlie's personal Buddhist perspective, the interpretation here pertains to an ultimate level of consciousness, and does not refer specifically to metaphysical existence.) Other great mystical traditions have similar interpretations of this holistic sea of energy. The Kabbalah teaches us that material existence extrudes from the subtle, non-dual and divine realm of *Binah* and *Chokmah*, the higher centers of the Tree of Life.

On January 18, 2013, Robbie attended a talk given by the popular physicist Brian Greene, author of *The Fabric of the Cosmos*, *The Hidden Reality*, and *The Elegant Universe*, and a proponent of string theory and the notion of parallel universes. The Paramount Theater in Austin, Texas, where he gave that talk was completely sold out to an audience of enthusiastic fans, many of whom were New-Agers, as we discuss above. During the question and answer session at the end, Robbie had such a pressing question that she stood up to catch his attention instead of just raising her hand like everyone else. It worked.

Her question was, "Where did the stuff that was in the original Big Bang come from?" Dr. Greene said that it was a great question, *the* fundamental question. His answer was first, that he didn't know (well of course he didn't—some questions are simply unanswerable, yet beg to be asked anyway). Yet then he went deeper to speculate about "nothing vs. something," noting that "nothing"—the absence of space, time, matter, energy, everything—might be an unstable state that requires "something." Later, at the very end of the session, Robbie opened her big mouth again, and asked if he might talk about God? Negative hoots, yells, and catcalls arose immediately arose from the audience—we suppose they thought Robbie was a Christian fundamentalist (who would be an anathema to that audience). Greene responded that he was simply too tired to address that question, to great audience approval. Unsatisfied, Robbie wrote an email to Dr. Greene, from which we excerpt the following:

> You were saying that you would be talking on Facebook and Twitter about lots of things, so I yelled out "Talk about God!"—not meaning for you to try to answer the question right then, just suggesting that you address the subject via your social media. I had no chance to explain why I asked the question—I almost didn't because belief in God is a matter of faith and you (and I) are all about science. But if you follow science all the way back to the Big Bang, or to millions of Big Bangs, you get to the question (if you think about religion at all), is there a God (or many) and were the ingredients in the Big Bang, "God"? That would imply that the ingredients in the Big Bang included a consciousness.
>
> I'm particularly interested in this question right now because I'm coauthoring (with Dr. Charles Laughlin, a neuro-anthropologist) a book called *The Power of Ritual: How People Think, What They Believe, and Why*. In that book we discuss how peoples enact and transmit their mythological/cosmological belief systems through ritual. The first draft of the book is out for review right now. In the section where we discuss the belief system of the Navajo, we note that their mythological system holds that First Man and First Woman gave birth to Changing Woman, who grew up rapidly and then created the world. A literal-minded reviewer asked, "But where did First Man and First Woman come from?"
>
> All such belief systems that I as a cultural anthropologist know about postulate that there was something before there was the something we know—something was there before the world we live in existed, and those somethings—gods, beings, monsters, whatever—created this world. (I'm sure you've heard the "turtles all the way down" story!) Rationally-oriented Westerners tend to dismiss all such stories as "primitive nonsense," yet they are all explanatory models that postulate something coming from something that preceded it, just as three of the major world religions (Judaism, Christianity, Islam) postulate via *Genesis* that God preceded the world and created it—just as scientists postulate that first there was all this condensed energy and matter, which then exploded in the Big Bang. They are all on a

parallel, as far as I can see, in terms of being very similar types of explanatory frameworks.

It's just that *science* leads us to the Big Bang, and not myth. Yet science cannot answer my question above, so you could not. There is an ancient Hindu myth which says something like "God breathed out, and the stars and galaxies went flying." Possibly that reflects an intuitive understanding of the Big Bang, thousands of years before the theory of the Big Bang was generated—a way of saying that there had to be something from which everything else came. Possibly the Navajo myth of First Man and First Woman, and all other such myths, reflect that same intuitive understanding that everything came out of something. Possibly humans hold that intuitive understanding because we are a part of our fully interconnected universe and our brains are "hard-wired" to know that in some archetypal way. So it might be entirely rational and reasonable that we construct these explanatory models because in some sense, we "sense" the fundamental truth underlying all of them.

I'm thinking about incorporating some of these thoughts into *The Power of Ritual*, and I would simply love it if you would give me some feedback on them!

Perhaps any feedback you might care to give could include an answer to this question: Does God form any part of your own explanatory framework? Full disclosure on my part: My own answer would be sometimes yes, when I'm desperate for something to believe in, and sometimes no, when I'm able to live with total ambiguity. I just can't get past my question about where the ingredients in the Big Bang came from without at least imagining a God, since I can't find any other answer—yet even that one is extremely unsatisfactory—if it was God who created the Big Bang and thus the universe, then where did God come from? Same issue!

Robbie has received no response from Dr. Greene, yet the questions—and their implications for the archetypal answers humans come up with to explain why we are here, and why our world and our universe exist—remain. Even eminent physicists, in the end, can do no better than "primitive" peoples—they all end up saying that there was something out of which everything else came.

Myth, Paradigms, Ritual Enactment, and Truing

Putting what we have said together in a single diagram, we can see from Figure 4.1 that the ritual enactments of mythical traditions and paradigms operate in a parallel manner. The mythic matrix is a traditional system of knowledge that is passed down from generation to generation through a people's cultural history, and has at its foundations the inherent wisdom encoded in the archetypal structures of the human nervous system, while the paradigmatic matrix is more the product of modern day scientific/philosophical, as well as socioeconomic and political factors. Yet, as both mythical traditions and paradigms are obviously the products of human cognition, they are merely different in degree rather than in kind.

Both the mythic and paradigmatic matrices are expressions of knowledge through symbolic media. If their expressions become enacted in ritual performances, the symbolism and the activity merge to evoke experiences in participants, who come to interpret what they have experienced in terms of the

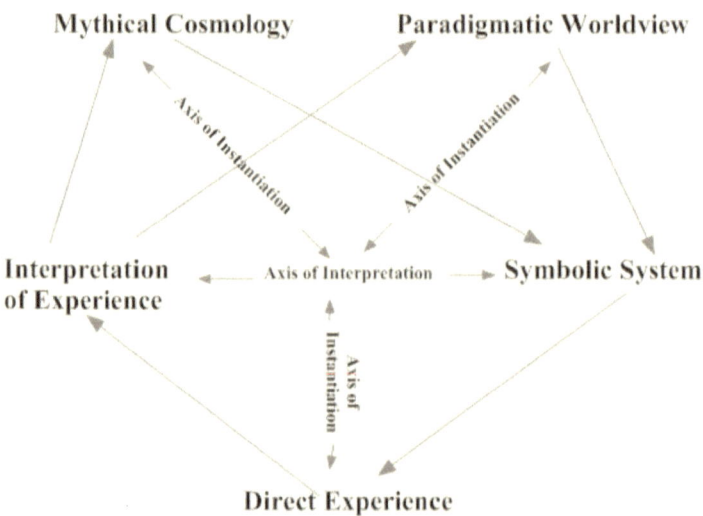

Figure 4.1. The Enactment of Mythical and Paradigmatic Matrices within the Cycle of Meaning. The traditional mythical matrix and the more modern paradigmatic matrix operate in much the same way when enacted in ritual. And the role of interpretation is similar as well. Two axes of relationship operate in the cycle of meaning to coalesce the system, one being the axis of instantiation that links knowledge and experience, and the other the axis of interpretation, which links ritual elements and interpretation of experience.

traditional mythical system or the modern paradigm. In a sense then, there is an *axis of instantiation* that we can draw vertically between the knowledge system (whether traditional or modern) and people's direct experience. The matrix comes alive in experience—experience evoked, conditioned and guided by ritualized social enactment—in other words, the matrix is *instantiated* (made immediately real) in the experience. The experience operates as evidence confirming the truth of the matrix, thus reinforcing the claims made in the matrix about the nature of the world or the self.

But there is another important relationship we need to point to here, and that is a horizontal *axis of interpretation* between the enactment of the matrix in ritual and the interpretive phase that naturally happens during or after participation in the ritual. Although the elements and events that make up a ritual may be initially meaningful before participation due to prior instruction (like receiving catechism before participating in the Mass, or the lecture before carrying out the lab "experiment"), the experiences that arise as a consequence of participation in the ritual quickly overshadow the initial instruction in importance. The memory of salient aspects of ritual experience becomes the meaning of the ritual and its elements for each individual participant. *Interpretation is information stored in memory* (especially if it carries the emotional charge that ritual often generates), and *it is very common for societies to act in various ways to standardize the interpretations that get laid down in individual memories.*

For instance, Tibetan Tantric Buddhist teachers (*lamas*) traditionally bestow their teachings in the form of a ritual called a *Wang Kur* or "Empowerment." These Empowerments are elaborate ceremonies in which the *lama* enacts the deity, whose essential mind-state or "vibration" is ideally being transmitted directly from teacher to student. The ceremony may require hours or even days to complete. And the experiences had during the process of receiving an Empowerment may be profound and life-changing. But interpretations of experiences had during or as a consequence of participating are not left to chance. Instructional sessions called *lungs* are given during the days following the Empowerment, in which precise interpretations of elements and events in the ceremony are repeated for the benefit of the student. In the Tibetan case, the alternation of experiences (instantiation) and explicit, canonical interpretation that make up the axis of interpretation may be considered as a meta-ritual sequence in which experiences are evoked and interpreted in a highly controlled manner. (In a similar fashion, fighter pilots will receive a briefing before they carry out a mission, and then receive a "debriefing" after the mission to share information and ideally reach a consensus view of what happened during the mission.)

Mythic and Paradigmatic Matrices: Revitalization and Change

Both mythological and paradigmatic matrices are largely conservative of meaning. After all, that is the point of emphasizing the systemic interrelations among knowledge, ritually evoked experience, and interpretation. All of these elements combine into a single living system of meaning for individuals and groups participating in rituals. But this does not mean that the cycle of meaning, in either its mythic or its paradigmatic format, is rigid and unchanging. Far from it! All of the components of the cycle of meaning are organic; they are part of a living system. Change may be introduced from within any of the quadrants. New information may be introduced into the society's or group's store of knowledge. New texts may be incorporated into the material that informs the people's knowledge pool, and cause a change in the knowledge that informs the ritual, thus altering the ritual-experience-interpretation relationships. Or the ritual itself may be altered due to imported symbolic elements and new techniques. The changed ritual may evoke novel experiences, leading to novel interpretations and thus a change in the society's knowledge. (See Chapter 10 for a discussion of ritual's roles in effecting social change.)

Moreover, human experience is never solely due to the ritual context in which it occurs. The cultural programming each individual brings into the situation, as well as their personal history and past experiences and proclivities, have effects on the experiences attained as a consequence of participating in a ritual. Novel dreams and visions, and novel linkages between ritual and non-ritual experiences, may require new interpretations that can alter both the knowledge store and the meaning of elements in the ritual. This organic and dynamic nature of the cycle of meaning potentiates what anthropologist Anthony F.C. Wallace (1966) called "revitalization." Without an openness to change, both traditional mythic and modern paradigmatic matrices would eventually become obsolete and unrelated to the real life conditions that confront people. In other words, without revitalization, the relationship between knowledge and experience along the axis of instantiation would increasingly produce dissonance between knowledge and experience (an inability to "true" knowledge and experience with new reality). One might argue that this sort of dissonance is precisely what has happened for many people who have turned away from orthodox organized religion in contemporary times. The religion's worldview, and thus the rituals that enact that worldview, may no longer "speak" to the everyday lives of many people. To address this problem, radical changes have occurred in many Christian and Jewish sects (for two examples) to revitalize their liturgy and increase their attendance. Occasional or frequent revitalization is required in order to true the matrix to a people's local reality so that the worldview will continue to have immediate and relevant meaning.

Nonetheless, the matrix and its ritual enactment normally provide an enduring conservative influence upon individual experience and understanding. This conservatism is the secret of the truing function of ritual in the archetypal mode, for its relative openness and ongoing revitalization allow the flexibility for knowledge and action to move with the changing times and conditions, at the same time maintaining a fundamental continuity that integrates universal properties and processes of reality with changing local elements. The world of relations is still coded in holistic terms; archetypal elements and constraints continue to populate the symbolic media; distinctions continue to be made in the primordial logic of binary oppositions, and in metaphorical association and metonymic substitutions—all these are aspects of the archetypal cosmology.

HOW THE CYCLE OF MEANING OPERATES ALONG THE TWIN AXES OF INSTANTIATION AND INTERPRETATION: THE SUN DANCE AND THE AMERICAN SPACE PROGRAM

As we previously described, there are significant differences between mythic and paradigmatic matrices (belief systems). The most important are that modern paradigms are neither narrated in traditional story form, nor are they necessarily informed from the deep psychological foundations of archetypal cosmology. Modern paradigms are nonetheless coherent and operate, as do myths, as templates for action. Both myth and paradigm must remain to some extent current (trued to their current circumstances) or they will drop away or be replaced.

Let us explore two more examples of cognitive matrices, one from a traditional mythical system and the other from a modern paradigmatic system, with a view to better understanding the cycle of meaning operating along the twin axes of instantiation and interpretation.

Sun Dance: The Twin Axes in the Mythic Matrix

For the mythical matrix, almost any traditional system would do as an example. Take for instance the Plains Indian Sun Dance. The Sioux people of the American plains have been quite innovative in their borrowing and reorganization of cultural materials. During the 18th century they incorporated horses (introduced into the Americas by the invading Spaniards) into their stock of resources, a technological borrowing that radically changed their patterns of subsistence and political relations and that also set the stage for borrowing cosmological and religious elements from both Spanish and other horse cultures, and reorganizing them into what became in the 19th century the Sun Dance religion. Elements centered upon corn and fertility were reorganized as befitted a migratory, hunting-gathering people who were now more concerned with buffalo, deer and other game than with gathering activities (Jorgensen 1972). Because hunting was now more important than gathering, male hunters became more highly valued, while still retaining their traditional role as warriors. Hence, traditional roles were adjusted to true them to the changes in means of subsistence.

During the Sun Dance, an annual festival, young male warriors would be tied to a pole by a lengthy cord passed through their pectoral muscles. The youths undergoing the ritual would walk and dance toward and away from the pole—the ritual center—straining on the rope until their flesh tore and they were free from the tether. The torn flesh would be treated and would eventually produce scars that were marks of courage, prowess and fortitude, qualities greatly valued by the Sioux. The American government forbade the practice of the Sun Dance in the 1880s, but it was reestablished years later in a new form—one that is practiced today. The more modern, peace-oriented version of the Sun Dance once again trued its intentions to the new demands of reservation life, and now emphasizes performing purification practices (like sweat lodge ceremonies) and dietary taboos prior to the ceremony, and then spending days dancing around a pole upon which the symbol of Buffalo, Eagle or some other religious icon is attached. Eventually the dancer may enter a trance in which visions occur that reveal to the young man his life purpose. This contemporary version of the Sun Dance has in one form or another spread widely among North American native peoples, for it is easily modified to true the cosmology of the people to local conditions.

The Sun Dance was originally a revitalization movement among the Sioux. Its intention was to bring about a golden age of prosperity and peace among the Plains Peoples. Over the nearly two centuries of its existence, the Sun Dance religion and ceremony have changed radically. Thinking about those changes in terms of the cycle of meaning, we can see that the worldview of Plains Indians has altered considerably over the years. The Sioux were eventually confined to a reservation, and the role of the hunter/warrior diminished, while the role of farming increased in importance, and therefore the role of the Sun Dance as a ceremony of defiance of incursions by the dominant Euroamerican culture dwindled. And yet the core symbols of Sioux cosmology remained, including Buffalo, the Sun, the importance of the high god *Wakan Tanka*, and so on.

The Sun Dance ritual itself has all along been directed at evoking visions and other alternative states of consciousness. Along the *axis of instantiation* (confirmation and vivification), we can see that the extraordinary states of consciousness many dancers experience bring the normally hidden aspects of the cosmology alive and thus "instantiate" (generate lived experiences of) the values and core symbols (Sun, Buffalo, etc.) of the people's cosmology. Yet, as the Sun Dance has changed over the generations, the form and significance of its elements have shifted along the axis of interpretation (reflection) as the spiritual and healing needs of the people have changed. The visions "driven" (see Chapter 5 on ritual drivers) by the privations, purification, and dancing have remained significant means of ascertaining information about the normally invisible spirit world, but have occurred in people of differing generations who have confronted different environmental and political-economic conditions. Interpretations of visions have reflected both the continuity of the archetypal cosmology and the shifting conditions of each generation's local, everyday lifeworld. So flexible has the Sun Dance become that it has spread beyond the confines of Sioux culture to many other Native American societies, and remains a very viable cosmological-ritual institution today.

NASA's Space Program and the Twin Axes in the Paradigmatic Matrix

In 1960, President John F. Kennedy expressed a vision that was later instantiated in experience—"send a man to the moon and return him to Earth within this decade." That vision galvanized the American space program into intensive action that did, in fact, result in the culmination of that vision. As NASA developed into a major institution, receiving billions of dollars from the federal government to help it make that vision a reality, its members developed a culture organized around achieving Kennedy's goal. "Making it to the moon" before anyone else developed America's technological abilities, leading to the inevitable cultural interpretation that "the U.S. is Number One in the world" in terms of technological prowess and global superiority and leadership. Yet once we had succeeded in making it to the moon via the Apollo program, our national priorities for further space exploration and leadership were suddenly unclear. We had made it to the moon, several times—what were we supposed to do now? The answer that NASA came up with was to build the shuttles and the international space station—a mission now accomplished—yet that mission and the others NASA developed were fuzzy compared to the clarity of "a man on the moon within 10 years." In part, this was because NASA no longer had a clear mandate from the executive branch, nor was Congress willing to provide the funds that would have allowed for a more ambitious vision.

During Robbie's years of conducting oral history interviews with some of NASA's pioneers (see Davis-Floyd, Cox, and White 2012 for abridged versions of some of these interviews, and www.davis-floyd.com for the full texts), it became clear to Robbie that they had "lost their way," in a sense, after the moon trips ended. They had built their entire culture and the vision that led that culture under Kennedy's mandate. The NASA culture that achieved that goal was based on the core value of "doing it yourself." The early NASA engineers were often hired because they were masters of building and flying model airplanes. Really! Young guys who won model airplane competitions were massively recruited during the late 1950s to join the National Advisory Committee for Aeronautics (NACA), the precursor to NASA, because during the early 1950s NACA was all about wind tunnels, in which model airplanes and small rockets were flown to determine how they would react to changes in air pressure, wind flow, and other factors, so that knowledge could inform the construction of actual airplanes and large rockets. Then, in 1957, the Soviets flew Sputnik 1, the first man-made object to enter low-earth orbit and circle the globe. In immediate response to this huge challenge to American technological, military, and visionary supremacy, NACA employees galvanized to beat the Russians in this entirely new game, and in 1958 NACA was transformed into NASA by federal mandate. The corporate rituals of the NACA had been minimal.

Bosses would overturn trash cans and sit on them next to the desks of their young, bright employees to check in on their progress and hear their many ideas. One phone call to the right person could result in the building of a major facility to test a round rocket—it was all about networking, and not at all about hierarchy.

That lateral, horizontal, networked early NACA/NASA culture got us to the moon—yet getting there led to the establishment of massive facilities and a massive bureaucracy. No longer would one phone call suffice, no longer could NASA engineers build what they designed on their own with financial support only from NASA. It became all about "outsourcing"—limiting NASA's former primary role in technology development in order to give government contracts to outside agencies that would do the work themselves. A single phone call was replaced with file drawers full of the paperwork that the federal government now required. Immediate "instantiation" of ideas was replaced by too much "interpretation" of those ideas by the recently created federal bureaucracy. Some of the most creative engineers and designers left in frustration. Others carried on and ended up facing the Challenger disaster, which, as Robbie learned in her interviews, was the clear result of that very same bureaucracy. As we know, it was the frozen O-rings that caused the disaster. But why was the Challenger launched under extreme cold weather temperatures? And more pertinently, why did the O-rings exist in the first place?

Because of the bureaucracy! Once NASA employees were no longer allowed to build rockets on their own, bids had to be taken from competing companies. The obvious thing would have been to build solid rockets all in one piece, with no O-rings to join the separated parts. But that would have meant going with the one company that was close enough to Cape Canaveral/Kennedy to get those huge rockets there in one piece. Having to "contract out" (i.e., ritualize) the bids for building those rockets meant having to accept a cheaper bid from a company far away, which would have to build the rockets in two pieces in order to be able to transport them to Florida, and to use O-rings to reconnect them. Ritual government protocol was followed, the cheaper bid was accepted, the O-rings were used, they froze in the cold weather, and the Challenger went down.

And what about the decision-making process that allowed Challenger to launch when it should have remained grounded on that too-cold morning? Again, it's a very sad story of conflicting corporate cultures that pitted the engineers, who insistently warned that the O-rings might fail in freezing temperatures, against the administrators who just wanted to "go for it" because everyone was there watching—the thrilling and very public ritual of launch was already in process, and they just followed that "ritual train." Challenger was scheduled to be launched around 4 am. The engineers wanted to let the sun rise and warm up the launch site to about noon that day. Yet a major senior NASA meeting was planned for Washington DC later that same morning, and would have to be canceled if the launch were canceled (Kenneth J. Cox, personal communication, April 21, 2012)—so the administrators prevailed and the ritual train proceeded (see Chapter 7 on "ritual inviolability and inevitability"). Launching the Challenger was supposed to be a successful ritual performance and mass celebration of American core values on technological innovation, prowess, and supremacy. Yet because of major dysfunctions within NASA's core culture and in NASA's cultural relationships with government employees and contractors, that planned mass ritual celebration turned into a massive and heart-rending disaster.

Returning to our twin axes of instantiation and interpretation, we can see how the instantiated belief in the supremacy of the U.S. space program led to the initial idea for the Challenger launch and to the idea that for the first time, an American space shuttle was so safe that it could carry an ordinary American citizen, school teacher Christa McAuliffe, into space along with the trained astronauts (whose training included the constant warning of the possibility of crisis, and even death). The ideal outcome of the Challenger launch would have been to re-instantiate American core values on technological supremacy and, additionally, to instantiate the access of an ordinary American citizen to America's highest technological achievement and to re-interpret, and thus true-up, the United States of America as Number 1 in the world.

We can see how ritualized (as in, affected by corporate culture and ritualized hierarchies and policies) miscommunications and the resulting *mis*interpretations led to the Challenger disaster. As Robbie's research shows, entrenched and ritualized hierarchies did not characterize the early years of NASA and did not get us to the moon. Yet the later bureaucratization of NASA did lead to massive, ritualized dysfunction and straight to the Challenger disaster. And NASA did learn from that experience, did restructure its corporate hierarchies and communication systems accordingly, and went on to accomplish many more successful shuttle journeys (although another shuttle was lost in 2003). The International Space Station does continue to reflect and embody the positive results of international collaboration and successful communication, and to symbolize what one united world can accomplish beyond its planetary boundaries.

SUMMARY: THE HUMAN NEED TO KNOW

Humans exhibit a universal need to know about and to understand the world they live in. Knowledge and understanding are first and foremost adaptive strategies that have been evolutionarily selected for over hundreds of thousands of years. If our systems of knowledge—our cultures—were not adaptively accurate enough for us to survive, were not sufficiently "trued" to the world we live in, we would simply die off as a species. The cultural (and individual) rituals we perform enable us to express and enact the understandings of the world that we develop, at the moment and over time. The role of ritual in truing knowledge and understanding is fundamental to revitalizing the paradigm or cosmology of the culture. Yet as we saw with the Challenger disaster, the truing-up may occur in the wrong direction—bringing bureaucratic intentions into impractical alignment with practical engineering intentions. This ever-present possibility of truing-gone-wrong underscores how the worldview of a group must be kept more or less current—more or less trued—with the daily experience of people on the ground (Hüsken 2007). Otherwise ritual fails in its primordial function, imposing the enactment of a world-as-we-want-to-force-it-to-be instead of an enactment of the world-as-is.

Suggested Reading:

Davis-Floyd, Robbie, Kenneth J. Cox, and Frank White (2012) *Space Stories: Oral Histories from the Pioneers of the American Space Program*. Kindle E-Book.

Davis-Floyd, Robbie and P. Sven Arvidson, eds. (1997) *Intuition: The Inside Story*. New York: Routledge.

Greene, Brian (2004) *The Fabric of the Cosmos: Space, Time, and the Texture of Reality*. New York: Vintage Books.

Radin, Dean I. (1997) *The Conscious Universe: The Scientific Truth of Psychic Phenomena*. New York: Harper.

Chapter 5

RITUAL DRIVERS: GENERATING AND CONTROLLING STATES OF CONSCIOUSNESS

States and Warps of Consciousness. Mimesis and States of Consciousness. Types of Ritual Drivers and How They Work. Ritual and Warp Control. Monophasic and Polyphasic Cultures. Transferring Information across States of Consciousness. Ritual and the Control of States of Consciousness. Ritual Drivers and the Cycle of Meaning. Portals as Ritual Drivers into Multiple Realities. Why Are Ritual Drivers So Compelling? Summary: SOCs, WOCs, and Ritual Drivers.

Philosopher and Vedic scholar Fritz Stall (1989) has made the argument that because ritual elements are "meaningless," therefore ritual cannot be communication, and thus cannot be performance. Rituals for Stall are more like grammar than semantics, rule systems rather than symbolic. Rituals more or less have a life of their own, unrelated to world views and religious beliefs. We argue that Stall has it all wrong. Rituals are full of meaning, both as total performances and as the locus of individual elements. How elements of ritual come together to communicate often profound meaning will be extensively addressed in this and subsequent chapters.

What is it about the elements that make up ritual that are so physiologically, psychologically and socially compelling and meaningful? That is the question we want to explore now. In order to do so, we have to reach an understanding of how the symbolism and repetitive behaviors embedded in ritual operate to influence the consciousness of participants. Let us begin by examining so-called "states of consciousness" and how they are changed from one state to another very quickly, or over time. Then we will return to our earlier (Chapter 2) discussion of symbolism, and follow that with a look at "ritual drivers" and the importance of both rhythm and repetition in effectively altering consciousness.

STATES AND WARPS OF CONSCIOUSNESS

As all of us will no doubt agree, our consciousness never remains the same from one moment to the next. Consciousness is forever changing. Because the shifting field of consciousness exhibits recurrent temporal patterns, we may become aware of "chunks" of experience which we recognize as distinct. The definitive quality of our awareness is *re*-collection, *re*-membering, or *re*-cognition of patterns in experience. We know where we are in our experience because to some extent we have "been there before," in the sense of pattern recognition. We recognize faces and places and things, we recognize the qualities of things like colors and textures and tastes, and we recognize feelings and thoughts, being excited and feeling fatigued, and all the other recurrent attributes of experience. The role of memory in our consciousness is both enormous and fundamental.

Furthermore, reflexive knowledge about consciousness itself involves knowledge of grand patterns of experience. In other words, if an episode is perceived as a salient unit of recurrent experience, then it may be cognized as distinct from other such episodes, and perhaps labeled: for example, we may say we are "awake," "stoned," "drunk," "depressed," "dreaming," "excited," "tired-out," "angry," "out-of-body," "playing," etc. These cognized and labeled categories of experience, and their underlying neurocognitive structures, are what anthropologists and others normally call *states of consciousness* (or *SOCs*). When we refer to SOCs other than those that occur in waking consciousness, we often speak of *alternative, or altered, states of consciousness* (*ASCs*), like dreaming, trance, hypnosis, getting high on drugs, fugue state (reversible amnesia), and so forth.

Any SOC is produced by a distinctive organization of brain activity. The organization of our brain when we are happy is not the same as when we are sad. Moreover, in order for one SOC to be transformed into another SOC, the underlying neurocognitive structures of the brain must reorganize themselves. This reorganization usually happens in the blink of an eye. Within a very short time we can experience a change in SOC from being hungry to being sated, from being on the phone with someone to being absorbed in a TV program, from feeling very sad to letting go of that sadness and experiencing happiness, or from our usual busy SOC to a deep meditation. The points of experiential and neurophysiological transition between states of consciousness are what we call *warps of consciousness* (*WOCs* or simply *warps*). The really important thing to remember about WOCs is that although they happen very rapidly compared to the longer duration of SOCs, they are crucial because the precise organization of warps can determine the organization and the qualities of the subsequent state of consciousness. Despite the importance of WOCs over our mind states, they generally happen unconsciously, so that we tend to be unaware of the warp processes that alter our SOCs. For example, the warp that produces the onset of sleeping may last for only a few seconds, yet its brief activity can determine the quality of the dream states that follow it.

MIMESIS AND STATES OF CONSCIOUSNESS

Much of the content of our states of consciousness consists of repetitions of happenings we have copied from other people—from peers, parents, co-workers, and so forth. It is very much human nature to learn by mimicry. The ability to mimic, also known as *mimesis*, is a fundamental expressive capacity underlying human cognitive evolution, mythic thought, and ritual action (Garrels 2011). The intimate association of ritual with chanting, music, and repetitive movement reflects the operation of the mimetic process that provides the remarkable human ability to *entrain* (that is, to link-up—or to synchronize—elements, organs and processes in the way that compartments are linked together to make a train) the body to external rhythms (Donald 1991), as well as to gestural and facial representations and the rhythmic behavior of others. The mimetic process provides a neurobiological basis for metaphorical symbolism—for representing through enacting. This communication system of the body involves a "rhythmo-affective semantics"—a rhythm-centered system of meaning that expresses the fundamental emotions (Molino 2000).

This mimetic process, expressed through imitation and ritual, produces an *ethos* (the fundamental character or spirit of a culture; the underlying sentiment that informs the beliefs, customs, or practices of a group or society; the dominant assumptions of a people or period) or system of collective belief that was enacted early in human evolution in activities involving collective participation. Vocal imitation of animals and group ritual dances were among the first of human mimetic activities. The shaman's uses of dance, imitation and drumming reflect the utilization of this innate mimetic process, which, again, provides mechanisms for integrating groups and maintaining coordination among their members. Mimesis—imitation—is still the principal mechanism through which humans learn social roles, physical skills, and engagement in sports and many expressive activities. The integrative functions of this innate mimetic process are manifested in the effects of music, which often include a compulsion to "move with the beat."

Songs and chanting are common aspects of shamanic healing rituals, and are found in ritual practices around the world. The non-verbal elements of music in ritual practices reflect a biological proclivity with deep evolutionary roots. Human musical capacities have their foundation in the hoots, songs, calls, and rhythmic expressive systems of other animals. Among the great apes, these vocalizations are used to express alarm, to modulate social contact and spacing, for mate attraction, pair bonding and territorial advertisement, and for enhancing group cohesion and unity (Geissmann 2000). In humans, music is part of a larger group of cultural activities (also including drama, poetry, dancing, and play) that share origins in common neural processes that provide rhythm, *affective semantics* (emotional meaning), and melody (Molino 2000:165, 173). Freeman (2000) suggests that music and dance coevolved to enhance communication of internal states and therefore social bonding, contributing means to induce altered states of consciousness that can transform—and collectively synchronize—habits and thought patterns. Music's adaptive capacity includes this ability to promote group cohesion through mutual cognitive and emotional expression that coordinates the behavior of different individuals into synchronized performances (Brown 2000; Merker 2000).

Thus far we have been discussing the role of mimesis in expressing internal activities occurring within a single SOC. But there is another kind of mimesis that is apparently unique to human beings, and that is what we can call *inter-state mimesis,* in which activities in one SOC influence experiences had in another SOC. This happens in poetry and music all the time. We might experience a pleasant, relaxing day at the beach and then at some later time write a piece of music or a poem that uses metaphor to express the feelings we had at the beach. In order for this to happen, memory of the activities in one SOC (say, being "awake") are retained across the warp and thus can inform experiences had in another SOC (say a "dream"). To illustrate, one evening Robbie had a talk with her 20-year-old daughter Peyton about how much her 16-year-old son Jason had changed in the last few years. And just before she went to sleep that night, Robbie glanced at a photo of her children riding on a merry-go-round when they were little. Not surprisingly, her subsequent dreams centered on vivid flashbacks to Jason's childhood. Upon waking, Robbie remembered the conversation and the photo, and thus understood what induced the WOC that led to her dreams. WOCs are crucial in the transformation between SOCs, for if the society (or the individual) can control the warp, it can control subsequent states of consciousness and the experiences that may arise in those states. What is required is that memory of what occurs in one state be retained across the warp and into the subsequent state (Laughlin et al. 1986). So if you want to make sense of your dreams, you might want to try to be aware of what you are thinking about just before you fall asleep.

TYPES OF RITUAL DRIVERS AND EXAMPLES OF HOW THEY WORK

For maximum effectiveness, either within or across states of consciousness, a ritual will concentrate on sending one basic set of messages that will be rhythmically repeated using different procedures and various codes. What is repeated in ritual can include the occasion for its performance (as in the Easter Mass cycle in the Catholic Church, an event that happens every year at the same time); its content (as in the Eucharist in the Catholic Mass); the form into which this content is plotted (as in the liturgy of the Catholic Mass), or any combination of these. This redundancy enhances ritual's efficacy in communicating whatever messages it is designed to send. As anthropologist Robert Redfield once pointed out, the Mayan farmer who hears the shaman chant the names of the gods twenty times in one hour, several times a day, is not likely to forget them!

Rhythm has long been recognized by anthropologists as a key feature of ritual. Rhythmic, repetitive stimuli affect the human central nervous system, generating (especially in safe, relaxed settings) a high degree of visceral arousal, limbic affect (emotion), imagery, cognition and motor activity, synchronizing these processes among the various participants (Chapple 1970). This process of entrainment may be experienced as a loss of self-consciousness and a feeling of *flow* (see Chapter 7). Ritual entrainment can lead to transpersonal bonding—a sense of the unity and oneness of the group and the world.

Rhythm and music are powerful "ritual drivers." You may have experienced this power at rock concerts—as the audience begins to entrain with the rhythms of the music, the huge auditorium may suddenly seem to shrink and be suffused with shared energy; you no longer feel yourself to be just one individual, but an integral part of a pulsating, organic whole. In *Drumming at the Edge of Magic* (1990), Mickey Hart, then-drummer for the Grateful Dead, described it this way: "Sometimes I felt that we were becoming a big noisy animal that made music when it breathed." The same entrainment and sense of oneness characterize many church services. When the congregation sings together and prays together, their neural rhythms entrain both with each other and with the religious messages conveyed during the service. In many societies, and especially in cults and religions, rituals are used to influence people's experience by specific design. Rhythm and its ensuing neural entrainment are powerful, and savvy pastors include large doses of them in the services they design.

The *ritual drivers* that can produce such neural entrainment are many and varied. They include, among others, drumming, chanting, running, singing, dancing, mantras, meditation, privations and painful ordeals, hazing, isolation, sensory deprivation, and drugs. The power of ritual depends in part upon the ability of these drivers to produce alterations in consciousness by penetrating into and triggering the metabolic and neural processes that can produce the desired experience. Let us consider how mantras operate as drivers. Once again, Fritz Stall (1989:208) argued that mantras are meaningless sounds. Nothing could be further from the case. For example, the simplest element in a more complex mantra like OM MANE PADME HUM, the famous Buddhist mantra of compassion, is the "seed syllable" (or *bīja*; see Pabongka Rinpoche 2006). For a ritual practitioner, the seed syllables OM and HUM are initially given dictionary-like definitions. OM may be defined as "the original sound of the universe," or "the name of God," but this is only an exoteric tag historically associated with the sound and with the sign (e.g., the Chinese character 唵) denoting the sound. The real esoteric meaning(s) of OM are memories of the experiences evoked by repetition of the syllable. If you were to play around with repeating OM (pronouonced "aowm"), you would find out that making the sound causes physical vibrations in your body, and that the vibrations move around. If you also contrast the OM vibrations with those produced by the HUM (usually pronounced "hunggg" or "hummm") seed syllable, you would see that the vibrations in your body are quite different. In fact the entire mantra, OM MANE PADME HUM, causes a myriad of physical vibrations in your body, repeating a pattern over and over again. A serious devotee of mantra yoga will tell you that eventually certain experiences may arise as a consequence of doing mantra work, and those experiences are the esoteric meaning(s) of the mantra (Paul 2004). We will return to a discussion of mantra in Chapter 11.

We define a *ritual driver* as *any recurrent element in a ritual that has a predictable effect on the bodies and minds of participants* (see also Winkelman 2010). There are essentially two different kinds of ritual drivers: *extrinsic drivers* that depend upon stimuli outside a person's body (drumming, flickering flames, the use of an icon like a mandala, the electronic fetal monitor in childbirth), and *intrinsic drivers* that are initiated from within the person's body (fasting, breathing techniques, meditation). Table 5.1 lists some examples of both kinds.

Ritual Drivers at Work: The Ancient !Kung Trance Dance and Contemporary Breath Therapy

The Ju|'hoansi of the Kalahari region of Namibia and Botswana (formerly called the !Kung Bushmen—theirs is a click language; the "|'" represents a particular kind of click, as does the "!") have an ancient tradition called by outside observers the "trance dance" and by the people themselves the "healing dance," which employs both extrinsic and intrinsic drivers. The outstanding anthropological ethnographies *Boiling Energy: Community Healing among the Kalahari !Kung* by Richard Katz (1982), and *Healing Makes Our Hearts Happy: Spirituality and Cultural Transformation among the Kalahari Ju|'hoansi* by Richard Katz, Megan Biesele, and Verna St. Denis (1997) document the process through which these formerly nomadic hunter/gatherers generate a powerful altered state of consciousness (ASC) in the dancers. While the women of the group clap in complex rhythms, male and sometimes female healers dance around a fire, often for hours. The clapping is an extrinsic driver, and its effects are enhanced by two intrinsic drivers—the stomping of the dancers and their heavy breathing. The healers say that as they dance, a healing energy that they call *"n/um"* begins to rise up inside them, eventually boiling over and spilling out of their hands, which they lay on other members of their community to transmit that energy to them for all kinds of healing purposes.

Rhythmic heavy breathing —the principal intrinsic driver employed by the !Kung in this dance—can produce profound altered states of consciousness on its own, as many practitioners of the New Age healing technique called "breath therapy" have found. Originally called "rebirthing" because its first practitioners used it to re-experience their own

Intrinsic Drivers:	Examples:
Breathing exercises	Buddhist meditation
Breath therapy	Holotropic breathwork
Chanting	Hindu and Buddhist mantra; Shouting and doing "the chop" at baseball games
Visualization	Tibetan "arising" yoga
Vision quest	Plains Indian initiations
Dream incubation	Ancient Greeks; Tsimshian shamanism
Active imagination	Jungian psychotherapy
High fever	Iroquois Handsome Lake movement, Tsimshian shamanism
Circadian rhythms	Biofeedback techniques for stress-reduction
Fasting	Purification for Sun Dance; annual purge among some alternative healing practitioners
Physical exertion	Long distance running; Tibetan trance-running
Fatigue	Use of exhausting exercise
Physical deprivation, sleep deprivation	Navajo all-night sing
Sexual abstinence	Many monastic traditions
Sensory deprivation	Kogi shamans raised in caves
Concentration	Navajo stargazing; Zen koan meditation
Directed intention	Tibetan *wang kur*
Seclusion	Tsimshian shamans; Benedictine monastic tradition

Table 5.1. Types of Drivers Used in the Ritual Production of Experience

Extrinsic Drivers:	Examples:
Rhythm:	
dancing	Ju|'hoansi *n/um* dance; American "raves"
drumming	Tsimshian healing rituals; fife and drum
marching events	Fourth of July parade
Group chanting	The "wave" at American sports events
Flickering light	Peaceful "trance" around the campfire at night
Psychotropic drugs	Ingestion of *ebene* by Yanomamo shamans
Imagery:	
art	Navajo sandpainting; Tibetan *tankas*; Acid rock concert "liquid emulsions"
Skrying	Shaman's "mirror"; crystal gazing
Kasina	Buddhist 10 meditations
Mnemonics	Tsimshian power songs; National anthems
Ordeal:	
scary task	Firewalking; snake handling; drinking poison
pain	Plains Indian vision quest ordeals; College fraternity "hazing" rituals
sweat bath	Plains Indian Sun Dance sweat lodge
Performance	Tibetan *cham* dances; Wagnerian Ring Cycle
Bloodletting	Maya ritual bloodletting; bloodletting in obsolete Western medicine
Continuous electronic fetal monitoring	Women giving birth in hospitals all over the developed world

births and to help their clients do the same, breath therapy involves focused deep breathing, sometimes for long periods, usually under the tutelage of an experienced breath therapist. After an initial twenty-minute period of intentional, connected breathing (meaning that one breath is immediately, consciously followed by the next, without the usual pause in-between), the person undergoing this process often finds that s/he is in a profoundly altered state of consciousness in which it is possible to "go anywhere" in memory in order to relive a given event or series of events in her life. The rationale behind breath therapy holds that individuals who have undergone deeply traumatic events like a terrible accident or some form of sexual abuse often cannot remember exactly what happened to them. As long as the memory remains blocked, the individual may find herself unable to move forward in certain areas of her life. The idea is to consciously re-experience the trauma, this time in a safe context, and to scream or sob out pain and anguish until the emotional blockage is released. There is no drumming or other stimulus. In this type of ritualized therapy, which many people find very effective, rhythmic breathing is the principal driver that produces the altered state, augmented by verbal suggestions from the facilitator to follow one's breath, focus on a particular memory fragment, and trust that the person is safe and it's okay to let the memories come. Similarly, Eye Movement Desensitization and Reprocessing Therapy, better known as EMDR therapy, utilizes electronic drivers—buzzers in both hands and sometimes a light pattern that flashes to the right and to the left, while the hand buzzers emit their buzz concomitantly. These synchronized stimuli easily facilitate brain hemisphere integration across the corpus callosum and a mildly altered state of consciousness that can facilitate access to the desired memory or cognitive process, often to great psychotherapeutic effect. (See Chapter 8 for a description of Robbie's extremely effective EMDR experience.)

Percussion and Transition: One Student's Intentional Use of Ritual Drivers

Across cultures, rhythm, whether established through an intrinsic driver like deep breathing or through external artifacts like drums, is utilized to induce particular states of consciousness and their accompanying experiences. Anthropologist Rodney Needham was the first to document this strong cross-cultural connection between *percussion* and *transition*.

And Michael Harner's popular book *The Way of the Shaman* (1990) offers a percussive formula that any individual can use for entering a trance state. For individuals who do not have access to a drum, Harner recommends tape recording rhythmic drumming with a spoon on a book and playing it back at high volume.

Some years ago when Robbie was teaching medical anthropology at Rice University in Houston, one of her students asked if he could do his term paper on shamanic trance and healing, with an experiential focus. Skeptical, Robbie insisted that he complement his experiential work with a hefty bibliography on shamanism across cultures, to which he agreed. Near the end of the semester, settling down at home with a large stack of term papers, Robbie found herself searching the pile for this student's paper, curious to know the outcome of his research. When she found it and started reading, she nearly fell out of her chair, and she learned a lot about how to create an effective combination of extrinsic and intrinsic ritual drivers to induce an altered state.

This student, whom we will call John, had begun the experiential part of his research by doing as Harner suggested: drumming on a book with a spoon and taping the sound. Then he laid in his bed and listened to the tape, but did not experience any significant shift in consciousness. The next day and the day after, he tried listening for longer and longer periods, still without success. Worried about making the deadline for the paper, he decided to escalate his use of ritual drivers in order to generate as much sensory and cognitive engagement as possible. He thought that employing some core symbols of shamanism might help him generate the experience he sought. His library research had taught him that shamanic religions are usually highly *chthonic*—grounded in the earth. So first he paid attention to setting, exploring the Rice campus and the nearby park until he found a secluded spot under some bushes where, lying down, he felt a sense of privacy and connection to the earth and its living creatures. Then he employed a traditional intrinsic shamanic driver—he fasted for three days, so that when he began his experiment he would already be in an altered state. He hoped that the combination of extrinsic (drumming, the proper setting) and intrinsic (fasting) drivers would allow him to experience a shamanic journey to the Underworld. On the third day of his fast, with tape recorder in hand, John walked to the park, laid down under the bushes, and turned on the tape.

The results were dramatic. He soon entered a deep trance state in which he perceived, to his surprise, a portal on the horizon of his consciousness that led, not to the expected Underworld, but to what shamans sometimes call the Middle World. He passed through this portal into a strange realm where he had all kinds of adventures, meeting animal helpers and others along the way. Eventually, many hours later, he traveled back through the portal and woke up, astonished, shaken, and delighted that at last he would have something exciting to write about in the experiential section of his paper!

A week or so later, John became aware that one of his friends was having severe emotional difficulties that were impeding her ability to complete her semester's work. He offered to help and she gladly accepted. So he again fasted, took his tape recorder into the bushes, and laid down, this time inviting her to lie down with him and put her head on his shoulder. Holding her tightly, he again journeyed into the Middle World, where he learned about the sources of her malaise and worked with his animal helpers to heal her spirit. After that experience, her emotional difficulties vanished and she successfully completed her semester.

John had these experiences in the context of an academic course that was certainly not intended to induce altered states of consciousness in its students, so he had no larger cognitive matrix within which to pursue his shamanic work. Robbie suggested that he look for a teacher, someone who could provide such a matrix, but after that semester Robbie and John lost touch and she does not know if he went any further. (She kept his paper for years, but lost it, along with a lot of other things, when her house caught on fire in 2009.) The failure of John's early efforts to enter trance with the aid of only one driver—the tape of him drumming on a book with a spoon—shows us that one simple driver is often not sufficient to induce an altered state; rather, a combination of drivers, which in John's case included a core symbol (the earth), fasting, and rhythmic percussion, proved essential to inducing the state of consciousness he sought.

Electronic Fetal Monitoring as an Extrinsic Ritual Driver

And finally we come to the last line on our chart above, the one that most of our readers will not immediately recognize as an actual "ritual driver"—continuous electronic monitoring of the laboring woman's contractions and her baby's heartbeat via hooking the mother up to a fancy machine complete with computer screen, called the electronic fetal monitor (EFM) in the U.S. and cardiotopography (CTG) in the UK and other European countries. To recap from Chapter 2, symbols work through the emotions. The EFM is the most powerful symbol of the rituals of hospital birth—it epitomizes our technocratic core values on high technology and the flow of information through machines. In most American hospitals, the entire labor experience is organized around the monitor. Stuck in bed tethered to the EFM and her epidural, the mother (and father, family, and nursing staff) are left with little to do but stare at the monitor and get kind of hypnotized by those glowing wavy lines rhythmically moving up, down, and sideways as contractions come and go and the heartbeat speeds up and slows down. The following quotations from two of Robbie's interviewees for *Birth as an American Rite of Passage* (1992, 2004) illustrate the symbolic "mapping-on" process generated by this powerful extrinsic ritual driver:

> From a nurse: *"I know it's irrational, but as soon as I put a woman on the monitor, I get afraid to take her off of it because I get the feeling that the machine is keeping the baby's heart beating."*
>
> From a mother: *"As soon as I got hooked up to the monitor, no one even looked at me anymore, they just stared at the machine. And pretty soon I started staring at it too, and then I got the feeling that it* was having the baby, and not me.*"*

The machine, in other words, becomes more than an instrumental means of checking on the wellbeing of the mother and the baby; it conceptually takes over the birth experience, mapping its meaning onto the mother's interpretation of her birth experience, as well as having complete influence over how nurses deliver labor care—they often must stare at banks of computer screens in the nursing station or the hallway to check on the labors of various women at once, without having to physically interact with those women for extended periods of time. (See Chapter 6 for an analysis of the EFM as a ritual technology and its instrumental effects.)

RITUAL AND WARP CONTROL

When a society wishes to exercise control over the recurrence, quality and attributes of a particular state of consciousness, it will tend to ritualize the individual's activity before and, if possible, during the warp preceding the SOC. This ritualization of activity is, as we have seen, the key to understanding inter-state mimesis in ritual. Ritual takes on the function of "warp controller." For example, so important is the moment before sleeping to determining the quality of dreaming that Tibetan dream yogis learn to control the warp and are thus able to exercise considerable control over the experiences they have during dreaming. Charlie was in fact a practitioner of this brand of dream yoga, and has written a description of his experiences in his book *Communing with the Gods* (Laughlin 2011). Tibetan yogis are able to *incubate* their dreams by virtue of practices carried out just prior to and while entering sleep. For another example, in church the minister lifts his hands and asks the audience to bow their heads—a WOC that produces, in devout members, a conditioned transition to the state of consciousness called "prayer." True prayer is not just a series of gestures (kneeling, bowing the head, clasping the hands together in supplication), but is a distinct ASC in which the member is more open to directly experiencing the sublime.

Because ritual plays such an important role in warp control, anthropologists working in other cultures have to learn to recognize shifts in SOCs in their hosts and ascertain what, if any, ritual activity has generated the shift. However, when dealing with complex religious practices, one must be aware *that while a certain ritual activity may be a necessary condition for an intended experience, it is likely not a sufficient condition*—there may be other ingredients required to evoke the intended experience. As Robbie's student John discovered, one may repeat the attempt many times without reaching the intended goal, because one or several of the requisites for the intended experience may be absent. It is not uncommon for practitioners to have to repeat a ritual activity numerous times, and sometimes for years, before the intended experience arises. This is often the case with practitioners of the Sun Dance ritual we spoke about in the last chapter. Participants may have to repeat the four days of dancing annually for years before the ultimate mystical experience occurs for them. The mere use of drivers, even multiple drivers, does not ensure that the desired state of consciousness will be obtained. Often the problem is internal—the ritual practitioner may need to develop a certain level of inner tranquility, for example, or to cultivate a state of receptiveness, or to drop all expectations or self-consciousness.

In addition, because experience develops over the course of life, rituals may be repeated over the course of years with the experiences intended by the guide or teacher changing in order to be appropriate to the maturational stage of the practitioner. Some rituals may be appropriate for puberty, and other rituals may be appropriate for women during childbirth, and still others for advancement into elderhood. Thus it is common for "life crisis" rituals to be designed with the age and maturity level of the practitioners in mind. And sometimes there is no precise design—profoundly significant states of consciousness can suddenly and unexpectedly arise, even when the ritual context is loose and unstructured. For example, Robbie chose to give birth to her second child at home. For her, labor and birth were more than painful physiological processes—they were profoundly significant emotional, psychological, and spiritual experiences as well. So the house had a sacred air about it, and labor felt both deeply physical and deeply holy to her as it proceeded. Near the end, Robbie, who had been laboring in a hot tub, got out to walk around for a while. Entering her bedroom, she noticed that the bed had been freshly made (by her midwives) with her favorite sheets and quilt. It looked so inviting that she dove in, face down. And then, in her words, "a miracle" happened:

> With my face buried in the quilt, which shielded me from external stimuli, I went deep inside myself. I realized that for two days I had been singing with the contractions, dancing with the contractions, breathing with the contractions—in other words, I had been trying to *do something* about the contractions. That maintained a separation between the contractions, the pain they caused, and me. Suddenly, and without any pre-plan, I said to the pain, "OK, I surrender. Take me, I'm yours!" Instantly I, body and soul, *became* the pain, and once there was no more separation between me and the pain, there was no more pain! There was only oneness.

Like John lying under the bushes, Robbie had powerful core symbols around her that aligned her cognitively with her own perceptions of labor and birth as sacred—her home, her family, her friends, candles, and an atmosphere of love. In her case the rhythmic driver was the contractions of labor, which had at this point been going on for almost three days (intermittently for the first two). The WOC was diving down into the bed, which had been ritually made up by the midwives to receive Robbie and her newborn after birth. The bed was beautiful, pristine, and to Robbie constituted the inner sanctum of her family life. It was the place where her children were conceived, where she read bedtime stories to her daughter Peyton, and where she cried out her sorrows and meditated upon her joys. Diving onto that bed in the midst of heavy labor felt to Robbie like diving into the inner sanctum of her own consciousness. Removed from visual connection with the outside world, that warp moment, suffused with ritual significance, took her into an unexpected and fully unified state of consciousness, one that monks in monasteries may take decades to attain. Of course, the monks who work so hard and long to attain this SOC are usually able to enter it at will, and/or are experienced in the use of the ritual drivers that help them attain it—for Robbie, it was a one-time, life-altering, gift.[4]

MONOPHASIC AND POLYPHASIC CULTURES

Normal, everyday states of consciousness naturally alternate between those that promote adaptation to the external world (being of and from our own culture, we lump these together and call them "being awake") and those that promote healing and integration within the body (we call these "being asleep"). As a consequence, our awareness tends to alternate between perceiving objects and relations in the world, and perceiving images in fantasies and dreams that perhaps represent internal processes, like stress or conflict or joy. Many societies integrate knowledge gleaned from awareness of events encountered in all states of consciousness within a single worldview. We saw in the last chapter that ideational and idealistic cultures manifest this kind of cosmological worldview. In these cultures, *all states of consciousness are of relevance to the people's understanding of themselves and their reality.* We might say that such cultures are more or less *polyphasic* relative to the range of alternative SOCs that human beings are capable of attaining and paying attention to. In this book we are using the word "polyphasic" to describe cultures that incorporate multiple states of consciousness into their worldview. Indeed, it is likely that prior to some point in human prehistory, virtually all societies were more or less polyphasic (see Lewis-Williams and Pearce 2004:Chap. 2).

For example, it is considered important among Tibetan Buddhists, at least for active practitioners, to be as aware as possible in all states of consciousness, whether they are "awake" or "asleep" from our Western

---

4. For Robbie's full birth stories, see Davis-Floyd, Robbie (2002) "Knowing: A Story of Two Births," unpublished ms. freely available at www.davis-floyd.com and soon to appear in Davis-Floyd, Robbie, *Robbie's Short Stories: Vignettes of My Magical Life,* forthcoming from Praeclarus Press.

point of view. Practitioners of dream yoga are sometimes taught to wander around while they are awake telling themselves that they are dreaming, and while they are dreaming to tell themselves that they are awake. The intention is to transform the stream of consciousness so that their awareness will be well-balanced between SOCs.

In contrast, modern Euroamerican societies and other sensate cultures typically give credence only to experiences had in what people consider to be "normal" waking states—that is, in the SOCs oriented primarily toward adaptation to the external world. Sensate cultures maintain the view that reality is the world which is present to the senses during normal waking states of consciousness—i.e., the reality of the table is the object as it appears to our senses and nothing more. Thus the kind of intense attention given by Tibetan Buddhists to their dream life makes little sense to the average sensate Euroamerican. After all, sleeping is what we do when we have had enough of daily experience and wish to "zonk out" and refresh ourselves. Moreover, we conceptually distinguish among feelings, thoughts, and actions in a way that those living in polyphasic cultures rarely do. We tend to consider knowledge that is not based upon language and reason as "irrational" and not worthy of consideration, at least for public credence. We tend to put feeling and intuitive stuff in the same category as "play," which we distinguish quite firmly from the serious stuff of "work." Thus we might say that we Euroamericans live in a relatively *monophasic culture*. Monophasic cultures are characterized by a marked concern for the world as presented to the senses and are all about material values, with relatively less concern for inner growth, spiritual development, and balance among states of consciousness.

Anthropologists who have been raised in monophasic cultures, and who find themselves working in polyphasic ones, may have a hard time learning how to access other states of consciousness. But if they do not do so, they may well miss precisely those experiences that inform and enrich the worldview of their hosts—and the experiences that are intended by their host's inter-state mimetic rituals (again, the rituals that drive the transition between SOCs). Such anthropologists may discover that they are experientially out-of-sync with the host culture in two obvious situations. One such situation is when they are out of touch with their dream life while doing fieldwork among a society whose members routinely track their dream experiences and consider dreaming to be a substantial source of knowledge about themselves and the spiritual world. The other situation is when the polyphasic worldview of the host society is enriched with experiences had while participating in rituals or drug-induced "trips" unavailable for whatever reason to the researcher.

One of the common errors made by anthropological theorists is failing to appreciate the extent to which common belief in spirits and animistic objects is grounded, not so much upon cultural representations, but rather upon direct experience of "other-than-human persons" (Hallowell 2002:20) in dreams, visions, trance states, drug-induced alternative states of consciousness, and so forth. Pascal Boyer (1996b) makes this error, we believe, when he insists that anthropomorphic (human-like) and animistic (things have a vital force inside them) beliefs are based upon *unnatural projections*—that we humans tend to project onto other beings and things attributes of ourselves (consciousness, soul, vital forces, etc.). What he misses is that people in polyphasic societies consider experiences had in all states of consciousness to be "real" in some sense. They may know for instance that there are ghosts because they see ghosts, interact with and communicate with ghosts. Likewise, Alcorta and Sosis (2005:327) repeat the same error when they contend that belief in supernatural beings is "counterintuitive." While belief in supernatural agencies and beings may seem counterintuitive to a Western scientist, they are simply experienced reality among polyphasic peoples (see Edith Turner 1996 on this crucial issue). This is a prime example of the trap that ethnocentrism sets for the unwary Western mind.

Sometimes learning to access the SOCs considered important in a polyphasic culture can be very daunting. For instance, the healer/sorcerer shamans among the Yanomamo Indians living in the rain forests of Venezuela and Brazil ingest a powerful hallucinogenic substance sometimes called *ebene* (*Virola* species, related to our Old World nutmeg) which allows them to access the *hekura* or spirit beings that inhabit the normally invisible spirit world. When they take the drug, they unite with their *hekura* and then are able to fly to distant places and see things and get things done. The shamans are also able to use the *hekura* to both heal their fellow kinsmen and group members, and kill their enemies. Anthropologist Napoleon Chagnon, who lived among the Yanomamo for years, had learned a great deal about their religion and had witnessed the shamans using the sacred green powder many times, but had resisted taking the drug himself. Only when certain political conditions pressured him into accepting the drug did he try it. He took the *ebene* under the supervision of the shamans and had an ecstatic experience during which he felt light and floaty, danced, sang, and chanted, and invited the *hekura* to enter him, reproducing the ritual activities he had witnessed the shamans perform so many times. In the end he fell exhausted into a hammock and reflected upon the considerable differences between Yanomamo religion and Euroamerican Christianity.

The thing to keep in mind here is that while the anthropologist in this case exhibited great courage in trying out the drug (very painful to ingest, as it is a powder that is forcefully blown up one's nostril and has the initial effect of making one extremely nauseous), he only did it once. And in doing it once he was already quite unusual among his peers, for most anthropologists shy away from taking unfamiliar and powerful hallucinogens. Yet the Yanomamo shamans take the drug, sometimes on a daily basis, over the course of years. It is unclear from Chagnon's report whether he actually perceived any *hekura*, and he certainly did not experience the at-oneness with the *hekura* that allowed his shaman hosts to fly around and "eat the souls" of their enemies. His experiences with *ebene* were actually quite limited, for there is, of course, a developmental aspect to learning how to use drugs in this way. To our knowledge, very few anthropologists have ever had that experience and written about it, much less taken the drug on a regular basis long enough for the physiological systems producing the shamanic experience to develop. Being raised in a society that is so extremely monophasic places severe limitations on the kind of experiences the anthropologist is open to in the field among a people who, like the Yanomamo, live in a polyphasic universe.

TRANSFERRING INFORMATION ACROSS STATES OF CONSCIOUSNESS

States of consciousness organized around the inner life of the polyphasic individual are frequently ignored, repressed, negatively sanctioned, considered pathological, or otherwise derided as "irrational" and "mystical" by people reared in monophasic cultures. Experiences in alternative SOCs may be lost or compartmentalized in memory when the individual has no intellectual framework for making sense of the experience in normal waking consciousness. Memory of experiences in one SOC (a dream, a trance, a vision, an intuition about the divine reality lying behind the world of appearances) may be lost to another SOC (our baseline state of being "awake") due to a radical transformation of the warp between SOCs. A radical transformation occurs in the brain when the neural systems producing experience change rapidly and totally during the warp from one SOC to another—as happens for most Euroamericans when they "fall asleep." Thus we are often unable to organize our experience of altered states in terms that our waking brains can understand. Some experimental evidence from sleep labs suggests that if we can retain even a minimal amount of organization as we move through the warp from the altered SOC to our normal waking state, we can integrate at least parts of the altered SOC into our memories. (That is why people who are trying to become more conscious of their dreams often write down whatever they remember immediately upon awakening—a technique that can help to lead to lucid dreaming.) Fragmented memories of altered SOCs tend to be common in societies that do not have ritualized methods for transferring memories across warps, nor a culturally transmitted, polyphasic worldview. Monophasic culture commonly stands as an impediment to inter-state mimesis (the transfer of memory or information from one SOC to another, e.g from waking to dreaming or vice-versa), because the natural process of symbolic penetration cannot operate as freely across warps between SOCs. Rituals that in a polyphasic culture may easily penetrate into, say, dreams have less effect in monophasic cultures whose members routinely ignore or disattend their dreams.

RITUAL AND THE CONTROL OF STATES OF CONSCIOUSNESS

Now that we better understand SOCs and WOCs, we can return to ritual drivers more fully informed, and begin to understand the influence of these drivers in terms of the hierarchy of neurocognitive functioning affected by ritual stimuli. The entire neuroendocrine system ("neuro-" refers to the nervous system *per se,* and "endocrine" refers to the body's system of glands and hormones) may be driven from the "top-down," so to speak, by means of symbolic penetration. This kind of ritual driving occurs very commonly in our everyday lives.

For example, the presence or absence of natural light can affect our moods. Indeed, a significant number of people in North America suffer from seasonally occurring bouts of depression (so-called "seasonal affective disorder," or SAD) due in part to insufficient daily levels of sunlight. Some SAD sufferers have found that if they sit under intense synthetic lighting (with the UV filtered out) for 20 to 30 minutes in the morning, their symptoms are relieved. We would say in this case that the light penetrates (from the "top-down") deeply into the limbic, pineal gland and endocrine systems controlling mood, and changes the internal organization of the SAD sufferer's emotions. It is important to understand that the experience of light is a construct of the visual cortex of our brain—there is no light "out there," only electromagnetic energies—and that these cortical processes are linked to lower neuroendocrine systems by pathways that are stimulated by cortical activity in the brain.

Also, symbolic activity mediated by the brain's cortex may be driven from the "bottom-up" by lower neurological, metabolic and endocrine activities. This kind of driving also occurs commonly in our everyday lives. Again, our mood may be affected by becoming very hungry. We may find ourselves inattentive, fatigued, and even cranky, until we eat some food. After "recharging our batteries" with a meal, we may find that our concentration returns, we feel energetic again and our mood perhaps shifts back to being "all sweetness and light." What we have done is drive our higher order cognitive and emotional systems from the "bottom-up" by providing nutriment that can be processed by our alimentary system and transported to our brain via our circulatory system.

Rituals employ both top-down and bottom-up drivers to effect alterations in SOCs. Fasting or the use of psychotropic drugs (bottom-up drivers) may be paired with drumming or sensory deprivation (top-down drivers) to produce a distinct SOC intended by those who designed the ritual. Indeed, one may find that a complex ritual contains an *orchestra of drivers,* the combined effects of which may result in a range of SOCs over time.

Theatrical performances are a type of ritual that may involve music, special effects, historical and archetypal symbolism, activity or passivity of the audience, and so on, to influence the audiences' state of consciousness. Above all, such performances are rich in mimetic devices—iconic symbols, themes, gestures, metaphors, stylizations, so forth—that drive home the message to participants and audiences alike, whether the intended experiences lie within or across the boundaries between SOCs.

Perhaps the most dramatic example of this kind of ritual in Western theatrical tradition might be the performance of Richard Wagner's *Der Ring des Nibelungen* ("The Ring of the Nibelung"). This is a cycle (Wagner's so-called "Ring Cycle") of four operas that are traditionally performed over the course of three days. Although they may be performed anywhere in the world, they are annually given at a special venue established by Wagner himself in 1876 in the little Bavarian town of Bayreuth in Germany. The Ring Cycle is a single and very complex story drawn loosely from German mythology that is enacted in music and drama, accompanied by much pageantry. Embedded within the musical score are numerous, recurring melodic "symbols" called *leitmotivs,* which represent characters, objects and relations in the story. All that is required to evoke the memory of one of the characters—whether or not the character is present on the stage—is the repetition of the leitmotiv associated with that character. For instance, during the first act of *Die Walküre* ("The Valkyrie"), the second of the four operas, two of the principals, Siegmund and Sieglinde, recover memories of their youth about the doings of their father, Wotan, the chief of the gods. The actual character of Wotan is not present in this scene, but the orchestra occasionally lapses into Wotan's leitmotiv so that his presence in the proceedings can thus be powerfully felt by the audience members who recognize that leitmotiv. (This particular melody of course has been paired with the actual presence of Wotan in the previous opera *Das Reingold*.) The musical score of this series of operas is in fact liberally laced—that is, *plotted*[5]—with an intricate pattern of these leitmotivs, to the extent that for the fully initiated Wagnerian aficionado, the entire plot may be "seen" to unfold solely in the course of hearing the music on CD. The leitmotivs are powerful auditory drivers that become associated with characters and events and thus are able to penetrate to visual and plot memories pertaining to the drama.

Operatic performances are only one of many forms of complex rituals in which we can trace the impact of drivers. Rock concerts, political rallies, games of sport (like baseball, American football, soccer, basketball, etc.) and church services are all forms of ritual in which we can isolate and analyze systems of plotted drivers that influence the SOCs of participants and audiences. Rock concerts often blend heavy repetitive rhythms, flashing lights, pyrotechnics, dancing, "moshing," and sometimes psychotropic drugs (e.g., "ecstasy") into a distinct state of consciousness that is avidly sought after by fans of that kind of entertainment. We note here, with curiosity, that the word "entertain" literally means "to hold someone in a particular state"—in this case a state of enjoyment and flow. A rock concert—or a sports event—then may be understood as a complex ritual that integrates a number of drivers in such a way that participants are "transported" into and maintained for a period of time in a desired and enjoyable ASC.

---

5. We are simplifying Paul Ricoeur's (1990:Chap.2) technical concept of "emplotment" here. Emplotment (hereafter our "plot" or "plotting") generally means that the elements of a narrative or ritual are arranged in an imaginative order, much like the plot of a novel.

Games are a ritualized form of play that is organized into roles and rules. In many cultures games have important religious significance; for example the Rājasūya dice game in Indian cosmology (Handelman and Shulman 1997:61-68), or the Apache Indian moccasin game (Reagan 1904). In our culture, games of physical skill are called "sports," and sports are a very important form of secular ritual. Individuals often learn to play sports as children playing on the playground, and in school where they enter team sports. Whole-hearted involvement in sports will produce a special sense of "fun" or elation—what the Germans call *Funktionslust*, or the natural pleasure felt by any animal doing what it does best. In professional sports this sense of pleasure or ecstasy may be part and parcel of a particular state of consciousness required for peak proficiency. One of Charlie's dear friends was the late Major League baseball pitcher Frank "Tug" McGraw, who often spoke of entering a "sweet spot in time" while on the mound during which he simply could not miss. If something happened to disrupt this state of mind, then his performance would fall apart. He said that his manager could tell when Tug lost the sweet spot and would pull him off the mound and replace him.

The drivers in the case of the opera, the rock concert, or the sports event may be extrinsic or intrinsic. Intense concentration upon a particularly salient symbol may (from the "top-down") result in profound transformation of the entire body, especially if the symbol has been paired in the past with intense emotion. The slow, ponderous movements of Wotan, the chief of the gods, the physical gyrations of the lead singer in a favorite rock group, or the tension generated by the player at the bat and the pitcher facing him, may penetrate into our psyche in such a powerful way that we lose our normal center and are transported, at least in the emotional sense, into a quite different felt space. Many other symbols also have this power of evocation. One's national flag or anthem may under the right circumstances trigger feelings of patriotic zeal. The operative symbol may be an object of meditation out in the world, like a picture of a guru or saint, or may be an image constructed before the mind's eye, like imagining a pleasant trickle of water entering the top of one's head and washing away bad things in the body. On the other hand, fasting (intrinsic driving) or imbibing psychotropic substances (extrinsic driving) may (from the "bottom-up") result in significant alteration of sensory and cognitive activity. The resulting transformed mind state may be requisite for full participation in the ritual and its cultural context.

Ritual drivers may be relatively extreme, like running to exhaustion, or may be quite subtle (chanting a mantra inside your head), depending on the effects upon consciousness intended. In fact in many of the world's mystical traditions, the lower the level of consciousness that one is trying to master, the more extreme or blatant may be the array of ritual drivers involved in evoking the state. By the same token, as the practitioner becomes "higher" or more mature, the range of drivers may become more and more subtle until a point in development is reached when the practitioner is able to reach a desired and very subtle SOC with little effort of will and without any apparent reliance upon any external drivers. There is a legendary story about the time when the Buddha held up a flower in the presence of his students, and that simple action caused one of his students, named Kassapa, to fully awaken to "the essence of mind." The flower was a symbolic driver that triggered a revolutionary transformation in Kassapa's consciousness. This is a case *par excellence* of a very subtle extrinsic driver having a profound effect upon the recipient.

RITUAL DRIVERS AND THE CYCLE OF MEANING

In the preceding chapter, we showed how a culture's worldview is incorporated in a system of knowing and enactment that allows people to experience directly the "truth" and efficacy of their way of viewing themselves and their world. We called this system the "cycle of meaning" and showed how traditional societies utilize myth and ritual to produce a range of experiences that instantiate and bring alive traditional ways of knowing their reality. We also showed how knowledge and experience interact to produce change within the cycle of meaning, ideally at least keeping the group's worldview in sync with contemporary experience. We are now in a better position to see how the myth-ritual complex actually works to control experiences that provide the instantiation of the group's worldview. We can now see how mimetic ritual enactments in one state of consciousness can penetrate symbolically into another state of consciousness, resulting in direct experiences that become the meaning of the mimetic elements for the ritual participants. We can also break down our understanding of ritual into its constituent elements and see that how the cycle of meaning works requires a distinct selection and plotting of drivers to produce and limit the range of SOCs that may be interpreted within the society's cosmological frame (see Figure 5.1).

The range of experiences that arise for participants in the ritual are actually evoked as a consequence of the joint effects of drivers and their

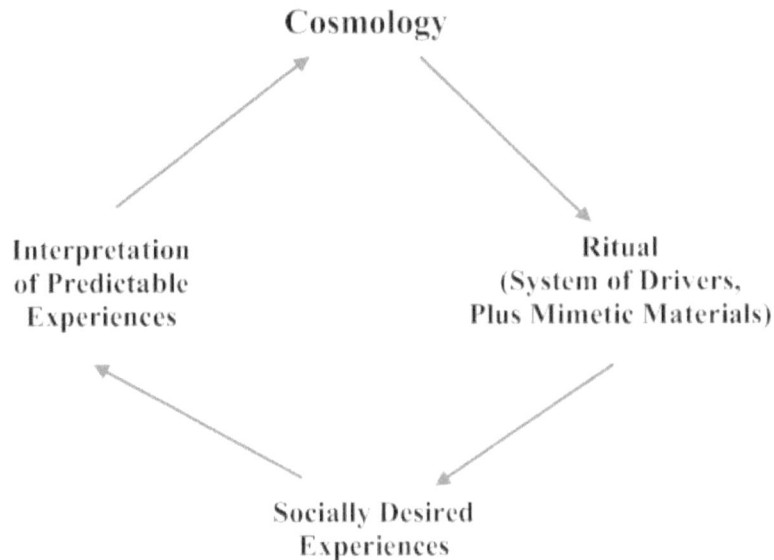

Figure 5.1. Ritual Drivers and the Cycle of Meaning. The society's cosmology is enacted in ritual, which is replete with drivers and mimetic materials that penetrate the neuroendocrine systems (brain plus glands and hormones) of a participant and lead to predictable experiences that are interpreted in such a way that the cosmology is instantiated (experientially lived) and confirmed.

plotting (placement) within the temporal unfolding of the ritual. The repertoire of drivers may be acting simultaneously from the top down with pageantry and spectacle and from the bottom up with drumming, fasting or drugs. All of these elements are orchestrated in such a way that the experiences produced are both spontaneous and predictable, and become illustrations for individuals of the accuracy, power and efficacy of the worldview, and perhaps the sociopolitical organization that sanctions and organizes the ritual event.

PORTALS AS RITUAL DRIVERS INTO MULTIPLE REALITIES

Important to our picture of the power of ritual is to remember that the cosmologies of traditional peoples are typically "multiple-reality" or *polyphasic* worldviews (see Chapter 3). That is, many peoples today (and in the past) believe that reality consists of a system of several worlds, sometimes stacked one upon the other. For instance the Tukano Indians, who live in the rain forests of the Amazon basin in South America, divide the universe into three realms—the upper world (celestial), the intermediate world (earth) and the underworld (paradise) (Reichel-Dolmatoff 1971). The sun is believed to travel a path along the Milky Way through the upper world, shedding its light upon the earth during its passage, and then through the underworld during the night. The creator god lives in the underworld and sends the divine blessing of energy to the people of earth through the flow of this daily solar cycle. Smoke is believed to unite the heavens and the earth. This cosmic scheme is not merely a conceptual invention. Rather, it is the sense that shamans in many cultures have made over the ages of visions they have had during periods of intense concentration and from the use of hallucinogens. They experience moving from realm to realm via the smoke of fires. (In a vastly simpler way, we could light a candle in a cathedral in memory of a loved one, as Robbie often does for her daughter Peyton in the many countries to which she travels, and feel more connected to that loved one through the channel opened between dimensions by the flame and the smoke it produces, which travels upwards and vanishes into the cosmic ether, hopefully carrying our messages of love and remembrance to the spirits of the departed.)

For the Tukano and many other ideational and even idealistic (and therefore polyphasic) cultures, individuals may have to access the different realms—the multiple realities—in order to maintain a balance, to correct some imbalance, or to heal the sick. Sometimes shamans will use meditation devices to aid them in moving from one realm to another—a process of transforming SOCs called *portalling*. A meditation object used to alter the SOC of a shaman or practitioner is called a *portalling device*. Portalling devices operate as a threshold, a *limen*—a passageway or tunnel through which the consciousness of a practitioner may pass to an alternative world. These devices are really symbols, and the experience of portalling is actually a form of symbolic penetration that produces a massive transformation in the organization of the neurocognitive structures mediating experience. Many different kinds of objects may be used to portal, including crystals and other gemstones, mandalas woven into sacred rugs, skrying bowls (sacred vesssels filled with water, mercury, liquid lead, or other fluid materials), cave mouths, "bulls-eye" concentric circles, labyrinths, etc.

Mirrors are among the most common types of portalling devices. Reflective pools, skrying bowls, polished metal objects, and the like can be used as meditation objects that have a potentially powerful evocative influence on the state of mind of the meditator. It is no coincidence that Lewis Carroll has Alice enter the strange mystical world of her adventures by stepping though a mirror in *Through the Looking-Glass,* or that C.S. Lewis has his children entering Narnia though a wardrobe or a painting. People are used to moving from one room to another through doorways; a meditative "doorway" is uniquely suggestive to a receptive mind of moving between inner spaces while in trance. In fact, architects and builders used to pay far more attention to the design of doorways than they do today because they were more aware of the significance of doors as thresholds of experience— the transition into a new space—and thus would decorate the lintel over the door with poignant symbolism. Indeed, the word "lintel" derives from the ancient word *limen,* meaning "threshold," which is itself a term that has survived to our present day and is used in psychology to mean a threshold of consciousness. Note the contemporary practice of the husband carrying his new bride over the threshold, which he often does even if they have been living there together for years! Actually marrying still remains a powerful and meaningful rite of passage for contemporary citizens of technocracies—we remain ritualistic, just as we humans have always been (see Grimes 2002).

One of the basic foundation practices (*ngon-dro*) in Tibetan Tantric Buddhist practice is the *dkyil-'kyor* or "mandala practice" which has to do with meditating on a portalling device. The practice involves repetitively constructing and destroying a mandala of heaped rice on top of a polished, translucent mirrored surface. The mirror (the *sa-gzhi,* which looks like a metal bowl made of silver or copper turned upside down) is held in one hand while the other hand constructs a mandala of rice and then sweeps the mirror clean of the rice. This practice is done over and over while repeating an appropriate mantra. For some practitioners this mirror meditation can be extremely powerful, for it invites visions and dreams that have to do with (from the Buddhist point of view) the illusory nature of the world.

Charlie undertook the mandala offering practice during the early days of his exploration of Tibetan Buddhism. He finished one hundred thousand repetitions of this practice during solitary meditation retreats. (Upon reading this statement for the first time, Robbie asked via email, "Seriously? 100,000 repetitions??" and Charlie replied, "Yes!") He used a round shaving mirror glued to a tea saucer and a large bowl of rice that had been stained yellow with food coloring.[6] Over and over, for five one-hour

---

6. See Laughlin, McManus and d'Aquili (1990:328) for a more detailed description of these experiments.

sessions a day for weeks, Charlie would take up a handful of rice from the large bowl in his lap and construct a mandala on the mirror—a mandala being a circular form with four cardinal points and a center. He would then offer the completed mandala up to the guru he visualized above his head, and then wipe the mirror clean—all the while repeating a mantra he had been taught by his teacher. At night Charlie would have lucid dreams of the mirror becoming a portal or a three-dimensional mandala-like form. The mirror would become a colorful tunnel down which he would fly, entering various dreamscapes and having various adventures. In one such dream, the rice grains became yellow flowers that sprang out of a circular mirror and emitted great energy. At other times the mirror would become a body of water or some other symbolic transformation. Charlie had hundreds of such experiences, which obviously were evoked by the repetitive action of constructing and deconstructing the rice edifice on the mirror. In our present terms, the rice and the mirror operated as extrinsic drivers, while the repetition of the mantra acted as an intrinsic driver, all plotted within the context of the "mandala offering" ritual.

Another set of experiments further underscores the power of ritual drivers to produce spiritually salient experiences. This time Charlie joined forces with his friend and colleague John Cove to help John explore the possible esoteric significance of what is termed the "shaman's mirror." John had spent years working with the Tsimshian and other peoples of the Northwest Coast of Canada and was fascinated by their shamanic traditions. During these researches, John encountered the phenomenon of the mirror. The shaman's mirror can take various forms, but the particular one Charlie and John were interested in is made of slate and is commonly found in the graves associated with shamans.

As these objects were no longer in use among the contemporary Tsimshian people, Charlie and John decided that the only way they could find out how they had been used by the shamans of the past was to try them out for themselves. They manufactured their own mirrors from black slate roofing tiles, and made them to conform exactly to some of the real objects that are found in museum collections. These look something like small paddles with one side ground down slightly so that it is concave, or spoon-shaped. They also incorporate a curious feature—a small notch at the top of the mirror. When John and Charlie wetted the concave side with water, it became very like a hand mirror. Held horizontally as the water evaporated, the reflective "portal" would shrink down to a dot and then disappear. At first they could see their faces in the mirror, but as the reflective circle got smaller and smaller, a tunneling effect was produced—their attention to their faces changed to attention to a tunnel, and they were drawn into the portal. It was like being poised on a threshold, quite able to pass over into another realm of experience or return to the normal state—quite literally a "liminal" state of mind (see Turner 1974 for a discussion of "liminoid" mind states). If you concentrate on your face in just the right way, the curious little notch at the top of the mirror causes a split representation of your face—a common motif used in Tsimshian art to represent supernatural beings.

Unlike the "mandala offering" technique used by Tibetan meditators, the Tsimshian shaman's mirror is no longer used in this way, and so John and Charlie really had no ritual context within which to embed the experiments with the slate "mirror." That is to say, they knew of no other drivers associated with meditating on the mirror. Nonetheless, their experiments demonstrated the robust effects of ritual drivers, even bereft of their traditional context. And undoubtedly, as in the case of the Tibetan practice, the shaman's mirror was used repetitively and within the context of some now-lost spiritual practice, intent, and cycle of meaning. Yet we can only speculate as to the "places" the mirror would take the ancient Tsimshian shamans.

What we do know from research on other systems of meditation is that over time, experienced practitioners become quite adept at controlling the experiences they have "on the other side" of the portal. In ideational cultures—cultures that are essentially polyphasic in their worldview—people who become adept at traveling to spiritual realms are frequently perceived as accruing great power. To touch the sacred or the numinous, to be in the presence of the divine, to be able to intervene between this world and the other worlds—all this leaves its mark on the practitioner, who may gain high status for his or her skill in accessing power and using it for the good of the community. And every time a shaman or a practitioner accesses the spiritual domain, he or she gives evidence of the existence of such places, and reinforces the society's belief in the world according to their polyphasic cosmology. It is an interesting and curious fact that the more contemporary quantum physicists and cosmologists delve into the dynamics of the universe, the more they seem to share this polyphasic view of multiple realities and dimensions, at least at the theoretical level, and the more common become multi-dimensional pictures of the nature of scientific cosmology. Quantum physicists like Brian Greene now quite blithely speak of the "10th dimension," parallel universes, superstrings, etc. (The interested reader might like to check out Jim Baggott's fascinating book *The Quantum Story: A History in 40 Moments*.)

The key to understanding just how the mind is able to access these normally hidden domains is to understand the power of ritual drivers to evoke WOCs and subsequent SOCs. Portals invite the liminal—they suggest to the mind an alternative view, and may evoke a WOC resulting in novel—even amazing—experiences. In a very real sense, portalling devices are doorways precisely because they symbolically penetrate to the structures that mediate experience and cause them to radically reorganize themselves.

A difference between real doorways and imagined doorways is that the penetration to an alternative space through an imagined doorway is not as simple as just walking through, and so may take some time and skill to achieve. Ritual activities performed in the waking state, like doing the "mandala offering" meditation, may lead to alternative SOCs in the dream state, as with the many suggestive dreams that Charlie experienced. Whether immediate or delayed, to go through the tunnel between the realms is to experience the radical transformation of one's own brain-state. And just as with a physical doorway, one may have to "knock" repeatedly upon the portal before one experiences entry. Diligence in the ritual repetition of drivers may eventually be rewarded by the experiences they are devised to activate—perhaps one of the meanings behind the esoteric promise "knock and it shall be opened unto you" in the Bible (Matthew 7:7). Drivers often only work upon the mind when conditions are auspicious—when things are just right (e.g., when the ambience is appropriate and the individual is fully able to concentrate). Repetition of the rituals and their drivers assures a greater chance that the intended experiences will occur. Ritual repetition lays the foundations for completing the cycle of meaning because it enables people to become more masterful at interpreting the experiences that ritual evokes in terms of the society's worldview.

WHY ARE RITUAL DRIVERS SO COMPELLING?

The power of ritual is in part the power of drivers, alone and in concert with other ritual elements, to compel/drive experience. Whether or not you think of yourself as patriotic, hearing the national anthem sung at a sports event may still cause you to experience a certain unbidden *frisson,* or even tears.

This emotional reaction reflects the power of ritual drivers to penetrate into and influence the physical processes that mediate experience. How drivers are able to generate an alteration in consciousness will vary depending upon the senses being affected. Moreover, it's important to understand that the sound, say, of the national anthem, is actually being produced in your head. There are really no sounds outside of our body, only vibrations that impinge upon our senses and that our senses interpret as music or whatever. *To make music is literally to cause vibrations that become music in the audience's heads,* explaining why certain sounds may be music to one person and harsh noise to another.

The process of penetration involves both the excitation of our sensory systems (our ear drums, the retinas in our eyes, the touch receptors in our skin, etc.) and an internal penetration from sensory systems to the cognitive, perceptual and emotional systems that make sense of the patterns of vibrations. So if you are conditioned in early life to feel and do certain things when hearing the national anthem, you may well feel and do those things all the rest of your life.

The effects that particular drivers have upon people are often very particular and predictable. Take for example "the blues." The curious thing about the blues is that while the lyrics are usually about suffering, pain and loss, the effect of the music (for those susceptible to that genre) is to produce joy and even ecstasy. This effect is produced by the characteristic rhythms and syncopation that constitute the structure of the music. Indeed, the blues may be interpreted both biologically and socially as a ritual for the transformation of depression and despair into happiness and joy. Considering that the historical roots of the genre called "the blues" lie in the terrible conditions of black slaves and sharecroppers on southern American plantations, the invention of the blues as a rite of emotional transformation was really quite ingenious. The music would be played at Sunday socials and in "juke" joints (both are ritual venues) throughout the American South, and when paired with imbibing alcohol and dancing, had a predictably cathartic effect upon a much downtrodden people.

Thus, some drivers compel experience by manipulating the internal biorhythms of the body, while others (like fasting and purging) manipulate the metabolic system and the quantity and variety of metabolites floating around in the bloodstream. Hot steam produced in sweat lodge ceremonies operates directly on the dynamics of the body's autonomic system. Even systematic, excruciating pain applied during ritual ordeals (like the Sun Dance) has the predictable effect of producing visions and alternative SOCs—that is the goal and the point of these ritual ordeals. (Intentional torture, by contrast, has no goal beyond the infliction of pain to obtain information or simply to cause suffering.) Orchestrating a balance among the plotting of ritual drivers and other more cognitive materials like symbolically rich stories and lore can act to guide participants into, through and out of a predictable and profoundly mind-altering experience.

SUMMARY: SOCS, WOCS, AND RITUAL DRIVERS

Ritual is essentially a mimetic (imitative) process, often rife with actions and elements that mimic reality, and that represent in waking consciousness elements and experiences had in alternative states. Rhythmic drivers, used repetitively, are also core characteristics of ritual. There are many different types of drivers, and they share important roles in producing warps of consciousness (WOCs) that can lead to altered states of consciousness (ASCs). A central feature of both intrinsic and extrinsic drivers is their ability to produce coherent, highly synchronized neural activities in various areas and levels of the brain. Cultures differ in the importance they give to this alteration of consciousness, ranging from polyphasic cultures that recognize and endorse many SOCs, especially dreaming, to monophasic cultures that only value the normal waking state of consciousness. In polyphasic (ideational, idealistic) cultures, people are developmentally prepared to take advantage of WOCs and the experiences of multiple realities they can produce. Certain members of these cultures have developed ways to ritually control the warps that alter consciousness and enhance information transfer back to waking consciousness. Such experiences can enhance health, establishing connections of the conscious mind with the usually unconscious processes of the lower brain systems, and can also produce life-altering and life-enhancing ways of thinking and being. Taking full advantage of SOCs and WOCs remains an option for individuals living in sensate, technocratic societies to employ the power of ritual towards individual and group psychological and psychic development—and perhaps, in time, for cultural and societal evolution toward more humanistic and holistic—and polyphasic—ways of thinking and living.

Suggested Reading

Garrels, Scott R. (Ed.) (2011) *Mimesis and Science: Empirical Research on Imitation and the Mimetic Theory of Culture and Religion.* East Lansing, MI: Michigan State University Press.

Hart, Mickey (1990) *Drumming at the Edge of Magic.* New York: Harper Collins.

Turner, Edith (1996) *The Hands Feel It: Healing and Spirit Presence Among a Northern Alaskan People.* DeKalb, IL: Northern Illinois University Press.

Chapter 6

RITUAL TECHNIQUES AND TECHNOLOGIES

Ritual Technique and Technology: Divination and Intent. What Is Technology? Ritual Technique and Technology. Instrumentality and Ritual. Summary: Ritual Technique and Technology.

You are now almost halfway through this book (if you've been reading the chapters in sequence). At this point, we wish to remind you of the nine characteristics of ritual—*the anatomy of ritual*—that the chapters you have been reading have sought to address. Again, they include:

1. the neurobiological basis of ritual behaviors as coordination and communication systems that first developed in animals;
2. the use of symbols to convey a ritual's messages;
3. a cognitive matrix (belief system) from which ritual emerges;
4. rhythm, repetition and redundancy: ritual drivers;
5. the use of tools, techniques, and technologies to accomplish ritual's multiple goals;
6. the framing of ritual performances;
7. the order and formality that separates ritual from everyday life, identifying it *as ritual;*
8. the sense of inviolability and inevitability that rituals can generate;
9. the acting, stylization, and staging that often give ritual its elements of high drama, the fact that it is *performed* and that it often intensifies toward a climax.

Just to keep everything in context, we note to you here that this particular chapter focuses on characteristic number 5: Ritual's use of tools, techniques, and technologies to accomplish its multiple goals, including its instrumental ones—the goals of achieving specific, often dramatic, effects and results in people's lives.

RITUAL TECHNIQUE AND TECHNOLOGY: DIVINATION AND INTENT

"Much of the work of religion is done by ritual," wrote anthropologist Anthony F. C. Wallace (1966:71). To emphasize that he did not mean "work" in just a metaphorical sense, Wallace went on to show how ritual often operates as a kind of technology. People carry out rituals not just to do things in a traditional fashion or to express symbolic meanings—they also act in ritual ways just to get things done. Ritual, in other words, has *utility* and *instrumentality* (which means getting things done in the world, as well as providing the means to do so).

Wallace offered several kinds of activities as examples of *technological rituals*. For instance, people often perform rituals that are designed to obtain information. They carry out a *divination* in order to find out where they are likely to find game to hunt, when the rains will fall, if their enemies might attack in the near future, to discover something that happened in the past—such as who committed a crime or perhaps what event in childhood might have produced the illness a patient is suffering from today. People also perform rituals and rites with the intent of increasing the quantity of game or the crop yield, to make the rains come or stop (for a contemporary example, Rick Perry, then-Governor of Texas, asked all state citizens to "pray for rain" to end the terrible Summer of 2011 drought), or to exorcize evil spirits that might be causing an epidemic or interfering with the smooth flow of everyday life.

Rituals of Divination: The Purloined Pots

An occasion during Charlie's time with the So illustrates how crucial this kind of ritual can be with respect to discovering important information. As mentioned in Chapter 1, when Charlie and his family arrived among the So in East Africa, his hosts were experiencing a serious drought, and food resources were very scarce for a period of some months. Charlie and his wife ended up feeding all the children who needed food on a daily basis. Every mid-day, they prepared huge pots of porridge for any children and pregnant women who showed up. But one morning, they discovered that the gigantic aluminum pots that they used to make the porridge, and that would be nearly impossible to replace, had been stolen. Searches by Charlie and his So friends came to no avail.

Finally, one of Charlie's So friends suggested that a famous Turkana (a tribe of people who live in Kenya, to the east of the So) diviner, who happened to be visiting relatives living on the mountain, could be consulted to find out where the pots might be. Having no confidence whatever in divination, but delighted at the prospect of watching a diviner "do his thing," Charlie consented. The next day at the appointed time, an old wizened man came to Charlie's compound and commenced throwing his sandals on the ground over and over and reading the patterns they made in the dirt. Finally he stated the obvious. The pots had indeed been stolen. All those present agreed that this was the case. Then he threw the sandals some more and said that the pots were no longer on the mountain. "Swell, that's a great help!" Charlie thought. More sandal tossing, and then the old man said that the pots were now located outside the house of someone in a particular neighborhood in the town of Moroto, the district capital at the base of Moroto Mountain where the So live. "Now that's more like it!" thought Charlie, and he gave the old man his fee and thanked him profusely for having taken the trouble to help the So people in their plight.

After the old man had wandered off, Charlie gathered some of his young warrior friends into the Land Rover, drove to the specified neighborhood, and within minutes spotted the purloined pots stacked on the side of a hut in the village. When confronted with the fact that the pots had been stolen, the woman of the house said that she had bought them in good faith from two young So men. Charlie compensated her for the money she had spent and returned to So with the pots just in time to prepare the porridge for the hungry kids. The information gleaned from the divination had proven to be both accurate and very fruitful.

Of course the interesting question is how the ritual specialist—the Turkana diviner—had known just where the pots were located. Did he read their whereabouts in the patterns made by the sandals, kind of like reading tea leaves? Or did he have prior knowledge about the theft of the pots, or just a good hunch as to who had stolen them? We will return to this question later on, for it suggests some interesting aspects of ritual as technology—as Wallace himself noted (1966:108), there is likely no society on Earth, including modern urban society, in which some people do not practice divination. After all, people in our society flip coins to make decisions and consult palm and Tarot readers to find out about the future. But first we want to get clearer in our minds what exactly we mean by technology and in what ways ritual can operate as technology.

WHAT IS "TECHNOLOGY"?

What exactly does "technology" mean from an anthropological point of view? Well, the truth of the matter is that we anthropologists are not always clear about what we mean by the term. In fact we tend to ignore questions related to technology, often choosing instead to focus on social relations. When the term is used, it is usually reserved for material objects, their manufacture, and their uses. But this commonsense notion of technology is not very useful to us here. Far more useful is to see technology in a more experiential, even a phenomenological way—to see *technology as an extension of how we act in and perceive the world*. Let us spend a moment generating the "tools" to look at technology through this experiential lens.

Internal and External Coordination

We have already said that ritual is a symbolic process. But it is *not* a process that is wholly internal to our mind or body. Symbolism usually involves physical activity in the world, and thus, like all physical activity, symbolism mediates between us and our environment. We humans interact with the world in multiple symbolic ways. Technological interactions between the mind and the world commonly involve activities that become formalized, not only to effect transformations in the world, but also to communicate between minds. Ritual is a special case of formalized behavior that usually requires participants to behave in a manner that is highly structured, repetitive, and stereotyped, and results in the coordination of elements of their lifeworld—elements of the activity, perception, cognition, feelings, and experience of people relative to some socially valued purpose.

Ritual effects two types of coordination among participants. Coordination may occur within each participant, and among participants (Chapple 1970). *Internal coordination* changes the activity of the neural networks, the endocrine and immune systems, and other body organs that affect the lifeworld of each of us as we participate in a ceremony. Ritual symbolism works to orient the individual's attention toward socially important activities, meanings, and goals. Life crises—such as puberty, marriage, birth, and death—are marked and managed in ritual ways. Ritual techniques are often used to transform the internal lifeworld of the individual, as is often the goal of healing rituals designed to repair injury or eliminate disease or to bring about a sense of close relationship to the divine. As we saw in Chapter 5, rituals frequently involve drivers like drumming, chanting, dancing and so on to evoke experiences intended by the designers of the ritual. In this way the role of ritual is fundamental to the social manipulation of experience, and knowledge about the self and world that is grounded in experience.

External coordination concerns our interaction with others—the organization and dynamics of our social relations. Ritual methods may be applied to change the course of events, or to remedy socially perceived imbalances in the cosmos—as when people act ritually to try to influence the outcome of a battle or to adjust the climate (as in praying for rain). They may also be used to evoke spiritual experiences upon which the continued vitality of the society's worldview depends. Rituals can evoke extraordinary experiences such as dreams and visions that may be publicly interpreted by shamans for socially useful purposes. As we have seen, some of the purposes to which visions and dreams may be put include divining future events, seeking the location of vital resources, revealing the future career or social role of the person having the dream or vision, and avoiding illnesses, wars and other catastrophes. In other words, rituals may be used by a people to achieve information and effects that otherwise would not be possible. So in a sense, rituals act in part as social glue—as techniques (like "throwing a party," which is our way of labeling holding an entertaining and social bonding ritual) for bringing people together and reinforcing social networks.

This mediation between the mental and physical aspects of our existence is what many scholars call *praxis*. Our mind not only interprets events and expresses itself symbolically, it also puts our symbols and interpretations to work, engaging them in praxis (practice that is socially embedded and meaningful). That is why social scientists like George Herbert Mead have long spoken of human beings as symbolic animals. Virtually all human activity is symbolically loaded— "pregnant with meaning" (Cassirer 1955).

Because we act in the world by way of symbolic filters, it makes sense to link symbolism and "technique" —the blending of which under certain circumstances produces ritual. When we say that he or she "has great technique," we mean that they do something very well and to good effect. Whether we are speaking of a tennis player returning a backhand, a dentist extracting a tooth, a farmer plowing a field, or a painter applying oils to a canvas, we are conscious of quality in how they go about their task. This quality of application derives from a developed interpretive framework within the person's mind that gets translated into action relative to the task at hand.

Some activities are augmented by tools—the tennis player cannot return the backhand without a racket, nor can the dentist extract the tooth without the aid of an extractor. Recall that the wheelchair used to transport pregnant women in hospitals mediates between the woman and the values underlying the hospital practices, the American health care system, and the values of American society. The wheelchair is not just a static symbol of disability; it is also used to mediate the symbolic activity of people involved in the formal practices of health care delivery. The pregnant woman sits in the wheelchair and is pushed around. She thereby becomes a "patient" with all that role implies. *Technology is thus essentially a symbolic process involving both activity in the world and feedback about the effects of such activity upon the world—the "praxis" aspect of symbolic activity.*

Experiencing Technologically

As philosopher Martin Heidegger (1977) pointed out, restricting our understanding of "technology" to tools, tool-use, or even practical, tool-like rituals, will result in our failing to get at the full symbolic nature of technology. The symbolic and interpretive activities of our minds make sense of, and give direction to, the techniques we use in the world to attain our goals, to achieve the effects we desire. As Heidegger jokingly noted, give a person a hammer and the whole world begins to look like nails! If you doubt the wisdom of this observation, watch a young boy play with his new tool kit—everything suddenly needs fixing.

Or, for another example, train a young obstetrician in the use of oxytocic drugs to induce or augment labor, and he may suddenly find that every labor he encounters is in need of artificial induction or augmentation. A full one-third of American births, which are mostly attended by obstetricians ("obs" for short), are in fact either induced or augmented with the Pitocin (aka syntocinon), an artificial form of the natural hormone oxytocin. And in most developing countries (in which birth practitioners pay far less attention to the scientific evidence than obs in the U.S.), medical custom and tradition (read: ritual) dictate that the vast majority of births will entail the use of

Pitocin simply to force the baby to come as rapidly as possible. Natural labors tend to take much longer—and obstetricians have no training in patience—so they use "Pit" to make the labor happen faster, often causing major problems in the birth process, as Robbie (Davis-Floyd 2004) has thoroughly documented, *because they can*. And in using an artificial hormone to speed labor, they are vivifying what Robbie calls *the technological imperative*: "If you *can* do it with technology, you *must* do it with technology.

In the absence of technology, we humans experience nature in a very human way. A birth may proceed according to its own rhythms. A tree may be something to climb, may provide us with fruits or nuts to eat, may offer us shelter from sun, rain, and wind. In this sense, our experience of the tree is pretty much the same as a chimpanzee's. If we were living in the rough in Africa without any of our modern gadgets to aid us, we might seek the upper branches of the tree as chimps do to build a nest at night so we could safely get some sleep. In a philosophical sense our relationship to the tree could be schematized as (where the arrow represents "relationship to"):[7]

I -----> tree.

Our relationship to the tree would be immediate and mediated only by (1) the nature of the tree, and (2) the nature of our very human lifeworld; that is, our self-limiting nature as a human organism with human senses, human hands with which to grasp things, a human metabolism that can digest fruits and nuts, but not leaves, etc.

But if we discover how to make and use an ax, we become *homo faber* (humans who make things), and the relationship we have with the tree changes. From "I ----> tree" our relationship becomes:

I + ax ----> tree

The tree not only provides shade and fruits, it also becomes a source of wood, and out of the wood we can make things like handles for axes, utensils like bowls and spoons, and shelters like huts and houses. And during this process the importance of the tree as shelter becomes reduced while its existence for us as a wood resource is amplified. *In fact all technologies—ritual and otherwise—both reduce and amplify aspects*

---

7. In discussing the Heideggerian phenomenology of technology, we are following the wonderful work of Don Ihde. See the Reference section.

of our lifeworld. Moreover, any change in our technology will have the effect of changing this amplification-reduction relationship. Change our technology and we have changed our lifeworld—we have changed our perceptions, interpretations, and activities.

An obvious example here is the contemporary cellphone, which has massively altered the ways in which its owners relate to the world. "Smart" phones enable us to contact or respond to contact from others almost anywhere in the world at almost any time, to search the Internet for information that comes to us within seconds, to listen to music or radio reports, to find directions to our driving goal, to get emergency assistance at any time and place, and so much more. (Robbie now tends to wear hers on a wristband during the day, and to sleep with it by her side—well, she gave up her landline home phone over a year ago due to relentless calls from telemarketers, so now her cell is her only connection in case of emergency, so of course she has to have it by her bedside at night, as so many of us now do.)

A less obvious example of how changes in technology can change people's lifeworlds comes from the damage that anthropologist Lauriston Sharp (1952) found after the introduction of simple steel hatchets into the Yir Yoront Australian Aboriginal society by missionaries back in the 1930s. What the missionaries had not realized was that stone axes and their use were pivotal in Yir Yoront social structure. Traditionally, only males could manufacture and own axes—when a female or a child needed an axe they had to borrow one from a male kinsman. This custom operated to reinforce the social status and role of the males, who knew where to get the right stones to make into axes, whereas most of the actual work done with axes was by women and children. Once steel axes were freely introduced by the well-intentioned missionaries, they tended to be passed around among people indiscriminately. The result was that the rug was pulled out from under the Yir Yoront interdependent social role cohesion, leading to major social and community disruption.

So, we *homo fabers* not only make things, we also experience the world through the medium of the technologies that we make. Because of this amplification-reduction effect, it is fair to say that we members of our contemporary technocracy experience our use of technology as *instrumental*. Our lifeworld without technology would be on the order of:

I perceive the world

but with technology:

I perceive [through the mediation of technology] the world

...becomes my experience of my lifeworld, because I am able to act in the world through technology. We (the authors) put the phrase "through the mediation of technology" in brackets because we humans tend to lose sight of this instrumentality. We simply take the world we are experiencing through technology for granted, because of the curious tendency of technologies to disappear from our awareness to the extent that they are efficiently doing their job. If the axe is of fine steel and very sharp, we lose our awareness of the axe per se and are focused instead on the act of chopping wood. Only after the axe gets dull and ceases to work well do we pay attention to it again to sharpen it. When our technologies go bust, then our awareness of them is sharpened. Anthropologists in the field often have this kind of experience with tape (now digital) recorders used in interviews. They are an essential tool in fieldwork, and yet they can largely be ignored when they are working well (you turn it on, show your interviewees how it works—if it's new to them, they exclaim a lot about it and play with it for a while, then get on with the interview and forget all about it, letting it recede into the background). But if the recorder breaks and the ethnographer is hundreds of miles away from a repair shop or a tech store, his or her awareness of the technology becomes agonizingly exquisite. And of course, the same with cellphones—if the battery dies, we tend to feel completely incapacitated and out of touch with the world until we can recharge it.

Our experience of the Earth has drastically changed since NASA's Apollo missions. When the astronauts showed us visually and in their verbal commentaries how tiny and beautiful and vulnerable "Spaceship Earth" is, it changed for all time our naive geocentrism. Yet few of us know much about the vastly complex technology that brought us those revolutionary views of Earth from space. Nor are we particularly aware of the even more complex satellite technologies that make real time weather pattern images show up on the evening news or on our iPhones, that make possible our billions of credit card transactions, and that enable us to find the best route to our destination via GPS devices. *Once we get used to them, these technologies disappear from our awareness of them as technologies.* As Heidegger said, they "withdraw" from our consciousness. Focused on pumping gas at the station, we do not reflect on the complex technologies that allow us to simply insert our credit card into the gas pump and our resultant ability to pump gas. We are simply unaware that the electronics in the gas station pump beam our credit card information to a satellite orbiting the earth, which beams it to other satellites that connect it to the credit card company's computers, which then validate the transaction and beam that validation back to the gas pump—all in a matter of seconds. These complex technological processes become salient for us only when the validation doesn't come through immediately, or if the transaction is not approved, leaving us feeling exposed and embarrassed (more so if we are trying to pay for dinner in a restaurant through those satellites and computers), taking very personally what is intrinsically an utterly impersonal process.

From Technique to Technology

Tools then are symbolic objects that have meaning to us relative to getting things done. More than that, our state of mind relative to a task is subtly conditioned by the tools we have at hand. In a sense, tools are really artifacts of our mind-states. *There clearly exists a biological and psychological continuum from technique (which may or may not involve tools) to technology (which implies the use of tools).* Even animals develop their particular techniques for getting things done, like hunting for food, or building a nest or a den. Some animals augment their techniques with tools (see Bonner 1980; Press, Kevin, and Galef 2009). Some birds use thorns and twigs to help dig for insects in the bark of trees. Sea otters crack open shellfish with pebbles. Baboons use stones to open hard husked fruits and to crush insects before eating them. Our closest biological relative, the chimpanzee, transports objects over long distances to complete a job. A chimp may carry a stick for as much as an hour over a distance of up to a kilometer, usually to get at termites in their nest—tender, tasty, and nutritious termites being a great delicacy to the chimp palate. Human beings share with other animals this strategy of physically extending the technique with physical objects ("tools"). And if we understand that to develop a technique for doing something is really a way of ritualizing the procedure (in the sense of symbolism and repetition), then we can see, as we have often previously expressed, that we share the capacity for ritual with animals as well (D'Aquili, Laughlin, and McManus 1979).

Techniques and technologies are both the expression of symbolic activity in our minds, and operate (when they work!) to fulfill our desire to be effective in the world. If we want to visit a distant friend, we hop in the car or get on a plane or train. We express our internal mental states by way of the techniques and technologies we use in the world. The painter expresses himself with the use of brushes, oils and canvas. And we may have our mental expectations fulfilled by these techniques and technologies. We are penetrated by and thus affected by the painter's finished canvas. In a sense, our technologies are material transformations of our inner mind-states, which then feed back into our minds and in turn influence our mind-states. By way of this materially augmented symbolic activity, we humans are able to open up, control, exploit, refine and otherwise extend what we can do with our bodies. These material transformations (tools, instruments, masks, regalia, icons, etc.) are therefore *artifacts of knowledge,* products of the material fulfillment and expression of the mental states of individuals in various societies directed at many different ends.

As symbolic fulfillment, an artifact may facilitate the occurrence of a desired event—a spear brings down a deer, a crystal is used as a meditation device to evoke divinatory visions of the future, the bread and wine are used to realize the body and blood of Christ in the Eucharist. As symbolic expression, an artifact may operate as a symbol in the very strict sense of the term—a signal flag is used to send a message, a painting is used to express a feeling, a wheelchair is used to assist the infirm. The policeman's uniform both symbolizes his status as a representative of the law and enables him to enforce it because the uniform entails body armor, as well as a gun, a stick, a flashlight, a Taser.

The same artifact may, of course, operate in both ways simultaneously—a stethoscope can fulfill the physician's desire to hear the heartbeat, and at the same time be a symbol of the physician's status. The electronic fetal monitor (analyzed as a powerful ritual driver in Chapter 5) can fulfill birth practitioners' desires to see the fetal heartbeat on the screen and the mother's contractions, and at the same time be a symbol of the power of technology to provide information. Unfortunately, the information provided is scientifically proven to be excessive—too much information that often leads to the performance of unnecessary cesareans, simply because the EFM records all fetal heartbeat decelerations, most of which are normal during the process of birth—yet if practitioners see every single one on the screen, they are likely to conclude that the fetus is in distress even though it most often is not, so then they rush the laboring woman to the operating room (OR) to perform an often completely unnecessary cesarean section. It is essential here to note that the cesarean section rate in the United States was a mere 6% in 1970, the year the fetal monitor was introduced. Ten years later, after the EFM had become pervasive in almost every labor ward, the cesarean rate had grown exponentially to 23%, largely due to the excessive information provided by the machine. A mountain of scientific evidence shows that nurses, midwives, or doctors simply listening to the fetal heart rate at 20-minute intervals produces quite enough information about the status of the baby and avoids unnecessary cesareans, yet the informational power and high technology resonance provided by the EFM still keeps it primary in hospital birth, making it a factor in the rise in the U.S. cesarean rate to over 32% first reached in 2009.[8] We must never underestimate the power of high-technology symbols like the EFM—our technocratic cultural faith in such technological symbols utterly ignores and transcends the huge body of scientific evidence against their routine use.

And in every case there is an evocative mode to the interaction, in that the artifact is perceived as meaningful prior to and during its use. This technological interaction between the mind and the world is facilitated and expressed by material fabrications in the world—fabrications that we normally refer to as "technology."

RITUAL TECHNIQUE AND TECHNOLOGY

Ritual is really a form of symbolically pregnant technique that frequently incorporates technologies to effect its goals—for example, the alleviation of suffering (healing rituals that include the use of herbs), the accessing of divine power and guidance (rituals of invocation using sandals, dice, or other "random event generators"), reinforcing group identity (patriotic ceremonies using flags, icons, and regalia), or the acknowledgment of a new social status at puberty (a rite of passage that perhaps includes shaving one's hair, scarring the body, or donning new clothes; see Chapter 8 for more on rites of passage). The technique of the ritual specialist may be augmented by physical objects, just as the technique of the artisan is extended by the use of chisels or loom.

The technical augmentation of human abilities may apply at the group level. Let us return to the example of the Navajo healing ritual that we introduced in the last chapter. What we did not mention there is that a traditional healing ceremony (a "sing") can only be held either inside or

---

8. http://www.childbirthconnection.org/article.asp?ck=10554. And see Davis-Floyd (2004:104-111) for an interpretation of the routine use of EFM as a ritual that enacts our technocratic core values on high technology and the flow of information those technologies produce.

around a traditional Navajo house called a "hogan"—a round, five-sided or eight-sided hut made of wood, mud, rocks, or more recently, brick or concrete. Today a majority of Navajo people no longer actually live in hogans, but rather in more modern styles of buildings like ranch-style houses, row houses, and mobile homes. Yet a healer will not consider holding a "sing" unless the family sponsoring the event owns or builds a hogan, because the myths and other texts that stipulate the techniques for symbolic healing also stipulate that it must be performed in a hogan constructed in the proper way, with its one door pointing east—the direction of the rising sun and the cultural heroine Changing Woman. All mandalas in Navajo sandpaintings likewise are open toward the east. When sandpaintings are constructed for use in a healing ceremony, they are made on the sandy floor of the hogan, and are oriented with the structure of the hogan in mind. The sandpainting is oriented properly within the hogan, and the hogan within the sacred homeland of the Navajo, demarcated by the four sacred mountains. Also, when people enter the hogan for ceremonial activities during the sing, they sit along the walls according to their gender, age, and status. Thus people become arranged properly relative to each other, relative to the sandpainting, relative to the hogan, relative to the homeland and ultimately relative to the entire cosmos—all of this simply because of the physical structure of the hogan. So you can see that the traditional hogan provides for the Navajo not only accommodation, but also a kind of ritual technology with great cosmological significance and efficacy in organizing social relations, activities and symbolism during a sacred ceremony.

In this way, the hogan is no different, say, than the temple is for Jews, the mosque for Muslims, and the church or cathedral for Christians. All are architectural forms of ritual technology that affect both the internal coordination of individuals participating in ceremonies, and the external coordination of people of different statuses and roles within the community. Within these edifices, people move and relate to each other in highly formalized and socially meaningful ways that reveal much about the social processes being expressed in the rituals that occur therein.

Just as mechanical technologies produce an instrumental lifeworld ("I ----> tree" becomes "I + axe ----> tree"), so too does ritual, both as technique and as the context of technologies. A simple, non-technologically mediated activity like social grooming (see below) or the "laying-on of hands" —an activity that we humans share with other primates—might produce an experience that could be schematized as:

I ----> patient

where the arrow stands for the experience of healing (picking lice, stroking, holding, talking to reduce stress, etc.). But in a healing ritual the experience may become mediated by technique and even technology, and the resulting experience of healing activity changes. This new relationship might be schematized as:

I + technology (herb, knife, sandpainting, fetal monitor, etc.) ----> patient.

In introducing the technique and technology into activity, certain attributes of the human being-as-patient are amplified, while others are reduced. Perhaps the patient is no longer held and stroked by loved ones to reduce his or her stress, but is administered a calming herbal tea, a tranquilizer injection by the healer, an injection of Pitocin, a surgery. In fact, the culture might lose track of the knowledge that touching and massage are effective stress-reducing techniques. The healer perceives the patient through the medium of the technology (in traditional cultures, smudging, rattling, making sandpaintings; in high-tech hospitals, x-rays, EEG printouts, vital sign monitors, CAT and PET scans and EFM). In extreme situations, as happens in modern hospitals, the patient may experience alienation when the medical specialists appear to be more oriented toward the information on computer screens than upon the patient as a person.

Ritual Reinforces an Instrumental Lifeworld

Virtually all rituals involve technique and technology. And the techniques and technologies thereby employed influence each participant's lifeworld. But just how these are conceived to cause things to happen will vary a lot depending upon the worldview of the culture in question. As we saw in Chapter 3 (on the cognitive matrix of ritual), people living in sensate/monophasic cultures may interpret causation quite differently than people living in ideational/polyphasic cultures. The former may interpret causation in materialistic ways while the latter may see causation in mystical terms.

Let us return for a moment to the mysterious case of the Turkana diviner and the purloined pots described above. We ended the story by mentioning that the real question was, how are we to interpret the fact that the old diviner appeared to know exactly where to find the pots? There are at least three explanations that have been put forward to account for this kind of phenomenon:

1. Prior knowledge. The diviner anticipates the question that will be asked and quietly obtains the requisite knowledge through his or her social network. S/he then presents the knowledge during the ritual divination, thus powerfully reinforcing cultural belief in the efficacy of divination. This anticipation would have the advantage in some cases of the knowledge becoming public in a ritual situation in which none of the diviner's informants could be blamed or negatively sanctioned.
2. Divine inspiration. The diviner uses "random event generator" techniques, like throwing sandals, bones, dice, stirring tea leaves, shuffling a deck of cards, etc., to invite the intercession of the spirits or the gods in answering the question through divine inspiration. The answer is read in the pattern produced by the random event generator. A genuine diviner lineage will likely transmit a system of interpretation of patterns from master to apprentice. In this sense the diviner is acting as a medium between the mundane world of everyday life and the divine realm (Rock, Thorsteinsson, and Tressoldi 2014). The divine will is read in the patterns produced by the actions of the diviner.
3. Vehicle for psychic powers or magical causation. The diviner is someone who has a special gift. S/he is able to access information through non-causal links to events distant in time and space. The information comes in a dream, vision, or intuition that may or may not be projected by the diviner upon the patterns made by a random event generator. In other words, the diviner appears to "read" the information in the patterns made by the sandals, but is actually projecting information gleaned through more subtle psychic powers.

Ritual and Prior Knowledge

If you are like most people reading this book, you were raised in a sensate culture and will likely be inclined toward the first explanation—that the diviner had known what he was going to be asked and had prior knowledge gleaned from gossip going the rounds the day before. But actually we have no way of knowing how the old man came by his information, and if we assume the prior knowledge scenario, we would be guilty of projecting our own cultural views on a very alien situation.

Of course we do know of other situations in which prior or consensus knowledge becomes publicly available and then apparently justified in ritual. Take for example the ritual use of masks in West Africa. Among some of the peoples living in Liberia, political control was long publicly held by a group of chiefs and a council of elder males (Harley 1950). But their real power at that time rested in the fact they were members of the *poro* secret society which every young man had to join at puberty. The *poro* society in turn was controlled by a hierarchy of elders. When the very most important elders died, the society had highly stylized death masks carved for them from wood. These allowed the dead members to continue as though they were still attending society functions and could be addressed through the medium of the mask when being appealed to for intercession with the ancestors.

Also, judges in these societies sat masked and robed, and spoke in falsetto voices so they could remain publicly anonymous. The mask represented the face of a great forest demon. Some chiefs had a mask of the forest spirits that was handed down with the office. When important issues were raised, the chief and elders met in the forest at night and discussed the issue thoroughly. Then they brought out the mask and reviewed the issue for the mask *cum* spirit. Addressing the mask, they would say something like: "If the cowrie shells we toss fall up you agree with us, if they fall down you disagree." Four shells were then thrown, and the decision of the mask spirit was supposed to be final and binding. (It was well known however that some chiefs learned to manipulate the shells so they would always fall the way they wanted them to.)

It is not too much of an exaggeration to say that ritual technologies and techniques such as consulting spirits through the medium of masks (consulting is the technique, the mask is the technology) are open to all sorts of influences. At least in some cases, as Scott Atran (2002) has shown, the outcome of the consultation puts the stamp of divine approval upon the decisions made in very worldly councils. Those in power are perceived to be doing their jobs, and their decisions and actions are perceived to be in sync with the will of the ancestors, spirits, and gods. In a sense, these kinds of divinatory rituals are a kind of ritual theater for acting out upon a public stage the proper relations and functions generally expected of leaders. So from this point of view, the old Turkana diviner may have given voice to commonly shared knowledge, but in a forum in which no one could accuse anyone of snitching.

Ritual as Divine Inspiration

But what of the alternative explanations for the old Turkana's divination? In order to comprehend how people might use a "random event generator" like sandal-tossing to divine important information, we have to mention that for most people "random chance" has no real meaning in their lifeworlds. Rather, "chance" is a term we in the contemporary technocracy apply to outcomes and decisions that more traditionally-oriented peoples would consider as having been made by supernatural forces. If we flip a coin to resolve some indecision, Western science would tell us we are randomizing our outcome—that is, there is an equal chance that one outcome (represented by "heads") will happen over the alternative outcome ("tails"). But to many people, to toss a coin that way is to invite divine intervention—to ask the spirit realm to make the decision for us.

To build a chance element into a game, for instance, is for most peoples not a simple matter of removing rational strategy from the game, but actually inviting decisions to be made by the spirits. In other words, games of strategy like chess and games of chance like poker or dice could be just two different modes of assigning the locus of decision-making. In a game of strategy, the outcome is determined by our own skill in reaching decisions and planning moves, but in a game of "chance" we are giving up the decision-making "to the gods." Actually, we members of sensate cultures are not that distant from this kind of attribution. How many gamblers carry a "lucky" piece with them when they go to the casino, how many baseball players wear the same dirty hat or socks because they believe that their "lucky" apparel brought them success in previous seasons?

Games of chance in some traditional societies are actually played as divining rituals, and their members pay close attention to the outcome for signs of important divine intervention. Random event generators like cards and dice, sandals and bones, are often ritual technologies used to invite divine intervention into problems and decision-making. There is certainly an element of this kind of invitation when some of us consult a Tarot card reader in order to clear up conflicts and ambiguities in our lives. A serious Tarot reader is intentionally using the cards to invoke the divine realm in informing the clients about their questions and uncertainties. Very commonly, the shuffling of the cards and the clients' handling of them is paired with standard, culturally received interpretations of patterns to effect a balance between divine decisions and human interpretations of those decisions.

Thus ritual technology may operate as a random event generator that may be perceived to remove ambiguity and uncertainty by inviting information and decision-making from divine beings. Ritual technologies can be used both as ways of randomizing the outcomes and as means for getting things done—reaching a decision or divining the will of the divine beings that are the "real" power behind events.

Ritual as a Vehicle for Psychic Power

The two above explanations of the old Turkana's divinatory skill are more acceptable to the Western sensate mind than is the final alternative—that ritual technology is a vehicle for application of psychic powers and magical causation. And yet there are many cultures that hold this kind of dynamic as not only possible but also primary. All of the meditation systems of the East—Hindu yoga, Theravaden Buddhism, Tibetan Tantric Buddhism, etc. —recognize the arising of psychic powers as a byproduct of spiritual practices. Australian Aborigines teach us that in the dreaming state, they are able to fly to places and do things at a distance.

The problem we have with this view of magical causation is that for most of us it is outside of our lifeworld. We are taught in our culture and in our schools that in order to cause something to happen, there must be some mechanical connection between the causal event and the caused event, like one billiard ball striking another and causing the second ball to move. The idea that the first billiard ball could cause the second billiard ball to move without ever touching it—so-called *causation-at-a-distance,* or *magical causation*—is alien to our thinking. Even more so, the notion that the causal event could happen *after* the fact of the caused event—so-called *backwards causation*—is simply anathema to us. And yet this very sort of thinking underlies many of the "magical" rites performed by traditional peoples, and is perhaps inherent in some of the ritual acts we experience in our own religious life. What else would one call the act of transubstantiation of the bread and the wine into the body and blood of Christ in the Eucharist but magic? Christians today would tend to eschew the term "magic" and speak perhaps of "divine intervention," but Christians living in the Middle Ages would have found no problem using the term "magic," for their cosmology was very different from ours today (see Huizinga 1996[1919]).

Moreover, there is now considerable scientific evidence that certain types of "magical" causation have a basis in fact. Physician Larry Dossey (1993) summarized the scientific evidence for the efficacy of prayer in healing in his book *Healing Words*. Citing scores of experimental studies, Dossey suggests that not only does prayer work for the benefit of those needing healing, but also that the religion of the person praying makes little or no difference. In fact, the praying person apparently need not espouse any religion at all, as long as he or she has faith in the act of prayer. Dossey's research is considered controversial in many scientific quarters, and is discredited by various scientists, yet for our purposes here is at the very least suggestive of what people do believe to be efficacious.

As an aside, Robbie suggests that well-meaning prayers are a way of sending "positive energy"—they may work or they may not, yet they do no harm, and they provide a way for individuals to try, in ritual fashion, to make a positive difference. The act of praying, whether or not it actually helps the person prayed for, can positively affect the psyche of the person doing the praying—we all feel better when we at least *try* to help someone (including ourselves). So, every time Robbie hears the sirens of an ambulance or a fire truck, she prays for the people for whom those vehicles are rolling. It's the only thing she can do; it might help or it might not. But at least she is feeling and sending compassion, caring, and love, and that act produces endorphins in Robbie's body, so at the very least, her prayers for others are helping her! She is very aware that her prayers for others are selfish in this very personal sense, in spite of the fact that she is trying to act selflessly. So very many people prayed for Robbie in the aftermath of her daughter's death—she just wants to return all those favors and to never be oblivious to the pain of others. Sending positive energy in whatever form can never do harm, and might just possibly be of help.

In similar fashion, if a baby is born and does not immediately breathe, many midwives will start neonatal resuscitation (in which all midwives are thoroughly trained) while at the same time asking the parents to "call the baby." Their underlying belief in doing so is that the spirit or soul of the baby might be hesitant to come into the world and need encouragement to make that decision. Certainly, "calling the baby" does no harm and has the positive effect of empowering the parents to play a role in this life-or-death situation. And, if in fact the spirit is hesitating, it might respond to the call. Many midwives and some neonatologists have experiences in which the baby begins to breathe as soon as the parents call to it; whether that act is causative or not, again it does no harm, and it just might work!

Returning to our discussion above, we note that causation-at-a-distance may also operate directly between minds. Scientists have demonstrated a phenomenon called "remote viewing." One person who acts as a sender may travel to some randomly selected location and then spend some time looking at the various landmarks around the area. Another person who is designated as the receiver may be back at the laboratory, and while the sender is experiencing the distant location, the receiver describes what they see in their mind's eye. Researchers have shown a remarkable accuracy on the part of some people in sending and receiving information about distant locations via direct mind-to-mind transmission (see Puthoff and Targ 1976; Targ and Puthoff 1977).

Results of this kind of research can get even more anomalous relative to our sensate and technocratic cultural expectations. Researchers at Princeton Engineering Anomalies Research (PEAR) labs at Princeton University generated over twenty years of research showing that the human mind is capable of influencing the outcome of random event generating machines. Whether the machine is a low-tech cascade of thousands of balls down a wall into pockets, or a hi-tech computer-generated set of random data, the human mind seems to be able to influence the outcome of the experiment to a small but significant degree. Even more startling, the PEAR researchers discovered that not only does the distance between mind and machine not affect the power of mind to influence machine, but also the time relation between running the machine and the operator attempting to influence the outcome *does not matter.* In other words, the intention to influence the outcome can occur before, during, or even after the machine is run, and there appears to be no difference in the effect. (See Jahn and Dunne 1987, 2011.)

What all of this evidence is telling us with respect to "magical" thinking in ritual is that there may well be good solid scientific reasons to suspect that causation-at-a-distance—and even backward causation—may prove to be factors in the potential efficacy of certain types of ritual—particularly those kinds of ritual activities intended to retrieve or influence information. From this vantage point, the old Turkana diviner might have been remotely viewing the purloined pots, giving voice to an internal image or intuition that he received while staring at the sandals.

We simply do not know, for we do not have the data to decide between the three possible explanations we outlined above. The lesson for us is that from the traditional cultural point of view, the first explanation—prior knowledge—does not exhaust the possibilities, and that we have to be sensitive to the biases built into our own sensate cultural conditioning when trying to understand the full extent of the power of ritual.

INSTRUMENTALITY AND RITUAL

As we shall see in Chapter 8, where we speak about the power of ritual to evoke transpersonal experiences, the efficacy of ritual can sometimes present anomalous results that our cultural position may find difficult to account for. Yet the main thing to emphasize here is that our bias in favor of the prior knowledge explanation is in part due to the kind of instrumental realism that we are taught—namely that the only way someone could know where the pots were located is if either they or someone they talked to had seen the pots while physically located near them (or had prior knowledge or a good guess as to who had stolen them). Our instrumental realism is a materialist and mechanical one. If one ball is to cause the other ball to move, they have to physically touch. There has to be a physical transmission of some kind of "force" from one physical object to the other. If one ball moves and the other moves without the two actually touching, we are inclined to call it a "coincidence" —meaning no causation involved. But this is not how people raised in ideational, or even idealistic cultures, think and perceive. Their instrumentalism includes the recognition that things can affect other things at-a-distance, as well as backwards and forwards in time. Their instrumental realism is quite different from ours, and may therefore radically alter their perception of the use and efficacy of ritual. Thus the variation in ritual instrumentality encoded in different cultures will predispose people from these cultures to experience their world quite differently and perhaps to believe more literally in their rituals than we might be inclined to do.

Spooky Causation in Modern Science

Yet lest we think that only "primitive" philosophies entertain such notions of a-causal relations, we need to reflect upon developments in quantum physics, which incorporates really "spooky" causation as well. There is for example a phenomenon called "the Einstein, Podolsky, Rosen effect" (aka "the EPR system"). In a 1935 thought experiment these three famous physicists modeled that once two parts of a quantum system are separated, they remain "entangled" and continue to act as a correlated unity no matter how far they travel from each other. EPR-type systems also confound commonsense notions of local causation, for there exists no clear mechanism by which the two parts can "interact" at a distance. Since that time, numerous experiments have upheld the EPR effect, and have thus disconfirmed to some extent the "local" causation assumptions of the more commonsense and classical Newtonian view (Selleri 1988).

Robbie's Spooky Quantum Physics Story: Peyton, the DFW Airport, and a Spontaneous Ritual Performance

This "spooky" quantum physics conclusion—that two particles, once interlinked and then separated in space and time, remain "entangled" and continue to act as a correlated entity (meaning, for one example, that if one particle changes its spin, the other will too)—had profound meaning for Robbie after the death (by car accident) of her 20-year-old daughter Peyton.[9]

> Three months after Peyton's death, I found myself walking the long corridors in the Dallas-Ft. Worth airport on my way to make my flight connection to Brazil, in a daze and sobbing. Suddenly, Peyton showed up in front of me, wearing a pair of blue-jean cutoffs and a blue halter top that I knew well, and walking backwards facing me. Laughing her head off, Peyton said, "Mom, you are sooooo not getting this!" Pointing at me and then at herself and back and forth, then making a circle with her fingers and holding one finger up, she said "Mom, I want you to repeat after me: I am you and you are me and we are One!" So, following her lead, I walked those long airport corridors facing

---

9. For a full description of Robbie's experience of her daughter's death, see Davis-Floyd, Robbie (2003) "Windows in Space/Time: A Personal Perspective on Birth and Death." *Birth: Issues in Perinatal Care* 30 (4):272-277. Reprinted in Weston, Robert (2007) *Vale of Tears*. New Wine, UK and freely available at www.davis-floyd.com.

Peyton, making the same hand gestures, and repeating aloud in wonder, "I am you and you are me and we are One."

Of course I got weird looks from the people around me, and of course my rational mind was racing like crazy: "No P-Pey, we are NOT One. I gave birth to you, I raised you, yet you were so much more than I ever could be—I am not you and you are not me, you are your own very special, very separate self!" while at the same time, my rational mind was also thinking, "Yet quantum physics says that if two interlinked particles are separated in time and space, a change in the spin of one can effect the same change in the spin of the other...so maybe it's possible..."

And while this dialogue between me and myself is going on in my head, Peyton is still laughing her head off and insisting that I continue to make those back-and-forth pointing hand movements and continue to repeat, "I am you and you are me and we are One." All the way to the gate—a very long way. And when I arrived at the gate, she, still grinning, vanished.

I was assigned a bulkhead seat, with plenty of room in front of me. After the plane took off, P showed up again, still smiling, and made me do the hand gestures and the words four more times, and then, slanting her hand horizontally, she made a circle with her thumb and forefinger, with the other fingers splayed out, and held it out in front of her, then moved it to her heart.

I knew that Peyton had been fluent in American Sign Language (ASL)—she had volunteered at the Austin School for the Deaf—so I figured that last gesture was some kind of "sign"—and so, trusting, I just waited to find out its meaning. Months later, I received an invitation in the mail to a dinner for bereaved parents hosted by our marvelous local counseling group, called For the Love of Christi. Well, I received those invitations every month and usually tossed them, but this particular one was *glowing*. I could barely let it out of my hands for long enough to tape it onto the fridge.

Of course this time I accepted the invitation and attended the dinner. Scanning the room, I saw a group of people signing to each other with a translator, who was also clearly hearing. Tentatively, I approached, and found the courage to show the sign P had made to the translator and to ask him what it meant?

He said with a huge smile that the sign was shorthand for "spirit," and that when she held it to her heart, she was saying

"My spirit lives in your heart!" (He also showed me the longhand sign for "spirit," which involves more movement.)

I could not speak. Instead I found a place to sit down, and simply sobbed from the intense feelings of both sorrow and joy that I was experiencing. My daughter was dead, and yet she was alive in some way and had communicated with me with the goal of teaching/showing me that her spirit lives in my heart!

At the time, if anyone had suggested to me that this vision, this marvelous Peyton apparition in the DFW airport, might be simply the product of my own imagination, my psychic longing for my dead daughter to be alive and in my presence again, I would have gotten furious. For me at that time, only three months after her death, seeing her in that airport was absolute proof positive that her spirit was still alive and well somewhere, somehow. I *needed* to believe that in order to survive.

Now, over fifteen years after her death, I can admit the possibility that perhaps I simply manifested her to myself to fulfill my then-desperate need to see her once again. Yet, says my rational mind, I don't know ASL and never have, so how could I possibly have imagined the sign for "spirit"?

I know that I could never have imagined that sign—yet I also know that occasionally I dream in other languages that seem very real in my dreams. I fly in my dreams sometimes. I live whole novels that I never could actually write—spy stories, action adventures, romances, historical novels—I dream them all in vivid detail. So could I have tapped some deep knowledge in myself to come up with those "visions" of Peyton in the airport, including the ASL sign—gifts from myself to myself? Or did/does her spirit actually live and manifest itself to me?

I *choose to believe* that Peyton's spirit does live, and did choose to show up for her grieving mother (as she has on other occasions, too many to recount in this book. I'm writing another book about my experiences around P's death, called *Grieving and Grace: A Chronicle*—it might take me some more years). My point here is that, as Charlie and I explain in this particular book, *belief follows emotion*. We generally do not intellectually choose our beliefs; rather, we tend to believe what we emotionally experience as "true." I, very emotionally, experienced Peyton's spirit as true and real, and I'm just like the rest of us—my beliefs follow my emotions. So I believe that she is alive and well and happy, dancing around the universe as she danced so excellently in life. I really have no choice—my sorrow would be greater if I could not believe that she is still alive somewhere, somehow, in some form.

Isn't that a lot like what religion and ritual are all about? We humans need to make sense of our suffering—we need to believe that the bad things that happen to us happen for good reasons. And the rituals that ritual designers (which any of us can become) create can show all the rest of us that they do—our rituals vivify for us that life has meaning even in death.

Perhaps now you will understand why I have so much passion for understanding ritual and explaining this human cultural universal to others as Charlie and I seek to do in this book. As I mentioned in the Preface, although sometimes ritual performance and ensuing belief have cost me dearly (e.g. when I was a participant in a cult), different kinds of ritual performance and ensuing belief did finally enable me to heal from Peyton's death.

I affirm that even spontaneous rituals that happen in sudden, unexpected visions of dead loved ones (like the hand ritual that Peyton made me do throughout that long airport walk, and like the EMDR healing I experienced at Sierra Tucson nine years later—see chapter 8) can be extremely instrumental for healing!

Taking a deep breath, we now return to our point about "spooky causation" in modern science—Robbie's section above is intended to serve as an example of how the same intuitions pop up in science—quantum physics—as well as in traditional ideas of causal relations.

The Implements of Ritual Practice

All human cultures are technological to some extent, whether they make their living by hunting and gathering in deserts or forests, by growing crops in fields, by fishing for resources in lakes or oceans, or by working in factories and offices. The instrumentality of each culture is part and parcel of their cycle of meaning. The techniques and technologies people bring to bear in solving problems and getting things done are integral to the ways in which they experience and interpret their world. Thus far we have emphasized the rituals themselves as techniques for getting things done—as technological rituals in Wallace's sense. Yet we also need to pay some attention to rituals as *contexts* for the use of technologies. For just as a hammer can turn a child into a carpenter and the world into nails, so too does the use of implements condition the mind-state of the ritualist, from carpenters to obstetricians to computer geeks and more.

We have already, during the course of these chapters, given numerous examples of the use of ritual implements. We have just examined the use of sandals as a means to generate random patterns that are then somehow interpreted in a way that produces information. Most of us would never think of using our flip-flops or Birkenstocks as tools in a divination, so obviously the instrumental mind-state of the old Turkana diviner was quite different from our own. For him, sandals are practical in more ways than merely protecting the feet—he sees possibilities that are invisible to us. We have also seen that objects like a mask, a mirror, a wheelchair, an IV drip, the electronic fetal monitor, a flag, a cross, a particular tree or a species of tree (like the oak or ash), a stalk of corn, even a person dressed as Darth Vader, can all act as ritual implements in the right circumstances.

Ritual conditions the application of the tools used in its enactment. Part of the context of the object is its physical surroundings. The mask used by a Japanese Noh player is perceived by the audience within the broader context of the actor's colorful costume, and mask and costume are viewed within the context of the stage and other actors. The object also gains its significance within the context of the story line and actions conveyed by the actors. In the same way, Navajo sandpainting, prayer sticks, rattles, and other ritual paraphernalia gain their significance within both the physical relations of the hogan and from the hogan outward to the sacred homeland and thence to the cosmos. Despite evidence of the importance of context for the effective use of modern medicines—much of this evidence includes the importance of the so-called "placebo" effect—medical practice today downplays this crucial ritual aspect to healing (but see Benedetti 2008).

Situating medicines and other ritual technologies within an appropriate ritual context is all-important for maximizing their effects regarding healing and other purposes. Nevertheless, most contemporary physicians choose to ignore the shamanic role that many patients wish to impute to them (they would never think, for example, of asking the parents to "call the baby" as they start resuscitation), and reject out-of-hand the conscious and deliberate performance of non-medical healing rituals, choosing to rely on the (unconsciously ritualistic) performance of medical procedures instead.

The context in which we encounter any ritual implement will certainly influence how the object works on us. A cross viewed in the midst of a Mass has a different impact than a cross worn around a friend's neck, or a cross brandished to protect herself by the heroine of a vampire movie. Context always conditions both perception and interpretation, and hence is always a factor in the practitioner's instrumentality. A mirror used to evoke the mandala offering in the Tibetan meditation is not the same even when that same mirror is used to shave with or put on lipstick. The same object, but different ritual context and different instrumental mindstates, are involved. A mask may be viewed as merely a prop in a theater production, but may also be experienced as the physical dwelling place of a powerful spirit. And how one views the mask will condition how one treats it and uses it. There are Northwest Coast Indian masks in the collection of the Canadian Museum of Civilization that are still considered by First Nations peoples to be repositories of powerful spirits. Every once in a while, a contingent of shamans visits the collection to ritually "feed" the masks—things that most visitors to the museum think of as only physical objects to be seen and then ignored. Just as we take germ theory for granted and will sterilize a needle before we use it to remove a splinter, those who perceive the mask as the actual face of a spirit or god will apply that knowledge to the use of the mask, and will interpret the outcome of procedures accordingly.

Despite the fact that they sometimes may not work in practice, ritual technologies are remarkably durable. One reason for the perseverance of ritual technologies is that often the implements used have actual physical properties that are part of their overall utility. Mirrors do indeed reflect light. Knives are sharp and can be used to cut. The stethoscope is not only a medical icon, it actually lets the physician hear the sounds of our heart. The electronic fetal monitor does record the mother's uterine contractions and the fetal heartbeat. And masks usually are designed to somewhat resemble actual faces. The sandals used by the old Turkana diviner, as well as tea leaves, a handful of dried bones, decks of Tarot cards, dice and roulette wheels are all physically capable of being manipulated by people to generate not-so-random patterns.

Moreover, we know from the study of ethnobotany that many, if not most, of the herbs used by traditional shamans actually do have biochemical properties that prove efficacious—our readers can find hundreds of them on the shelves of Whole Foods and other such alternative stores (bringing up more issues involving the exploitation of traditional peoples and their knowledge and resources than we can even begin to address here). And of course, all the psychotropic plants and concoctions used by traditional peoples to alter the SOCs of ritual practitioners are known to have biochemically induced hallucinatory effects (see Rudgely 1993; Schultes and Hofmann 1980; Devereux 2008).

A caveat: Much of the power of ritual implements has more to do with the features of their symbolic design than their inherent physical properties—a fact most clearly demonstrated in the use of art in ritual. Art for most peoples on the planet also involves practical use—or as anthropologist Alfred Gell (1998) called it, "art as agency." Gell was getting at the same thing we are saying here, that art as well as its ritual context is used to get things done. One type of art Gell found interesting was the kinds of symbolic implements used by some peoples to influence the minds of other people, especially their trading partners or enemies. Gell (1992:40-67) called this use of art the "technology of enchantment." Just as when the job of putting a child to bed is made easier if "the bed in question has sheets and pillowcase richly embellished with spaceships, dinosaurs, or even polka dots, be they sufficiently jolly and attractive" (Gell 1992:74), so too does the trading expedition tend to go better when one dazzles one's trading partner with magical symbolism at the very beginning. Thus the Trobriand Islanders of Melanesia in the South Pacific, who (to this day) go on lengthy, dangerous trading expeditions in huge ocean-going canoes, have intricate prow boards carved and painted with magical symbols so that the first thing their trading partners see coming over the horizon at them is a phalanx of beautiful, magical images that have the effect of demoralizing them and making them more compliant in the economic transactions to come.

In the same vein, 19th century warriors from the Marquesan Islands in the Polynesian Archipelago used to decorate their bodies and shields with intricate and highly abstract symbolism designed to work on the psychology of their enemies. The intent was to directly cause lack of morale, loss of confidence, and confusion because of the magical significance of these dazzling motifs. In a certain sense, the Marquesan's intent was little different from that of the Scots regiments who went into battle during World War II to the haunting (and to their enemies, terrifying) strains of the bagpipe. Marquesan body tattoos and Scots bagpipes are examples of ritual "technologies of enchantment" designed to affect their enemies' mind-states. The ritual aspect of warfare is of course more obvious when carried out by traditional peoples for whom battles were highly regulated by rules and prescriptions, most of which have been disappearing in modern warfare since the time of the American Civil War. Even weapons may have this dazzling, psychological effect—for example, common knowledge in military history holds that the use of rocketry by the British during the Napoleonic Wars generally caused more terror in the enemy than physical destruction.

Hi-Tech and Virtual Rituals

It is clear from what we have said about instrumental realism that the invention of more and more complex technologies in our contemporary world must impact the nature of human interaction in general and ritual in particular. In Chapter 2, we alluded to the remarkable effects that Princess Diana's funeral and her son's wedding to Kate Middleton had upon millions of people who neither knew these royals personally nor were physically present in London for the events. Nevertheless, people viewing these events on their television, computer, or tablet screens all over the world had the sense of having participated in the ceremonies—of having in some way been "present" and "participating" in the ritual. And in a psychological sense, these people *were* present, for they were experiencing what we call a *virtual ritual* (see Kapferer 2004). By "virtual ritual" we mean that *most of the elements of ritual are operating in the experience of the participants, except for the intimacy of actual physical presence.*

Examples of virtual rituals abound in modern life (see Goethals 2003; Grimes 2013; Wagner 2012). People become involved in and are influenced by such televised events as football, soccer, and ice hockey games, televangelist religious programs and church services, real life court cases, parliamentary and legislative debates, etc. People become even more interactive in ritual dramas on the Internet when they participate in MUDs, blogs and on-line real-time computer games (see Goethals 2003).

But the notion of virtual reality, especially with respect to ritual, is not so straightforward as these examples might suggest. From another point of view, *all reality is virtual in the sense that our individual lifeworld is the product of our own body's nervous/neuroendocrine system.* Our internal lifeworld is not all there is to reality. Our individual lifeworld is a partial view of reality, hence "virtual" in the literal sense of the word. (The word "virtual" derives from the Latin root for "possessing certain virtues" —meaning that many, but not all, of the attributes—qualities or "virtues" —of something are present.) The world of our experience arises between our ears, in our bodies, within the space produced by our sensory systems, regardless of whether the funeral, wedding, baseball game, or presidential inauguration we are "attending" is actually before our eyes, or technologically reproduced in images before our eyes. Hi-tech virtual rituals may be extremely effective, for much of the sensory experience triggered by the images on the television, laptop, iPad, or smartphone are very close to the experiences we would have if physically present at the event. Because our technologies tend to "withdraw" from our awareness when they are working efficiently, what is left in our consciousness is the event—the ritual itself.

The more interactive the technology allows us to be, the more our illusory sense of reality is heightened. Viewing a televised sports event and listening to a concert broadcast over the radio are fairly passive events. But with the advent of the Internet, even these relatively passive virtual rituals are "heated up" by being associated with interactive websites. The sense of interaction with either real or virtual persons is crucial to the sense of virtual participation. We have all had the experience of talking with a distant loved one over the phone or via computer for so long that the virtual conversation slips into being very real, and we experience a sense of loss when we eventually do hang up. Indeed, we may call the loved one repeatedly in order to reinforce that sense of virtual closeness—especially nowadays when we are communicating via Skype and can actually see images of each other during our conversations. The more intimate the interaction over the phone or the computer, the greater the sense of shared relationship—understanding here that a conversation may range from being a formal exchange of information to actually making virtual love with each other (having so-called "phone sex"). Intimate conversations via technological media amount to very simple virtual rituals—in this case, virtual rites of intensification (see Chapter 8).

SUMMARY: RITUAL TECHNIQUE AND TECHNOLOGY

Ritual is almost always instrumental in the sense of "instrumental realism." Because it is so often instrumental, ritual influences our experience of the world. Part of the ritual package, the cycle of meaning, is the technological immanence that penetrates both our consciousness and our experience—

our experience of the world is mediated through the technology. As with germ theory—we take it for granted because it has been proven to be true—germs that are visible via microscopes cause diseases that can be cured by getting rid of the germs.

All ritual is technique, and most rituals are also technologized—we experience them not just through activity and symbols but also through physical objects and the manipulation of the causation lying behind events. Modern rituals often involve high technology, and thus express the changes in a society's technology just as they enact changes in its members' core values. Modern electronics have even made "virtual" rituals possible (Grimes, Hüsken, Simon, and Venbrux 2011:Chap. 6). Video games like *World of Warcraft* and *Skyrim* provide an outlet for both conscious and unconscious feelings and proclivities while at the same time conditioning players to an underlying set of rules of virtual behavior. The games make certain virtual technologies (swords, healing potions, communications technologies) available to the player and exclude other alternative technologies, all the while limiting what players can do with these objects and what actions they can take while utilizing them. Just so with the old Turkana diviner and the purloined pots!

Suggested Reading

Dissanayake, Ellen (1992) *Homo Aestheticus: Where Art Comes From and Why*. Seattle: University of Washington Press.

Dossey, Larry (1993) *Healing Words: The Power of Prayer and the Practice of Medicine*. San Francisco: Harper.

Sharp, Lauristan (1952) "Steel Axes for Stone Age Australians." *Human Organization* 11(2):17-22.

Chapter 7

RITUAL FRAMING: ORDER, FORMALITY, AND INVIOLABILITY

Physical and Non-Physical Frames. Ritual Frames: Energy and Power. The Meaning and Power of Shrines and Altars. Formality and Order in Ritual: Why They Matter. Inviolability and Inevitability: "The Ritual Train." Breaking Frame: Purposeful Disruption of Ritual. The Ludic Dimension of Ritual: Breaking the Frame to Enhance the Energy. Framing and Flow. Ritual Order: Enhancing Courage and Confidence. When Rituals Fail. Summary: Ritual Order and Ritual Failure.

Formal rituals differ somewhat from everyday ritualization. One of formal ritual's primary characteristics is that it is framed—set apart from the realm of the everyday, in a special building, room, or specially marked space, and/or held at a special time. Order and formality intensify this sense of set-apartness, and are the dominant modes in ritual. You know you are in the presence of ritual when things are no longer casual but precise, when order matters, when the feeling is formal—that is, when you have to start paying special attention to your body movements to be sure you are behaving appropriately, as in church or at a formal dinner ("formal" means "attention to form"). A formal dining room with the table fully set indicates that a highly elaborate dinner ritual is about to take place. The dining room serves as a frame, setting this ritual apart from everyday life. The kitchen, by way of contrast, while often also a ritual space, is one of multiple functions—food is prepared there as well as eaten. So dinners at the kitchen table are culturally marked as more casual than dinners in the dining room—the frame is less clearly demarcated and the ritual is concomitantly more diffuse. We do not mean to imply that the boundaries of a ritual frame are precise—indeed, as Don Handelman (2004) has pointed out, the frame may have fuzzy boundaries; one may slip, say, almost seamlessly from a non-ritual public event into a ritual. What is critical to framing ritual is the intention to generate a sense of formality, and thus an intensification of the ritual, via the framing—for example, moving the questioning of crime suspects into an interrogation room instead of simply querying them on the street. The significance of the ritual frame became most evident to Robbie while she was working, in the early 1990s, with a Mexican *curandero*, Don Lucio (now deceased), who performed ceremonies every year in a grotto on the side of the volcano Iztaccihuatl to bring the rains. It bothered Don Lucio that there was no clear demarcation of the grotto from the open field in front of it because there was no clarity about where the ritual space ended and began. So he had his followers construct a portal through which all had to pass to enter the special space that could now be defined as sacred because it had been formally separated from the world of the profane. On the field side of the portal, casual conversation and movement were appropriate. But a few inches away, on the other side of the portal, one had to stand up straight, keep one's eyes focused on the altar built into the side of the grotto, refrain from speaking to others, and do whatever the other participants in the ritual were doing—silently listen to Don Lucio pray and chant and do so along with him at the appropriate times. One's spatial relationship to the ritual frame, in other words, determined the kind of behavior in which it was appropriate to engage.

Figure 7.1. Don Lucio's portal, early 1990s. Photo by Robbie Davis-Floyd

PHYSICAL AND NON-PHYSICAL FRAMES

Ritual frames can be physical or non-physical. Physical frames include such devices as church or temple sanctuaries, Navajo hogans, sacred caves or grottos, auditoriums, theaters, concert halls, stadiums, the garden patio adorned by the ivy-covered wedding arch, and so forth—and, for virtual rituals, the plastic frame around the TV or computer screen. Such architectural frames keep the ritual contained within a demarcated space and are symbolically loaded with expectations and rules for what kind of behavior is expected and appropriate in that particular space. These rules or expectations facilitate the work of ritual, as they predispose people entering those spaces to behave in ritually appropriate ways and thus to begin to enter the psychological mindset the ritual is constructed to generate. The mere act of entering an obviously ritualistic space can constitute a sort of ritual—once inside the frame, people will alter their behavior accordingly even if they don't plan to actually participate in a full-fledged ritual performance.

Imagine that you are sightseeing in a European or Mexican village and you decide to visit the local cathedral. As you walk up the steps, you start scanning the interior for signs that a church service is in progress, so you can avoid disrupting it. Perhaps you cover, or uncover, your head, depending on the local rules and whether you are a woman or a man. If there is a service in progress, you will probably enter to the side, and try to scan the interior as unobtrusively as possible. If there is no service, you likely will enter in the middle, so as to obtain the most complete view of the interior, and walk directly down the central aisle. But you will at the same time be scanning for people kneeling in prayer, and will respectfully keep your distance from them. Here you are encountering a smaller ritual frame. A person kneeling in prayer inside a church (or even on the street) constitutes a ritual microcosm—the space immediately around her or him is perceived by themselves and by others as sacred and inviolable. People engaged in performing rituals, with or without technological accoutrements, often generate what Charlie and Robbie like to think of as *invisible lines of energy running around the space they inhabit*. Other people walking by will notice this non-physical frame, and will generally go out of their way to avoid breaking or violating it. Sacred icons, art, and altars can generate a similar kind of non-physical frame. In their presence, you keep a respectful distance, you don't touch the icon or altar, and you behave in relatively formalized ways until you move outside of the frame.

This sense of the sublime can arise anywhere, really—it does not require the physical presence of a sacred building (hogan, tipi, pyramid, church, etc.), but only the sense of an aura—an energetic frame—around someone or some event, triggered by ritual elements. Suppose we go on a picnic and there is great merriment and boisterous fun going on while the table is set for the feast. Once seated, someone says, "Let us pray" and holds out their hands to their neighbors, a circle is formed, all play ceases, and everyone bows their heads while a prayer is recited. The ritual words and the forming of a human circle are sufficient for many to have the sense of a holy event, a sacred space and time in which there are strict rules of behavior and attitude (Grimes 2007). In the Islamic world, daily activities cease with the call to prayer five times a day. The devout Muslim is expected to stop what he is doing, roll out his prayer rug if he has one, and do prostrations toward the sacred city of Mecca. The rugs may have woven into them sacred symbols, including portals of one sort or another. The call to prayer and the ritual activities constitute a ritual and a frame within which the sense of the sublime may arise, depending upon the proficiency of the practitioner.

Theater history was made in 1972 when the famed British director Peter Brook took a troupe of his actors (including Helen Mirren and Yoshi Oida) on an adventure to sub-Saharan Africa (Heilpern 1999). Over the course of months and more than 8000 miles, the troupe set up shop in tiny villages and market places. They would lay down a carpet in the village and do their performances upon it. They found that the villagers would sometimes insist upon doing their own performances, which were frequently more interesting than those of the professional actors. The only rule was that when one stepped onto the carpet, one had to act a part in the ongoing, unfolding play. The carpet became the ritual space, and surprisingly, many of the African villagers, unfamiliar with European stage productions, nonetheless quickly got into the act. They seemed to intuit the notion of the carpet as a ritual space which required of them extraordinary psychology and action.

RITUAL FRAMES: ENERGY AND POWER

Those who participate fully in a ritual, either within or outside of a physical frame, will often describe a sense of spiritual "power" that may surround them and enter them during the ritual. You may be wondering by now if we are speaking metaphorically about the "energy" generated by ritual, or if we think that energy is in some sense real. Hal Puthoff, the physicist we mentioned in Chapter 5, would say that all physical objects are "peaks of coherence in the energy sea" —in other words, all physical objects— all matter—are coalescences of energy—everything and everyone is energized out of the quantum sea. One of the implications of this view is that we humans are normally aware of only a tiny fraction of the energies that envelop us. Other animals are clearly able to perceive energies we are unable to. Just prior to an earthquake, animals on a farm or in a zoo may act strangely, exhibit agitation for no perceivable (to us humans) reason. Certain fish in the ocean perceive electromagnetic energies that humans do not without the aid of technology. Sea turtles and many migratory birds sense electromagnetic forces we are only able to measure through technological means (such as compasses). Philippine tarsiers, another of our primate relatives, are able to communicate using sounds much higher than humans can naturally hear, using frequencies in the high ultrasonic band. Thus far, we have been speaking of the "power of ritual" in the sense that rituals done properly can be extremely efficacious. But there is this other sense in which the term "power" is used by traditional peoples—the access to normally invisible, but perhaps real energies that may be tapped through ritual means, and that may be used for common purposes.

Framing is essential to the power of ritual because the energy that ritual generates (whether physical, psychic, or metaphorical) is much more palpable when it is contained within a defined space (see Driver 2006). And when ritual spaces are permanent, like churches, temples, and hogans, the energy of every ritual ever performed in that space lingers and can be sensed when one enters. Such places are thought of by the cultural groups who use them as *power spots, power centers,* or *power places.* As we have mentioned, simply entering such a place is often enough to generate a strong sense of ritual participation. This pattern of perception and behavior has an ancient history, as Paul Devereux describes in a number of his books, including *The Sacred Place, Sacred Geography: Deciphering Hidden Codes in the Landscape,* and *Symbolic Landscapes.* Devereux has traced the sacred landscape frame all over the planet, and back to at least the beginnings of the Neolithic, thousands of years ago. Common to these many traditions seems to be recognition of "power places" that are the source of spiritual guidance, energy, and efficacy. In ancient times, these places were marked by the construction of buildings and monuments, like the famous Stonehenge in southern England.

Modern folks too are able to sense such power. Years ago, Robbie had the good fortune to visit a church in the small English village of Isleham where, she had learned, a number of her ancestors were buried. To her surprise, she discovered that they were buried not in the graveyard outside, but inside the church, in crypts on top of which rest their marble effigies. The earliest crypt is dated 1484. Standing alone inside the church, Robbie got goose-bumps thinking of the long and tenuous chain of life events that led over the centuries and across an ocean from their genes to her birth in 1951. Had they lived or died differently, she—and her children—would not exist. And here she was, in the very church where these people had knelt in prayer, joined hands in marriage, and baptized their children—and who were now her ancestors. The energy traces of these ritual lives seemed to shimmer in the air as she reached out to touch the cold marble of the stone effigies of her direct ancestors. Moved to her core, and wanting both to honor her sense of connection to these ancestors and to leave her own ritual trace to mingle with theirs in that sacred space, she lifted her arms and sang a hymn of praise.

Inside that frame, this act seemed to make perfect sense; once outside, she felt embarrassed and hoped no one had heard—*because behavior that is appropriate in a ritually framed space is generally not appropriate in the everyday world.* We tend to react negatively to preachers yelling their ritualistic words on the street corner or in the park, yet positively to a preacher standing at his podium in a church. What works within a ritual frame usually does not work outside of it.

Physical ritual frames can be generated not only by the landscape and by technological artifacts, but also by human bodies. Have you ever stood or sat with others in a circle and clasped hands? When you did, you were participating in creating a ritual frame. People who often use this technique to create ritual frames are generally aware of the *power of framing*—in other words, of the energy generated and contained within the frame. So if an individual has to leave the circle—break the frame—she will generally back out slowly and make sure to pull together the two hands of the other participants that she has been holding together until they clasp, in order to minimize the energy rupture. Members of various Wiccan communities often create sacred circles as part of their ritualizing. At the conclusion of the ritual, they will likely say "The circle is open but unbroken!" to indicate that although the ritual is over, the energy it generated will live on for its participants, forming threads of connection and continuity between each of them and the ritual they collectively performed.

THE MEANING AND POWER OF SHRINES AND ALTARS

The smaller the frame, the more focused and intense can be the energy generated by the ritual performed within it. Frames work like lenses in their capacity to focus attention and energies. Altars are particularly important ritual frames. Because they are small in size (compared to the church, the temple, or the rooms in which altars are constructed) and visually compelling, they are effective focal points for focusing energy around various phenomena, from religious icons to secular mementos. Charlie was once the student of the famous anthropologist and photographer John Collier Jr., one of the founders of the modern field of visual anthropology. In his courses, Collier taught his students to photograph what he called peoples' "shrines"—specific spaces in homes and other places that reflect and display their values. These shrines were not necessarily religious foci, but spaces that for the people who create them are pregnant with meaning—shelves with souvenir spoon collections reflecting their travels, collections of family photographs on tables and pianos, various objects grouped together on mantelpieces, a wall full of framed diplomas and certificates. All such shrines, whether sacred or secular, draw the eye and trigger memories that enhance the meaning of the shrine.

Religious altars are a special category of shrine that have very special efficacy. Before his death, Don Julio (a compadre of the aforementioned Don Lucio) and his family lived in a village in central Mexico in a small house with one large room containing the family dining table, the double bed in which Don Julio and his wife slept, and the family living area with sofa and TV. At the far end of that room, near the door, was an altar that took up a whole wall of the room. The altar consisted of a large blue table covered with a flowered plastic tablecloth, on top of which rested statuettes of various Catholic saints, flickering candles in tall glass candle holders, dried flower arrangements, and paper cards depicting still other saints. In the middle of the table, toward the back, stood a tall wooden cross. On the wall above the table, and on either side of the cross, hung multiple pictures of Jesus, the Virgin of Guadalupe, and still more saints. If a family member, or a visitor, happened to pass within three feet of that altar, he had to kneel down and cross himself before he could go on. The altar, in other words, defined the space around it as ritual space in which certain behaviors were appropriate and others, like normal conversation, were not.

Figure 7.2. Don Julio's home altar, early 1990s. Photo by Robbie Davis-Floyd

Like Don Julio and his family, millions of people construct altars in their homes. These home altars serve as sacred spaces for focusing the spiritual energy of whatever religion or belief system the household participates in—the spiritual realm inhabits a physical space within the secular realm. The altar reminds the family of their beliefs by making these beliefs manifest both visibly and psychically, generates further entrainment with those beliefs, and provides a sense that the religious or spiritual figures honored by the altar are watching over the family. In other words, altars serve as multi-dimensional portals, bringing the spirits into worldly space and carrying messages and prayers from this world to the spirit realm. More secular altars may simply hold mementos and artifacts that link us to people and memories we treasure—or to ourselves and our accomplishments and those of our children or other family members and close friends.

The power and utility of altars became evident to Robbie in February, 1993. All day she felt out of sorts, as if something were missing or dreadfully wrong, but she couldn't put her finger on exactly what. Arriving home in the late afternoon, she happened to glance at the calendar on the fridge, and realized that it was Feb. 7, the day on which, twenty years ago, her father had suddenly and unexpectedly died. Twenty years! (Regarding important anniversaries, we Westerners tend to think in terms of decades because of the structure of our numerical system.)

Robbie was overwhelmed with a need to mark the occasion in some way. Without forethought, she moved about the house gathering up mementos of her father, Walter Gray Davis: two large photos of him riding his palomino stallion on the small ranch he had owned in Wyoming, his cowboy boots with the elaborate stitching and the silver inlay over the heels and toes, the scrapbook containing photos and newspaper articles describing his work as an independent oil operator in Wyoming in the 1950s and 1960s, the cocky green felt hat with the red feather he had so often worn when he served as ringmaster at horse shows in San Antonio, Texas, after his retirement from the oil business. Robbie found herself carefully arranging all these mementos on a table next to a wall, on which she hung the two large photos. She scrounged for candles, placed them, and lit them. Then she sat on the floor, stared at the altar, and sobbed for an hour, flooded with the memories of her father's strong presence, his wit, his characteristic East Texas accent (*"Ah cain't hep it!"*), his strong and steady arms around her on the horse as they galloped like the wind when she was a small child, his anger over a boyfriend he didn't like when she was 16, his joy over her marriage at 19 to a man he did like, his untimely death when she was 23. After a while it almost seemed as if her father Walter was physically present with Robbie—she could see the tweed checks of his favorite jacket, feel its rough texture, smell his Old Spice aftershave, revel once again in the ruddiness of his cheeks and the twinkle in his grey-blue eyes. She could even see the scar on his arm put there by the neighbor's guard dog, who escaped from his backyard during a post-wedding garden party her parents were hosting and terrorized the arriving guests until her father grabbed the dog and wrestled him to the ground. Once he had the dog subdued, Walter dragged him back to the neighbor's backyard and locked him in his pen, went into the bathroom and poured hydrogen peroxide over his torn and bleeding arm, wrapped two bandanas around it and tied them tightly, changed shirts, and went on with the party, cheerful as ever. When all the guests were gone, he went to the hospital and ended up with 23 stitches in that arm. (He didn't tell Robbie and her new husband about that tangle with the dog until weeks later, as he didn't want to spoil their honeymoon.)

When Robbie's children Peyton and Jason came home some time later, they found Robbie sitting on the floor in front of her makeshift altar and smiling through her tears. She nestled them close and began to tell them stories of their grandfather, who had died before they were born. She explained every artifact she had placed on the altar and its place and meaning in her father's life, so that her children could have some sense of the life and personality of the grandfather they had never known. (And at the next school Costume Day—a ritual that allows participants to play with other identities—Jason chose to dress up as a cowboy, because that was the identity he had gleaned from the photos of his grandfather Walter on his stallion.)

As this story makes clear, even simple, makeshift home altars can serve as powerful focal points, helping us to focus energy and attention on the symbolic meaning of the artifacts we place upon them. Thus, as Robbie experienced, altars can make the elements they represent a stronger part of everyday life, open lines of communication between dimensions, and help people achieve emotional catharsis around specific events. Home altars can take many shapes and forms, and are often not specifically recognized as such. Look around your house and ask yourself where your shrines and altars are. Have you hung all your diplomas and certificates above your desk, along with various other memorabilia commemorating your life accomplishments? Is there a special wall, shelf, or piece of furniture filled with photos of family or friends, or sports trophies? All such commemorative spaces serve as frames for focusing attention and energy on the things they celebrate or commemorate. These are the very spots that Charlie's teacher, John Collier Jr., taught his students to photograph and analyze. Through creating such sacred spaces in our homes, we demonstrate, honor, and more deeply align ourselves with what we consider to be some of the most important aspects of our families and ourselves.

In contrast, degree and award certificates hung in professional spaces (offices, restaurants) are generally placed there as symbols of the competence of the professional in question, not so much about the expression of values through ritual as about exhibition, showmanship, and proof of professionalism. Yet many professionals also choose to create small "altars" in their offices or cubicles displaying photos of family and friends as a way of interlinking their professional and private lives, and often also as a powerful reminder of why they are working so hard—for their loved ones.

For another take on altars, Buddhists in Thailand, Bali, and Burma believe that certain spirits can cause people travail if they are not given gifts and other ritual observances. Hence they will place a small temple or spirit house on the property, usually on a small pedestal, where the spirits can gather and be ritually "fed" with daily offerings, believing that this practice keeps the spirits from gathering in the human's restaurant, business, or home. Tourists visiting these countries often marvel at the beauty and intricacy of these spirit houses, while Buddhists will often pause to bow and pray to the spirits before entering the establishment. Robbie saw many such spirit houses during a recent visit to Bali, and was consistently impressed by the fresh flower petals that appeared on each one of them every morning. Few Westerners would go to such daily trouble to honor the deceased! The ritual motif of *propitiation* (acting to evoke divine favor) is widespread across the world's cultures where the forces of the spirit world are considered to be both dangerous and helpful, depending upon how they are approached and placated.

FORMALITY AND ORDER IN RITUAL: WHY THEY MATTER

In their book *Secular Ritual,* anthropologists Sally Moore and Barbara Myerhoff suggested that ritual's insistence on repetition and order evokes the perpetual processes of the cosmos, thereby metaphorically implying that the belief system being enacted has the same permanence and legitimacy as the cosmos itself. We would add to this argument that almost everyone on the planet experiences undertaking projects that require the plotting of activities and symbolic materials in a proper order. If we want to have shelter from the rains, we have to seek out building materials, then plan a shelter, build some kind of frame, and put a roof on it. Only then can our goal of being sheltered be experienced. Likewise, if we are farmers and wish to have food for next winter, we have to grow food during the spring and summer. In order to grow food, we have to clear the land, plow the field, plant the seeds, weed and weed again, and then harvest our produce. We then have to store the food so that rodents and other competitors cannot get at it. So many of the things we do during the day are intended to bring about some goal, some outcome, and those things have to be done in the right order to accomplish our goal.

The same is the case for rituals in human culture. If we believe that our rituals have real utility—and most people who carry out rituals do believe in their efficacy—then they are just as important to the outcomes of our lives as plowing, planting, or harvesting. If religious people wish to build a church or temple, the job is not finished merely by putting a cross or some other symbolic instrument on the roof. The building must be consecrated by way of appropriate rituals in order to link the building and the activities going on inside the building with the sacred.

The Trobriand Islanders: Fishing, Canoes, and Cranking Gears

For example, one of the first anthropologists to actually participate within the culture he was studying, Bronislaw Malinowski, lived among the Trobriand Islanders for over a year and published his work in a book called *The Sexual Life of Savages* (1925)—a brilliant title given that he was writing for a generally Victorian culture whose members could not officially deal with their own sexuality but who would be thrilled to read about "savages" who "obviously" had nothing to do with the august members of Victorian society—hence a book that provided free vicarious enjoyment and lots of book sales! Most of Malinowski's book was straightforward ethnography—how the Trobriand Islanders lived, what they ate, their customs, rituals, economic exchange systems, and so on. (Only one chapter—indeed a most lascivious one—dealt with their sexual customs.) Much of his book in fact dealt with the Trobrianders' rituals in relation to obtaining food. He noted that the lagoon they enjoyed was placid and full of fish—albeit small ones—and they often put their small canoes into that lagoon, as the fishing was easy—yet the yield always as small as the fish that lived there—enough to feed a family for a day or two.

Much greater rewards awaited in the deep ocean—huge fish that could feed a family for a week or more. Yet the dangers were significant—one large wave could collapse the small boat, and sharks were ever-present. So, how to gain the courage to fish in the deep, rewarding, yet fearful ocean? The Trobriand response was to create an altar on the beach containing symbolic artifacts, and then to chant the names of the gods in a particular sequence for an hour or so. This ritual action, at least in their minds, would ensure that the gods would respond by keeping them safe during their dangerous ventures. They could engage the gods with the ritual, thus (hopefully) binding them to respond. Likewise, when the Trobrianders built those large ocean-going dugout canoes we mentioned in the preceding chapter, knowing that sea voyages were very perilous (many such expeditions never returned), they performed an elaborate series of rituals during the construction of the canoes to make them impervious to calamity and protect those aboard. These ritual ingredients of construction were for them as utilitarian as the physical construction of the canoes, and each ritual had to occur in its proper sequence in order for it to protect the boat and its crew.

In other words, ritual technology has cosmological efficacy. These ritual technologies and performances served for the Trobrianders like cranking gears serve for contemporary machines—you set the little gear in motion with your careful ritual performance, and get the psychological and very comforting feeling that that little gear will set a larger process in motion— you do your part, then the gods will be obliged to do theirs.

Bolivian Tin Miners: "The Devil is in the details"

Another excellent example of using ritual for efficacious, instrumental purposes comes from the work of anthropologist June Nash (1979, 1992), who studied Bolivian tin miners with the profound question, "How do you gain the courage to go down so deep into hot and potentially explosive mines every single working day?" The answer she discovered was that the miners conceived of the mines as the "Devil's territory," so they worked hard to make the Devil their friend. They coded him as *Tio*, "Uncle," and left offerings of coca leaves, candy, gum, and cash to him on altars at the entrance of every mine shaft. In our terms, the miners acted to engage that little gear and give them the courage to go down into what they conceived as "Hell." You give a gift to the Devil, then the Devil is obligated to protect you.

But what happened when there eventually was a major mine explosion and dozens of their colleagues died? Did these miners then throw away their belief system, reinterpreting it as unreal and useless? No, of course not! The fault was theirs, for they obviously had failed to properly perform the rituals. People had failed to leave appropriate offerings (ritual symbols and technologies) at the altars, had failed to invoke and honor *Tio* sufficiently, so he was angry! The solution: hold a huge community feast, sacrifice a llama and cook its meat, build a huge altar on which to offer the llama meat and many other delectable foods so that the spirit of the devil could consume the spirits of the food. Then the community consumed the "leftovers" and held dances and prayer ceremonies in honor of *Tio*—and of course, the mine company having taken some care, it would be months or years before another such disaster, so of course the ritual would appear to have worked to accomplish its instrumental end.

Contemporary Obstetricians, Ritual, and Danger: The Power Is in the Rituals

We find another, very powerful use of ritual's cranking gears in the many ritualized procedures that contemporary obstetricians utilize to keep their fear of the natural birth process and its many unpredictabilities at bay. In previous chapters, we mentioned the ritual uses of the electronic fetal monitor—a powerful symbol that speaks with many voices, promising to provide full information on the strength of the laboring mother's contractions and the condition of the fetal heart rate, representing the vast corporation that created it and all of the technological know-how that went into making it, and giving women a sense of psychological and emotional trust in the information it provides. (Reviewer Henci Goer aptly suggests that the EFM is a "high-tech divination tool masquerading as a diagnostic evaluation.") In Chapter 3, we described the technocratic, humanistic, and holistic models of birth and health care, noting that the dominant, hegemonic technocratic model defines the body as a machine, the woman's body as an inherently defective machine (after all, this model was developed in already-patriarchal Western Europe during its industrialization phase), and birth as an inherently dysfunctional process that can go wrong at any point. Since its inception, as Robbie points out in *Birth as an American Rite of Passage* (2004), Western obstetrics has always been all about controlling the chaotic and therefore "dangerous" process of labor and birth.

From the moment a laboring woman enters a hospital to give birth, the staff begins the process of "damage control." As in all initiatory rites of passage, the woman is stripped of her individual identity—her own clothes are removed and she is dressed in a hospital gown and put into a hospital bed, symbolizing her "patient" status. An IV (intravenous line) is inserted—a symbolic representation of the umbilical cord—the woman is now dependent on the institution for her "lifeblood." If she is still in the early stage of labor, Pitocin will be administered through that IV to speed up her labor. (As we mentioned previously, the technocratic model places no value at all on patiently waiting for the mother's own natural hormones to kick in.) In many American hospitals (and indeed in most hospitals around the world), she will be deprived of food and drink—well, she is "hydrated" through the IV—yet hunger can make her weak and unable to face the medically-termed "trial of labor" that she is now enduring. The common use of Pitocin to hasten birth has been shown to interfere with normal physiologic labor and can play a detrimental role in the so-called "snowball effect" of medical intervention in the labor process. This snowball effect continues with our laboring mother asking for pain relief and receiving an epidural (in resource-poor countries, the mother will often have to endure the intense pain of the Pitocin-induced contractions with no pain relief at all). The epidural will usually take the pain away, yet if given too early (before five or six centimeters of dilation), it can slow labor, necessitating an increase in her Pitocin drip. Of course, she will now be hooked up to the electronic fetal monitor, because that's hospital protocol (reinforced by insurance company requirements). While mountains of scientific evidence show that women in labor should be up and moving around (movement assists fetal descent, the effectiveness of contractions, and cervical dilation), even if the woman knows that evidence, she will find herself in bed tethered to the monitor and the IV, with nothing to do (she's no longer in pain) but stare at the monitor and measure her own labor progress according to its vascillating lines and beeps. She will receive regular vaginal "checks" to make sure that her cervix is dilating appropriately (at the rate of 1 cm per hour). If it is, she will go on to give birth vaginally. If it is not, her Pitocin drip will be increased, the now back-to-back induced contractions will likely cause the baby to go into fetal distress, she will end up with a cesarean section (as 32% of American women currently do), and she will thank her obstetrician for saving her baby's life— usually never realizing that the "cascade of interventions" (what we call the "ritual train") that she experienced were *the cause* of the baby's distress.

In Chapter 3 of *Birth as an American Rite of Passage*, Robbie explains and analyzes this powerful ritual process in detail, likening it to damming up a river to keep it from flooding. Because none of these ritual obstetrical procedures have any scientific basis or actual medical efficacy in (what otherwise would likely have been) normal births, in her effort to understand why such practices have become so routine for so many decades, Robbie was forced to interpret them as rituals that enact our core cultural values on the supremacy of high technology and our profound cultural fear of untrammeled nature. She said:

> If we stop a moment now, to see in our mind's eye the visual and kinesthetic images that a laboring woman will be experiencing— herself in a bed, in a hospital gown, staring up at an IV pole, bag, and cord on one side, and a big, whirring machine on the other, and down at a steel bed and a huge belt encircling her waist—we can see that her entire visual field is conveying one overwhelming perceptual message about our culture's deepest beliefs and values:

technology is supreme, and you are utterly dependent upon it and the institutions that control and dispense it. (Davis-Floyd 2004:109)

(For full descriptions of the scientific evidence in favor of normal, physiologic birth, go to www.childbirthconnection.org).

The technocratically-trained obstetricians Robbie has interviewed over her 30 years of research on childbirth, midwifery, and obstetrics seemed to have learned little from their attendance at normal, unproblematic births. But they learned a lot from the fetal deaths and maternal hemorrhages they all experienced. These are extremely rare in developed societies, yet they carry such a powerful emotional charge that the obstetricians who experience them will do absolutely anything to avoid experiencing them again.[10] Like the Trobriand Islanders and the Bolivian tin miners we described above, contemporary obs depend on their rituals to engage those cranking gears to carry them through danger to safety. Not once did a technocratic ob interviewee of Robbie's ever say that perhaps the problem happened *because* of the interventions they performed. On the contrary, they consistently expressed the belief that if they had only performed more rituals—paid more attention to the EFM, given more Pitocin, done the cesarean sooner—the mother or baby would not have died. So great was their belief in the power of the rituals they routinely performed that *they always believed that intensifying their ritual performance would have saved them and their patients from danger.* (This belief is belied by the excellent outcomes achieved by the holistic obstetricians that Robbie and her colleague Nia Georges recently interviewed, who pay great attention to the scientific evidence in favor of facilitating and supporting the normal, physiologic, process of birth and eschew the technocratic model and the multiple interventions it demands. See Chapter 10.)

INVIOLABILITY AND INEVITABILITY: "THE RITUAL TRAIN"

The exaggerated precision and careful adherence to form and pattern that set ritual apart from more casual modes of social interaction work to establish an atmosphere that feels inviolate and an order that feels

---

10. See Davis-Floyd 1987, 1990, 1991, 2001, 2004. Most of these articles are freely available at www.davis-floyd.com.

inevitable. One would find it hard to imagine, for example, stopping a graduation ceremony, interrupting the Pledge of Allegiance, standing up in the middle of a church service to argue with the minister, or walking out of the hospital in mid-labor. Participants understand that the sequence of events is laid out and will proceed as planned; interruptions are generally neither permitted nor thinkable. As we have previously mentioned, this unstoppability of ritual has been likened to getting on a train—once it starts moving, you can't get off. Think of a graduation ceremony, a wedding, a Presidential inauguration. Once the graduates begin their procession, once the bridesmaids start walking down the aisle, once the orchestra begins to play, there is consensual agreement among all participants that things must proceed as planned and no individual would dream of trying to stop the ritual progression, except in the case of a dire emergency like an earthquake or a fire. How often have you sat all the way through a ceremony or performance (or a boring lecture) you desperately wanted to leave, yet you did not wish to break the ritual frame? And if you do dare to disrupt the ritual by leaving, you do so bending at the waist, as if to make yourself as small and invisible as possible. This body language, while completely useless in making you take up less space, at least communicates to others that you are sorry to be so disruptive, letting them know that you respect the ritual norms and rules even as you violate them by leaving.

A Wedding and a Cesarean Section: Riding the Ritual Train

Robbie's first experience of this sense of inevitability that ritual can generate occurred when she was 18 and her boyfriend proposed marriage. She was a senior in high school and he a senior in college. It all seemed so romantic at the time! She accepted. She knew she was perhaps too young to be making this commitment, so she set a wedding date a year into the future, thinking that during her first year of college, if she so desired, she could change her mind at any time. But she was completely unprepared for the ritualistic sequence of events that then began to unfold. Once the date was set, her mother and mother-in-law-to-be flew into action. They reserved the church and the minister, the country club for the rehearsal dinner and the hotel banquet room for the wedding reception, which was to be a seated formal dinner complete with an orchestra for dinner entertainment and dancing. Within months, the wedding invitations were ordered, the bridesmaids' dresses picked, and Robbie increasingly began to feel that she was indeed on a moving train and couldn't get off. By the time she started to realize that she was making a mistake, she found herself completely unable to stop the sequence of events that had been started. So she got married in spite of her doubts, and four years later, got divorced. From this experience, Robbie learned firsthand about the power of ritual, and that it takes tremendous strength of character to stop a ritual process once it has started—a strength she did not have at the age of 19.

Nineteen-year-old girls are not the only ones who find themselves unable to stop the ritual juggernaut. Even middle-aged and mature medical practitioners can find themselves highly susceptible to the sense of inevitability generated by ritual. Consider the following story told to Robbie by midwife Sandra Morningstar:

> A family practice physician in my home state, who herself had had a home birth, found herself faced with a pregnant patient whose baby was breech (bottom instead of head first). Since obstetrical protocols prescribe cesarean section for breech, surgery was scheduled for Elaine at 38 weeks. [Full term is 40 weeks; the physician did not want her patient to go into labor, so the operation was scheduled well in advance of her due date, but within what was then considered to be the safety zone.] On the morning of the surgery, the doctor found herself full of doubt about its appropriateness. Her intuition told her it should be stopped, but the patient was already being prepped—in other words, the ritual process was already in motion. After the epidural was administered and Elaine was on the operating table, the physician checked the baby again and found that it was no longer in the breech position—it had turned. Thus there was no reason to perform the Cesarean section. With the patient prepped and ready, surrounded by an expectant medical staff, the doctor found herself saying "Why don't we get on with this? We can have this baby out in fifteen minutes." Acquiescing, the patient signed the papers and the operation proceeded as scheduled. In spite of repeated ultrasounds, it turned out that the age of the baby had been severely overestimated: the newborn was only 32 weeks old—dangerously premature—and had to be flown out to the nearest neonatal intensive care unit (NICU). (Sandra Morningstar, personal correspondence, Oct. 12, 2002).

Such events are common in contemporary medicine. Once a ritualized sequence of events like an elaborate testing procedure or an operation has been started, people start behaving in stylized, choreographed, pre-sequenced ways and it becomes very difficult to stop the process, even when you know that you should.

BREAKING FRAME: PURPOSEFUL DISRUPTION OF RITUAL

This sense of inevitability that characterizes a ritual's progression is enhanced by the sense of inviolability generated by the ritual frame. At a friend's wedding, you may have been casually chatting with one of the bridesmaids outside the sanctuary before the ceremony began, but you wouldn't dream of trying to talk to her while she is walking down the aisle. As we previously noted, once established, there is a clear sense among the participants that *the ritual frame must not be broken*. Children generally learn this rule at their parents' knees—they have no sense of the existence of ritual frames until their parents instill such a sense in them by constant admonishments not to make noise or interrupt—i.e., not to "break the frame." The sense of inviolability that ritual can generate means that some of the most interesting and exciting behaviors humans can perform involve violating or "breaking" ritual frames. The stronger the frame, the greater the charge you get—and everyone else gets—when you break it. Many movies climax with the breaking of a ritual frame—the jilted suitor zooms into the church on a motorcycle and stops the wedding, the graduation ceremony is stopped just before the unworthy candidate is awarded his diploma, the darker side of the dastardly politician is found out just before he wins the election. And new religions are often started by religious reformers who deliberately break the ritual frames of the older one.

Consider Jesus, who generated a new religion in part by smashing the categories and ritual frames of the older religion, Judaism. According to the Christian Bible, Jesus overturned tables in the temple, violated the Jewish rule of not working on Saturday (the Sabbath), and commanded his disciples to drink his "blood" when any form of consumption of blood was expressly prohibited in Judaism. Perhaps he intuitively understood that when you break a ritual frame, you release the energy that it has been holding it in place and if you are quick, you can grab that energy and turn it to your own purposes, which Jesus and many other creators of new religions have proven most adept at doing.

For another instance, there once lived a Seneca Indian named Handsome Lake (1735-1815) who was an alcoholic and, as a consequence of his drinking, became very ill. During his illness he received a series of visions. Upon recovery, he began to preach lessons based upon those visions and eventually transformed the religion of the entire Six Nation Iroquois Confederacy, melding the traditional *Haudenosaunee* religious beliefs with a new and more up-to-date system meant to revitalize their culture in the context of colonization by Europeans (Wallace 1969). That religion, the Code of Handsome Lake, is practiced to this very day. It grew out of a previous religious system that had become moribund and incapable of handling the new conditions imposed by the European interlopers. The new system incorporated proper responses, moral perspectives and interpretations appropriate ("trued") to the new times.

THE LUDIC DIMENSION OF RITUAL: BREAKING THE FRAME TO ENHANCE THE ENERGY

In spite of their serious formality, rituals often intentionally incorporate an intensely ludic (playful) dimension. In some cultures, like the Mescalero Apache of New Mexico, during their most sacred ceremonies a clown mimics and mocks the singers as they perform the ritual acts in the required sequence, while the watching participants laugh uproariously at the clown's antics. The Mescalero do not feel that their laughter decreases the sacredness of the event, but rather *increases* it through the revitalizing energy that laughter brings to the culture's most deeply held beliefs. A parallel can be found in the rodeo clown (see also Handelman 1998: Chap. 10). Rodeo bull riders ritually display the manly heroic virtues that their subculture holds dear; the clowns whose task it is to divert the bulls while entertaining the audience mock those manly traits, even as they themselves exemplify them. When Don Lucio and his group held their annual ceremonies to bring the rain, there always came a much anticipated moment when the chanting and the praying ceased, bottles of orange soda pop mysteriously began to appear in people's hands, and those in the know started to smile. Suddenly, at a signal from Don Lucio, those holding the pop bottles began to shake them vigorously, then pop off the lids and spray the assembled multitude while everyone ran around laughing and screaming and trying either to escape the spray or to obtain a pop bottle themselves so they could spray others.

Robbie experienced the ludic/playful dimension of ritual for the first time during her very fun attendance at Camp Cimarroncita in New Mexico when she was 10 years old. With all campers gathered in the large Kiva (a big room designed for plays, dances, etc.), the counselors instructed the campers to get down on their knees and chant the following phrase: "OWA TA GOO SIAM." And then, chuckling to themselves under their hands, they waited to see when we would "get it." True believers all, at that young age, we dutifully chanted the mantra over and over, lifting and lowering our arms to the floor as instructed—thinking that we were actually performing some kind of sacred Native American ritual and duly excited. (Charlie had the same experience in Boy Scout camp.) We are not going to tell you what that chant was actually about—repeat the "mantra" for yourselves until you get it too, and then laugh your head off, as we did when we got that we had been totally "had"!

Often the ludic, or playful, dimension of ritual is reserved for the very end, when for example university graduates simultaneously throw their caps high into the air, screaming and cheering. Robbie had a very different experience when she attended the May 2000 graduation ceremonies for Yale University. The elegant old buildings surrounding the huge courtyard provided a beautiful frame for what Robbie expected to be a serious and austere ceremony. The long procession of black-robed-and-capped undergraduates and the multi-colored robes and capes of the faculty did nothing to alter this expectation. But then the graduate students began to enter the courtyard. The Divinity students all had gold tinsel halos tacked to their black caps. The Forestry students had long green ferns growing out of their caps and trailing down to the ground. Little plastic balloon globes bobbed above the caps of the Earth Science students. Nor was the students' employment of the ludic dimension mitigated by the commencement of the ceremony. Throughout the proceedings, even during the formal speeches, huge inflatable balls were periodically tossed about, balloons were batted from row to row, and occasionally various graduates would rise and shoot off cans of a ribbon-like substance that arced over the group, forming temporary and very colorful rainbows in the air.

Intrigued, Robbie asked some Yale faculty members why they tolerated this behavior, and was told that after years of intense work, the students who completed that work were fully entitled to play! And of course, the students' play had high entertainment value, bringing life and celebration to what might otherwise have been a dry and dull ceremony. In other words, the Yale faculty and student body shared a belief in the value of play and celebration, and mutually delighted in its enactment during their graduation ceremony. And the audience benefited as well, as the energy thus generated was tremendous, and everyone left "on a high," as one student quite aptly expressed it.

The linking of play with learning is hardly fortuitous—all higher animals play during their early life and then later on with their offspring. Play has distinct neurocognitive functions (Blanchard 1986). Bouts of play allow developing animals to vary and practice their behaviors freely without serious consequences, thus giving them valuable experience and learning, which then may be used in more important situations. In other words, play and fun form essential ingredients in the power of ritual. They lighten up the seriousness, poke fun, evoke laughter, and release tension and stress, all by generating the production of endorphins in our brains. Remember, *ritual is very much about affecting and effecting emotions.* When you experience fun and joy during an otherwise serious ritual, your emotions, and thus your perceptions and beliefs, will be all the more engaged, and you will be all the more open to internalizing the messages of the rituals you are experiencing—a good thing when you actually want to internalize those messages, and not so great when you don't.

FRAMING AND FLOW

We have seen that ritual behaviors often encompass decisive acts; when they are effective (when they work), they can help the individual enter a state of consciousness that psychologist Mihaly Csikszentmihalyi (1975) has called *flow*. The flow state is one in which there is no inhibition, repression, fear or hesitation. Flow is the experience of fully "letting go" into the action, which in turn results in creativity and happiness. According to renowned anthropologist Victor Turner (1979:154):

> Flow is the holistic sensation present when we act with total involvement, a state in which action follows action according to an internal logic, with no conscious intervention on our part. Flow is experienced in play and sport, in artistic performance and religious ritual. There is no dualism in flow....Flow is made possible by a centering of attention on a limited stimulus field, by means of

bracketing, framing, and often a set of rules. There is a loss of ego, the self becomes irrelevant...Flow is an inner state so enjoyable that people sometimes forsake a comfortable life for its sake.

Flow occurs when the central nervous system is totally involved in an act or course of action. There is no interference by alternative systems in the body. Metabolic, motor, emotional and cognitive-imaging systems are all entrained (synchronized) in a single, unitary and unfolding activity.

The role of ritual in generating flow experience is pivotal. If it is a social ritual, flow may arise when the central nervous systems of participants fully entrain with each other and with the movement of the ritual—in other words, when they enter a mutually shared ASC (altered state of consciousness). Time seems to slow down, all participants act as one (think of a rock concert, a mosh, a spiral dance, the entire congregation of a Baptist church praying with arms uplifted, the free flow of play in children's ritualized games, or even the altered state you enter when playing a video game and become so engrossed that you feel part of that virtual reality and win, time after time). All that is required aside from the ritual action itself is intense and single-minded attention. When attention (please note: attention = energy—*when you pay attention to something, you focus your energy on it*) is powerful enough, all impediments to flow disappear. The basketball player or the long-distance runner—or any athlete—may also experience this flow, as do birthing women who are not interfered with during labor and thus can fully immerse themselves in the physiologically-induced flow-state of normal labor and birth.

Artists often enter a state of flow while writing, painting, dancing, singing, or sculpting; their mind-states are inextricably associated with "setting loose" the creative muse. Many successful writers have a series of ritual acts they go through before they ever write anything. Poet Gertrude Stein used to sit in her automobile for inspiration and scribble her poems on scraps of paper. Throughout her working life, world-famous anthropologist and childbirth educator Sheila Kitzinger (1929-2015) would arise at 6 am, have her morning tea by her bedside, then sit in her huge four-poster bed writing on a yellow pad for two hours, by hand—this ritual process worked for her because by the time she actually got out of bed, she had that satisfied feeling of having spent two full hours in a process of creativity, no matter what the rest of the day might bring. (Only later would she or her secretary transcribe what she wrote into her computer.) Somehow for Sheila, the act of creativity required the sensory feel of pen and paper.

In dramatic contrast, Robbie, a terrible penswoman, channels her words through her fingers' connection with the computer keys—it feels like her brain is connected to her computer through her fingers. A total night person, Robbie ritualizes her days at home by getting up around noon, cooking herself breakfast and reading mail and email, then a long walk with her dogs on the trails around a creek near her house—she draws energy from the Austin sunshine and the beauty of the trails and the creek, especially the waterfalls. She settles down to work on her books or articles in the evenings into the wee hours of the morning. When Robbie is confronted with references to find, footnotes to attend to, flow does not happen for her. Yet when she is free just to write, to immerse herself in that creative process, she does, mercifully, enter a state of flow in which time does indeed seem to stop and the words simply come. Asleep around 3 am, she dreams about the chapters that are up for working on, and returns to them with renewed energy the next night, when the world closes down around her again and she is free to focus within what she experiences as the sacred ritual frame of her small-but-beautiful office.

Because flow is the natural outcome of concentration, meditators of all religious persuasions experience from time to time a state of intense bliss or ecstasy that adds the sense of *numinosity* to religious symbolism involved in the practice. Ecstatic bliss is transportive to other realms of being, and is often associated with altered states of consciousness, as well as more permanent alterations in personality and self-understanding. Hence, this kind of experience is frequently one of the goals of religious (and other types of) ritual—to transport the mind of the practitioner from one state to another through flow. This transportive effect is fundamental to religious initiations, as well as to the application of many traditional healing rituals. There is considerable evidence that ritual evocation of certain flow experiences can transform the balance of autonomic functions and other factors and literally transform, even heal, ritual practitioners and participants.

RITUAL ORDER: ENHANCING COURAGE AND CONFIDENCE

The courage- and confidence-enhancing function of ritual is as pervasive in the contemporary world as it always was in the past. It is especially obvious in sports, as when the pitcher turns his cap sideways and eats pancakes before every game, because the first time he did that, he pitched a no-hitter, and doing it again gives him the feeling that he has started those gears in motion and they will carry him safely through the pitfalls of the game.

The following story demonstrates the importance of *awareness* in the deployment of ritual. Perhaps some of you remember when American figure skater Debi Thomas was positioned to win an Olympic gold medal in 1988. She was in first place, and all she had left to do was the last, long figure-skating performance. Every time she had gone onto the ice, the TV cameras had shown her skating over to her coach before her performance. He would give her a quick pep talk, she would hold out her hands, he would slap her ten, and she would skate off and do a terrific job. This last time, she skated over to her coach, he gave her a quick pep talk, and she held out her hands for him to slap her ten, but he missed and their fingers glanced off of each other—their hands did not connect. In other words, the ritual sequence was not completed, the small gear was not fully cranked. She skated off, fell twice, and won a bronze medal instead of the expected gold. The moral of this story: *if you are going to use ritual to enhance your courage and increase your chances of success, it is wise to be conscious about your use of ritual and to be sure that you complete the process fully and properly, so that small gear will engage the larger cosmic (or psychological) gear and your desired outcome will result.*

Watching the 2012 London Olympics, Robbie was fascinated to see another very clear example of the intentional use of ritual to enhance performance in the pre-performance rituals enacted by gymnast Daniel Leyva and his stepfather/coach Yin Alvarez. In the seconds before the beginning of each set, Alvarez would tap Daniel on the head, pull swiftly up on his ears, and whisper to him, "Trust your training!" The rituals worked—the gears got engaged, and Leyva won his expected bronze medal in the individual all-arounds.

Obviously, these ritual "gears" we are talking about are metaphorical. The courage-enhancing function of ritual is deeply psychological. Whether or not there are gods or devils or spirits that can bring one safely through danger in return for ritual chants and offerings, for sure humans have brains; performing rituals in carefully sequenced ways to bring about desired outcomes—often neurophysiologically complex outcomes (Fauconnier, and Turner 2002)—will affect the output and condition of those brains. Moreover, rituals may incorporate and bracket decisive acts in such a way that the ritualized behaviors before the decisive act (throwing the ball, skating a program, etc.) influence the act before it is even attempted. Basketball fans may be aware that free-throw masters often prepare to shoot the ball by various, apparently inessential ritual acts before the throw. Experiments carried out by sports anthropologists have shown that interfering with the ritual context of free-throwing will decrease accuracy and confidence in players (Southard and Miracle 1993). The reason for this decrease is that the brain does not behaviorally delimit where ritual behavior stops and decisive action begins. Rather, there is an entire sequence of actions in which the decisive act (actually throwing the ball at the hoop) may be embedded among other plotted activities that are crucial to the success of the decisive act. Stripped of the sequence of plotted acts, the efficacy of the decisive act is reduced or even eliminated. Continued practice of the ritually embedded decisive acts results in a habituation of neural circuits and motor sequences that facilitates carrying out the decisive act without the need for planning or thought. The downside is that changing or correcting the sequence of the ritual is difficult. For instance, it is often far harder for a golf instructor to improve an experienced golfer's swing than to teach a beginner to swing correctly in the first place.

This confidence-enhancing role played by ritual is even evident in much subtler form in cultural greeting rituals ("Hello, how are you?" "Good, thanks. You?"). Although such standardized performances may appear trite or insincere to the analytical intellect, they nevertheless perform an important service. The rhythmicity of greeting rituals facilitates rapid entrainment of linguistic and bodily rhythms that is accompanied by a sense of comfort and security—all of which happens before an actual conversation takes place, thus facilitating the actual exchange of information.

For example, when a stranger stops you on the street, you may react with fear. But if he is courteous and polite—in other words, if he engages you in the performance of greeting rituals that you recognize as known and familiar—your fear may subside. Through his skillful use of these rituals, he has demonstrated that he shares the same cultural universe as you. This apparent sharing metaphorically suggests that he abides by the same cultural rules and is therefore safe to interact with. You will then tend to relax, and have friendly open feelings toward him (for better or worse, for correct ritual performance does not guarantee honesty, as ritual can easily be manipulated for sinister ends). In this capacity, ritual has for eons served humans well by "greasing the wheels" of their social interaction. Ritual is the symbolic form through which trust between strangers can quickly be established, so that information can be exchanged, the friendship initiated, the business deal closed.

WHEN RITUALS FAIL

Well, as we have seen, what happens when a mining tunnel collapses in spite of multiple offerings to the devil, or when the obstetrician follows ritual procedure, but the baby dies anyway—in other words, what happens when cranking the little gear fails to engage the larger one and produce the desired outcome—is *not* that the participants realize that it was all nonsense, throw out their belief system, and stop performing the rituals that enact it.

One of the most powerful aspects of the rituals that people design is their flexibility. It is almost always possible to find a reason why the ritual failed, and to assure yourself that if you only perform it right the next time, it is bound to work (see Hüsken 2007). You didn't make the altar right, you skipped a verse or two of the chant, you didn't leave enough coca leaves for the devil—or if *you* did, then it wasn't enough because *other people* didn't, and so the devil is very angry and decides to punish the people for their transgressions. So now, clearly (within the belief system—the matrix underlying the ritual), restitution must be made so that balance and order can be restored. Logic would dictate that if the devil is angry, it must be because he is hungry because people haven't been feeding him enough—not enough coca leaves, not enough tobacco, etc. So, as we mentioned previously, in response to a major mining disaster, the Bolivian tin miners Nash wrote about gather the whole town together and sacrifice a llama to the devil. They take the animal to the bottom of the mine shaft near the area of collapse, kill it, and offer its spiritual food essence to the hungry devil, then hold a big feast and eat the physical remains. Now the devil's stomach is full, he is happy, and he will surely protect those who have realized their transgressions and are now once again giving him his due.

That's the way it almost always is with ritual—if it doesn't work, you don't assume that the belief system underlying it is faulty—rather *you assume that you or others haven't been doing the rituals right*—something was out of order, or not done properly—and thus you *intensify ritual performance* in an attempt to set things right. If an obstetrician experiences a fetal or maternal death, he never assumes that it might be because he performed too many ritualistic interventions into the birth process—instead he always assumes that if he had gone immediately to the very most powerful ritual—a cesarean section—the outcome would have been good (Davis-Floyd 1987, 1992). One such ob/gyn of whom we have heard had a patient whose first baby had died of severe congenital anomalies. He persuaded her to plan a cesarean for her next birth so that he could ensure her a healthy baby! Such is the nature of ritual—we almost always assume that it works, and that if it doesn't, it's not because our belief system from which our rituals stem is wrong, it's that we simply didn't pay enough attention to the proper performance of the rituals (Hüsken 2007).

Our readers will know about Jim Jones and the cult he founded and its tragic outcome. Another, less tragic, yet also extreme example of too much faith in ritual comes from a 1950s sect Robbie once heard about, whose members were absolutely convinced that they were in touch with an alien spacecraft whose crew would transport them aboard if they met certain conditions, including the removal of all metal of all kinds from their clothing and teeth. So these cult members removed their metal fillings and cut off their metal zippers, and spent countless hours in backyards filled with believers ready for transport. Incident after incident, year after year, the reason given by the cult leaders for the failure of the ritual was that someone—maybe you!—had not fulfilled the conditions and thus had ruined the experience for the entire group. Most of the group members, true believers all, hung in there for over five years before finally concluding that the whole thing had been a massive hoax perpetrated by people who only wanted the life savings they had committed to the enterprise of "space salvation." These types of charismatic cults are quite common (see Lalich 2004). Another such group, the so-called Heaven's Gate cult, made news in 1997 when the group's founder (like Jim Jones) talked his followers into committing mass suicide. The members apparently believed that they were actually aliens who were waiting for a spaceship that would accompany the comet Hale-Bopp. By killing themselves, they would set their souls free to be transported to the spaceship. They performed all sorts of ritual preparations, including buying matching shoes and dwelling in the dark to simulate the conditions they expected after transportation.

When ritual fails, the most threatening outcome is not the potential results of the failure of that particular ritual, but rather the potential loss of the entire belief system—the entire cycle of meaning—through which a group of people organizes its lifeworld. It's one thing for some individuals to die in a fishing accident or a tunnel collapse, and another for an entire social group to come smack up against the question of whether their cosmology is true or false, whether their whole cycle of meaning is valid or not. When individuals lose their worldviews, they often plunge into doubt, depression, and despair. As the world has witnessed over and over again during the last four centuries, cultures die when their belief systems crumble. When ritual fails (see Hüsken 2007 for examples), there are only four possible explanations: (1) the belief system on which the ritual is based is wrong, and the rituals that enact that belief system are therefore meaningless and invalid; (2) the ritual participants didn't perform the rituals correctly; (3) it was the wrong ritual for that particular situation; (4) the lifeworld is so out of whack that one ritual isn't enough—the ritual process must be *escalated* so that the larger balance can be restored. The consequences of accepting the first alternative are dire and must be avoided as long as possible, because accepting them will mean the dissolution of the group. So in most cases and in most places, for as long as they can, people turn to the other three. They repeat the ritual performances, only more carefully this time, or they try other rituals, or they escalate to a much larger ritual, like sacrificing a llama and holding a community-wide feast (or for many obs worldwide, just do cesareans for almost every mother—cesarean rates around the world have now risen to epidemic proportions).

It is perhaps useful to run through the cycle of meaning model we presented earlier for purposes of the present context. A worldview generates lore and rituals that are intended to bring about expected outcomes—distinct experiences—that are then interpreted in such a way that they instantiate and confirm the worldview, and reinforce the meanings contained in the ritual. But in the cases we describe above, and many others, the expected outcome does not happen—something bad happens instead. The survival of the cycle of meaning depends upon how the people interpret the unexpected outcome, and as we say, most societies have built-in explanations for why the ritual did not cause the desired effect.

An evangelical talk-show host named Harold Camping prophesied that the Rapture and Judgment Day would happen on May 21, 2011 and that the world would end on October 21, 2011. He based his predictions—not the first he had made in his career—on numerology (the spiritual meaning of numbers). The Rapture, according to some Christian groups, is the point during the End Days at which God will take his Chosen People into Heaven, leaving all the rest to experience the horrors of "the great catastrophe." Well, as the existence of this book and your reading of it will attest, the world did not end in 2011. So you might reasonably think that the evangelist's prophecy would be debunked and his followers scattered to the winds. Not so, for the failures of his predictions were explained away by his having gotten the math wrong, and many people continue to follow his guidance to this day.

Camping's mistake is hardly a unique example of prophecy gone awry. Social psychologist Leon Festinger and his colleagues studied such a phenomenon back in the 1950s. This time it was a clairvoyant named Marian Keech (aka Dorothy Martin) who received messages by way of "automatic writing" from an entity living on the planet Clarion, who predicted that the end of the world would be caused by a great deluge on December 21, 1954. Keech and her followers were instructed to await a visitor who would guide them to a spaceship that would save them from the cataclysm. Mrs. Keech's followers joined her at her home on the night of December 20th and waited until it was obvious that the visitor would not appear, at which point Mrs. Keech received a new message from her correspondent on Clarion telling her that the earth's destruction had been cancelled because of the good work she and her followers had done (Festinger, Riecken, and Schachter 1956).

This kind of ritual cult is not limited to Western societies. Indeed, there is a common phenomenon called a *millenarian movement* that has popped up all over the planet at one time or another. *Millenarianism*, loosely defined, is the belief that if the group carries out certain changes and actions, the society will transform itself into a new age. Technically speaking, and as the name implies, some of those groups think in terms of thousand-year cycles. But anthropologists are interested in studying any religious group that predicts fundamental changes in the society and the world if certain practices, usually ritualized ones, are carried out.

For example, a Paiute Indian prophet named Jack Wilson (or *Wovoka*) created the Ghost Dance religion in 1889, a movement that spread throughout many western North American native cultures. Wilson's original teachings were about how a new age of love and harmony would arise in which whites and Indians (they did not call themselves Native Americans at that time) would cease to do battle and live together in peace. At the heart of the Ghost Dance teaching was the circle dance, an ancient ritual that incorporated many of the drivers we have discussed earlier. There are groups that continue to follow Wilson's teachings to this very day. One of the important spinoffs of the teaching, however, was the transformation of the Ghost Dance taken up by the Lakota Sioux Indians, who interpreted the teachings as bolstering their resistance to the white invaders. They developed the concept of the Ghost Shirt—a symbolic garment thought to be bullet-proof. Many of the Indians who fought and died at the Wounded Knee massacre in 1890 were wearing those shirts. The failure of the shirts to protect those warriors was taken by most as a sign that the teaching was false, and they ceased to believe in it. Their cessation of belief is one more clear indication that sometimes, when rituals fail to work in a very dramatic, perhaps deadly way, people are capable of ceasing to believe in them and the belief system that underlies them.

SUMMARY: RITUAL ORDER AND RITUAL FAILURE

Framing, order, and a sense of formality are primary characteristics of ritual that are essential to its efficacy. Ritual spaces and places are generally culturally acknowledged as such, and thus tend to be respected, even by passers-by. Most often, architecture designed to create ritual spaces generates this cultural acknowledgement. Yet invisible lines of energy that are nonetheless felt both by participants and observers can define these spaces and places even when architecture does not do it for them. Shrines and altars created in individual homes can demarcate ritual spaces that constitute the focusing of energy on family religion, beliefs and values, cherished memories, and individual and family accomplishments. Consider the millions of people who have visited the Vietnam Veterans Memorial Wall in Washington, D.C. in order to find their relative's name and pay homage to their sacrifice for their country. The wall is a shrine, and its visitors are in a very real sense worshippers at that shrine and supplicants for the souls of their deceased loved ones.

The Trobriand sea fisherman who makes elaborate offerings and incantations in precise order before embarking into perilous waters believes that, if he does his part correctly, so must the gods of the sea do their part to bring him safely home. For the same reasons, the batter turns his cap backwards and clutches his rabbit's foot before he steps up to the plate. The Bolivian tin miner, before descending into the hot and dangerous mines that he thinks of as the devil's territory, makes an offering of candy or tobacco to the devil so that the devil will be obligated to reciprocate by protecting him. Each and every one of these ritual performances invokes a sense of inviolability—the ritual must proceed according to prescribed formulas. Laughter and play form important components of this ritual process, generating, via endorphins, a feeling of wellbeing in the ritual participants.

When ritual fails, its human enactors will tend to intensify ritual performance in an attempt to set the world right via more focused attention on the proper (ordered and formal) performance of ritual. (Please keep in mind that ritual often involves very little rationality. It is much more about rationalization than rationality, more "primitive"/embedded in the core brain than rational adaptation.) As we have shown, when ritual continues to fail, the adaptability and flexibility of the human mind will incorporate this failure, leading eventually to abandonment of the ritual complex and the worldview underlying it. The resulting cultural chaos resulting from the dissolution of a culture's (or an individual's) worldview will be addressed in following chapters.

Suggested Reading:

Atran, Scott (2002) *In Gods We Trust: The Evolutionary Landscape of Religion.* Oxford University Press.

Handelman, Don and David Shulman (1997) *God Inside Out: Śiva's Game of Dice.* Oxford University Press.

Hicks, David (Ed.) (2010) *Ritual and Belief: Readings in the Anthropology of Religion.* New York: Rowman & Littlefield.

Chapter 8

RITUAL AS PERFORMANCE: GENERATING EMOTION, BELIEF, AND TRANSFORMATION

Ritual, Belief, and Emotion. The Excitation and Relaxation Nervous Systems: Ritual, Flow, and Ecstasy. Ritual Mechanisms for Engendering Emotion and Belief. Rites of Passage and Religious Conversions: Transformation Through Ritual. Ritual and Cognitive Transformation. Summary: Ritual, Emotion, and Belief.

RITUAL, BELIEF, AND EMOTION

Many cosmopolitan individuals would like to think that they choose their basic beliefs with intellectual caution and precision. But in most cases the opposite is true. *Belief follows emotion—* we tend to believe in our heads what we feel in our hearts (Atran 2002). In addition, people are far more likely to remember events, and to absorb lessons from those events, if they carry an emotional charge (Reisberg and Hertel 2004). Ritual, especially formal ritual, can generate that charge—it can focus the emotions on the symbolic messages it presents. Of course, individuals can go through the motions of a ritual—sit through a funeral, a Mass, a patriotic rally—and be unmoved, may not believe in the belief system behind the ritual, indeed may even be bored to death. But we are speaking here of how rituals work *when* they work.

The focusing process in ritual is enhanced by the rhythmic repetition of the ritual's messages, which will often intensify toward a climax. If the ritual is successful, belief will be generated or enhanced through the symbolic "mapping on" process described in Chapter 5, in which ritual and its drivers can penetrate the consciousness of the participants and heavily influence or determine their perceptions and experience. And because of the emotions associated with belief, neither the experience nor the belief are likely to be forgotten. This design has proven to be remarkably adaptive throughout our evolution. When something new suddenly pops up in our consciousness, we commonly become more alert, and perhaps a bit wary. If the new perception is identified as something either attractive (food, friend, etc.) or aversive (a threat, danger, etc.), the perception rapidly links to a feeling that has been previously associated with the perception in our memory. For example, the second Charlie even hears about someone standing on a precipice, his body reacts negatively with fear, as though he were standing above the abyss himself (he is a tad acrophobic, meaning that he experiences discomfort with heights).

Ritual Healing from Soul Loss through an Indigenous Shamanic Ceremony: Juan the Chamula

As a youth, Juan had left his family and his Tzotzil culture in Highland Chiapas (Southern Mexico) to work in the coffee plantations in the another part of the south of Mexico for many years. Upon his return, he felt alienated from his old associations, and eventually fell ill. His community was concerned, so they brought the local shaman to see him. The shaman diagnosed Juan as suffering from "soul loss." In his biography *Juan the Chamula,* anthropologist Ricardo Pozas described the healing ceremony that the shaman performed to cure Juan of soul loss—a long and elaborate series of rituals involving careful placement of ritual artifacts, lots of chanting, prayer, and storytelling, and the sacrifice of a rooster. At the climax of the ceremony, the shaman twisted the neck of the rooster, killing it, and Juan exclaimed, "Suddenly, I felt free!" This experience of ritual healing constituted for Juan an important step in his reintegration into the cultural system he had left years ago, and to which he was now returning.

As this example demonstrates, healers can use ritual's ability to generate belief to map their interpretation of the illness into the mind-body of the patient. When these fuse, healing can be achieved, *as the body responds to what the mind now believes.* Another way to describe this phenomenon is as *healing through story-telling*—or what psychologists might call "visualization." The healer tells a story about the illness (in Juan's case, the story was that the warlocks stole his soul to eat it and the shaman sought to trade the soul of the rooster for the return of Juan's soul) and dramatically enacts that story through ritual. The success of the ritual depended on Juan's emotional and psychological identification with the story that the ritual was enacting. Because this resonance did happen in Juan's psyche, he came to experience his illness through the story, or in terms of the story; thus, when the story reached its climax, Juan's body healed as his soul returned. "Soul loss" is still today regarded as a real phenomenon by many contemporary New Age and other types of healers, and the "retrieval of the lost soul" via ritual and visualization is a common psychotherapeutic technique.

Ritual Healing from "Soul Loss" through Contemporary Psychotherapy: Robbie the Anthropologist

Her daughter's death took from Robbie more than her daughter—in her experience, it took away what she thought of as "a huge part of my being." She writes:

> The knock on the door that every parent dreads came for me on Sept. 13, 2000 at 12:30 am. In great irritation—who would be calling at that hour?—I answered the door to find two people—a woman and a man—in gray T-shirts bearing the insignia "Travis County Sheriff's Department." I let them into my dining room, and there, as I stood on a square foot of gray carpet, they informed me that, "There was a car accident in Virginia, and Peyton didn't make it."
>
> In a state of shock so intense that I could barely see or breathe, I raced to the phone to call Peyton's father Robert, and then to Jason's bedroom to awaken my sleeping 16-year-old and call him to the table so he could hear the news for himself. Robert and his new wife Debbie arrived in what felt like seconds, the house filled with people, and it was all about action. The hospital in Roanoke, where her body lay, called: her body had been so decimated by its exit through the smashed windshield of the Mitsubishi jeep she called "Big Blue" and by its 50-foot skid down the highway that the only organs left to donate were her eyes. Would we be willing to donate her eyes?
>
> In a moment of lucidity, Robert and I both realized that any human being who could see the world through Peyton's

eyes would be blessed, so, still in total shock, we agreed. By 5:00 am I was packing to get on a 6:30 am flight to go be with her body in the Roanoke hospital; by 9 am I was there. And then there was so very much more to do—to spend hours hugging her dead body and begging her to breathe, to put the phone to her ear so that Robert and Jason, who stayed behind to arrange her Memorial Service, could say their last goodbyes, to pull off all the electrodes and wires in a frenzy of cleansing and to bathe her dead body, inch by inch—a very conscious ritual of purification.

Then, that next horrible day, driving to the scene of the accident to try to understand how the hell, on a perfectly clear blue day, her 19-year-old friend Kara, who was driving at the time, could possibly have steered off the highway enough to cause her to violently swing the wheel, causing Big Blue to flip 4 times and sending Peyton's body through the windshield and 50 feet down the highway before the truckers who saw it happen could call it in.

Then nothing but action in the ensuing days—gathering P's luggage from the wrecked car, coming home to plan an amazing Memorial Service—the most awesome ritual celebration of her life that we could possibly have planned, and then another one for her New York friends two weeks later—well they planned that one so of course we had to show up—the logistics of getting 12 people to NYC, finding us a place to stay, getting to the Service—well the action went on and on, for a very long time. And those rituals *did* work, and they did carry us through for the next weeks and months. Indeed, they carried me for a year, during which I finally got back to work.

Yet all the while, a part of me stayed frozen on that square foot of carpet where I received the news of Peyton's death. A HUGE part of me simply stayed frozen there. And that "me" that froze—well, that was the "me" that I had worked for many years to become—a happy, fulfilled, and self-actualized person who jumped out of bed in the morning to teach her classes or do her research or write her books and articles (see www.davis-floyd.com). Years of therapy had finally enabled me to heal all my childhood and adolescent issues. I was happy, in a great relationship, and full of enthusiasm every day for whatever that day might bring.

That was the "me" who got frozen in place on that square foot of carpet, and the "me" who carried on, doing everything that needed to be done, was a pale and broken reflection of the *me* who used to be. What I called "being frozen," shamans would call "soul loss"—and I agree.

Fast forward nine years to 2009—the "me" who had remained present to life had gone on to write lots of widely-read articles and books, to travel the world giving talks, to become a "culture hero" and a "rock star/icon" in the childbirth and midwifery movements—yet I was not whole. I had suffered two massive nervous breakdowns in the years after P's death, had recovered more or less (with the help of Lexapro, Klonopin, and psychotherapy for my grief), yet I still felt shattered and broken into pieces—a mere shell of my former self, glued back together in a very tenuous way.

Then came the ultimate melt-down. My arthritic left knee became swollen to the size of a large cantaloupe. I could barely walk. So, knee surgery with a titanium and plastic knee replacement—I was totally unprepared for the ensuing pain—and that pain, in horrible addition to my psychological grief and agony over Peyton's death and many other really, really bad things that happened to me in the years after she died—well I simply cratered into a totally suicidal depression. And on one terrible night, when I couldn't bear the physical and psychological pain any more, I took 11 strong sleeping pills (all I had, fortunately) and wrote myself a note: "I just want to sleep for a very long time and wake up in rehab at Sierra Tucson." And when I did wake up, late the next night, I saw the note, got it that I needed help, called Sierra Tuscon, and got on the next plane in a very simple and straightforward effort to survive.

Help! I'm trapped in this horrible place (well really it was a wonderful place, yet it's horrible to feel trapped *anywhere*)—yet every time I want to check myself out and go home, the question they ritually tell me to ask myself is, "Do you really want to go back to the way it was?" And of course, I did not. It was a place too terrible to go back to. So I fully committed myself to all the healing therapies they had to offer. I *am* an anthropologist, so I interviewed everyone who was leaving (people were always coming and going)—"Did you get what you came for?"—and every single answer was "YES!"

For the first two weeks, I was sure that I would be the only person to leave without getting what I came for, which was to heal from Peyton's death and to find again the happiness I had lost when she died—it seemed an impossible goal!

And then came the turning point—a 3-hour session with an EMDR (oh, just Google it!) therapist named Maureen. She put buzzers in my hands and had me watch a blue light that went from one side of my vision to the other—when the light went to the right, the right-hand buzzer went off, and vice-versa. Once my brain hemispheres were thereby coordinated, I easily entered an ASC. And Maureen put me right back on that square foot of carpet where I was standing when I received the news of Peyton's death. And that was when I fully understood "shock."

In that instant of hearing the news, I had been shocked out of my mind and also out of my body. The fully shocked part of me—the formerly self-fulfilled, self-actualized part of me—simply froze on that square foot of carpet, while the rest of me went on to do what had to be done. Nine years later, in the safety of the therapist's room, I am standing in front of her/me 9 years earlier on that terrible night—I could see me in that moment, frozen in space and time—I could even see the gray dress I had been wearing with the embroidery down the front—and I could see the look on her/my face. I narrated my experience to Maureen. And Maureen said, "Can you move toward her, can you embrace her?"

I could, so I did. I stood with her on that square foot of gray carpet, I put my arms around her/me—she was sooooo cold! I hugged her hard and tried to warm her up. Eventually, she opened her eyes and looked at me, and she said, "Oh, I get it, you are *me* from the future! Does it get any better?" Regretfully, I said, "No, it only gets worse from here. I've lived what you haven't, and I have to tell you the truth—it only gets worse." Then she said, "OK, I don't want to live through what you have—could we just please lie down and die, right here, right now?"

Knowing that this was only a highly ritualized and very safely framed visualization, I agreed. We both laid down together on the floor, arms around each other—at least I had gotten her to move off that square foot of carpet!

We stayed like that for a while until I felt her warming up in my arms. And then I said, "You know, *we can't stay here*. We are *not* going to die right now. And I have gone on, while you have stayed here frozen in place. And the *you* that froze was the best of *me*, the best that I was before P died. I NEED YOU. Please, please, let's get up off this floor and go back to my reality, together. I need you to wake up, be alive and alove, and come back inside of me. I lost so much when I lost you—please come home to me."

Well, really she had no other option, which she got. Slowly, slowly, we got up off the floor together, arms still wrapped around. And then we were standing, and then I started to freak, and I said to Maureen, "OK I've got her in my arms, we are standing, but still on that carpet—how do we get out of here?"

In a flash of insight, Maureen said, "Do you see any colors around you?" And I looked at the air around us, which had also frozen when she/me froze—and in fact, there *were* colors, amazing and beautiful colors, swirling all around in the molecules of air which were finally unfreezing. I verbalized that to Maureen, and she said "OK, can you use those colors to get yourselves back here?"

And then suddenly Peyton's voice said, "Look up!" And I did, and there was my precious P-Pey, grinning from ear to ear. She squatted down and extended her right hand—colors flew from that hand, and those swirling colors turned into a rainbow that swirled and curled around us, and lifted us, still embracing—and then we were 4 feet off the carpet, and then 12 or so, and then, higher and higher till we were flying through the air until, BAM!, we landed together on Maureen's soft sofa, and there she/me was, on top of me in a full-body embrace. And Maureen nodded in satisfaction.

And then I said to her/me, "Come inside me, be part of me again—I've missed you and I've needed you so much!" She nodded, then started to melt into me. As her left leg melted into my left leg, she stopped in surprise and said, *"What the hell is that?"* And I said, "Oh, I failed to mention, we had a total knee replacement—what you are feeling is titanium and plastic—our new knee. It's working well—can you be OK with that?" And she said, "Whatever!" and continued to melt into me.

Left side complete, she started melting into my right side. As her right hand melted into mine, it felt like pulling on a glove *inside* my hand. And then, encountering the ring on my right ring finger, she stopped in surprise and said, "What is that ring?" And

I explained that it had been Peyton's, and she said, "But that's not possible—Peyton never ever wore gold jewelry—silver was her thing!" And I said, "I know, but this ring was there among P's jewelry when it came back to me—the only gold thing—and I put it on my hand, and it fit perfectly, and I've been wearing it ever since—and guess what? Over time I figured out that the four large loops on the ring represent the four times Big Blue rolled over, and the flower to the side represents P's spirit flying free, out the side window—I figure that she got what was happening and just flew away before her body rolled down the road. So this ring is a hologram of her death and new life."

And she/me said, "Ooooh, too much information—I'm so very tired!" And I said, "OK honey, just ooze on into the rest of my body, and then lay your heart on mine"—and she did, and then I said "OK, now just come on into my heart, and then just rest, for as much and as long as you need." And when she entered my heart, she lifted her head for the last time and said, "OH, Peyton is here, right here in your heart!" And then she slept. And over the next days, I began to feel whole again—I knew that I had turned the corner in my healing process. I no longer felt so fragile and fragmented, and after many more healing sessions, I left Sierra Tucson no longer suicidal and very glad to be alive and alove and returning to wholeness.

Robbie the Anthropologist and Juan the Chamula: Healing from Soul Loss across Time, Space, and Culture

Shamans (and others) would call these experiences soul loss and recovery. Maybe you can kill a rooster to reclaim the part of the soul you lost when you left your community, and maybe you can do a powerful EMDR visualization like the one Robbie just described, with the same result. Robbie is glad that it didn't take a rooster's death to unfreeze the frozen part of her—but it did take a marvelous therapist, a technology-induced ASC—and a very, very safe ritual frame (Maureen's lovely office with its soft sofas and pillows and buzzers and light flashers, and Maureen's loving and comforting presence, all tucked safely inside the protected premises of Sierra Tucson) to bring the part of Robbie that she had lost to shock back home to Robbie's body. Nine years of suffering Peyton's death, nine years of feeling frozen on that square foot of carpet, and suddenly, just like Juan the Chamula, Robbie felt free! Robbie says: "And of course I still miss my daughter, yet not in that desperate, I-can't-live-without-you way. I *am* living without her, and in recovering and re-warming that frozen part of myself, I am finding my way back towards happiness, day by day." The power of ritual performance brought healing to both Juan the Chamula and Robbie the anthropologist, as it has to so many others across human history, in both traditional and contemporary societies.

Western Medicine: A Differing Perspective

Western medicine usually tells a very different sort of story about illness—a story of germs or cancerous cells invading the body. This story too can be marshaled to aid healing: some researchers (see Simonton, Simonton and Creighton 1978; Kingwatsiaq and Pii 2003; Trakhtenberg 2008) have found that teaching people to visualize the invading germs or cancer cells and zap them like the monsters in a video game can powerfully affect their healing process. But all too often in Western medicine, the doctor ignores his shamanic potential for storytelling and ritual healing, expecting a pill or surgery to do the work (which they sometimes do) without enlisting the healing power of the mind. (Indeed, Robbie's psychiatrist treated her "depression" with anti-depressant drugs for many years. It never occurred to him, or to her, that soul loss might be involved. It took the much more open-minded therapists of Sierra Tucson to go there.) Many Western practitioners treat the body as a machine with a mind in it. They fail to comprehend that body and mind are two aspects of the same being. There is more to the mind than just the brain because our nervous system literally goes everywhere. Our whole body is permeated with nerves that constantly transmit messages from the body to the brain, and back again. In fact, our central nervous system *is* our brain, extended all over our bodies. This is precisely why the so-called *placebo effect* is so important in medicine (Benedetti 2008). Over and over, medical scientists have found that *belief in the efficacy of a medicine has a powerful effect on how well that medicine works* in a given patient. And medical anthropologists have found that it does not matter which culture the patient comes from—there is always a placebo effect operating in healing (Moerman 2002a, 2002b). One of the most critical aspects of healing, therefore, is *belief that the medicine or healing technique will work.* We will be clarifying a lot of this information with respect to ritual below, but first let us look at how *affect* (feeling or emotion) itself works.

THE EXCITATION AND RELAXATION NERVOUS SYSTEMS: RITUAL, FLOW, AND ECTASY

The affect generated by ritual can do much more than merely emotionally charge a belief. Our brains come equipped with two subsystems, the *excitation* and the *relaxation* systems (Gellhorn 1967; Laughlin and Throop 1999). Under normal everyday conditions, these two systems operate alternatively—when one is active, the other is quiescent. But the repetitive stimuli of ritual may actually cause both systems to become active at the same time. Under the right social, environmental, and ritual conditions, this simultaneous activation of both nervous systems can produce an intensely pleasurable, perhaps ecstatic and almost orgasmic sensation (indeed, both subsystems do simultaneously discharge during orgasm).

This ecstatic state occurs in ritual when our physical, emotional, and intellectual experiences of the symbolic messages we are receiving become one (as in the *flow* we described in Chapter 7). The pleasurable feelings may be very brief, experienced only as goose bumps popping out as the banner-bearing choir marches down the aisle on Easter Sunday or a shiver down the spine as you salute your country's flag during a parade. (Many Americans, especially those who supported the Presidential candidate who won the election, report experiencing just such feelings during presidential inaugurations.) It may happen only once during the ritual, or may be repeated at numerous focal points. Or this ecstatic state may be prolonged, as in meditation and religious trance or dance. Here we revisit the quotation that we used at the beginning of this book:

> As Glenna began the opening conjuration of the ritual, a silence fell over the circle. Through the castings and chargings of the circle, through the invocation of the Goddess, it grew, and as Albion and Loik and Joaquin Murietta hammered out a dancing rhythm on their drums, as we whirled in a double sunwise ring, that silence swelled into waves of unseen lightness, flooding our circle, washing about our shoulders, breaking over our heads. Afterwards we wandered about the gardens, laughing and clowning, drunk on the very air itself, babbling to each other: it worked! (Adler 1986:164)

These ecstatic sensations become experientially associated by ritual participants with the belief system enacted in the ritual. Charismatic Christian groups are filled with the Holy Spirit, !Kung trance-dancers with the boiling energy they call *n/um,* and Wiccans with the energy of the earth and the Goddess, as in the quote above. Concert and opera attendees who entrain with the music and the songs will feel uplifted. Participants chanting slogans like "Four more years!" or "Yes, we can!" in political rallies find their ritual "high" in ritually enacted shared belief in a particular candidate. Biological research has established that during such altered states of consciousness (ASCs), high levels of endorphins—natural pain-relieving, pleasure-producing chemicals—flood the central nervous system. This ritually induced experience of ecstasy is one of the most powerful experiences available to humans.

As previously described in our discussion of flow, once you experience this state (especially the prolonged version) during a ritual, you will never forget it, and you are likely to want more. This desire can be a powerful incentive to begin regular attendance at the ritual events that can induce this feeling. The reader should know by now that attaining these feelings entails (necessitates) actual participation in the ritual—doing things, sometimes arduous things—not merely sitting around and watching. Full-bodied ritual participation may involve full attendance at political conventions for days on end, or seemingly nonsensical practices like dancing for hours or days, walking on hot coals, running until exhaustion sets in, and all the other kinds of drivers we discussed in Chapter 5. The participant may ingest psychotropic drugs (for instance, taking the drug "ecstasy" while attending modern raves).

Even an activity like sexual intercourse generally involves beginning with various ritualized behaviors termed "foreplay" before the activity can proceed on to ecstatic bliss. In such cases, the ritualized behaviors are biologically wired-in to transform the emotional, metabolic, and perceptual state of the individuals involved so that union can occur. Foreplay is a precursor to sexual intercourse throughout mammalian and bird species, and, generally speaking, the more complex the brain, the more complex the pre-copulatory ritual. Bottlenose dolphins, for instance, have been called the "sexiest animals on the planet" because their bouts of foreplay can go on for hours before copulation actually occurs. For humans, foreplay ritual can be so entraining that it can work even at a physical distance—over a telephone or via the Internet. So powerful is the urge to feel sexual ecstasy that it pervades the online industry, where various forms of erotic and pornographic imagery are big business (see Quayle and Taylor 2003).

From ritualized sexual foreplay to ceremonial performance, ritual's rhythmic repetition, evocative style, and precise manipulation of symbols and sensory stimuli enable shared rituals to focus the emotions of participants on the calculated intensification of their messages (see Chapple and Coon 1942 on "rites of intensification"). Remember that *belief follows emotion*. Ritual generates intense emotion in humans, even ecstasy, and intense emotion, in turn, generates belief. As we will discuss further below, *the more people's emotions can be engaged through ritual, the more they can be prevented from questioning its messages or examining alternative views.*

RITUAL MECHANISMS FOR ENGENDERING EMOTION AND BELIEF

Ritual Performance

A major characteristic of ritual is that *it is performed*. You cannot fully participate in a ritual by reading about it—you have to *be there*, either in person or through some virtual technology like computers or television. Rituals are embodied (see Bell 1992:Chap. 5, 2008), sensory—and thus must be *experienced*. The more compelling the performance of ritual, the more fully its participants will entrain with the symbolic messages the ritual is sending. A major part of ritual's job is to imbue participants with a strong sense of the value, validity, and importance of the belief system being enacted; in so doing, ritual must also work to preclude challenges to that belief system and the social structure it supports.

Ritual can be high drama—its performers often stage it like a play (well indeed, plays originated via ritual performance) that intensifies toward a climax. The more dramatic ritual is, the more effectively it engages the emotions. These qualities enable ritual to command the attention of participants and audience, while at the same time serving to deflect skeptical questioning or the presentation of alternative points of view.

Masters of Ritual: Charisma and Ritual Command

Masters of ritual are thus master performers, from traditional shamans to fundamentalist preachers to the high Priestesses of Wiccan rites to many politicians, presidents, and totalitarian and cult leaders. They have both total command of the belief system being enacted—indeed, they often have a part in creating that belief system—and dramatic, often charismatic, flair. Their effectiveness rests on their ability to entrain groups—to take individuals of disparate backgrounds, rhythms, and beliefs and unify them into synchronous adherence to one belief system. Adolf Hitler's ability to accomplish this cognitive entrainment through ritual was so profound that within a few years he was able to restructure the symbolic system of an entire nation around the cognitive matrix of German dominance and Aryan supremacy, represented by one powerful symbol, the swastika.

The secret to understanding the power that such a leader can unleash in a population takes us back to the issue of archetypal symbols. The charismatic leader (the guru, the teacher, the tyrant, the pastor, the priestess, the chief, the politician, the President, etc.) is a person whose physical form and behavior penetrate directly into the archetypal King (or leader) in everyone's brain (see especially Ludwig 2002), whatever that symbol may be called within any particular language and by any particular culture. The tipoff that the charismatic leader is receiving projected archetypal King or Queen status is the fascination that he/she holds for us—we tend to be fascinated with people and things that trigger archetypes in us.

Hitler was extremely charismatic—people continue to be fascinated by him to this day, especially when watching his speeches. His messages were simplistic, yet he was explicitly operating in a mythopoeic venue with the goal of creating himself as an icon of his country, in which he massively succeeded. Hitler practiced his gestures over and over—he even had a series of pictures taken of himself in different noble poses, and then studied them to discover the best ones to include in his public displays. Germans never saw the real Hitler in public, only Hitler playing to the archetype. It is likely that he became possessed by his own King archetype, and that it ended up controlling him. This danger is ever-present in our own unconscious minds, for if we over-identify with an archetype, we can lose our sense of identity and personhood. You might do the same thing vicariously if you over-identify with a leader—you might end up doing things you'd never otherwise dream of doing if you lose your character and personality to the charismatic person and his or her message (as Robbie did during her participation in that cult—see pp. 291-295).

Whether the process of over-identification with a charismatic leader is a good thing or bad thing, of course, depends on the intentions of the leader. Some charismatic "gurus" do lead people to a wholesome lifestyle and righteous ends. Charlie had the opportunity to meet and spend some time with Martin Luther King when he visited Austin, Texas, during the early days of the civil rights movement there. In a private, one-on-one meeting with Dr. King, Charlie found him to be a warm and friendly—quite a normal—person. Later, Dr. King mounted a stage before several hundred people and, utilizing the ritualized black Baptist preaching style (returning to a simple repetitive phrase over and over, as he did in his famous "I have a dream!" speech), he gave a sermon centered on the idea, "We have come a long, long way, and we have a long, long way to go!" At the beginning of Dr. King's talk, the mostly white audience was quiet, welcoming and polite. By the time the speech was over, the audience members were ecstatic, on their feet, and cheering at the top of their lungs. Dr. King's charisma was an example of the kind of charisma that leads toward positive, life-affirming ends.

Contrast that with the destructive ends of malignant narcissistic leaders like Jim Jones, the head of the Peoples Temple cult, who persuaded over 900 of his followers to commit mass suicide at Jonestown, Guyana, in 1978. The question always arises, how could so many people be so deluded that they would kill themselves just because Jones told them to do so? (If you read the messages that Jones repeatedly gave to his followers, they will almost inevitably seem stupid and "crazy"—well, you are reading them lucidly and interpreting them through the left hemisphere of your brain, a process that enables you to analyze them intellectually because you are not experiencing the right-brained gestaltic ritual experience of hearing Jones himself expound those messages.) The explanation of course is that the charismatic leader is the focus of such intense fascination that everyday commonsense, including the instinct for personal survival, is overcome, and people cease to use their critical faculties, opting instead to let the leader do their thinking for them—a surrender of the intellect that is always potentially dangerous. We note here that the Book of Matthew takes up this issue when it warns the reader about "false prophets," using the metaphor of good and evil fruits:

> Ye shall know them by their fruits. Do men gather grapes of thorns, or figs of thistles? Even so every good tree bringeth forth good fruit; but a corrupt tree bringeth forth evil fruit. A good tree cannot bring forth evil fruit, neither can a corrupt tree bring forth good fruit. Every tree that bringeth not forth good fruit is hewn down, and cast into the fire. Wherefore by their fruits ye shall know them. (Matthew 7:16-20)

Mohandas (Mahatma) Gandhi led millions of Indians into freedom from British imperialism without killing anyone, and without ever aspiring to or attaining political office. Adolf Hitler thought himself the embodiment of Germany and led millions to their tragic deaths on the battlefield and in extermination camps. "By their fruits shall ye know them" indeed!

Ritual's ability to generate belief, and thus cultural consensus—and their mastery of that ability—is a major reason why totalitarian leaders manage to retain control of entire countries. And here looms again the shadow side of ritual—its potential to be exploited for good or ill. *Ritual can be used to open the mind to new ways of thinking or to close the mind around only one way to the exclusion of all others.* Totalitarian dictators, cult leaders, and others exploit the power of ritual to prevent their followers from questioning their messages or examining alternatives. If through the manipulation of ritual and symbol a leader can get people to associate him with "the nation" in their minds and emotions, even if they hate him they will find it difficult to imagine the country without him.

Fidel Castro's political power in Cuba, for example, is as much rooted in his symbolic association with that nation—an association by now deeply rooted in Cuban people's minds and hearts—as in the army or the police forces he used to command. It becomes unimaginable to have one without the other, so opposition movements can't get off the ground. We could say the same for China under Mao (massive posters of him adorned many buildings, schoolchildren were taught to memorize his *Red Book*), Iraq under Saddam Hussein (every family was required to have a picture of him hanging in their homes), North Korea under Kim Jong-il (and now his son), Syria under Bashar Hafez al-Assad, and many more. (Yet obviously change can happen, totalitarian leaders can be overthrown—we will address ritual's roles in effecting social change in Chapter 10.)

On a much simpler and smaller level, we need to note that parents too can be "masters of ritual"—orchestrating dinner, homework, play time, bath time, story and lullaby time, and bedtime in ways that accustom their children to follow this ritual sequence, get tucked in, and go to sleep without protest (well, most of the time). Many families organize their night lives around such rituals, which enact their family values and beliefs on the importance of shared family time, eating healthy foods, cleanliness, learning to appreciate the magic of stories and song, learning to read and sing—while at the same time leading their children straight to the parents' desired goals—sleep!

Ritual and Emotionally Charged Beliefs

At the risk of oversimplification, we state here that there are two types of belief: those that have no emotional charge attached and those that do. For instance, Charlie believes that his daughter's new car is blue because he saw a picture of it on the Internet. But he has no emotional capital invested in the belief that the car is blue. If it turned out that the car were actually green, he would just update his belief and that would be that. But Charlie also believes in the right of every citizen to own and bear handguns, while Robbie believes that handguns present a danger to their owners that neutralizes their ability to protect the homesteader. We both have strong emotions around handguns, and we could argue with each other to the point of frustration and anger (instead, we avoid the issue to keep the peace). Each of us might attend a ritualized rally in favor of his/her respective side. Well, the kind of beliefs that are engendered and reinforced by rituals tend to be of the latter kind—those paired with emotion. Rituals are designed to present symbolic material in ways that generate emotions.

The reader might naturally wonder who invents rituals in the first place? A very good question, but not one that is easily answered, for when anthropologists go into the field to study social and cultural behavior, the rituals are usually in place, and have existed more or less changed or unchanged, over generations. One of Charlie's friends, Father Ronald Murphy at Georgetown University, author of *The Owl, The Raven, and the Dove: The Religious Meaning of the Grimms' Magic Fairy Tales* (2002), is an expert on the history of the Catholic Mass (see Murphy 1979). He can carry out a Mass from any century over the long history of the Church. Clearly, although that ritual has existed for centuries, it has also continued to change over time. And of course, it is people, acting in concert, who change such rituals. It is very rare to find a ritual that has been created out of whole cloth. The more common situation is that a ritual becomes transformed—the plotting or symbolic order is changed, bits are added, moved or removed—so as to alter the message in some way, or to bring the message up-to-date. Yet humans invent new rituals almost every day to encompass new realities. For example, there are appropriate ritualized ways to utilize the Internet, Facebook, Linked-In, etc. that are in constant development and flux

Human beliefs are linked to language. Beliefs are models of the world that we can talk about with each other. While all vertebrate animals dream, only human beings can share dream content with others. Hence we humans have developed rituals designed to influence our dream lives. The ancient Greek oracles were places where people could go for advice and insight, assisted by the priests who controlled the fasting, purification rites, and preparations for dreaming insightful dreams while sleeping in a cave or other sacred space. This conscious preparation for dreaming is what is called "dream incubation." Dream incubation continues to be practiced today at retreats and other venues, and, just as in the time of the ancient Greeks, if the ritual preparations do their work, the practice evokes vivid dreams which the dreamer then talks over with a priest, a traditional dream interpreter, a contemporary psychotherapist or psychiatrist (especially one of a Freudian or Jungian persuasion) so as to discover important information, perhaps about the future or to better understand our past (Laughlin 2011).

Not only are beliefs sharable, they are also performable—expressible through symbolic media and meaningful action. As such they are part of a society's cosmology and cycle of meaning. Beliefs about the origins of the people, important resources like game, staple crops, water, herbal remedies, etc. are more or less spelled out in the belief system and articulated in rituals. If you ask Navajo people whether they believe it's true that Changing Woman was the mother of the Hero Twins who went to the Sun in order to get the power to fight the monsters, the people will simply reply, "That's what they say!" Referring to the elders, to sacred stories, to the annual ritual cycle, people will say that their beliefs are true because *that's the way it is*—it is what we've been taught and what we have been enacting in our rituals since childhood, thereby learning to incorporate and embody our cultural and social beliefs.

Ritual as a Generator of Collective Effervescence

People in traditional societies are raised to accept certain stories about reality as being "the way things are" because "the way things are" is reinforced over and over by emotionally poignant myths and rituals. The great French sociologist Émile Durkheim (1858-1917) called this process "collective effervescence" —socially shared excitement and other intense emotions (Durkheim 1995 [1912]). While most objects we encounter daily are mundane and "profane" (kitchen cabinets, a hammer, the car, etc.), we also encounter objects like the Bible, the Quran, crosses, crystals, beads, cassowary feathers, holy water, etc. —as well as particular social roles—that we are taught to see as sacred. They are elevated out of the ordinary, and derive their sacredness because of communal rituals in which, according to Durkheim, the emotional charge generated within participants by various driving mechanisms is projected into the objects and roles. Repeating the rituals renews the collective effervescence, which continues to imbue the objects with sacredness.

One of the most successful systems of ritual that Charlie has experienced is the cycle of Easter Masses carried out in the Eastern Orthodox Catholic Church—its liturgy dates back to the 15th century and before (and was not affected by the Vatican II modernization of Roman Catholic rites). Imagine, if you will, the cycle of Masses as they were performed before the discovery of electricity, when literally all the light was gone from your town, church, roads, and home from Friday night to Sunday morning. At a Friday night Mass, the priest would hide the host (the bread or wafer representing the Body of Christ) under his raiment instead of in the sepulcher, walk out of the church, and all lights would be extinguished, to be rekindled on Sunday morning. Imagine the power of the message: with the death of Jesus all of the light disappears from the world, and only returns with His resurrection from death and ascendency to Heaven. The message is powerful to believers—"just as our life is without fire, so too is our life without Jesus."

Fire is a primordial driver. A person entering into the liturgy might not understand any of it at a conscious level, but because the ritual drivers are often archetypal (fire, light, water, the smoke of incense), they can affect people emotionally whether or not they understand the liturgy. Christian missionaries commonly used embodied participation in church rites to convert the natives. Some missionaries came to understand that intellectual presentation of the core beliefs and values of Christianity could not work due to language barriers and profound differences in ways of thinking—only embodied ritual performance could work to engender belief and effect conversion. Rather than relying upon rational persuasion or textual presentations, these missionaries relied upon the right-brained, gestaltic association of symbolic material and intense positive emotion during rituals. These emotionally-charged experiences could then be interpreted as the "presence of the Holy Ghost" or some other Christian interpretation.

On a much simpler level, Robbie wants to speak here of ritual as a generator of collective effervescence in terms of her experience with Mexican and Mexican-American ritual performances during the singing of songs, either by mariachis or by the group as a whole. Much as Black Americans will ritually murmur or shout phrases of encouragement or affirmation of his messages to the preacher during his sermon or the speaker during his talk, so Mexicans and Mexican-Americans will often offer *el grito* ("the yell, or "the cry") at appropriate places during a song. Robbie vividly remembers a graduate student paper by her then-fellow student José Limon describing his intense discomfort during such ritual performances. He was an acculturated Mexican-American, raised by a traditional family yet then attending graduate school at the University of Texas Austin; he later went on to become a Full Professor with a distinguished career. As he reported in that grad school paper, he was often coded by his fellow Mexican-Americans as a *bolillo*—a piece of baked bread that is brown on the outside yet white on the inside. So during the performance of traditional songs, he experienced additional pressure to yell the *grito* to show that he was still "brown on the inside"—a huge cultural challenge for this very intellectual scholar. Robbie, a scholar herself yet far more extroverted than José, took such opportunities as a chance to exhibit, as spectacularly as she could, her chosen assimilation into Mexican culture and its songs. So while José continually hung back from performing *el grito*, Robbie took every chance she had during sing-fests to yell it out loud at the top of her voice—*aaayyyayy ahhhhh—ah a ha eee aaayyy!* (for a poor written facsimile of her totally awesome performances of *el grito*—according to her, anyway). And she was always massively applauded by the Mexican, or Mexican-American audience, for her efforts to show that she "got" their culture and really wanted to participate in it. Robbie certainly experienced collective effervescence as a result of her efforts, and can only hope that her audience did too (or perhaps they were just being kind to an outsider who was trying so hard to fit in).

Raw Ritual Experience and Its Cultural Interpretation

As we have seen, often the generation of belief through ritual includes inducing alternative states of consciousness that produce powerful transpersonal experiences. Such raw experiences are then interpreted for the individual by ritual leaders in terms that are consonant with the society's world view. *The experience is raw, and the culture is ready and willing to impose the appropriate interpretation.* Conversion can happen when ritual produces an extraordinary state of consciousness that then begs interpretation, and the society (or group, or cult) is usually right there to tell the person what it means, to "code" the experience for them. Keeping in mind the "rule of multiple interpretations"—that is, there is no such thing as an experience amenable to one and only one interpretation—we note nonetheless that *when the society structures the ritual to produce an extraordinary experience, it will inevitably also structure the interpretation.*

Back in the 1960s, Charlie had a friend who came very close to suicide. She was extremely depressed, took drugs, and had the classic tunnel and light "near-death experience." She interpreted this experience as a blessing from Christ, and subsequently embraced a "born again" Christian ideology. The experience and her interpretation of it changed her life. However, any experienced Buddhist meditator hearing the description of the raw experience would tend to recognize it as a *samadhi* (absorption) experience that is associated with a particular level of development. In other words, a Christian will interpret such an experience within the Christian cycle of meaning, while a Buddhist will make sense of the same experience within the Buddhist cycle of meaning.

Beauty as a Ritual Mechanism

The claim that "beauty is in the eye of the beholder" certainly has a strong cultural component—aesthetic standards vary widely among and within cultural groups. Nevertheless, it is fair to say that across cultures, the performance of important cultural rituals demands that people dress in their "Sunday best" and employ artifacts that meet the aesthetic standards of the community (see Dissanayake 1992). Trashy, ugly, ordinary things are generally not found in rituals (unless the ritual designer chooses them to be there for particular meanings, in the way that Robbie kept a few pieces of Peyton's smashed jeep Big Blue on her altar for years—she had found them in the grasses beside the highway near the spot where the wreck occurred). Rather, the technologies and the trappings of ritual are usually as beautiful as the members of the social group in question can make them.

For one example, driving through Kingston, Jamaica on a Sunday morning, Robbie was impressed to see Jamaican citizens emerging from their tiny homes, hovels in some cases (from Robbie's middle-class American point of view), extremely well-dressed even in the suffocating heat—the men in suits and ties, the women in elegant outfits complete with matching shoes, purses, and hats, the children dressed equally as well (the girls with exquisitely braided hair)—walking in what Robbie perceived as an aesthetic parade to their respective churches in honor of their religious beliefs and in full display of their cultural and community values.

What is difficult for Westerners to understand is that although the aesthetic sense is universal to peoples on the planet, the modern Western notion of "art" is not—if by art one means some object (painting, sculpture) or performance (play, movie) that is made solely for aesthetic viewing. Craftsmanship and competence in making things beautiful are recognized in all societies, but the manufacture of objects to hang on the wall and be appreciated merely for their beauty is generally not a part of traditional societies. Rather, as Ellen Dissanayake (1992) shows, art among most traditional peoples is the application of aesthetics to ritual or sacred objects to "make them special." When we dress up for a ritual ceremony (going to church or temple, attending a funeral or a marriage, etc.), we are making ourselves "special" for the ritual occasion—doing our part to make the occasion beautiful.

Ritual spaces are often made special by enhancing their beauty. Although a Catholic mass can be performed anywhere (in a living room, in a vacant lot or open field), the ceremony is most often carried out in a church. This creates the requisite beautiful, special, and hence sacred background to the rite. To recap from Chapter 7 on ritual frames, when we pass into a sacred space, our behavior changes. We become more circumspect and reverent in our actions. A Muslim carrying out his or her daily prayers (*Salah*) should take certain steps to make the prayers effective. Often a sacred space is delineated by a special prayer mat (*sajjāda*) which assures that the space in which one carries out prostrations and prayers is both special and clean. Before stepping into this sacred space, one is supposed to carry out various ablutions and be dressed in clean clothes, for by doing this ritual, one is facing God in direct communion. (Likewise, some Christians dress up to pray, putting on their best before God and kneeling in a special place that is sacred to them.)

Beauty and the Mandala of Perception

If you look carefully at a lot of Muslim prayer mats, you will see that they almost always include geometric designs that are intended to remind the supplicant of God. Because Islam forbids icons depicting the figure of

Figure 8.1. Catholic Mass (image courtesy of Priestly Fraternity of Saint Peter, available from http://fssp.org)

God or the Prophet, God or The Divine is represented by patterns that are both beautiful and meaningful to the practitioner. Sometimes a geometric pattern will take the form of a *mandala*—a circular form that has a center and lines that radiate outward from the center to the periphery. The classic mandala looks something like a pie that has been sliced into sections. Most people perceive mandalas as beautiful. Study the stained glass windows in a church, which are often mandalic in form—it is highly likely that even if you do not share the belief system they represent, you will nevertheless find them aesthetically appealing. Mandalas are found everywhere in the iconography of peoples, and are universal because they are fundamental structures of perception and imagination, and also because they are a kind of shorthand encapsulating beliefs and aesthetics in one economical form. In some more complex mandalic forms, the radians may be construed to be binary oppositions (right vs. left, up vs. down, east vs. west, etc.) Psychodynamically speaking, a mandala may represent the opposition of aspects of our being such as giving vs. hoarding, love vs. hate, proper thoughts vs. improper thoughts, etc.

Cultures will often define their world as a system of opposites that are at the same time part of one great unified whole. For instance, the Navajo conceive of the world as existing as a set of opposites, some of which are given gender attributions—like Mother Earth and Father Sky, Blue Corn Boy and Blue Corn Girl, night animals and day animals, and so forth. In their healing ceremonies, the healer will create an intricate mandala on the floor of the *hogan* using ground stone of various colors (called "dry paintings" by the Navajo and "sand paintings" by others). These drawings are often circular and have oppositional images around a central figure. When done properly, the drawing is magically transformed into a portal through which the Holy People can come and help heal the patient, who is placed in the middle of the mandala. After the ceremony is finished, the drawing is destroyed and the colored sand is swept up and discarded. A traditional Navajo would not dream of keeping a true healing drawing to hang on the wall no matter how beautiful the creation, for to do so would be considered dangerous in the extreme—allowing a non-ritually controlled portal into the spiritual world to remain open. Mandalic forms, however, are not perceived as dangerous in and of themselves because they do not attract the attention of the Holy People. Indeed, the Great Seal of the Navajo Nation is a simplified mandala (not unlike a healing drawing) and represents the masculine principle (the circle of arrowheads pointing outward in defense of the nation), and the feminine principle (the rainbow

Figure 8.2. The Great Seal of the Navajo Nation

path of Changing Woman around the four directions, the four sacred mountains defining Navajoland, the important animals and corn plants).

Why do we find mandalas all over the planet, and why are they so common in rituals and sacred spaces? The answer is actually quite simple. Each and every moment of perception is mandalic in form. Focus your attention on anything—your computer screen, this book, a tree, a mug of coffee—and reflect upon the fact that the object you are focused upon is not all that you are seeing. Your act of perceiving, say a coffee mug, places the mug in the middle of your perceptual field. That means there is stuff to the right and left of the mug, stuff above and below the mug, stuff in front and in back of the mug. Voilà—a mandala! You can make this even more interesting, for as you walk down a path or hallway, your gaze focused on something ahead of you, you will find (if you look) that things are passing by you to the left and right, above and below, in front and behind you. You are in the middle of a dynamic mandala, which in this case takes on the 3D form of a mandalic tunnel. Even more interesting is that whatever you focus upon, whether moving or stationary, is the center of the mandala and everything else around it is its context. The mug is sitting on a table, which is standing on a rug, which is centered on a floor, etc. The mandala of perception simultaneously defines the object of interest and its context, and the context always refines the meaning of the object. Change the context and the meaning of the object changes. Place the mug in the sink and it connotes "dirty and needs to be washed"; put the mug on a shelf—it now connotes "clean and ready to be used." If on the other hand you are looking at the mug in a store, the connotation is "this mug is for sale."

This notion that changing the context of an object changes its meaning within the mandala of perception is obvious, isn't it? But what is not so obvious to most of us is that when we learn to perceive our inner selves, our perceptions, imagery, and intuitions quite naturally take on mandalic forms. Indeed, mandalas found in Buddhist iconography specifically depict the inner nature of consciousness and being. Thus, the mandalic forms we encounter in Buddhist architecture (temples, stupas, sacred spaces) are specifically intended to remind us of our true inner nature—a nature that takes the form of oppositions, relations, and the constant struggle of the self for unity. The mandalic nature of perceived space is common throughout the world's religions. When we focus our attention on any altar, then everything else becomes peripheral to that altar, but also constitutes the context or frame of the altar. The message is usually that the altar is the center of the mandala of sacred space. Just a moment's reflection will show you that every time you shift your gaze, you create a new mandala before your mind—now this tree, now this cloud, now this piece of music or person's voice—a constantly shifting mandala of perception of every object we focus upon is contextualized by everything else around it in our perceptual field. How natural then, if we wish to focus upon the divine or sublime dimension of things, that we focus our attention upon a divine object, which then becomes the center of a sacred mandala, whether that focus is upon a visual form (Christ on a cross), a musical form (a hymn), an olfactory form (incense), or a tactile form (the feel of the prayer mat under us, the prayer beads passing through our fingers). What mandalic forms do you focus on, if any?

Drama: Acting, Stylization, Staging, Intensification

Ritual can be high drama. Its performers must often stage it like a play that intensifies toward a climax. The more dramatic ritual is, the more effectively it engages the emotions. These qualities enable ritual to command the attention of participants and audience and work to ensure their engagement in the ritual performance.

In Chapter 7, we explored ritual frames—a characteristic ritual shares with theater in general. In many ways, the spaces in which ritual is performed (from hogans to stadiums, from prayer mats to great cathedrals) function much like the stage in a theater or concert hall, helping to focus the energy and attention of both participants and audience on the actions going on inside this bracketed space. As in a good play, when the ritual is effective, for participants and audience the world narrows down to the reality enacted in the ritual, and for a while, everything else disappears from consciousness and perception. When it works, the ritual evokes the intended states of consciousness that constitute the living reality mirrored in the ritual.

As mentioned earlier, it is common knowledge in stagecraft that there should never be a superfluous object on stage during a play or in a novel. By the same token, all the objects, persons and behaviors at or surrounding the altar—all of which take their place within the presentational mandala—must have their assigned meaning and play their part in the sacred drama. As we sit in our pew in a church and gaze at the priest doing his thing at the altar, we see the stained glass window behind the altar above, the roof arching above to the heavens, the stone or wood floor below, and symbolic objects and persons to the left and right. For those drawn into the ritual world, the effect is to produce a portal into the sublime. By the very structure of our own perceptual system, we create before our mind the mandalic sacred space with its focus, context and over-arching meaning.

RITES OF PASSAGE AND RELIGIOUS CONVERSIONS: TRANSFORMATION THROUGH RITUAL

The most profoundly transformative of all rituals are initiatory rites of passage and religious indoctrinations (Driver 2006:61-62). These break down the belief system of the initiate, then rebuild it around the beliefs and values of the group—a process known in religion as a "conversion experience." Whether the individual is converted to Islam, Christianity, Judaism, the Moonies (or any other sect or cult), or initiated into the Marines, the Navy, the Ku Klux Klan, a terrorist group, or a fraternity or sorority, the ritual process is very much the same.

A *rite of passage* is a series of rituals designed to conduct an individual (or group) from one social state or status to another, thereby effecting transformations both in society's perceptions of the individual and in the individual's perception of her- or himself (Van Gennep 1966; Turner 1967, 1969; Grimes 2002).

Ritual's role in rites of passage is fourfold:

1. to give humans a sense of control over natural processes that may be beyond their control by making it appear that natural transformations (e.g. birth, puberty, death) are actually effected (or at least powerfully shaped) by society and serve society's ends (Malinowski 1954);
2. to "fence in" the dangers perceived cross-culturally to be present in transitional periods (when individuals are in-between social categories and therefore call the conceptual reality of those categories into question), while at the same time allowing controlled access to their energizing and revitalizing power (Douglas 1966; Abrahams 1973);
3. to convey, through the emotions and the body, a series of repetitious and unforgettable messages to the initiate concerning the core values of the society into which he or she is being initiated through the carefully structured manipulation of appropriately representative symbols, and thereby to integrate those values, as well as the basic premises of the belief system on which they are based, into the inmost being of the initiate (Turner 1967, 1969). As Roger Abrahams (1973:24) noted, "What distinguishes a full-blown rite from all other ritualized behaviors is the number of [central symbols] resorted to, and the willingness—indeed the felt necessity—to repeat so often the message of the enactment through these [central symbols]";
4. to renew and revitalize these values for those conducting, as well as for those participating in or merely watching, the rituals through which these transformations are effected, so that both the perpetuation and the vitality of the belief and value system of the society in question can be assured (Turner 1967, 1969; Geertz 1973; Abrahams 1973).

Rites of passage generally consist of three principal stages, outlined by van Gennep (1966) as: (1) separation of the individuals involved from their preceding social state; (2) a period of transition in which they are neither one thing nor the other; (3) a reintegration phase in which through various rites of incorporation they are absorbed into their new social state. Van Gennep states that these three stages may be of varying degrees of importance, with rites of separation generally emphasized at funerals, and rites of incorporation at weddings.

Yet the most salient feature of all rites of passage is their transitional nature, the fact that they always involve what Victor Turner (1967, 1979) has called "liminality," the stage of being betwixt and between, neither here nor there—no longer part of the old and not yet part of the new (from the Latin word *limen,* which means "threshold"). In the "liminal phase" of initiatory rites of passage, "the ritual subject passes through a realm that has few or none of the attributes of the past or coming state" (1979:237). Of this liminal phase, Turner (1979:238-239) writes:

> The passivity of neophytes to their instructors, their malleability, which is increased by submission to ordeal, their reduction to a uniform condition, are signs of the process whereby they are ground down to be fashioned anew and endowed with additional powers to cope with their new station in life....It is the ritual and the esoteric teaching which grows girls and makes men....The arcane knowledge, or "gnosis" obtained in the liminal period is felt to change the inmost nature of the neophyte, impressing him, as a seal impresses wax, with the characteristics of his new state. It is not a mere acquisition of knowledge, but a change in being.

One of the chief characteristics of this liminal or transitional period of any rite of passage is the gradual psychological "opening" of the initiates to profound interior change. This change is so profound that ritual expert Ronald L. Grimes (2002) uses the metaphor "deeply into the bone" to refer to the effects of rites of passage. In many initiation rites involving major transitions into new social roles, this openness is achieved through rituals designed to break down the initiates' belief system—the internal mental structure of concepts and categories through which they perceive and interpret the world and their relationship to it. Ritual techniques that facilitate this process of cognitive breakdown include *hazing*—the imposition of physical and mental hardships (familiar to participants in military and fraternity (and sometimes sorority) initiation rites), and *strange-making*—making the commonplace strange by juxtaposing it with the unfamiliar (Abrahams 1973). A third such device, *symbolic inversion,* works by metaphorically turning specific elements of the belief system upside-down or inside-out, so that the high is brought low, and the low is raised high, and the world in general is thrown into confusion (Babcock 1978:13-32):

> As this process is continued over time, the cognitive reality model begins to disintegrate. Learned versions of reality and previously instrumental responses repeatedly fail the initiate. Confusion and disorganization ensue...introducing a relatively entropic state. At this point the individual should be searching for a way to structure or make sense out of reality, and in terms of the initiation, his search constitutes the launching point for the transformation of identity. (McManus 1979b:239)

The breakdown of their belief systems leaves initiates profoundly open to new learning and to the construction of new categories. Any symbolic messages conveyed to an initiate during this opening process can thus be imprinted on his or her psyche as deeply "as a seal impresses wax" (Turner 1979:239). Once broken down, their cognitive structures can then be rebuilt around the beliefs, values, and approved behaviors of the group. (This cognitive de- and re-structuring is not metaphorical—quite literally and physically, the networks of neurons in the brain are broken down and re-organized during intensive initiation rites.)

For example, in the rite of passage of Marine basic training, the initiate's normal patterns of action and thought are turned topsy-turvy. He is *made strange* to himself: his head is shaved, so that he does not even recognize himself in the mirror. He must give up his clothes—those expressions of individual identity and personality—and put on a uniform indistinguishable from that of other initiates. Constant and apparently meaningless hazing (e.g., orders to dig ditches and then fill them up) break down his cognitive structure. Then through repetitive and highly symbolic rituals (such as sleeping with his rifle), his physical habits and patterns of thought are literally reorganized into alignment with the basic values, beliefs, and practices of the Marines.

Cross-culturally, the most prominent type of rites of passage are those dealing with life crises. They accompany what Lloyd Warner (1959:303) has called

> the movement of a man [sic] through his lifetime, from a fixed placental placement within his mother's womb to his death and ultimate fixed point of his tombstone...punctuated by a number of critical moments of transition which all societies ritualize and publicly mark with suitable observances to impress the

significance of the individual and the group on living members of the community. These are the important times of birth, puberty, marriage and death.

The sequence of these life-crisis events which Warner uses refers to the baby's birth and not to the *woman's* giving birth nor to *her* transition into motherhood. Thus this sequence reveals a strong male bias that may be one reason for the general anthropological overlooking of the significance of the rites of childbirth across cultures. Arranged from a female-oriented physiological perspective, the sequence would have to read: birth, puberty, marriage, childbearing, menopause, death.

RITUAL AND COGNITIVE TRANSFORMATION

Transformation for ritual participants can be both mental and physical. It can be external in the eyes of society, and/or internal in the psyche of the participant. Some kind of transformation can be said to occur in *all* types of ritual. For example, the ritual handshake and "Hello, how are you?" open a previously non-existent channel of communication between two individuals, resulting in almost immediate entrainment of their bodily rhythms. But ritual's true potential for transformation, of course, goes much deeper than this example, entailing profound possibilities for individual interior change.

Deep transformation for ritual participants occurs when the symbolic messages of ritual fuse with individual emotion and belief, and the individual's entire cognitive structure reorganizes around the newly internalized symbolic complex (as Juan the Chamula's did at the ritual climax of the sacrifice of the rooster, when suddenly he felt "free"). Although this may sound final, as if it could happen only once, it is not. Human neural structures are not made of cement; they are relatively fluid. As most religious adherents know from experience, belief waxes and wanes, and must be continually reinforced through ritual if it is to retain a significant role in shaping individual cognition and behavior. Each time you attend a religious service or a political rally, you can experience this process anew, diving deeper and deeper into the symbolic constellations of belief of the religious, spiritual, or political system.

Religious and Cult Conversions

Intensive religious and cult indoctrinations can tear apart the prior belief system of the initiate through prolonged exposure to the beliefs of the new group that results in cognitive breakdown and reorganization (*hazing*), the induction of altered states of consciousness (*strange-making*), the extreme denigration of the initiate, or his exaltation to a place of exaggerated honor and importance in the group (*symbolic inversion*). These tactics can result in a *conversion experience,* in which the entire cognitive structure of the initiate reorganizes itself around the beliefs, values, and approved behaviors of the group. Such religious conversions can evolve slowly, over years of repeated exposure to a given set of beliefs, or can be made to happen very fast.

For example, Mark Galanter (1989), a sociologist studying the Moonies (followers of the Korean evangelist Reverend Sun Myung Moon) found that potential new members were often selected to pick on because they were socially isolated, frequently as a result of being new students on a college campus without a strong social network. They were initially recruited by what this sociologist called "love-bombing" —showering the potential recruits with multiple messages of appreciation—and thus thrilling and bewildering them and making them want more—in order to entice them to attend a five-day workshop. Fascinatingly, around one-third of those who did attend such a workshop (ostensibly offered to explain the religion to interested newcomers) ended up converting—*even if* their original reason for going was to learn enough about the religion to talk a loved one into getting out!

How could such previously unintended conversions happen? Participants sat through many hours of lecture, during which they were bombarded with an overload of confusing information, resulting in a narrowing of their cognitive abilities (see the following chapter). Interspersed between lectures were periods of playful fun—volleyball, dancing—during which the newcomers were made to feel wholly important, wholly wanted, wholly loved. Allusions were made to Rev. Moon in connection with the Second Coming of Christ, and it was repeatedly suggested that if the workshop participants were truly blessed, they might see visions of Rev. Moon himself during their regularly scheduled meditation periods. Not surprisingly (due to symbolic penetration), many did! Those who did not sign up after the five-day "workshop" often wanted to, but all had at least one highly significant friend or relative pulling them away.

Robbie's Unwanted Conversion Experience

I am lying on the floor and Steven is above me. "Breathe, breathe," he tells me as he presses on my chest and massages my arms. "I don't want to," I tell him—"This is too hard, it hurts too much. I'll never clear this issue, I can't!" "I am not my negative thoughts," Steven intones. "I am not my negative thoughts," I repeat dutifully. "I am not my negative thoughts—I am unlimited," Steven chants. "I am unlimited," I repeat, over and over. It seems clear that his intention is to get me past my limited notion that I will never heal the emotional pain that led me to request this rebirthing session. His hands press my sternum—"Breathe, breathe," he tells me, again and again. I take one deep breath after another, inhaling as much air as I can get into my lungs and expelling it slowly, completely. Breath after breath, in and out, in a rhythm that opens my psyche and eventually releases the pain in my throat and chest, which seems to float out of my body on the waves of air I expel. Fused as one with the rhythms, Steven breathes with me, urging me to keep repeating "I am unlimited." As my pain floats away and my emotions calm, I feel deeply unified, deeply alive, and wide open.

Turning aside to find his glass of water, Steven muses, almost to himself, "Yeah, you know, it's like the white flame that burns without consuming.*" The symbol he has just articulated penetrates my consciousness like a wheel of fire. My entire cognitive universe immediately reconstellates around this core symbol, and in an instant, I go from not believing anything the people in this New Age group have been telling me for years to believing it all. Flying into a rage, I leap from the floor, grab a pillow, and start pounding it against a wall, screaming "Father André, you son of a bitch, you tricked me!" Steven is startled and alarmed. "Damn you!" I scream at him. "How could you do this to me? I didn't choose to believe this stuff, and now it's too late!"*

Let us explain. Shortly after the birth of her second child Jason (in 1984), feeling somewhat isolated and overwhelmed by the realities of mothering two young children, Robbie had joined a mother's support group she had been told about that met weekly in a house just down the road. It turned out to be led by a woman named Karen, who had begun to channel a spiritual entity named Father André. Robbie was fascinated—here was the New Age happening full force, just a few miles from her house in a conservative middle-class neighborhood! The anthropologist in her wanted to know more. Plus she was enjoying the companionship of the other mothers, and her older child (Peyton) seemed to enjoy playing with the other kids, for whom activities were always provided.

So she continued her attendance, and as time passed and she got to know other members of this group and their husbands or significant others, she began increasingly to utilize the services they offered: massage, Chinese medicine, nutritional counseling, and rebirthing, which nowadays is more often referred to as breath therapy (see Chapter 5 on ritual drivers). Eventually, as Robbie became more familiar with Father André's teachings, she began to request individual counseling sessions with "him," primarily to deal with difficulties she was experiencing in her marriage. But all through this process, Robbie merely "suspended disbelief" in order to gain maximal advantage from the healings and the counseling sessions. She maintained cognitive distance from the belief system of the group, which centered around the core notion of "ascension." Father André taught that just as Jesus Christ had ascended—in other words, "had expanded out to become one with all" —so every human being had the potential to do the same. In fact, said Father André, the point of Jesus' ascension was to demonstrate that it could be done and thus encourage others to work toward this ultimate goal.

Members of the group, which we will call World Healing Services (WHS—a pseudonym), would occasionally channel other entities besides Father André, who recounted remarkable "ascension stories." One was channeled from an Indian warrior whose best friend betrayed him by raping his wife. He tracked his betrayer into the desert for three days, and finally caught up to him, finding him weak with thirst, hunger, and exhaustion, and unable to fight. Lifting his knife to kill his former friend, the young brave looked into the other man's eyes and, in a profound moment of illumination, knew that they were brothers, indeed, that *all people were one*. In that instant, he "ascended"—became "one with all." Another ascension story, "channeled" by another group member, came from a young Icelandic maiden who was punished for some transgression by being left alone on an ice floe to freeze to death. "As the ship and the sailors who left me there to die sailed off into the distance, my heart reached out to forgive them. With the ice as my support, the wind to empower me, the grey skies to lift me up, I encompassed them with my consciousness and knew that we were one. In love and ecstasy, and without effort, I understood that I was one with all, and so I did not die, but rather ascended."

Robbie found these stories fascinating. She didn't believe them for a second, but she thought they were terrific *stories*—indeed, she intended to record them and to write an article for a folklore journal analyzing what she called "ascension stories" as a New Age storytelling genre. And she had plans to write another article about this New Age group that would analyze its belief and value system and compare it with those of other cults and new religious movements. But then came the fateful counseling session with Father André, during which he specifically advised that to work on her marital problems, she should do a rebirthing session that week with Steven. Deep into the rebirth, in a deeply altered SOC, Robbie found that Steven's musing about "the white flame that burned without consuming" suddenly, somehow, made all this "nonsense" about ascension make sense. She saw Moses standing before the burning bush that burned but was not consumed, and she understood something essential and profound about energy and eternity that she still has no words to articulate.

As we noted above, such experiences are raw but almost always, the culture or social group is there to interpret them, to tell you what they mean. Steven did not spell it out for her—he did not even have to say "the white flame that burns without consuming indicates that ascension is possible." Robbie had been hanging out with this group for three years at this point, had been hearing their stories and listening to them discuss and work through rebirthing/breath therapy to "clear their issues" in order to achieve ultimate ascension—in the flesh, just like Jesus. So, in a flash, her mind interpreted that raw experience in terms of ascension, and the meaning the symbol of the white flame took on for her was that ascension, like eternity, exists and is possible and can be represented and evoked by the white flame, which exists in perfect balance between producing and consuming—constantly emitting just enough energy to sustain itself without destroying anything else.

In retrospect, what Robbie finds so amazing about this experience is that she knew the instant that it happened that *she had been converted, she did not want to be converted, indeed was furious about it, but it happened anyway!* Without wanting to or choosing to, she went in an instant from not believing to believing, all because in a state of psychic openness induced by heavy rhythmic breathing (and preceded by three years of exposure to this particular belief system), one core symbol penetrated her consciousness, mapped itself onto her worldview, and changed the way she perceived the world and the meaning of life.

After that intensely transformative experience, Robbie moved ever deeper into the belief system of the group, attending more and more of their weekend seminars, meditation and rebirthing sessions, and starting herself to rebirth others (she got pretty good at it!). During this time, Robbie had more fun and experienced more intimacy and more ecstasy than ever before in her life. She was a full participating member in a community dedicated to healing where she truly felt that she belonged—to such an extent that for a while, she even wanted to move in with them, give them all her money, and put her children in their school as their other members had—the classic reaction of the recently converted. But in addition to being a true believer, Robbie was still an anthropologist. She knew she had been "had," as it were, and her intellect never did accept the validity of her conversion experience nor of the belief system into which she had been converted. Most of her being—her emotions, her perceptions, her sensory experiences—resonated with that belief system, but intellectually she understood that it was just one story among many that had been invented by humans, and that ultimately it could be no truer than any other such story.

Nevertheless, it took her six whole months to un-convert herself—with much associated trauma and pain. She was massively assisted in that process by her then-husband, who was adamantly opposed to her participation in WHS, for obvious and very accurate reasons. WHS was still in its early stages when Robbie was participating—later, after she withdrew, they did turn into a full-fledged cult with disastrous results, including bankruptcy and homelessness for some of the longest-enduring members—but that's a story for another time. Nevertheless, for many years Robbie missed that sense of specialness you feel when you believe that only you and a few others *really understand* the meaning and purpose of life.

Conversion Experiences and Ritual Socialization

Robbie's conversion experience was the result of a long, slow socialization process that crystallized suddenly through one powerful core symbol. Mechanisms for generating belief through ritual include this kind of slow socialization, which involves repeated exposure to the beliefs and values of a group over time, but also include much faster and more radical mechanisms like deliberately and rapidly breaking down the individual's pre-existing cognitive system, then rebuilding it through the careful manipulation of ritual drivers paired with specific symbols that penetrate the individual on multiple levels—intellectual, emotional, physical—with the desired messages.

Robbie's conversion experience was very negative for her, as have been the conversion experiences of hostages who experience the well-known "Stockholm syndrome"—identification with their captors and eventual conversion to their belief system (Patricia Hearst is perhaps the most famous example). Yet many others experience very positive conversion experiences, to Christianity, Islam, Ba'hai, Judaism, the Jehovah's Witnesses, Christian Science, Mormonism, and multiple other sects and religions. Many such experiences happen in much the same way as Robbie's—repetitive bombardment over time with symbolic messages and then a sudden flash of opening and acceptance. While the ritual process may remain the same or similar, the final result will depend on whether or not the newly converted individual welcomes the conversion (for example, receiving Jesus Christ into their lives as their personal Savior, or realizing that all of the perceptual world is an illusion from the Buddha point of view), and finds it cause for celebration and positive life transformation.

The successes enjoyed by many religions, sects, and cults that employ such conversion tactics demonstrate the extreme malleability of the human central nervous system. *Under the right conditions, any of us can be made to believe almost anything.* Understanding human susceptibility and the power of ritual to influence belief can leave you free to choose.

SUMMARY: RITUAL, EMOTION, AND BELIEF

In this chapter, we have described ritual healing from "soul loss" for both Juan the Chamula and Robbie the anthropologist, showing how the sensory manipulation of repetitive and symbolic stimuli facilitated those healings. We have described the excitation and relaxation nervous systems and shown how ritual can cause them both to discharge simultaneously, producing a strong sense of flow and sometimes even ecstasy—which can keep ritual participants coming back for more. We have described ritual mechanisms for generating emotion and belief, including ritual performance, extrinsic and intrinsic drivers, charisma, beauty, mandalas of perception, ritual socialization, collective effervescence, and ritual drama. We have discussed rites of passage and religious conversions, and shown how raw individual experiences can be (and almost always are) interpreted in cultural and religious terms to give them socially-shared meaning.

Their rhythmic repetition, evocative style, and precise manipulation of symbols and sensory stimuli enable collective rituals to focus the emotions of participants on the calculated intensification of their messages. Remember, once again, that *belief follows emotion.* Ritual generates intense emotion in humans, even ecstasy, and intense emotion, in turn, generates belief. In conclusion, we repeat: *The more people's emotions can be engaged through ritual, the more they can be prevented from questioning its messages or examining alternative views.* Yet please do not misunderstand us here. We applaud and celebrate ritual conversions to belief systems that individuals truly want to hold (when their intellectual faculties are also engaged) because we understand that belief can benefit human beings and add light, even illumination, to our lives. These belief systems, when both ritually effected and consciously welcomed, can bring to us ways of cognizing (thinking about) our lifeworlds that we may well find helpful within the larger scheme of things—a topic that we will discuss at length in the following chapter.

Suggested Reading

Ludwig, Arnold M (2002) *King of the Mountain: The Nature of Political Leadership.* Lexington, KY: The University Press of Kentucky.

Moerman, Daniel E. (2002b) *Meaning, Medicine, and the "Placebo Effect."* Cambridge: Cambridge University Press.

Rush, John A. (Ed.) (2013) *Entheogens and the Development of Culture: The Anthropology and Neurobiology of Ecstatic Experience.* Berkeley, CA: North Atlantic Books.

Chapter 9

RITUAL AND THE FOUR STAGES OF COGNITION

Cognitive Simplification: How Rituals Speak to the Masses. Concrete and Fluid Thinking: The 4 Stages of Cognition. Ritual and the 4 Stages of Cognition. Ritual, Cognition, and Stress: Substage and Stabilization. Summary: Concrete and Fluid Thinking, the Four Stages of Cognition, Ritual, and Stress.

COGNITIVE SIMPLIFICATION: HOW RITUALS SPEAK TO THE MASSES

In any culture, ritual participants will differ from each other both in intellectual ability and in cognitive structure. Individuals of high cognitive complexity, for example, may adopt a relative view of reality tolerant of multiple interpretations of a given phenomenon, while individuals with simpler (or simply different) cognitive systems may tend to insist on one and only one correct interpretation (Harvey, Hunt and Schroder 1961; Ievers-Landis *et al.* 2006; Faiola 2002; Sias, Lambie, and Foster 2006). Straightforward didactic communications must take these differences into account if their messages are to be understood. But *ritual must work collectively, for the masses.*

Ritual overcomes this problem by working to reduce its participants, at least temporarily, to the same cognitive level, at which they will all see the world from within the confines of one cognitive matrix/belief system. Some social scientists (including us) have called this "rigid" or "concrete" thinking. Individuals who are thinking at a rigid/concrete level will tend to see the world in terms of black and white, interpreting others as either "with them" or "against them" (a type of thinking that is typical of religious fundamentalists). This sort of either/or thinking does not allow for the consideration of options or alternative views—except perhaps to refute them. For examples, there are multiple ways in which anti-evolutionists/creationists deconstruct biological and anthropological theories about evolution to point out their failings and use those issues to promote creation theory. Fundamentalist preachers and politicians will dissect their opponents' arguments not to seek the truth of the matter, but to find ways to discount them.

We are not saying that concrete thinkers lack intelligence—only that they are so attached to one particular viewpoint, or one belief system (especially when that belief is emotionally charged) that they will disregard reasonable and evidence-based arguments to the contrary. Think for example of the massive resistance that Copernicus and Galileo encountered in their efforts to prove that the Earth was not the center of the solar system, but only one planet among several orbiting around the sun—a "theory" that has been proven to be fact.

Returning to the subject of ritual and its effects on the human psyche, we note that *cognitive simplification* generally precedes the conceptual reorganization that accompanies true psychological transformation (see Chapter 8 on rites of passage). The most common technique employed in ritual to accomplish this end is the rhythmically repetitive bombardment of participants with symbolic messages, as described in earlier chapters. The advantage of this cognitive reduction of ritual participants to concrete thought is that *only one ritual structure is now sufficient to communicate social norms and values to a wide variety of individuals.* In other words, even complex thinkers can be reduced by ritual to concrete, either/or thinking; thus they may not tend to question the symbolic messages they are internalizing. This process is most clearly visible in the performance of religious rituals such as the Catholic Mass, which can be deeply felt and equally convincing to individuals of all levels of cognitive complexity. (Classic joke: How many Catholics does it take to change a light bulb? Answer: Change? You've got to be kidding!)

Perhaps the most remarkable uses of ritual to bring about concrete thought and behavioral regimentation were the massive rallies mounted by the Nazis prior to World War II. Students of ritual today can learn a lot by watching the 1935 propaganda documentary directed by Adolph Hitler's pet filmmaker, the brilliant Leni Riefenstahl, entitled *Triumph des Willens* (*Triumph of the Will*).[11] The film covers the 1934 Nuremberg congress of the National Socialist (Nazi) Party, showing hundreds of thousands of people marching,

---

11. This classic film has been reconditioned and is available on Netflix, YouTube and DVD.

standing at attention, shouting "*Heil Hitler*" ("Hail Hitler!") and "*Sieg Heil!*" ("Hail Victory!"). The regimentation of behavior, scripted presentations, and the ensuing intensification of a single belief system are all obvious to the anthropological eye, augmented by the rich symbolism of authority (such as Hitler and other leaders of the party elevated above the rank and file of party members), uniformity (everyone dressed in uniforms, hence literally *uni-formed*), an emotionally charged hand gesture (the *Hitlergruß*—the right arm raised at an angle with the hand flat out, a gesture erroneously attributed to the Ancient Romans). The film also shows the Nazi emphasis upon controlling the thought, opinions, loyalties, and proper behavior of Germany's youth—a critical use of ritual to form future public opinion. The rally was attended by the *Hitlerjugend* (Hitler Youth, or HJ) which was the organization for boys (ages 14–18), as well as the younger boys' section *Deutsches Jungvolk* (ages 10–14) and the girls' *Bund Deutscher Mädel* (League of German Girls, or BDM). We can think of no case in which ritual was relied upon more to revolutionize and then intensify concrete thinking among a mass population.

CONCRETE AND FLUID THINKING: THE FOUR STAGES OF COGNITION

Thus far we have been speaking of "concrete/rigid thinking" without doing very much to clarify the notion. Because it is critical to understand how thought may range from very simple to very complex, and how ritual may act as a buffer to cognitive disintegration, we need to clarify what we mean by "stages of cognition." We cannot emphasize enough that the *structure of thought is independent of the content of thought.* In other words, thought can be relatively simple and concrete, or very complex and abstract, regardless of what we are thinking about.

Concrete Thinking: Stages 1 and 2

For our purposes, there are two stages of concrete thinking, Stages 1 and 2. Concrete (or rigid) cognitive structures exhibit a

> ...tendency to standardize judgments in a novel situation; a greater inability to interrelate perspectives; a poorer delineation between means and ends; a poorer capacity to act "as if" and to

understand the other's perspectives; and less potential to perceive the self as causal agent in interaction with the environment. (Schroder 1971:257)

Let us look at each of the levels of concrete thinking and how they influence the individual's view of "reality."

Stage 1 Thinking: Naïve Realism, Fundamentalism, and Fanaticism

Stage 1 thinking results from a rigid, hierarchical cognitive structure that necessitates fitting everything one experiences into one and only one explanatory structure/worldview. Stage 1 thinking tells one cohesive story about the world that does not allow for options or alternatives to that basic story—yet there may be many depths and many layers of meaning to be found in exploring that one story, as scholars and seekers of every religious persuasion have discovered.

Here we identify three kinds of Stage 1 thinking: (A) what anthropologists call *naïve realism;* (B) *fundamentalism;* (C) *fanaticism*. Naïve realists, fundamentalists, and fanatics all believe that *their way is the only real and right way*—yet there are profound differences among them. *Naïve realists* are raised in one culture with one unified belief system and *simply do not know that there is any other way to think about the world,* or have so little exposure to other ways of thinking that they discount them as irrelevant or simply misguided. (Given the increasing globalization of contemporary society, there are fewer and fewer true naïve realists left in the world.)

In contrast, fundamentalists of any religious persuasion or political ideology (Jehovah's Witnesses, Southern Baptists, Mormons, some Islamists, Orthodox Jews, the far right or far left politicians of the U.S., etc.) know perfectly well that there are other belief systems and ways of thinking out there in the world, but deeply believe that *their worldview is the right one*. Yet these religious sect members (and fundamentalist politicians) are generally non-violent—they may proselytize in an effort to convert others in order to "save them" by putting them on "the one true path," yet (generally speaking) they would never dream of hurting or killing them because they are not on that path—they just feel sorry and sad for the "non-believers" who will not "be saved" and often work hard to "save" them by converting them to the "proper" way of thinking.

In even more dramatic contrast, Stage 1 *fanatics* believe so strongly that their way is the only right way that they want to make everyone else fit inside their conceptual box, or disappear. Such fanatics, from the medieval Crusaders through Hitler's Nazi movement to today's jihadists feel totally justified in killing people who are openly opposed to or simply do not share their beliefs, values, and cultural mores—suicide bombers are a case in point.

Stage 1 thinking at its best provides individuals and groups with a strong sense of safety, stability, order, and meaning in life. All questions are answered and everything is held under tight control. Examples of groups or societies for which this kind of concrete thinking can be adaptive (or at least useful under certain circumstances) include:

1. small-scale societies living in conditions of relative environmental stability, in which there is little need for individual thinking, because everyone shares the same worldview and it works for everyone because there is sufficient food, shelter, and social satisfaction regarding group activities and social interactions. (There are fewer and fewer such societies left in the world because modern "development" constantly encroaches against them);
2. small- or large-scale societies in conditions of high stress or crisis, such as war or environmental disaster (see below), as shared concrete thinking enables people to join together for concerted action (World War II is a perfect example, while the Vietnam War constitutes a perfect counter-example, as there was little shared concrete thinking about that particular war);
3. soldiers (or others) trained to obey orders without question, so that they can immediately respond to those orders (as John McManus (1979:221) noted: "The army private who is complex and flexible in his thinking may find himself less adapted to rigid, authoritarian army life than his less complex friend");
4. particular fundamentalist religious groups who live somewhat apart from the rest of society. Examples include Christian, Mormon, Amish, and Hutterite families in the US and other countries who seek to raise their children in their religion and worldview only. Adults strive to minimize connections to the outside world by homeschooling their children and prohibiting radio, television, and Internet access to ensure that they are not exposed to heretical ideas or views during their formative years while their belief system

is concretizing. Some Muslims choose to have their sons attend what we would call Stage 1 schools in which only the Quran is taught. In these schools the students do learn to read and write and to think—yet only in the terms of their fundamentalist religion. We must ask, is this kind of Stage 1 thinking and learning adaptive in the contemporary world?

Stage 1 Thinking: Maladaptive Manifestations

Concrete/rigid cognitive structures are vulnerable to at least two types of potentially maladaptive manifestations. In the first place, concrete thinking—most especially fundamentalist and fanatical thinking—is often accompanied by intense negative emotion. Indeed, it is commonly the case that concrete thinking is a rationalization for, or a masking of the real reasons for the belief system—fear, anxiety, loathing, despair, anger. Fear that one's cherished belief system might be subsumed by another; anxiety that one's culture or society might be threatened; loathing of those perceived as a threat; despair that the world may be coming to a very bad end because nobody but you and your group knows "the real truth"; anger toward those who don't "get the truth" and about the "unjustness of it all." (For one example, it is very common for racism and anti-ethnic/immigrant feelings to erupt when the global economy tanks and people are in fear for their jobs.)

In the second place, concrete thinkers systematically misunderstand information coming at them from a much higher level of cognitive organization. Not only do concrete thinkers over-simplify the information coming at them, they also often unintentionally distort it. This distortion is produced by unconscious cognitive structures (neural networks) that lead concrete/rigid thinkers to latch onto and incorporate information that fits into their worldview and to misunderstand or dismiss information that does not—the message heard is not the message sent. For evidence of this kind of processing, one need only track far-right or far-left radio and TV "talk shows," where evidence is twisted and distorted through a system of very simplistic assumptions and political beliefs. One senses that behind these views is intense emotion—anger and hatred toward those of a different political or ideological persuasion ("You idiots! Why don't you think as I do—can't you see the real truth?"). The hallmark of such emotionally charged concrete thinking is that no matter how much objective evidence there may be that their views are false, "true believers" persist in holding these views by either ignoring or explaining away all evidence to the contrary. For one brief example, some people, most especially in the UK, believe that "man never went to the moon"—that it was all an elaborate hoax, despite the many pictures, witnesses, historical records, space capsules, and moon rocks on exhibit in various museums.

Conspiracy theories are on the rise in modern society, and are often the result of emotionally charged, very rigid thinking during periods of dynamic events in the world. Canadian journalist Jonathan Kay has written a fascinating study of conspiracy theories entitled *Among the Truthers* (2011). In that book he describes people who believe fervently that the Holocaust was an elaborate hoax, that "global warming" or "climate change" are either not happening or are not human-induced, that the official explanations for the assassination of President John F. Kennedy or the events of 9/11 are lies and cover-ups for conspiracies perpetrated by the Mafia, the CIA, and so forth. We are making no judgments here about the latter two of these theories—some of our friends believe in them and we are no experts on the fall of the Twin Towers or JFK's death. Our point here is simply that dozens of conspiracy theories are floating around the world at any given time—some, like denying that we ever landed on the moon or that the Holocaust never happened—are so far from reality that they need to be accounted for via investigation into why humans construct such ideas. Kay accounts for the appeal of conspiracy theories by referring to a natural human desire for certainty in a very uncertain world. "Conspiracism is a stubborn creed because humans are pattern-seeking animals. Show us a sky full of stars, and we'll arrange them into animals and giant spoons. Show us a world full of random misery, and we'll use the same trick to connect the dots into 'secret conspiracies'" (ibid:316).

Stage 1 thinking is of course difficult to maintain in culturally diverse societies, yet can easily persist when members of a Stage 1 group simply isolate themselves from the wider society and keep, as much as possible, to themselves without persecuting or molesting others. For one small example, when members of a Jehovah's Witness sect choose to leave, they are not hurt in any physical way; rather, they are simply "shunned" — treated as invisible by their former community and friends. Of course the psychological and emotional pain of such shunning can be terrible to bear, but at least no physical harm is done. In contrast to jihadist-type fanatics, as we mentioned above, naïve realists and religious fundamentalists living in contemporary, diverse societies are generally non-violent—they simply protect their boundaries by keeping away from others with differing points of view, and by ignoring or explaining away any evidence or information contrary to their belief system. Their unconscious mental structures often cannot evaluate or incorporate conflicting information. Putting it another way, they have no neural networks complex enough to process that information because of their intense socialization into one particular worldview—meaning that their neural networks are organized to interpret everything in terms of that one view. (Again, we do not mean to imply that Stage 1 thinkers are stupid—they can be extremely intelligent within their own belief systems/worldviews.)

Stage 2 Thinking: Ethnocentrism

Stage 2 thinking is more flexible than Stage 1 thinking, for it allows for varying views of the same experiences or sets of information, yet tends to favor one view over the others—a type of thinking that anthropologists call *ethnocentrism* and that is common to all societies on the globe. Ethnocentric thinkers recognize that other groups and other worldviews can and do legitimately exist, but still insist that "our way is the best way." Psychological studies suggest that most human beings on the planet are incapable of transcending Stage 2, ethnocentric thought (Schroder and Suefeld 1971; Rest et al. 1999)—the vast majority of human beings are ethnocentrists at our core.

Ethnocentrism at its most adaptive allows cultural groups facing the prospect of assimilation into another culture to retain their own identities by taking pride in their own traditions and mores. Ethnocentrism is thus the natural cost societies pay for the conservative aspect of culture and ritual. Culturally diverse societies like contemporary Canada, the EuroZone, and the U.S. encompass a tremendous variety of ethnic groups. While some members of such ethnic groups (usually first generation immigrants) work very hard to assimilate—sending their children to English-speaking schools, for example—most of them also work hard to maintain or recreate their culture, or as much as they can of it, by forming ethnic communities—hence we have Chinatowns, Little Italies, and many other such "hoods." Any immigrant family that wants its children to have a sense of cultural continuity will take pains to teach them the language of their culture of origin and to create family life, especially holidays, around their own cultural traditions. Yet some of the many rituals of ethnicity are extremely minimalist for those who have mostly assimilated into American society and culture. Consider that on March 17th each year, tens of thousands of Irish-Americans may celebrate St. Patrick's Day by wearing green clothing and drinking green beer. For many, this is their sole acknowledgement of their Irish heritage throughout the year.

Stage 2 Thinking: Maladaptive Manifestations

At its worst and least adaptive, ethnocentrism allows the members of one group to exploit and dominate others while feeling justified in their "superiority." This sense of superiority can be dangerous and result in damage and great harm. Take for instance the trans-Atlantic slave trade that lasted for roughly three hundred years. Western Europeans and Americans of European descent came to believe that the slave trade was justifiable because African people were "sub-human"—little more than animals—and thus subject to the same treatment as animals. They did not hate "Negros" in a fundamentalist way—they just needed to feel justified in exploiting them. What is especially interesting is that this belief arose as a rationalization of the practice, not as the reason for initiating it. Studies of documents including ship's logs and letters during the early years of the trade—back in the 16th century—suggest that African people were not referred to in derogatory ways until long after the slave trade got going. Many American racists of the 18th, 19th and early 20th centuries were what we would call naïve realists—they simply assumed the sub-humanity of African peoples because they were dark-skinned "like monkeys" and lived in Africa in "primitive cultures." Robbie vividly remembers her American Southern-born-and-raised parents justifying slavery during her childhood with the following phrase: "They sold their own people!" It took her years while growing up to realize that her parents simply had no clue that Africa was as diverse as any other continent and that there was no one "African people"—there were many different African peoples, some of whom exploited the others just as peoples on every continent have done at different times in human history.

Again, ethnocentrism at its best simply allows people to value and appreciate their own cultures more than others, while leaving others alone. (We repeat that in truth, most of us humans are ethnocentric—because most of us value and appreciate our own cultures and would not choose to live in another one.) At its worst, ethnocentrism can lead to ethnic cleansing/genocide, as in recent decades in Rwanda, Nigeria, and the former Yugoslavia. Negative, fear- and anger-based ethnocentrism often arises or intensifies in many nations (including the U.S. and Europe) in the wake of economic decline and sociopolitical conflict, usually out of fear that those "others" are taking things away from "us."

Fluid Thinking: Stages 3 and 4

Fluid thinking is a type of post-conventional cognition that readily deals with diversity and change. In multicultural and constantly changing societies like ours, fluid thinking is far more adaptive than rigid naïve realist, fundamentalist, or fanatical (Stage 1) or ethnocentric (Stage 2) thinking. Here we identify two developmental levels of fluid thinking (Rubinstein, Laughlin and McManus 1984) that are representative of true abstract thinking.

Stage 3 Thinking: Cultural Relativism

Stage 3 thinking is produced by cognitive structures that are capable of encompassing multiple points of view—an attitude that anthropologists call *cultural relativism*. This kind of relativistic thinking occurs in people who realize that a society's point of view about something (healthcare, gay and lesbian marriage, the proper role of the state in human affairs, gender roles and relations, etc.) is but one of a set of possible views that are conditioned by a society's customary childrearing.

In its positive form, cultural relativism honors the existence of many ways of interpreting the world and insists that *no way is more right or better than any other*. While this kind of relativism is important to life in a multicultural society, it gives equal validity to all cultures and all cultural traditions and beliefs, including those that institutionalize behaviour that many find morally repugnant. For examples: it is the custom in some rural villages in Pakistan and Romania for men to beat their wives regularly in a ritual display of dominance. It is the custom, especially in rural areas, in Somalia, Sudan and other countries to circumcise young girls in an extraordinarily painful way. Torture and maltreatment are common elements of prisoner capture and interrogation in many societies. Within prison culture, these violent and damaging behaviors are considered customary and acceptable. Yet, like wife-beating and female circumcision, they are fundamental violations of human rights—well, to even consider that *all humans have rights* requires a search for a higher standard than cultural relativism (see Rest et al. 1999)—hence we move to Stage 4.

Stage 4 Thinking: Global Humanism

Stage 4 thinking produces views that transcend cultural relativism in its search for a higher point of view that does not depend on any particular culture or religion. It is the kind of thinking reflected in the words of St. Augustine ("Against the Fundamental Epistle of Manichaeus"):

> Let us, on both sides, lay aside all arrogance. Let us not, on either side, claim that we have already discovered the truth. Let us seek it together as something which is known to neither of us. For then only may we seek it, lovingly and tranquilly, if there be no bold presumption that it is already discovered and possessed.

Stage 4 thinking underlies today's *global humanism*. Stage 4 thinkers know better than to lay any claim to defining "reality" in any absolute sense, for to do so automatically produces *anomalies*—an "anomaly" being any information that "just doesn't fit" the current view. Concrete thinkers are quite capable of ignoring anomalies while asserting that their view is the correct one. Stage 4 thinkers can handle multiple perspectives and anomalies within the same cognitive frame. A person operating at Stage 4 can speak in terms of the "likelihood" of a point of view being correct, given the preponderance of evidence, while simultaneously acknowledging evidence that may point in another direction. (An example of the difference here would be the tendency of concrete-thinking police detectives picking out one subject and expending all their efforts to "prove" their suspect guilty. In contrast, Stage 4 detectives would be able to focus on likely suspects while at the same time able to acknowledge anomalous evidence suggesting the innocence of said suspects, freeing them to look beyond "the obvious.") Stage 4 thinkers are aware of the limitations of cultural relativism (Stage 3 thinking), which gives equal value to all cultures and customs, no matter how brutal or exploitative—and of the need for universal and global moral standards that may help humanity evolve to a higher, fairer, and more gratifying way of life for all.

In regard to wife-beating in Pakistan, wife-burning in India, female circumcision in Sudan and Somalia, the gassing of Jews in death camps, and the routine torture of common prisoners—to offer but a few examples—the higher cultural standard proposed at the 1985 Women's Conference in Beijing insists that (1) all humans have basic, fundamental rights; (2) women's and children's rights are human rights; (3) cultural systems that do not recognize or honor basic human rights (as defined by the UN) should be transformed. The challenge of this kind of Stage 4 thinking is to identify, aim for, and help develop "high ethical standards"—*humanistic* standards not based on any one religion or worldview, but on what works to guarantee the rights of all humans to be treated with dignity and respect and to live their lives as best they can without persecution or mistreatment, and without the imposition of the rigid/concrete belief or value system of one group on others.

Because Stage 4 (globally humanistic) thinking advocates higher standards than those set by many cultures and religions (see Kohlberg 1981; Rest et al. 1999), Stage 1 thinkers often clash with Stage 4 thinkers. Fluid, globally humanistic, Stage 4 thinking can be anathema to Stage 1 (fundamentalist-type) thinkers because it seeks to refute their deeply held beliefs that *their way is right and therefore, no other way can be right*. Stage 4 thinkers hold a space for a higher moral ground that acknowledges the human rights of all human beings—again a view that can easily clash with the views of Stage 1 thinkers, especially the fanatics. (To recap, Stage 1 *naïve realists* simply believe that their way is the only way that exists. Stage 1 *fundamentalists* just want everyone to believe as they do, without violently hurting them to achieve that aim. Stage 1 *fanatics* want to eradicate (or convert) everyone who does not believe as they do.)

So, Stage 1 fundamentalists and fanatics work very hard to *reinterpret and remake* Stage 4 thinking into an "alternative" and distorted concrete system. For instance, right-wing true believers may code global humanists as "left-wing do-gooders," "pinkos," "socialists," and the like, while left-wing fanatics may code global humanists as bourgeois capitalists, Western puppets, etc. Yet people of any party and any persuasion can be Stage 4 thinkers, in the sense of people who "think beyond" fundamentalism, true-believing, ethnocentrism, and even cultural relativism, who are open and willing to explore all thoughts and all possibilities even while they identify themselves, in socio-cultural terms, with one party or another, one religion or another, one culture or another. The quote from St. Augustine that we provided above gives one example. The famous Republican commentator William F. Buckley provides another, as he had the gift of intelligent insight that led him to the pithy essence of many political issues of his day—for instance, when he said, "Even if one takes every reefer madness allegation of the prohibitionists at face value, marijuana prohibition has done far more harm to far more people than marijuana ever could." Republican President Dwight Eisenhower offers another example—he famously said in his "Chance for Peace" speech (April 15, 1953), "Every gun that is made, every warship launched, every rocket fired signifies, in the final sense, a theft from those who hunger and are not fed, those who are cold and are not clothed...."

The always-possible conflict between Stage 1 true believers and Stage 4 fluid thinkers lies behind many of the troubles that pervade our contemporary global society. Ethnocentrism (the product of Stage 2 thought) simply leads people to live the lives their cultures tell them is right. They may be tolerant of other cultural systems and let others alone to live by their own cultural lights, or their ethnocentrism may lead to cultural conflict, either within a nation or between nations. (Some traditional societies have lived peacefully in their environments for many generations, while others have engaged in internecine and usually ritualized warfare over years and even generations.) Many modern nations pride themselves on being "multi-cultural"—Canada being a good example. Yet even in relatively peaceful nations like Canada, the struggle to actualize a uniform tolerance of "difference" has often proved very difficult.

Cultural relativism (generally the product of Stage 3 thinking) lets everyone "do their own thing," without blame or judgment that any one way is better than any other way—a system in which ideally at least everyone has the right, as Rodney King famously put it, "to just get along" without harming anyone else. Yet this view, however tolerant it may seem, faces the challenge of handling those knotty moral dilemmas we mentioned above—blatantly harmful customs like refusing medical treatment for women and children based upon a very concrete interpretation of scripture, surgically removing little girls' clitorises so that they cannot "shame" themselves by enjoying sex or sewing closed their vaginas so they cannot have sex until they are married, or advocating ethnic cleansing or even genocide in order to bring about a utopian social system. Again, Stage 1 thinking can at times produce a virulent form of fundamentalist fanaticism (socially organized "true believers") based upon a very simplistic desire to impose their ways on everyone else or get rid of them. In contrast, Stage 4 fluid thinking often produces social movements to create a world in which we do so much more than "just get along" and tolerate difference —a world in which higher ethical, humanistic standards guarantee basic human rights to every global citizen, regardless of their racial, ethnic, cultural, religious, political, or socio-economic background or gender/sexual orientation.

RITUAL AND THE FOUR STAGES OF COGNITION:
Stage 1: Naïve Realism/Fundamentalism/Fanaticism, Stage 2: Ethnocentrism, Stage 3: Cultural Relativism, and Stage 4: Global Humanism

It is important to understand that ritual can support each of these stages of cognition by enacting the belief and value systems generated at each level of complexity. Ritual is a primary supporter of naïve realism, continually enacting in every ritual performance the beliefs and values of a given culture and the myths that underlie and explain those beliefs and values. Ritual performance vivifies fundamentalists' and fanatics' sense of righteousness, reinforcing the tenets of their belief system in the hearts and minds of true believers and thereby strengthening their "true belief." Rituals are also essential to ethnocentrists, helping each and every group to enact, intensify and thus reinforce and transmit its belief in its own worth. Rituals can also express cultural relativism, as when Christians deliberately replace "Merry Christmas" with "Happy Holidays" to honor and respect non-Christians during the holiday season. And ritual can enact, display, and transmit globally humanistic belief systems, as it did at the Women's Conference in Beijing, and as it does in a small school in New England where people gather every year

Stages of Cognition	Anthropological Equivalents
Stage 1: Rigid/concrete thinking	Naïve realism, fundamentalism, fanaticism
Stage 2: Self- and culture-centered thinking	Ethnocentrism
Stage 3: Relative thinking	Cultural relativism
Stage 4: Fluid thinking	Global humanism

Table 9.1. The Four Stages of Cognition and Their Anthropological Equivalents

on a giant map of the world laid out on the playground to light candles for every nation on earth, and in peace-circles held around the world in which participants name every nation and call for that nation to have peace with all other nations.

Examples of Stage 4 Rituals: Midwives and Women

Like any other profession, midwifery today around the world is plagued by political and ideological conflicts and divisions. Some midwives highly value university education and graduate degrees, whereas others value apprenticeship—learning experientially from other midwives. Some midwives attend home births and seek to support home birth mothers by learning skills like external version (manually turning a breech baby in utero to a head down position before birth), vaginally delivering breech babies who can't be turned (standard obstetrical procedure for breech babies is a cesarean section in most developed countries), supporting women with one or more previous cesarean sections to give birth at home or in a birth center instead of in a hospital (where they will almost surely have another cesarean due to hospital policy). Other midwives discount such efforts as "irresponsible" and "dangerous" and choose to follow obstetric protocols and rituals (such as the use of the previously-discussed electronic fetal monitor) and to become expert in those rituals and procedures. Some midwives continually challenge obstetric dominance over birth, citing the large body of scientific evidence that supports the humanistic, woman-centered, "midwifery model of care," which is focused on facilitating normal, physiologic birth (see Davis-Floyd et al. 2009:441-462 for a full description of this model). Other midwives prefer quiescent patients who are happy with their epidurals, even if those epidurals (when given too early in labor—before 5 or 6 centimeters of cervical dilation) often lead to unnecessary cesarean sections.

When these differing types of midwives come together at midwifery conferences around the world, their ideological differences often lead to conflict and dispute. Yet all midwives want the best for mothers and babies—a healthy mother, a healthy baby—and hopefully, a fulfilling birth experience. So at such conferences, particularly those held around the world by an organization called Midwifery Today, during the closing ceremony the midwives often form a huge circle around the auditorium, join hands, and sing this song (usually repeated 4 times to facilitate ritual entrainment):

> *Humble yourself in the sight of your sister*
> *You need to bow down low (everyone bows down) and*
> *Humble yourself in the sight of your sister*
> *You need to know what she knows, and (arms rising in synchrony)*
> *We shall lift each other up!*

This Stage 4 ritual expresses and enacts midwives' shared values on refraining from assuming that any one particular view is right and on the importance of learning from each other.

Likewise, for some years, a few dozen Israeli and Palestinian women weekly enacted a ritual in which they all dressed in black and stood in parks and other places, simply holding hands, in a silent statement of solidarity in their desire for peace and reconciliation. And here is another Stage 4 ritual song, sung by women's groups in many countries:

> *If every woman in the world had her mind set on freedom*
> *If every woman in the world sang a sweet song of peace*
> *If every woman, of every nation, young and old, each generation*
> *Held hands, in the name of love, then we would all have peace*

And another one:

> *Circle round for freedom, circle round for peace*
> *For all of us in prison, circle for release*
> *Circle for the planet, circle for each soul*
> *For the children of our children, keep the circle whole!*

These are Stage 4 social movement songs, expressing a desire for universal human rights, including those of women and children. Other examples of Stage 4 rituals can be found in Native American sweat lodge proceedings, in which all participants of every race and ethnicity call upon "all my ancestors" to be present to the ceremony—those ancestors could and surely do include colonialist conquerors and many more. Stage 1 rituals are exclusive, honoring only the true believers who perform them, whereas Stage 4 rituals are inclusive, honoring all. Who are you and where do you want to stand along that spectrum? And how will you use ritual to enact and facilitate your particular stance?

RITUAL, COGNITION, AND STRESS: SUBSTAGE AND STABILIZATION

When humans are subjected to extremes of stress (see below for a definition of stress), they may, at least temporarily, retrogress into a dysfunctional cognitive and emotional condition that we call *Substage,* in which they become panic-stricken, unreasonable, or simply out of touch with reality. Whenever the danger of such retrogression is present, ritual plays a critical role, for it stabilizes individuals under stress by giving them a conceptual handhold to keep them from "losing it." When the airplane starts to falter, even those who don't go to church are likely to pray! The simple act of rhythmically repeating, "Dear Lord, please save us," can enable terrified passengers to avoid the panic that might increase the likelihood of disastrous behaviors.

Ritual stands as a barrier between cognition and chaos (between Stage 1 and Substage) *by making reality appear to conform to accepted cognitive categories*—that is, by making the world look the way we think it ought to, even a little bit. In other words, to perform a ritual in the face of chaos is to restore conceptual order. Even a small semblance of order can enable individuals to function under the most chaotic of conditions. Hence the following section describes the "cognitive anchors" that individuals and cultures can "hold onto" in extreme situations in order to cognitively ground themselves—in other words, to keep themselves stable and functional in the face of chaos, at least at a Stage 1 level.

Cognitive Anchors: Earthquakes and House Fires

Ritual action in the face of disasters is not as irrational as one might think. To repeat a familiar and ritualized action may keep the person from cognitively bottoming-out and descending into Substage irrational thinking and panic. Think of the earthquake victim sweeping off her front steps when the entire neighborhood lies in ruins around her. Those steps represent one ordered cognitive category. To make them clean is to ground oneself in a little piece of the known and the familiar. To repeat a familiar and ritualized action may keep the person from "losing it" —descending into panic or hysteria. From that cognitive anchor, one can then begin to deal, a little at a time, with the surrounding chaos as the brain frantically creates new neural connections to enable the individual to grasp the larger chaotic reality.

When Robbie's cherished home of 30 years burned down in 2009, she got a good dose of "cognitive anchoring." Just after the fire alarms went off, dressed only in her strawberry-patterned nightgown and her blue, pink, and green paisley sleep socks, she grabbed her purse (which she always kept right by the front door in case of exactly such an occasion) on the way out. Standing in the driveway in front of her burning house, she looked down at her body to take stock. "Good," she thought—"I'm not barefoot, so the driveway won't hurt my feet. Oh, and I'm wearing my nightgown, so at least I'm not naked. And I have my purse in my hand, which means I have my cellphone, my car keys, my drivers' license, my credit cards—which means that I can still function in the world—oh, WOW, I have everything I need!" Of course she was in shock, yet she found some grounding and calm in those cognitive anchors, few as they were compared to all that was going up in flames behind her.

Two days in the hospital for smoke inhalation gave Robbie even more calm and grounding because family and friends were constantly there to support her. Her son Jason came to say, "Mom, you need to *get this*—the house is barely there—the fire went into the attic and the ceilings collapsed, so everything is buried in gray muck." Those words gave Robbie the chance to form new neural networks—new images—that helped her to face what she would find when she returned to her house two days later to begin the salvage work. She was prepared for the horrible mess, yet totally unprepared for the new cognitive anchors that would gradually emerge from the muck—the tiny figurine that had belonged to her mother sticking its hand out of a huge pile of ashes and emerging undamaged while all its former companion figurines laid in ruin, her long-collected Mexican pottery shining fresh and clean in the dishwasher (which she had turned on before going to bed) in the midst of a shattered kitchen, and, most importantly, Peyton's altar (which was in a closed closet with an intact ceiling) impeccably preserved, along with the beautiful urn that contained Peyton's ashes and all the small mementos—her Guatemalan wallet, her passports, her journals, her dolphin sculptures, her dream catchers—that so indelibly evoked Peyton's personality and spirit. Tiny islands of cohesion in the face of the utter chaos that lay all around—cognitive anchors that Robbie clung to during the 10-day cleanup of the ashes and muck that later became meaningful ritual artifacts that Robbie could incorporate into her new home, evoking continuity between her past and her present home lives.

Most ironically, the house burned in a very disordered way after Robbie and her Jewish partner Alan had hosted a Rosh Hashanah dinner for a group of Alan's friends from his synagogue—a lovely and well-ordered ritual, after which Robbie and Alan left the ashes cooling in the charcoal grill outside on the wooden deck. Evidently a hungry raccoon climbed up to get that last sweet potato, knocking the grill over and spreading the still-burning ashes over the deck, which caught fire, and the fire then spread up the outside walls to the attic. In that attic, Robbie had stored all the ritual artifacts that she had hoped to give to her grandchildren when they arrived—her christening gown, her wedding dress, the Christmas velvet outfits her children had worn each year, her own favorite toys and dolls from childhood, with which she had played for many happy hours, and all of her mother's Christmas decorations, collected over 40 years. Few of these ritual artifacts had any monetary value, yet they all had ritual value to Robbie and to her son Jason. It speaks to the power of ritual and its symbolic artifacts to note that the loss of these mementos caused Robbie more emotional pain than the loss of the many practical and daily-useful items that vanished in the fire.

Cognitive Anchors and Rituals of Stabilization

Rituals (such as prayer, or crossing oneself, carefully setting the table, lighting candles for loved ones in danger, pulling out the Christmas decorations or the Passover Seder plates, holding a feast for the devil after the mine shaft collapses (see Chapter 7), or a healing ceremony when illness strikes) provide their participants with many such cognitive anchors. Ritual thus has high evolutionary value: it is a powerful adaptive technique that our ancient ancestors 100,000 years ago must have utilized to help them continue to function at a survival level whenever they faced conditions of environmental or social stress (like earthquakes, volcanic eruptions, grass and forest fires, and the deaths of loved ones). Archaeological discoveries show that mortuary rituals may go back as much as 300,000 years to the earliest periods of Neanderthal and ancient *Homo sapiens*. For one example, when archaeologists excavated Shanidar Cave in the Kurdistan Region of Iraq, they found evidence that Neanderthals carried out mortuary rites and ritual burials around 80,000 years ago, burying skeletons in the fetal position and showering the dead with flowers (Trinkaus 1983). And by 40,000 years ago, ritual burials, as well as cave art and ritual iconography, were common (Giacobini 2007).

For many thousands of years, therefore, humans have understood that *groups that believe together can act together* to meet and overcome crises and danger. When belief is not shared, joint action is much more difficult—perhaps impossible—to achieve. Even warring armies often rely on a number of shared beliefs, symbols, and rituals—the Geneva Conventions, the red cross or red crescent of medical facilities, the white flag of truce, the process of formal surrender. These are rituals of stabilization that can work even in the face of the chaos of war.

Eustress and Distress

In this section we present a case in point of the adaptive significance of a people's myth/ritual complex. Generally speaking, cultures "build in" ritual responses to potential dangers. Prior knowledge and ritualized responses prepare people to "weather the storm" by making sense of events within their scheme of things, and knowing what to do to survive. People deal with what their environment hands them in ways that help them to avoid *information overload*—that is, too much information coming at them too fast. By putting all of the above together, we are able to see why the famous endocrinologist Hans Selye (1907-1982) insisted upon distinguishing two types of stress. *Eustress* is "good stress" in that it challenges us to peak cognition, positive feelings, and adaptive action (see Selye 1974). *Distress*, on the other hand, is "bad stress" that can drive us to hyper-emotional, Substage thinking and reactions, and can lead to physical breakdown, heart attacks, cancer and other nasty diseases and mental problems.

Distress often arises when a person feels trapped and is unable to adaptively respond to the environment. For instance, highly stressful jobs like those of paramedics, emergency room physicians, police officers, fire-fighters, and soldiers may easily lead to not being able to "leave it at the office" —becoming unable to "let go" and take a rest from the environmental stressors such individuals are forced to deal with day in and day out. We know that we are under some degree of distress at least if it takes us a week to "come down" from the job when we are on our two-week vacation. In this sense, a "vacation" amounts to a ritualized break from the daily stress—a period of time during which we may actually have to "vacate" our homes and go somewhere else in order to de-stress. Coffee breaks, regulated work hours, guaranteed lunch hours, etc. are rituals that buffer to some extent the distress inherent in the job. Successful businesses take the need for these ritual buffers fully into account and increasingly offer, in addition, on-site gyms, walking trails, and day-care centers. (Those businesses that don't institute such ritual buffers suffer the consequences of employee dissatisfaction and "burnout.")

As we mentioned above, open-minded, fluid-thinking individuals who normally function at Stage 3 or 4 can be reduced to Stage 1 thinking, and even Substage, by *stress*. Persistent stress can cause information overload and the development of "tunnel vision"—the need to shut out extraneous stimuli and focus on one thing only. In other words, *stress can make fluid thinkers become rigid/concrete,* if only for a while. Usually rest or a vacation will restore us to our normal fluid state. But if the stress continues, we can disintegrate into Substage—again, a condition antithetical to clear thought, one of hysteria, panic, a nervous breakdown (also known as "losing it"). Under such conditions, *ritual can stabilize us at Stage 1, thereby preventing us from degenerating into Substage behavior.* In times of crisis, of information overload, of too much stress, the most stabilizing behavior is at least a temporary return to Stage 1 rituals (often those of our childhood, like a return to the church in which we were raised) that generate a sense of peace and calm (and renewed hope for a brighter future) and allow us to regroup and recoup. Individuals facing extreme loss may suddenly become extremely religious, even fanatical, when they never were before. Other individuals facing extreme stress may suddenly develop obsessive-compulsive disorder (OCD), ritualizing their every move in an enormous effort to stabilize their lifeworld. The trick is not to stay in Stage 1 too long! Once the individual is stable, change can be tried at a gentler pace. When the stress subsides, we can move back into fluid thinking, secure in the knowledge that there is order in the world (most of the time).

Contemporary democratic societies are structured in accordance with the need to strike a balance between rigid and fluid thinking—between the need for stability and the need to adapt to rapid change. Democracies across the globe structure their legislative decision-making so that the rituals of governance (e.g., public parliamentary debate, transparent rules of procedure, public voting on laws and policies, and so forth) require rulers to at least appear to take alternative points of view into consideration and make their decisions in an open, public, and transparent way. Public legislative governance forces higher cognitive functioning by ritualizing communication. Furthermore, such systems tend to recognize the importance of a diverse education for developing fluid modes of thought.

We suggest that contemporary humans, especially those living in modern, industrial, or post-industrial technocratic societies, must be able to move up and down the rigid-fluid continuum in order to cope both with high levels of stress and with the need to keep up with our constantly changing world (a major stressor). Conscious use of ritual can make all the difference. Stage 1 rituals can ground and stabilize us in times of great stress and confusion. (Americans can vividly remember the flags flying from almost every household after 9/11—powerful symbolic and ritualistic expressions of love of country when that country was attacked on its own soil, for the first time in over two centuries.) Stage 2 rituals can reinforce our belief in the "okay-ness" and goodness of our own, culturally influenced lives—Jews celebrate the Passover Seder to honor and celebrate their exodus from Egypt and the 3000 or so years of cultural continuity they thereby gained. Christians celebrate Easter—a reminder for them of the "risen Christ." Muslims fast during the month of Ramadan and strive to make the pilgrimage to Mecca at least once in their lives, thereby vivifying their religion and their religious beliefs. Wiccans stage rituals to honor the Summer Solstice and the ever-repeating cycles of the Earth, Our Mother. (And on and on). Stage 3 (culturally relative) rituals can expand our consciousness to encompass the notion that many other peoples have lives just as rich and full as our own, even though they are profoundly different from "us." And Stage 4 rituals can enact the core values of humanism—that all people have rights, that no one should suffer unjustly, that justness does or can exist, that we can strive to be fair even when life is not.

Ritual and Stress Reduction

The relationship between the level of complexity of cognitive functioning and performance on the one hand, and the amount of environmental challenge/stress on the other hand, may be represented by an inverted U-curve (see Schroder, Driver and Streufert 1967; McManus 1979 and Figure 9.1). What the *inverted U-curve* shows is that we do not do our best, either in thinking or doing, unless the environment around us presents a sufficient challenge. "Challenge" in this sense has to do with the amount of information coming at us. Most of us are used to thinking of information in digital and electronic terms—it just comes at us through print media and the wires and airwaves that make our computers, TVs, and smartphones work. Yet there is an older, and for our purposes much more experiential, sense of the term "information." Something is *informative* to us if it can potentially influence our perceptions, feelings, decisions, and actions. Information is whatever is coming at us that we have to pay attention to as relevant. All brains work on this principle, be it our human brain or the brains of our pet dog, cat, parrot, or goldfish. We seek to reduce our perceptions of a situation to manageable patterns and then assign action appropriate to those patterns.

Seeing information in this more commonsense way allows us to distinguish between stuff coming at us that is redundant (nothing new) and that is novel (new). If we are dealing with the same situations, day in and day out (making breakfast, driving to work, doing our job, bathing the baby, etc.), our brain tends to routinize—quite literally *ritualize*—its activities.

We feel that we have to stop a moment to note again, as we did in Chapter 1, that we see routine, habit, and full-out ritual performance on a *spectrum of ritual*. It is the essence of "habit" not to think about the actions we are performing, allowing us just to perform them in routine ways. Yet how often do we talk about our morning or night-time "rituals"—the simple self-grooming ways in which we start our days, and the simple, routinized ways in which we end them, perhaps by reading bedtime stories to our children, taking a hot bath, or enjoying that last glass of wine? Such tiny acts of individual habit or routine may be unconsciously or consciously performed,

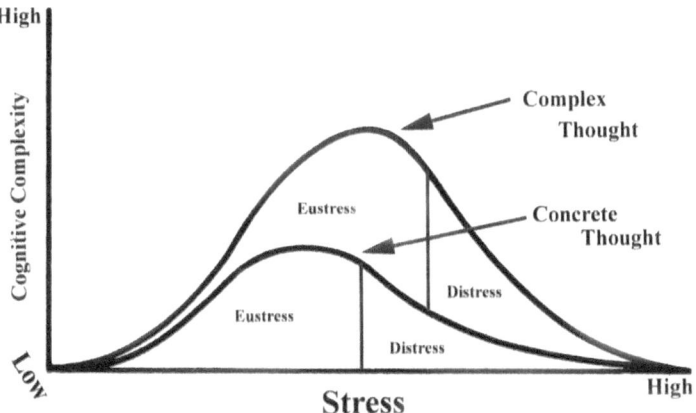

Figure 9.1. The complexity of a person's optimal level of cognition in part determines how easily he or she adapts to increasing stress. The more complex the mind, the greater environmental stress may be encountered and processed before the cognitive system is overwhelmed (adapted from Schroder, Driver and Streufert 1967: Fig. 10.4)

yet we insist in this book that all these activities are in fact rituals—*patterned, repetitive, and symbolic enactments of cultural or individual beliefs and values*—that exist on a spectrum ranging from habit and routine to full-scale ritual ceremonies. All such acts are ritual performances of our beliefs and values, no matter how grand or how mundane.

When a woman shaves her legs, she is enacting her culturally-induced belief that shaved legs are more attractive than hairy ones. When she chooses not to shave her legs, she is enacting a counter-cultural value on "natural" appearance—letting the body do as it will and appreciating the results. When a man shaves his face, he is enacting his equally culturally-induced belief that a shaved face is more appropriate than a bearded one in his particular case. When we brush or floss our teeth, we are enacting our cultural and individual values on dental hygiene (not shared in many other cultures). Our Foreword author Betty Sue Flowers suggested to us that "It is the essence of ritual that we pay profound—I would even say 'sacred'—attention to the action being performed." We respond that most people reserve their sacred attention to ritual for their very most special weekly, seasonal, annual, or ceremonial rituals, from baptisms in whatever faith to Presidential Inaugurations. Most humans perform most of their daily rituals in a relatively unconscious state, simply following the ritual sequence already laid out by themselves or their culture. Such habitual rituals make life easier to live—*the fact that the rituals have become habits or routines does not diminish their ritual import.*

Returning to our present topic of ritual and stress reduction, we note that the information coming at us is mostly considered redundant by our brain. We end up doing the same things in the same way with little thought because we are ritually habituated to that way (in other words, our neural networks have constellated to facilitate that particular way of doing things). But when some novelty pops up in our environment, perhaps placing an obstacle in our way (ran out of eggs, the car won't start, the computers are "down" at work, there are no more diapers, etc.), our brain perks up, gets interested in what is happening, and perhaps applies some creative thinking to resolve the problem. Our brains, in other words, are designed to operate at peak efficiency when the environment is complex, novel and challenging—in a word, "stressful" in a positive sense.

But our tolerance for novelty has its limits. If things get too complex, too novel, and information is coming at us too fast, then our brains may start to shut down and cease to operate effectively. We begin to experience information overload (Klingberg 2008; Eppler and Mengis

2004)—known in the common American vernacular as "TMI"—"too much information." One of the most important factors in our experience of information overload is our emotional state. As Figure 9.1 indicates, if our environment provides us with insufficient information, we will tend to experience boredom. Boredom is a sure sign that what we are doing at the moment is not interesting to us. When the environment is more information-rich—that is, of sufficient interest to us to perk-up our cognitive processes—then we tend to feel energized, we experience excitement and enhanced focus—we may even experience "flow" (see Chapter 7 on ritual framing and ritually-induced flow). But if the environment becomes over-rich with information—is perceived to be coming at us too fast, or in bundles of information that are too complex for us to deal with—we tend to react with anxiety and may even panic/regress into Substage.

Most people attempt to order their lives so that their environments are sufficiently information-rich that they feel good, enjoy themselves, stay interested in things, and complete the tasks at hand in a focused way—perhaps even, as we mentioned above, in a state of flow. But how many of us are able to control every aspect of our lives so that we are never bored and never anxious? How many of us rely upon media to entertain us and keep us from the depths of boredom? If we examine our lives closely, most of us will readily admit that *we have ritualized our activities to escape boredom on the one hand and to avoid information overload on the other hand.* We will plan ahead so that our meals occur at specific times and are enjoyable. We may watch favorite TV programs, play interesting video games, take long walks, play card games with friends, attend sporting events, have sex with an amiable partner, in patterned, repetitive, and symbolic—in other words, ritualized—ways.

Any reader who has followed a spiritual path that requires lengthy (weeks, months) meditation retreats can attest to what happens to our minds when suddenly all external entertainment, daily busy activity, and endless distractions stop. Most meditators eventually have to confront what Charlie calls the "boredom barrier" in their retreat work. That happens when you require your mind to chill out and just watch its own machinations. Gone are the ritualized daily activities that keep the mind busy and entertained, replaced by ritualized meditations that turn the mind inwards. Often boredom sets in for a while until the mind decides to make its new activity interesting. Eventually the mind becomes very interested in its own processes, aided by rituals of concentration (meditating on a mantra, the breath, a sacred image, etc.). Now the mind itself is providing information that feeds its own internal curiosity.

One of the major factors in determining information overload is the stage of cognitive complexity we are capable of bringing to bear in processing environmental information (Schroder, Driver and Streufert 1967). Peak efficiency for the concrete/rigid mind occurs at a level below that of a very complex mind (everything else being equal). Notice in Figure 9.1 that it requires more environmental challenge to stimulate peak complexity and efficiency in the complex mind than for the concrete mind. As the environment begins to "heat up" (that is, becoming more complex or more information rich), the concrete mind will peak out earlier than the complex mind, but if the challenge becomes too great, eventually both kinds of minds will begin to decrease in efficiency and complexity of information processing until they both bottom-out and are in danger of Substage reactions.

One of the functions of ritual is to act as a buffer between environmental challenge and cognitive effectiveness—again, *ritual stands as a buffer between cognition and chaos.* Take for instance the conditions faced by soldiers in a firefight. How is it possible to get reasonably intelligent humans to face enemies doing their very best to kill them, when the intelligent thing would seem to be to get out of the line of fire and run away to hide? The answer is that society puts the warrior through an intense "boot camp"/initiatory rite of passage designed to build-in ritual buffers to normal reactions to danger. If we examine how boot camps are designed, we will always find rituals paired with indoctrination sessions in an alternating sequence—all the ingredients of a rite of passage we discussed in the preceding chapter. First the trainees are put through ordeals and other activities (marching, hazing, weapons drills, etc.) to break down their individual sense of self and their former worldview, and to physically habituate them to new ritualized responses to danger until they become automatic. And then they sit through classes and perform ritualized activities that offer an alternative worldview, including new interpretations of events, a new social structure, a new set of values, and so forth—the soldier's worldview.

The great anthropologist Anthony Wallace (1956a, 1957) once researched individuals' reactions to a tornado in 1953. He found many people so stressed-out that they completely denied that something horrible had happened. To give that phenomenon a name, he coined the term "disaster syndrome." It was as though the terrible destruction had wiped people's minds of any reality grounding and effective responses. He observed peculiar behaviors, such as a woman carefully sweeping her front steps when the house behind her had been completely blown away (an example we mentioned above as a search for a "cognitive anchor"). The other really important thing he found was that *those people who had gone through disasters before were much more able to cope with the tragedy than those who had not.* In our terms, such individuals had formed new neural networks while dealing with the original tragedy or trauma that stayed in place and were thus available to help them more rapidly adapt to a new tragedy or trauma. For other examples: it turns out that veteran combat soldiers are far less likely to succumb to PTSD than non-veterans; and Charlie's work (along with that of Ivan Brady) among the So, who had repeatedly experienced devastating droughts throughout their history, showed that cultures confronting periodic disasters tend to be ritually structured so as to buffer the effects of the disaster on their people (Laughlin 1974; Laughlin and Brady 1978).

Robbie's personal experience comes in handy as another example of developing new neural networks to deal with an original tragedy that, once in place, facilitate a family's ability to deal with subsequent tragedies. As Robbie puts it,

> Since my daughter Peyton died in 2000, our family has experienced other significant losses. We have almost become used to dealing with death, so we have developed a formula that we ritually follow. First we collectively write the dead loved one's obituary, then we plan a family viewing, and then we plan a beautiful Memorial Celebration of that loved one's life. (We are not into "funerals" but rather Life Celebrations.) We have collectively developed neural networks for dealing with death, which develop further with each new death and help us to know what to do, how to proceed. Of course we are still massively shocked by the bad news when it comes—yet we have been through this enough times that we are perhaps more prepared than others to process the shocking information and channel our shock into rituals that we know will carry us and others through that initial shock.[12]

---

12. Robbie has written a manual for dealing with death and grief called *The Art of Grieving Gracefully*. It is freely available at www.davis-floyd.com, under "Articles," and also in revised form as an Appendix to Hass, Robyn and Robbie Davis-Floyd eds. (2016) *Surviving the Death of Your Ex: Managing the Grief That No One Talks About*. Praeclarus Press.

Stress and the Myth/Ritual Complex

Distress is not peculiar to modern life, although it is certainly exacerbated by the demands of modern economic and social uncertainties. Traditional folk frequently encounter severe stressors in their environment and their social relations. In 2004, as our readers will know, a huge, magnitude 9.1 earthquake struck Sumatra in Indonesia (the "Sumatra–Andaman earthquake"). It produced horrible damage on the island, and caused a tsunami (gigantic wave) that struck coastlines all over the Pacific. It is estimated that 230,000 people lost their lives in 14 countries. As rescue efforts unfolded, anthropologists who had lived among the peoples of the Andaman Islands feared that their hosts might have been badly harmed or wiped out. Quite to the contrary, virtually all of the people in those islands had retained folklore about past massive tsunamis and hence knew the signs immediately. Some saved themselves and their fishing boats by heading far out to sea where the giant waves just passed harmlessly under their keels; the rest immediately headed inland, away from the coasts. Few sustained casualties, with the exception of the Necobar Islanders, who had given up their traditional culture and had converted to Christianity, and hence were unprepared to recognize the signs of impending disaster and take appropriate action. We cannot emphasize enough that the knowledge of their environments gained over many generations by traditional societies (always encoded in their rituals) is simply invaluable, and often can't be replaced once it is lost.

Nevertheless, traditional societies may generate systemic distress in the form of tensions inherent in social and political structures. One of the most common sources of tension in many societies is between the power elite and the governed. In traditional societies, these tensions may take the form of class or caste conflict, tension between the hereditary leadership (e.g., when the role of chief or king is passed down from father to eldest son) and his or (more rarely) her subjects, conflict among clans, etc. The tensions in such societies may be expressed in witchcraft accusations, a build-up of resentments between the haves and the have-nots, social frustration and unrest. Ritual plays an enormous role in ameliorating these potential sociopolitical tensions. One of the most common forms of this kind of ritual activity is the *rite of reversal*—"...institutionalized behavior that is the inverse, reverse, or in some way conceived by their actors or by anthropological observers as the 'opposite' of behavior normal at other times" (Norbeck 1979:51).

For instance, the role of the ritual clown has been that of a "contrarian" throughout history and across the globe. The clown may wear royal raiment inside-out, mimic the behavior of sacred practitioners (priests, shamans), doing so clumsily or in contrary order. The intent is to poke fun at the source of tensions in the society and relieve the tension through comedy and laughter. (Keep in mind that science has shown that laughter causes the release of endorphins, naturally produced morphine-like substances, into our bodies that make us feel good.) Among the Lakota Indians, the *Heyókȟa*, or sacred clown, makes fun of conditions, ceremonies and political roles with impunity. During the Sun Dance, the *Heyókȟa* will appear and dance backwards and in the opposite direction than the dancers (Wallis 1996). In the past, if the people were facing famine and hunger, he might sit around complaining that he was "too full." Among the Iroquois there were "dream rites" during which desires expressed in dreams were ritually acted out, thus releasing repressed emotions resulting from normally forbidden behaviors. The Ndembu people of Zambia carry out a *Wubwang'u* ritual during which men and women throw insults at each other, impugning the other's sexual prowess while extolling their own, thus acting out the tensions that grow between men and women in that society. The great social anthropologist Max Gluckman (1911-1975) showed that the tensions among South African societies that might lead to actual rebellion are acted out in rites of social role reversal and rites of rebellion (2006), thereby "bleeding off" social tensions before they can erupt. All of these rituals and ritualized roles may be interpreted as forming a buffer against distress and the ever-present potential regression to Substage—to repeat once again, for we cannot emphasize this enough, *ritual stands as a buffer between chaos and cognition.*

Stress and the Modern Paradigm/Ritual Complex

Ritual continues to function as a buffer against distress (between chaos and cognition) in modern technocracies in which peoples' ways of life are rife with tensions based upon class, gender, age group, occupation, and position in the sociopolitical power structure. It is often said that we now live in an "information age." As John Feather (2008) notes, the technologies that have come "on-line" in the last six decades have increased peoples' information load higher than ever before in history. More people have more information to deal with on a daily basis than our ancestors could even imagine. The results of this technological boom have both good and bad aspects. Enhanced information flow makes the world "smaller" and for many people more interesting. On the other hand, information flow can produce, as we said above, information overload. What determines whether the flow of information produces eustress or distress has to do with (1) how that information is buffered; (2) how much control individuals have over the quantity of information they have to deal with; and (3) the stage level of cognitive processing the individual is capable of at that moment. The role of ritual in all three of these aspects is crucial.

In the first place, ritual activities such as family or business meetings can spread out the responsibility for handling information, can set priorities for dealing with information, reach conclusions that eliminate sources of information leading to overload, and so forth. Ritualized assignments and instructions—like briefings and establishing "terms of engagement" in military campaigns—can give the individual the tools necessary to pare down the amount of information that has to be processed. In the second place, it makes a world of difference how much control individuals feel they have relative to the amount of information coming at them. When people feel that they have little or no control over the amount of information they have to process, information overload can lead to increased anxiety and a lowering of cognitive processing. Information becomes noxious rather than usefully challenging ("TMI"). Individuals engaged in certain occupations—air traffic controllers, emergency room triage nurses, battle field commanders, soldiers, and SWAT teams, etc. —have to routinely face the possibility of overload and a potential decline in their cognitive capacities. Such occupations have built within their training and deployment ritualized buffers to help them cope and not crash.

And in the third place, many occupations select for Stage 3 and 4 cognitive abilities because concrete thinking is not adaptive in many contemporary professions. Astronauts, test pilots, university professors, researchers, systems analysts—all these and many more must be able to think fluidly and to adapt rapidly to intense flows of information and changing circumstances. There really should not be an astronaut, test pilot, triage nurse, university professor, or systems analyst who is incapable of complex thought within their professional domain. If there is such a person, they are in the wrong occupation, for they are highly susceptible to noxious stimuli and information overload. (Yet we have to note that professionals who operate at a high cognitive level in their jobs might also operate at a concrete level in their family, political or religious lives. For instance, an excellent, highly competent and cognitively complex triage nurse could also be a Stage 1 Christian or Muslim "true believer." The human brain is flexible!) In general, various ritualized methods are used to ensure that people of high cognitive complexity make it into such occupations. Psychological testing is very common these days to select people with sufficient (and sufficiently flexible) intelligence and personality characteristics to carry out the highly stressful duties of certain professions.

SUMMARY: CONCRETE AND FLUID THINKING, THE FOUR STAGES OF COGNITION, RITUAL, AND STRESS

In this chapter, we have described two basic types of thinking—concrete/rigid and fluid—and four stages of cognition, and more or less equated those four stages to the anthropological categories of naïve realism/fundamentalism/fanaticism (Stage 1); ethnocentrism (Stage 2); cultural relativism (Stage 3); and global humanism (Stage 4). For Stage 1 thinking, we have described the deep differences between naïve realism (not knowing any other way), fundamentalism (knowing that there are other ways of thinking and believing, yet truly believing that your way is the only right way), and fanaticism (believing so much in the rightness of your way that you also believe that all other ways, most especially those most opposed to yours, should be eliminated if they cannot be assimilated). We have shown that positive ethnocentrism simply results in a culture's celebration of itself and in attempts on its members' parts to preserve and perpetuate that culture, while negative ethnocentrism can result in one group persecuting or attempting to persecute, enslave, impoverish, or eliminate other groups (especially when those groups occupy the same geographical territory).

We have also shown the weakness of Stage 3 cultural relativism—simply acknowledging the right of every culture to exist and to have its own lifeworld and lifeways can result in accepting behaviors like wife-beating and torture as okay in a general sense because they are okay within the parameters of that culture. And we have described global humanism as Stage 4 thinking: the ongoing effort to find that elusive "higher ethical ground" that ensures universal rights to all human beings.

We have shown how ritual can be utilized to enact, display, and transmit the beliefs and values held by Stage 1, 2, 3, and 4 thinkers, as well as to stand between cognition and chaos by stabilizing every level of thinker at Stage 1 in times of crisis and distress, in order to prevent them from regressing into Substage—to keep them from "losing it." And we have noted that fluid thinking is a type of cognition that readily deals with diversity and change. In a multicultural and constantly changing society like ours, fluid thinking is far more adaptive than rigid naïve realist, fundamentalist, or fanatical (Stage 1) or ethnocentric (Stage 2) thinking. We have also shown that even fluid thinkers can be reduced to lower cognitive levels by daily stress overload or major disasters, and how the conscious performance of ritual can help them find "cognitive anchors" to keep them from regressing into Substage and "get a grip" on their new reality, giving them time, space, and the energy needed to grow the new neural networks they will need to cope with the distressing challenges they face.

We conclude this chapter by noting that ritual, among other things, is a set of tools and techniques that can be used in multiple ways to justify and perpetuate multiple ways of thinking, multiple worldviews, and all of the 4 Stages of Cognition, and with the suggestion that ritual be used consciously and wisely to achieve its desired function while "doing no harm."

Suggested Reading

Feather, John (2008) *The Information Society: A Study of Continuity and Change* (5th edition). London: Facet Publishing.

Rest, James, D. Narvaez, M. Bebeau, and S. Thoma (1999) *Postconventional Moral Thinking: A Neo-Kohlbergian Approach*. Mahwah, NJ: Lawrence Erlbaum Associates.

Schroder, H.M., M. Driver and S. Streufert (1967) *Human Information Processing*. New York: Holt, Rinehart and Winston.

Chapter 10

RITUAL'S PARADOXICAL ROLES: PRESERVING THE STATUS QUO AND EFFECTING SOCIAL CHANGE

Cognitive Simplification: How Rituals Speak to the Masses. Historical Relationships vs. Ecological Adaptation: The Consistent Human Choice to Preserve the Historical Status Quo Through the Rituals That Enact It. Cultural Mnemonics, Cultural "Memories." From Big-Men to Kings to Dictators: Changing and then Preserving the Cultural Status Quo Through Ritual. Ritualized Control through Social Consensus—or Not! Effecting Social Change Through Ritual: Revitalization Movements. Revitalization Movements and Collective Rituals: Failure and Success in Effecting Social Change. Revitalization Movements Among Traditional People. Current Revitalization Movements. Ritual as Adaptive Technique. The Contemporary Invention of Ritual: Effecting Social Change. Summary: Ritual, Cultural Preservation, and Social Change.

COGNITIVE SIMPLIFICATION: HOW RITUALS SPEAK TO THE MASSES

Culture is essentially conservative, and yet the world is ever-changing. Thinking of culture as a system of relatively stable knowledge and of the transmission of that knowledge down through the generations, we can see how today, in spite of the massive technological changes many societies on earth have experienced, most of us still lead lifestyles that are more like our own ancestors' ways of life one hundred and even two hundred years ago than they are like those of historically unrelated people elsewhere on the planet. Indeed, anthropologist Joseph Jorgensen (1983) once tested whether it is ecology or cultural history that is more powerful in molding cultural similarities among historically related peoples living in different environments. He found that historical relationship trumped ecological and economic adaptation every time.

HISTORICAL RELATIONSHIPS VS. ECOLOGICAL ADAPTATION: THE CONSISTENT HUMAN CHOICE TO PRESERVE THE HISTORICAL STATUS QUO THROUGH THE RITUALS THAT ENACT IT

In *Collapse: How Societies Choose to Fail or Succeed* (2005), Jared Diamond provides various profound examples of how historical relationship trumps ecological and economic adaptation. One of them tells the story of the early Norse settlers in Greenland, who were historically and culturally accustomed in their country of origin to keeping livestock—cows, goats, sheep, chickens—so they brought their livestock with them on their overseas journeys to Greenland. They survived and prospered there for around 450 years, living off their livestock, wild game, and occasional trade with Norway when the ships arrived. Yet (to make a long and complex story very short and simple), in order to feed their livestock during the winters, the Norse settlers cut down trees to have more land on which to grow hay, eventually depleting the forests and the wild game animals that survived within them. And the more the livestock grazed during the summers, the less of the delicate and superficial tundra there was to graze on, especially when the climate got colder.

Significantly, the Norse Greenlanders never gave up their historical association of themselves with Europe—they thought of themselves as "Europeans" and thus, according to Diamond, were prejudiced against the Inuit settlers who also appeared on Greenland, and who were surviving quite well on the abundant fish—a resource the Europeans apparently chose to ignore, possibly because of their European prejudice, so they never developed a ritualized system of trading with the Inuit that could have enabled them to survive. Thus their European and Christian-oriented myth/ritual complex—their cycle of meaning and charter for culturally approved behavior—failed to undergo the changes it would have needed to in order to "true" the Norse to their Greenland environment and enable them to adapt to that environment and survive within the abundant resources it in fact provided. With the lands they had claimed eventually overgrazed and the forests depleted, eliminating other sources of food, and because of their culturally-motivated refusal to work with and learn from the Inuit cohabiters of Greenland, the Norse's 450-year tenure on Greenland ended with them eating all their remaining livestock and then starving to death.

Similarly, Diamond theorizes how the ritual tradition of building the massive statues that still populate Easter Island—constructed and carefully sculptured to honor the tribal chieftains after their deaths—eventually led to the extinction of the people who constructed those statues. So many trees were cut down to roll the statues to their final resting places, reasons Diamond, that eventually the entire island was completely deforested and the people, who had lived from the forest, died out. (There are alternative theories about how the great stone heads were moved; see Hunt and Lipo 2011.) We might imagine that these indigenous people of Easter Island would eventually have become aware that cutting down trees was destroying the environment that sustained them on their part of the island—yet they could still see trees on other parts of the island, so they could not imagine that one day all the trees would be gone. As is usually the case with historically-entrenched rituals that vivify the culture's values and beliefs, subsequent dying chiefs wanted to intensify the ritual performance of honoring their death by having their followers build ever-larger statues in commemoration of themselves (just as the Pharaohs of Egypt wanted ever-larger pyramids). And their followers willingly carried out these desires because the larger and more impressive the statue representing the chieftain they followed, the more their own importance as a follower of that chieftain would be enhanced. Thus any ecological concerns they may have had were consistently trumped by historically and ritually socialized desires to construct the best statue ever and to place it where they wanted it to be, no matter how many trees it took to roll it there.

In both cases—the immigrant Norse Greenlanders and the indigenous people of Easter Island (and so many more throughout human history; see Charlie's and his friend Ivan Brady's 1978 book *Extinction and Survival in Human Populations*), *historical relationship trumped ecological adaptation*. As Diamond (2005:75) put it, "The values to which people cling most stubbornly under inappropriate conditions are those values that were previously the source of their greatest triumphs over adversity." To Diamond's statement, we add that *the more inappropriate the conditions, the more people are likely to cling to the rituals that have historically enacted their core values and belief systems and thereby sustained them* (until they reach the possible tipping point that we describe below).

Cultural Conservatism and Cultural Change

So yes, culture is essentially conservative, and from the above examples we can clearly see how that conservatism, while it may lead to initial success and long life for a number of generations, can also lead to that society's demise when it does not adapt rapidly enough to changing life and environmental circumstances. And of course, again, the world is ever-changing. We can recall how things have changed over the course of our own lifetimes or those of our parents or grandparents. We no longer ride horses to get from one place to another (most of our great- or great-great-grandparents lost the option to do so after the automobile was invented and became incorporated into life in industrialized societies, resulting in the building of highways far too dangerous for horses and buggies). As a direct result of industrialization, we can no longer assume that a lovely mountain stream's water is clean to drink, we no longer have to go through a telephone operator to call one another (or even use a telephone, given Skype), we can't fix our own automobiles without the aid of specialized training and sophisticated computers, nor live without our own personal computers and cellphones. A diagnosis of AIDS is no longer a death sentence, and being infertile does not necessarily stop us from having babies.

Change happens, and societies either develop new myths or paradigms, and new rituals to enact them that can help them to adapt to that change, or they do not. And if they do not, in the end they may well disappear, as have many thousands of traditional and other societies over the past several centuries. (If you had lived in the heyday of Ancient Rome, when the Pax Romana stretched across continents, you might never have imagined that one day, Rome itself would fall.) The possibility of disappearance confronts us today: nuclear or chemical warfare, air, water, and ground pollution, climate change, a new epidemic disease, even an asteroid collision—any of these and more could destroy some or all of us, or profoundly change life as we know it. Our ability to survive and thrive will depend in large part on our ability to tap our human flexibility and creativity and the power of ritual for its adaptive capabilities.

For a very mundane example, if water becomes scarce in developed countries due to global warming and subsequent drought, can we find more creative ways to perform our daily rituals of dish-washing and bathing—like the four-minute shower already obligatory in some parts of Australia, where water is already scarce? Could we learn to live without non-renewable resources like oil, gas, and coal? The huge global dialogue about such issues has resulted to date in not enough concrete action, because the citizens of contemporary technocracies are accustomed to the comforts that come from consuming such non-renewable resources and to the billion-dollar businesses they sustain. Our daily rituals and large-scale ceremonies depend on those resources, not to mention our lifestyles and the technocratic worldview on which they are based.

Within our lifetimes, we may all have to acknowledge that human actions have played a major part in environmental change, to completely revamp our lifestyles in order to adapt to our changing environment, and to change our rituals to enact new values on conservation and living well with less—what one of Robbie's friends, Robert J. King, calls "the prosperous way down." Many of us are engaged in such ritual change (see Grimes 2003a)—we religiously recycle everything we can (yet have to use the precious resource of water to rinse much of what we recycle). We turn off our taps while brushing our teeth instead of letting the water run (a huge ritual/habitual change for those of us who were raised to let that water run while we took our sweet time to brush our teeth). We support organic, especially local, growers by buying their products or encouraging our local grocery stores to do so. We purchase cars that use less gas, grow our own gardens, refuse those ubiquitous plastic bags still so freely offered in American stores (yet not in Europe, where you have to bring your own bags, as we Americans are just now learning to do). "Freegans" forage for food inside the trash bags that grocery stores throw out, finding lots of packaged food discarded simply because the package was damaged in some way. Lots of us in the U.S. are changing our daily rituals in environmentally conscious ways—yet our efforts still constitute only a tiny drop in the vast ocean of human over-consumption. We must do better. Large corporations must change their ritualized practices of generating massive amounts of waste—these practices enact their core values on showing profitability at the expense of all else (some are trying), and on and on. Whether our contemporary technocracies prove to be sustainable or not will depend in large part on profound changes in thinking and belief, and on the rituals that may come to enact those changes.

CULTURAL MNEMONICS, CULTURAL "MEMORIES"

As we saw in the preceding chapter, information stored within sacred stories and folklore over many generations may make the difference between high casualty rates or no casualties at all among people confronting potential disaster. Some scholars have interpreted this cultural transmission of information as a kind of "cultural memory" that not only determines our reactions to events in the now, but influences our very identities (see e.g., Assman 2011). We do not follow this loose usage of the term "memory" here, for the only memories that we actually have exist inside our brains/bodies. But these scholars have made a very valid point: many cultural institutions operate as *mnemonics* derived from the past—that is, cultural artifacts and institutions like art, monuments, writing, story-telling, architecture, folklore, etc. can operate as *reminders* of information relevant to both the past and the future. The duration of cultural "memory" can go back hundreds, even thousands of years. Some Australian Aboriginal myths tell of the time far back in the past when "the earth exploded." These myths seem to refer to the eruptions of volcanoes in various places in Australia—for example, of Mount Wilson near modern day Sydney—that happened thousands of years ago yet are still encoded in contemporary aboriginal myths, just as Genesis still encodes the historically forced transition from hunting and gathering to large-scale agriculture, and the folktale of the "Three Little Pigs and the Big Bad Wolf" more elaborately encodes the transition from hunting-gathering to horticulture to agriculture.[13] The most powerful system of cultural mnemonics among traditional and modern peoples alike is their myth/paradigm-ritual complex. Through explicit performance of a culture's cycle of meaning, ritual works both to preserve and to transmit the society's belief system, and so becomes an important force in the preservation of the status quo in any society (see Taylor 2003). Moreover, when one sub-group within a given society gains control over mnemonic performances, it can exercise a great deal of political control over its members.

In the early years of the formation of the Christian church, for example, there was a struggle for control over scriptural interpretation and the liturgy. Those who wanted people to share equally in the practice of their faith were labeled "Gnostics" and declared "heretics" (and even killed) by the patriarchal priesthood whose members wished to control access to both the scriptural canon and the liturgy—and of course the wealth accumulated by the Church. Those testaments that seemed to reinforce

---

13. Didn't know that? Well, Robbie, who is also trained in folklore, figured it out and wrote about it at length; see Davis-Floyd, Robbie and Melissa Cheyney (2009) "Birth and the Big Bad Wolf: An Evolutionary Perspective." In *Childbirth across Cultures,* eds. Heleine Selin and Pamela Stone. Dordrecht, The Netherlands: Springer Science, pp. 1-22.

the "natural" power of the clergy were gathered together into what came to be called the Holy Bible, and alternative testaments were disavowed and relegated to the historical trash pile (see Pagels 1989). It was not until the 15th and 16th centuries that the German monk Martin Luther and others fomented what came to be called the Protestant Reformation, which essentially pivoted on the notion that everybody has the right to read and interpret the scriptures. This "Re-Formation" led to the wresting of power from the hands of Catholic priests and the formation of many of the Protestant sects that have flourished to this day, and to the creation of multiple rituals that enact, reinforce, and transmit the newer belief systems of the Protestant sects that developed out of the Reformation.

FROM BIG-MEN TO KINGS TO DICTATORS: CHANGING AND THEN PRESERVING THE CULTURAL STATUS QUO THROUGH RITUAL

As we saw in the preceding chapter, anthropologists who have studied literally thousands of cultures around the world usually find that those in power in a given social group tend to exercise unique control over ritual performances. They utilize ritual's tremendous power and influence to reinforce both their own importance and agendas, and the importance of the belief and value system that sustains them in their positions. Let's look at an example that is very far removed from our everyday Western lives. Societies throughout the Western Pacific have political systems centered upon what has been called a *big-man* (Sahlins 1963). Unlike the more feudal-like chiefdoms and kingdoms found elsewhere in the Pacific and around the world, most traditional societies in Western Oceania remain at the tribal level of organization, in which a few hundred or so people are integrated into a loose and somewhat informal political structure. We can do no better than quote anthropologist Marshal Sahlins' description of a big-man:

> In the several Melanesian tribes in which big-men have come under anthropological scrutiny, local cultural differences modify the expression of their personal powers. But the indicative quality of big-man authority is everywhere the same: *it is personal power.* Big-men do not come to office; they do not succeed to, nor are they installed in, existing positions of leadership over political groups. The attainment of big-man status is rather the outcome of

a series of acts which elevate a person above the common herd and attract about him a coterie of loyal, lesser men. It is not accurate to speak of "big-man" as a political title, for it is but an acknowledged standing in interpersonal relations—a "prince among men" so to speak as opposed to "The Prince of Danes." In particular Melanesian tribes the phrase might be "man of importance" or "man of renown," "generous rich-man," or "center-man," as well as "big-man" (Sahlins 1963:289, emphasis added).

The personal power of the big-man (occasionally also a big-woman) comes from two aspects of his nature: his ability to persuade others to his point of view, and his generosity. Big men tend to be natural leaders (but cannot order anyone to do anything), and they understand the fundamental rule of gift-giving—giving gifts creates obligations on the part of the recipient. Really important giving is ritualized in these societies, as it sometimes is in our own society (e.g., Christmas and birthday presents), and it is the personal power of the big-man that makes the rituals possible. An example of how this works out in real life and how ritual intensifies sociopolitical relations is the effort that big-man Ongka had to go through to mount a great *Moka* ceremony among his Kawelka tribe of New Guinea (Strathern 1971, 1979).[14] Ongka had spent much of his life helping others accumulate pigs, giving kinsmen pigs as an "investment" for the future (pigs being the major source of traditional wealth among the Kawelka and surrounding groups). The only ways in which one could obtain pigs were by stealing them from enemies, being given them by kinsmen, and by natural accumulation. However, as pigs were rarely killed and eaten, and thus had to eat the same food as did people, there was a limit to how many pigs one family could support. Therefore, the major problem for Ongka in mounting his great *Moka* (meaning "giving" in Kawelka)—a ceremony that required giving away hundreds of pigs, plus huge amounts of money in cash and other valuables—was to persuade others of his kin to donate their pigs, and even their cash etc. to the effort. Ongka could not just tell everyone in his group to cough-up pigs and wealth the way, say, a feudal lord might have done. They had to willingly participate in making the great *Moka* happen. During the build-up to the main ceremony, the giving up of pigs (in little *Mokas*)

---

14. This is a particularly apt example because a wonderful documentary of this event was made in 1976 for the Granada Television's *Disappearing World* episode, *Ongka's Big Moka: The Kawelka of Papua, New Guinea.*

to Ongka was also a cause for minor ceremony and feasting. When all the requisite wealth was accumulated by Ongka and his family, the day for the *Moka* was set, and invitations were sent to the recipients of the wealth—that being another tribe who had themselves given a great *Moka* for the Kawelka many years before.

A great *Moka* ceremony demonstrated to everyone in Ongka's social world that indeed, Ongka was a big-man. His social status soared to supreme heights. Such ceremonies constitute a recognition and re-enforcement of the status-quo, and at the same time ritually enact the social dynamics and social values that made life among New Guinea tribal peoples possible: namely, sharing, reciprocity, generosity, and modeling oneself on the charismatic leader who embodied these values. Ongka was a big-man because, despite all the vicissitudes of everyday life, including political struggles between himself and other big-men, and despite the fact that he could not order the thing done, Ongka was able to muster his personal power and social networking skills to bring together the resources to make this once in a lifetime event occur.

Fast-forwarding from Ongka, the big-man of horticultural New Guinea, who presided by strength of personal charisma and deep understanding of the gift-giving rituals of his people and their meanings, through the feudal lords and kings and queens of Europe, to today's totalitarian dictators, we can perhaps understand how all of them both utilized and manipulated ritual to enhance their status and their power—in other words, to establish and then maintain a societal status quo (to their liking and benefit, of course). Europe's feudal lords organized annual ceremonies during which their peasants/serfs presented their tributes in the great hall and received acknowledgement and recognition of their services. Europe's kings and queens received the tributes brought to them with great ceremony and royal recognition—often knighthood and/or admission to one or another prestigious group. Their status was enhanced by any personal charisma they might have had, yet the social structure was so tightly organized around the king's God-given right to hold the throne and the many rituals that supported that right (e.g., coronation) that they could hold that position even if they were dull, boring, non-charismatic people.

In contrast, 20th and 21st century totalitarian dictators often arose from humble beginnings. Like the big-men of New Guinea, they used their personal charisma, the ritualized techniques of gift-giving (and bribes), and a deep understanding of their native cultures to develop/invent rituals that could tap the core values of their respective cultures and associate themselves with those core values to rise to ultimate positions of leadership that gave them close to total control of their respective nations. Hitler of Germany, Mao Zedong of China, Pol Pot of Cambodia, Idi Amin of Uganda, Saddam Hussein of Iraq—all (and many, many more) are cases in point. They all heavily manipulated ritual to put them in positions of control and to keep them there, as Vladimir Putin of Russia is doing today. And then they continued (and some still continue) to manipulate the power of ritual to keep their populations under subjugation and control. A strong case in point comes from the very moving book *The Girl with Seven Names: A North Korean Defector's Story*, by Hyeonseo Lee (2015:220). She writes:

> One day early in the first semester our teacher had an announcement to make. Training and drilling for the mass games would soon begin. Mass games, he said, were essential to our education. The training, organization, and discipline needed for them would make good communists of us. He gave us an example of what he meant, quoting the words of Kim Jong-il: since every child knew that a single slip by an individual could ruin a display involving thousands of performers, every child learned to subordinate their will to that of the collective. In other words, though we were too young to know it, mass games helped to suppress individual thought.

RITUALIZED CONTROL THROUGH SOCIAL CONSENSUS—OR NOT!

Yet we must emphasize that it does not take a totalitarian leader to keep a population under control through ritual (and the myths and paradigms that rituals are designed to enact). *All societies on earth work to maintain social order through ritual.* The laws intended to enforce order cannot be fully maintained solely by the judicial system of any society. Most people in developed countries ritually/habitually stop at STOP signs and red lights and refrain from speeding, not because they are afraid of getting caught and ticketed, but because they have been socialized into doing so and recognize that this socialization is reasonable because it prevents traffic accidents. They *consensually choose* to obey the laws and to enact the rituals (patterned, repetitive, and symbolic behaviors) that obey and reinforce those laws, especially when the laws seem reasonable to them. But when laws appear to be unreasonable, many people *choose to disobey* them. And when too many people in a given society choose to disobey a given set of laws, those laws in general cease to have any great effect on societal behavior.

The prohibition against alcohol in the United States during the 1920s is a case in point—although there were laws against the manufacture, selling, and drinking of alcohol, so many people defied those laws that eventually the laws were rescinded. Today, so many people in the contemporary United States defy the laws against growing, selling, and smoking marijuana that those laws are now in question and are giving way to the legal sale of marijuana "for medical reasons" in a number of U.S. states, including California. And now the sale and use of marijuana for whatever reason have recently been legalized in Colorado and Washington State. These laws constitute the simple recognition on the part of lawmakers in these states that popular use and opinion trump previous official policy. Likewise, increasing numbers of women in the U.S. are choosing to give birth at home with midwives in attendance. Their choices have helped lead to the legalization of home birth midwifery practitioners in many states, with others on the way (see Davis-Floyd and Johnson 2006).

In all these cases, ritual has played a significant role. Americans in the 1920s desiring to drink alcohol and have fun went to "speakeasies"—a window opened in the door when they knocked, they gave the proper ritualized information, and were admitted. And the dances they participated in, while drinking alcohol, were ritualized enactments of their values on altering their states of consciousness through alcohol in order to let go of their socialized inhibitions and to have fun as a result of that letting go. Marijuana growers and smokers hold annual conventions in The Netherlands to both celebrate and ritualize the practice of marijuana smoking. Homebirthers often hold New-Age adaptations of Native American Blessingways to honor their choices for autonomous birth and celebrate the midwives who choose to attend them, and, during the birth process, they may perform (or have friends perform) many rituals, such as lighting candles and "throwing their fears into the flames," drumming, chanting, dancing, ringing bells—all designed to help them entrain their psyches with the physiological rhythms of labor and thereby to achieve the normal physiological births that they desire.

EFFECTING SOCIAL CHANGE THROUGH RITUAL: REVITALIZATION MOVEMENTS

As we mentioned previously, although culture is conservative, it is also dynamic. Culture *has* to be dynamic and flexible in order to prepare each generation to confront the realities of contemporary life and to "true" its members to those realities. Paradoxically, ritual, with all of its insistence on continuity and order, can be an important factor not only in individual transformation (as we have shown in previous chapters) but also in social change. New belief and value systems are most effectively spread through new rituals designed to enact and transmit them. Even if a ritual is being performed for the very first time, its stylistic similarities with other rituals make it feel tradition-like, thus giving entirely new belief systems the feel and flavor of being strongly entrenched and sanctioned by ancient tradition (a phenomenon that some anthropologists call "invented tradition;" see Hobsbawm and Ranger 1992) —especially when the new rituals take their place within an altered cycle of meaning.

How is a cycle of meaning changed? We hope you remember that in Chapter 3 (on the cognitive matrix of ritual), we said that the cycle of meaning includes the ongoing experiences of participants. When people's experiences begin to diverge from the ways things are expected to happen, new information in the form of new interpretations begins to enter the system. Eventually the society's worldview shifts. For one instance, apparently the only members of the U.S. military who opposed the end of so-called "don't ask, don't tell" policies pertaining to gays in the services were older people, especially older noncoms and officers. The younger generations in the military have little or no trouble with openly gay soldiers because the values of their generations have changed over time, due to increased openness about the issue as they were growing up. And for another, peculiar instance, eating dog meat in China—a food tradition that has been around for millennia—is now being challenged by a new generation of middle-class Chinese who are increasingly keeping dogs as pets. Today there is a whole social movement growing in China (with its concomitant rituals) to keep dogs from being slaughtered for human food—a phenomenon that is very bewildering to the millions of Chinese who have long considered dog meat an entirely appropriate source of protein and tasty delights. (Members of this new movement use social media to galvanize participants to surround trucks carrying dogs to slaughter, toting placards, chanting slogans, and sometimes negotiating to buy the dogs themselves.) And we are certain that our readers can come up on their own with many other examples of recent examples of significant changes in their own societies' cycles of meaning, for the contemporary world is in a process of rapid technological and sociocultural change.

Moreover, *entrenched belief and value systems are most effectively altered through changes in the rituals that enact them*—again because of the systemic relations among the various components of the cycle of meaning. Indeed, ritual represents one of society's greatest potentials for the kind of revitalization that comes from internal growth and change in response to changing circumstances. The great American anthropologist Margaret Mead (1901-1978) took the view that when we examine any culture over lengthy periods of time (say, over several generations), the culture is so constituted that it at all times both *transmits* and *transforms* knowledge (Mead 1979, 1989[1955]). Her point becomes obvious once we see that for young people growing up, culture is only part of the information they have to process on a daily basis. As Turner and Bruner (1986:33) wrote, "...meaning arises when we try to put what culture and language have crystallized from the past together with what we feel, wish, and think about our present point in life." And as John Cove (1987:28), an anthropologist and student of Northwest Coast Indian mythology, noted: "...the relationship between mythological and lived-in realms is never completely isomorphic. Each is *more or less* than the other. If the first has particular significance, it is in giving a foundation for meaning in the second." Keeping in mind that a culture is a pool of information more or less available to individual members of the group, we can see that not everyone shares exactly the same information, or understands things in exactly the same way, or has the same experiences, opinions or memories, or for that matter agrees about the meaning of things. In many societies there are recognized specialists who are considered to know more about the cosmology (or corporate culture) and its implications than everyone else, and they are often the very same people who are in charge of ritual—perhaps the shamans, chiefs, or CEOs, depending on the society in question. Below we provide two examples of the power of individuals to effect social change through their manipulation or creation of myths, paradigms, and the rituals that enact them.

REVITALIZATION MOVEMENTS AND COLLECTIVE RITUALS: FAILURE AND SUCCESS IN EFFECTING SOCIAL CHANGE

Nobody is a passive "culture-bearer," for culture is entangled with direct experiences of contemporary social and physical life, both of which change over time. As we saw in previous chapters, ritual is used in various ways to re-enforce the group's belief system (rites of intensification), to transform people as they grow up and age (rites of passage), and to foment revolutionary change (rites of transformation). Yet each of these types of ritual uses the same drivers (see Chapter 5) and other operations to attain the intent. Moreover, it is well to keep in mind that all human beings make an effort to interpret their daily experiences as meaningful in terms of their worldview. When a society's worldview becomes out-of-date, there usually will arise a movement to change things to make that worldview up-to-date with—trued to—contemporary life. For example, the Roman Catholic Church has steadfastly outlawed the use of contraception in family planning, yet numerous polls in various countries suggest that a majority of Catholic women are in favor of the use of contraception. Insofar as the Catholic Church remains intransigent on the issue, there will continue to be a mismatch between what the Church says people ought to do and what a majority of people actually do. In time it seems likely that the Church will be forced to update its views and teachings if it is to continue to have credibility with much of its membership. If it does not, it is highly likely to lose credibility. (Yet people do not abandon their deeply-held religions lightly—mostly they just choose to ignore some of their religion's tenets while continuing their religious practice in selective ways.)

Anthropologist Anthony Wallace (1956b:265) called such a shift in a people's worldview a *revitalization movement*, which he defines as a "deliberate, organized, conscious effort by members of a society to construct a more satisfying culture" (see also Harkin 2007). As his definition implies, revitalization movements (which include prophetic, nativistic, messianic and millenarian movements) tend to crop up in situations in which people are suffering chronic distress, as well as where groups or classes of people perceive themselves to be undergoing *relative deprivation* compared with another group or class (Walker and Smith 2001).

REVITALIZATION MOVEMENTS AMONG TRADITIONAL PEOPLE

Cargo Cults as Failed Revitalization Movements

The classic and heart-rending examples in anthropology of failed attempts at cultural revitalization are the millenarian-type movements called "cargo cults" (Trompf 1990). During World War II, the Allies suddenly appeared on many islands of the Pacific and built airfields so that soldiers and war materiel could land. The natives on these islands had little choice in what was happening to them, so day after day they watched the great material wealth of the war effort magically stream in from the air in the holds of the "great birds" (cargo planes). At the end of the war, the Allies disappeared just as suddenly. Gone were the "great birds" that brought such wealth. The natives were left behind in whatever poverty conditions prevailed at the time. Feeling deprived, and wanting the "cargo" to come back, some native groups developed rituals that involved acting out perceived "white American" mannerisms and re-creating the airfields with the flashing firelights and other features, the intent of which was to attract the great birds to return. Some groups, led by charismatic cargo cult leaders, sold or abandoned their homes and their possessions and went to sit on an airfield at the appointed time to await the arrival of the great cargo plane. And of course the sad tragedy was that the "great birds" did not return, and the cult members who had believed that the power of their belief and the rituals they developed to enact and express that belief would bring back the cargo, just for them, were left utterly bereft and massively disillusioned. Their belief system did not "true" their imagined worldview to the world they actually lived in.

There have been many examples of revitalization movements in history and across cultures, some of which (like the Sun Dance) caught on and "worked," and some of which failed. The Protestant Reformation began with a revitalization movement against the wealth, power and privilege of the clergy (Hillerbrand 2009). Back in the 16th century, the Catholic Church was far more split than it is today, with more than one figure claiming to be Pope, and with clergy selling "indulgences" (clerically granted forgiveness of sins) to bring in wealth and clerical control of the liturgy and scriptures. As every informed Christian knows, Martin Luther and others demanded changes in the Church, and when their demands were not granted, they created their own protesting (hence "Protestant") organizations with transformed liturgy and ritual that "trued" their worldview to the new one that Martin Luther and others had created.

A Paiute Prophet: Wovoka and the Creation of the Ghost Dance Religion

In a similar vein, in the wake of draconian 19th century U.S. government policies pertaining to Native American societies that drove native peoples onto smaller and smaller reservations, a Paiute Indian prophet named Wovoka (aka Jack Wilson) accumulated practices and beliefs from various Native American cultures and reformulated them into what became known as the Ghost Dance religion (Kehoe 2007). During a solar eclipse, Wovoka (already a trained "weather worker") had a vision in which the great god gave him instructions on how the people should change their lives to make things better. Keep in mind that no Native American language has a word that means exactly what our English word "religion" does. The closest one can get in many of these languages is something like "moving around ceremonially." Hence, the central ritual of the Ghost Dance was the ancient "circle dance"—dating back to prehistoric times, these dances symbolized the sun's cyclical movement around the sky and involved drumming, whistling, and chanting. (The Ghost Dance was originally called "Dance in a Circle" or "Spirit Dance"—the word "spirit" was translated into English as "ghost.") Wovoka's vision was that if the people carried out the right activities—living clean and honest lives, and especially if they danced properly—a new era would arrive in which the white man and the Indian would come to love one another and live in peace, and prosperity would reign with the return of the buffalo and other crucial resources. As the Ghost Dance spread from its original source among the Nevada Paiute, Native American tribes synthesized selective aspects of the ritual with their own beliefs—a process that often created change in both the society that integrated it, and in the ritual itself.

The Lakota Sioux adaptation of the Ghost Dance, for example, took on a millenarian tone and ended tragically during the 1890 massacre at Wounded Knee Creek in South Dakota. Fearing that the Ghost Dance was a source of social unrest and potential uprising, the U.S. government sent troops to Wounded Knee to stop the dancing, yet the Lakota continued to dance in the hope of salvation. (The crops they were supposed to produce on the reservations to which they had been confined failed because the soil was too poor, the buffalo were gone, and the people were starving.) A tragic series of mistakes, miscommunications, and the accidental firing of a gun led to the massacre of 153 Sioux, most of whom were women and children. The special "ghost shirts" the Lakota wore were supposed to magically ward off bullets, but failed to work, leading to the Lakota's rejection of the Ghost Dance religion. Nevertheless, that religion is still alive and well among some Native American groups—it remains essentially a pacifistic religion advocating love and proper behavior. (Interestingly enough, it was never picked up by the Navajo, who have an intense dislike of "ghosts.")

Charlie Yahey: A Dane-zaa Dreamer and His Invention of a Myth

Another way that a cycle of meaning may be changed is by changing the stories that express a people's worldview. For instance, the Dane-zaa Northern Athapaskans (also known as the Beaver Indians) are a First Nations/indigenous people living in the Canadian Subartic. They were seasonally nomadic hunter-gatherers until white colonizers forced them onto reservations after World War II. In an effort to explain this historical circumstance that so massively affected the lives of his people, one of their "Dreamers," a man named Charlie Yahey, came up with a story about how the Dane-zaa could view their own adaptive strategy compared to that of the newcomers from Europe. According to anthropologists Robin and Jillian Ridington (2006), who have long studied the Dane-zaa:

> The story relates that long ago, the creator gave the people a choice of how they would make a living. One option was to write a design for whatever they wanted on paper and have it come true without further effort. The other was to make a living using the tools of "dogs, snares and cartridge belts." The story illustrates both essential features of Dane-zaa technology and also its adaptability. Here is the story as [our Dane-zaa colleague and interpreter] Margaret Davis translated it:
>
> God made everything on this world
> by drawing out the design for it
> on a piece of paper.

He made dogs, snares, and cartridge belts.
Then, he took these and the paper for drawing designs
to the people of long ago.
He put these things before the old men. He said,
"Anything you want from this land
    when I have finished making it
    I will write down on this piece of paper.
    You can choose which gifts you want;
    the paper to make anything you want,
    or the dogs, snares and cartridge belts."
    But the Indians said to the paper,
    "We won't get anything from this piece of paper,"
    and they took the other gifts instead.
Dogs barking.
    People can live from the dogs.
    When people go to hunt they take the dogs with them
    and the dogs show them where to hunt.
    "From this paper we will get nothing," they said.
    So they took the snares and cartridge belts
    and they knew about them.
    The white people took the piece of paper.
    They can make everything: wagons, stores.
    He wrote it down on that piece of paper for them.
    Even these airplanes he made for them.
    This world is not big enough for them.
He made us Indians to live in the bush,
to do hard jobs and to make our living.
    We just do our own lives,
    but the whitemen started growing crops.
    They made plants that would grow and started to copy them.

The white people, Charlie Yahey says, can make everything from a piece of paper. Now, the white people, with their paper-based technology that produces "wagons, stores, and airplanes..." have taken the world back to a condition of ecological imbalance. It is "not big enough for them." Indians, according to Charlie Yahey, chose dogs, snares and cartridge belts. When I heard Margaret Davis's translation of this story, I was initially surprised and disappointed to hear cartridge belts listed as part of an original Dane-zaa technology. Surely, the people of long ago used bows and arrows, not breech-loading rifles. Other stories told clearly of a time, not so long ago, when the Dane-zaa first learned about muzzleloading muskets.

Then I asked her what word in Beaver Charlie Yahey had used. She replied that it was "atu-ze" which she told me confidently was how you say "cartridge belts" in Beaver. Both she and I knew, of course, that "atu" means "arrow" and "ze" means real, proper to or belonging to. Thus, atu-ze could be translated literally as something like "belonging to real arrows" and may have once meant either arrow holder or bow. But Margaret insisted that atu-ze is "our word for cartridge belts." Suddenly it dawned on me that rather than being an example of cultural contamination and anachronism, this story demonstrates a continued cultural vitality and adaptability. It is about the essence of Dane-zaa adaptive strategy and how it differs from that of the white men.

Indians make their living from their knowledge of the environment. They make it through negotiating social relations with sentient non-human persons. The particular instruments of this technology are not essential to its successful operation. Once, people used bows and arrows. Now they use rifles and cartridges. The essence of their technology is situated in the mutually understood social relations of production they negotiate with human and non-human persons, rather than through the possession of any particular artifact. "Real Indians" are not constrained by the artifactual inventory of their ancestors. Real Indians, Dane-zaa, use whatever instrumental extensions of their intelligence that are available to them. (Ridington and Ridington 2006)

This creative thinker, Charlie Yahey, gave his people a story within which their present subjugation made sense, not to mention empowering them through this story because *they were the original people and the original choice was theirs.*

A similar story comes to us from the Ju/'hoan San people of the Kalahari (formerly known as the !Kung) that describes how the Black people who showed up in their traditional hunting-gathering grounds ended up with cows that they could milk while the Ju/'hoan got stuck with "gathered raisins" instead of milk:

/'Oma /'Oma, a Ju/'hoan man, had the first cattle and herded them alone, but they had no kraal [corral]. A Black man came and asked whose cattle they were. The Ju/'hoan man said they were his, but agreed to herd them back to the village with the Black man to spend the night. One of the cows had given birth, so the Black man said, "Let's milk her and taste the milk." /'Oma /'Oma was afraid of the cow, so he asked the Black man to tie her up with a leather riem [thong] . . . Then /'Oma /'Oma gave the Black man a leather reim that was tied to a piece of string. The two of them together pulled on its opposite ends. It soon broke, and the Black man got the reim, while /'Oma /'Oma got the string. The Black man said that he would keep the cows and the Jul'hoan man would be his servant. /'Oma /'Oma had to go off and eat little things like the three kinds of raisin berries, and the Black man began to cultivate sorghum and maize and ate them along with beef and milk. (Biesele et al. 2009:39)

This story, told to anthropologist Megan Biesele some years ago by its creator, a Ju/'hoan man named Di\\xao Pari \Kai, encapsulates the struggles of the Ju/'hoan people to adapt to the presence of Black Herero cattle herders, who took over Ju/'hoan traditional watering holes for their cattle plus a great deal of their land for planting crops, often leaving the Ju/'hoan people without sufficient water and greatly diminishing their ability to hunt and gather, as they had previously done in that area of Botswana and Nambia for many thousands of years.

Subjugated people like the Dane-zaa and the Ju/'hoan can feel empowered if their creation stories tell them that they had the original choice, even if that choice eventually led to their disempowerment. At least, it was *their* choice! Here again we can detect the "truing" function of myth—such creation stories "true" people to their present environments by helping them make sense of why those environments currently exist and, thereby, to adapt to those current environments. Similarly, Wovoka's Circle/Spirit/Ghost Dance helped thousands of Native Americans adapt to their own radically changed circumstances. It did not tell them *why* they had been so subjugated, as Yahey's story did for the Dane-zaa and Di\\xao Pari \Kai's story did for the Ju/'hoan, yet it did offer them a way to "true" themselves to their present environment by giving them *something to do* about it—live a good life, live in harmony and peace with others, and dance to revitalize their cultures and themselves. (In contemporary American youth parlance, "True dat!")

CURRENT REVITALIZATION MOVEMENTS

Revitalization movements continue to arise in modern societies, especially those in which people in sufficient numbers suffer relative deprivation of resources, wealth, and political power. Modern movements, just like those in the past and those among traditional societies, inevitably ritualize their responses in the form of patterned, repetitive, and symbolically meaningful rallies and demonstrations of their alternative, counter-hegemonic values and beliefs. In recent years, social turmoil has overcome several Middle Eastern nations in what has been called the "Arab Spring" —a series of social movements in various countries that have led or are leading (or trying to lead) to profound social change. The "Arab Spring" had one of its beginnings in Egypt in 2011 with the massive social protests in Tahrir Square—powerful collective spontaneous ritualized performances enacting beliefs in democracy and individual rights of expression that did successfully lead to the overthrow of the then-current government. We can usefully contrast this public revolt, which was successful in the short term at least, with the unsuccessful 1989 revolt in China that revolved around Tianamen Square. (Note that both Tahrir and Tianamen Square are socially recognized ritual frames.) The success of the revolt in Egypt and the failure of the revolt in China reveal both the power of collective rituals to effect change, and their impotence in the face of draconian measures to repress them.

Collective rituals can always express the changing beliefs of the masses and their desires, yet they cannot always effect change. In order for them to do so, there has to be a "tipping point"—a point at which the government in power has reached the limits of its ability or its willingness to repress change. That tipping point was recently reached in Libya and appears to be imminent in Syria. Very recently, the government of Burma/Myanmar has opened itself to change—primarily through releasing from house arrest the primary leader of the movement for change, Aung San Suu Kyi. There could be no greater symbolic gesture on the part of the Myanmar government than releasing her and allowing her to participate in politics. She is the widely-acknowledged political leader of the social movement for change, and a ritual leader as well, as she embodies/symbolizes the hopes of her people. Her release could not more powerfully signify the government's current willingness to allow change.

In dramatic contrast, the death of the dictator Kim Jong-il in North Korea, culturally and socially honored with massive nation-wide rituals, seems only to have led to the ascension of his son Kim Jon-Un. The hugely public rituals that honored the dictator's death were designed, of course, to enhance his reputation as the father and leader of his country, and to transfer his ritual power of authority to his designated son and heir. Nothing in the rituals performed around his death seemed to indicate any potential change of heart, plan, or policy in North Korea—only more of the same.

RITUAL AS ADAPTIVE TECHNIQUE

As we showed in Chapter 6 on ritual techniques and technologies, rituals often derive from the *institutionalization of techniques*—a *technique* being an action or set of actions by which the body gets something done, and a *technology* being a technique augmented by physical objects (hammer, rattle, drum, spear, etc.). When a technique seems to work just fine, it tends to be done that way with only slight changes from then on. Some readers will remember when they first learned to tie their own shoes and brush their teeth. Once these techniques are internalized, we no longer have to think about them. We just do them, more or less the same way, more like a robot than a conscious being. We also saw that rituals have *utility*—they don't just happen, they are experienced by people as *making things happen*.

One of our reviewers noted here: "That's the difference between a habit and a ritual. You pay attention to a ritual. I don't think there's anything symbolic about brushing teeth." We again beg to differ, arguing that whereas brushing your teeth obviously functions practically to prevent cavities, gingivitis, discoloration, and bad breath, it also symbolically enacts your internalized cultural value on having and maintaining healthy teeth, and therefore qualifies as a ritual, albeit on the looser end of the ritual spectrum.

Sometimes the effects of ritual may be different in the real world than what is thought to be happening by the participants. In a classic work, anthropologist Roy Rappaport (1926-1997) analyzed the utility of ritual in managing change among the Tsembaga people of highland New Guinea (Rappaport 1984). Like so many western Oceanic peoples, such as the Kawelka described above, the Tsembaga are a tribe with no hereditary leaders, nor do they have big-men in the strict sense defined by Sahlins. Of course, as with all human groups, the Tsembaga do have leaders in the sense of charismatic individuals who wield more influence than others. Moreover, they have a cycle of rituals that help to regulate ecological relations between the people and the land. It works something like this: In good times people raise more and more pigs (yes, pigs again!), but the more pigs one has, the more garden produce goes toward feeding pigs and not people. There develops a pressure for more land upon which to grow more crops, but the Tsembaga, as well as their neighbors, are hemmed-in by tribal boundaries. This pressure for more land, according to Rappaport, leads to warfare, and to carry out effective warfare, a tribe turns to its allies for help. In order to maintain warfare alliances over time, the people slaughter pigs and feed the allies so as to gain not only their material help but also the help of the allies' supernatural spirits. Thus during warfare-related ritual feasts, the proportion of pigs to humans is altered, a great deal of animal protein is consumed during this period of distress, land boundaries may be adjusted, and more crops may be available for humans to eat. In addition, the people pay back to their allies the pigs that they themselves once received for their aid in mounting warfare. Of course the people themselves do not see their rituals in this way because they are focused on what they see as needed in the moment, and not on the larger picture. Rappaport's interpretation is a larger, ecological way of understanding the point and utility of Tsembaga ritual. This larger view allows us to see some of the ways in which rituals may effectively operate to regulate human-land and human-wealth relations, thereby preserving the status quo or effecting limited social change.

THE CONTEMPORARY INVENTION OF RITUAL: EFFECTING SOCIAL CHANGE

As we noted in Chapter 3, those who seek to accomplish a "paradigm shift" within a culture or company fail if their retooling does not address the rituals, visible and invisible, that keep the old paradigm in effect. *If you want to change the paradigm, you must change the rituals first.* Here we provide examples of exactly how that can be done, from Robbie's latest fieldwork project.

The Paradigm Shift of Holistic Obstetricians: "The Good Guys and Girls" of Brazil

In Chapter 3, "The Cognitive Matrix of Ritual," we described paradigms and presented as examples "the technocratic, humanistic, and holistic paradigms of medicine." Here we ask, why do some obstetricians choose to change? In other words, why would obstetricians fully trained and socialized into the technocratic model choose to switch ideologies and style of practice, from the technocratic/mechanistic to the holistic/integrative approach to maternity care, thereby going against the cultural grain and risking persecution and ostracism from their obstetrical colleagues and employers? This question is most poignant in Brazil, a country with one of the highest cesarean section rates in the world (56% in 2014, compared to 32% in the U.S., 23% in the U.K., and 16% in the Netherlands). In December 2011 and July 2012, Robbie and her colleague Nia Georges (Chair of the Department of Anthropology at Rice University in Houston) conducted 31 interviews with Brazil's holistic obs, who today call themselves "the good guys and girls" (Georges and Davis-Floyd 2016).

Robbie started to call them by that name when she first met a group of them at the 1st International Congress on the Humanization of Birth, held in Fortaleza, Ceara, Brazil in 2000. They liked the name and immediately adopted it for themselves, as it fully differentiates them from the "bad guys"—obs with extremely high cesarean rates (often 80% or higher), who practice obstetrics according to their technocratic ideology and their own convenience (cesareans take only about 20 minutes to perform, whereas waiting at the hospital for birth to proceed normally, or going back and forth, can take many hours). During their interviews with "the good guys and girls," Robbie and Nia found that these dedicated and committed holistic obs generally have extremely low cesarean rates because they dedicate themselves to helping mothers and babies to achieve normal, physiologic birth. They practice in varied settings—some of them will only attend home births, others attend births in both home and hospital, and some only in hospital, where they train staff to give holistic and humanistic "evidence-based" care. They were all trained—heavily socialized—in the technocratic paradigm. So how did they change their internalization of that paradigm?

Well, again, *if you want to change the paradigm, you first have to change the rituals that enact it.* For many of them, that change in ritual performance started with giving up episiotomies. An episiotomy is a cutting with scissors of the vaginal tissue that opens the perineum more widely and gets the baby out faster. Many obs still today, especially in developing countries, believe that it prevents injury to the baby and preserves pelvic floor function for the woman and thus greater sexual satisfaction for the man. These beliefs are erroneous. There is a huge body of scientific evidence that shows that there is no need whatsoever in the vast majority of cases to perform that ritual procedure. Our interviewees actually read some of that evidence, were intellectually convinced, and so stopped performing episiotomies. (Most of them were additionally motivated to do so by emotional appeals from their patients who wanted to avoid episiotomies.) They found that only patience was required to replace the episiotomy—if they just waited for the perineum to stretch on its own as the baby's head crowns and recedes, then crowns again, they found (sometimes to their actual amazement) that the perineum did in fact stretch sufficiently and the baby could be easily born. Of course, they had to sit or stand in front of the birthing mother for extra minutes waiting (obstetricians are not trained to wait but rather to get in there and "do something"—perform the episiotomy, apply the forceps or the vacuum extractor—anything to get that baby out as quickly as possible and get on to the next job). Yet, intellectually convinced by the evidence, these obs chose to start waiting, and were richly emotionally rewarded by normal births in which they did not have to do harm to women to "get the baby out." Their emotions were now engaged in their process of paradigm-shifting.

They were encouraged by the happy results of letting go of the ritual performance of episiotomy (well, they had all either read Robbie's books and articles or descriptions of her work by others [e.g. Jones 2005, 2012], so they understood that episiotomy and the other "routine procedures" they had been trained to routinely perform were rituals). And they read more of the scientific evidence and over time became intellectually convinced that birth works better in upright positions. So they began to abandon the traditional lithotomy position (flat on the back with feet up in stirrups)—a huge shift for them as it meant that they had to change their own physical position (and thus their social status) relative to the woman. They could no longer be "on top"—they had to become willing to get down on their knees, or sit or squat down, in front of upright women—to actually and symbolically serve them instead of dominating them. Realizing over time (from reading the evidence) that women usually get exhausted during labor because they are hungry or thirsty, they started encouraging women to eat and drink during early labor at least.

Reading more, they started encouraging women to move around a lot during labor to assist fetal descent and pelvic/cervical expansion. A moment of further enlightenment occurred for these "good guys and girls" when they realized that women *can't* move around when they are attached to the electronic fetal monitor, so they let go of continuous monitoring unless the woman chose to have an epidural—in which case, continuous monitoring is absolutely required by hospital protocol. Reading and experientially observing that the epidural necessitates many other interventions, they started encouraging their patients to use doulas (women trained to give labor support) and get into showers or baths for pain relief instead of resorting to an epidural. And through additional reading and further experiential observation, these obstetricians came to realize that most of the time, there is no reason to artificially speed up labor with Pitocin. In fact, they realized, artificial induction or augmentation of labor causes problems down the line, because if the woman's body is not ready to go into full labor on its own, forcing it to do so through drugs often results in a dysfunctional labor that ends with the baby going into distress and a cesarean section that was "needed" because the interventions they performed caused that fetal distress—the "snowball" or "ritual train" effect we mentioned previously, which Robbie calls "the vicious circle of technocratic birth."

As these obs became known in their communities as supporters of normal birth, more and more women who wanted normal birth started seeking them out. And the more these doctors saw normal birth, the more they were thrilled when they could facilitate women to achieve it. Over time, these obstetricians let go, one by one, of the ritualistic interventions they had been taught and learned to find delight and personal fulfillment in attending normal, physiologic, vaginal births that, most importantly, delighted and fulfilled the women who achieved them and their partners. Massive emotional engagement on the part of all parties!

To summarize the process of the paradigm shift of these "good guys and girls": first, they stopped performing the rituals that enacted the technocratic paradigm of birth. As a result, they started experiencing the joys and happy outcomes of normal birth. And as a result of those happy experiences, they changed their paradigm of birth from technocratic to holistic. And over time, they invented new rituals to enact their new holistic paradigm—spending lots of time with the mothers they attend, engaging in deep conversations with them, developing strong personal relationships with them, and enacting the values they placed on those relationships by choosing to let go of their busy schedules to spend many hours with those women when they went into labor. Some of them informally call themselves "midwives" (*parteiras*) because they are practicing what is internationally known as the midwifery model of care (again, see Davis-Floyd et al. 2009:441-456 for a full description of this model). These obs now limit the number of clients they take on per month in order to ensure that they will have that time to spend, and many of them accept only clients who truly want the kind of normal, physiologic births these obstetricians offer—an ideological match that benefits them and their clients. (Yet some of them accept every client who seeks their services, no matter what kind of birth she wants, because they believe that every woman deserves the very best and most holistic care, whether she wants a home birth or a scheduled cesarean.) They usually make less money than their technocratic colleagues, but according to their own reports, they are much happier in their practices—in spite of the persecution they often experience from their technocratic colleagues and "the system."

Changing from an established and culturally hegemonic paradigm like the technocratic model of birth (and health care) to a countercultural model (like the holistic paradigm of birth and health care) often entails massive persecution by the dominant system. Brazil's holistic obs, who live and work in the modern technocracy, are not subjected to torture or burning at the stake, yet they are often fired by their hospitals and sued, not by their patients but by other doctors who object strongly to their countercultural and counter-hegemonic practices. They find their much-needed social support from their holistic colleagues, who by now can be found in almost every Brazilian city and who are all members of the national network ReHuNa (Network for the Humanization of Childbirth), and, in their own communities, from local birth activists, doulas, and midwives (if they are present—professional midwives currently attend only around 6% of Brazilian births), and their usually very happy clients.

One of them, a holistic obstetrician named Jorge Kuhn, expressed public support for home birth in a national media interview in Brazil in early 2012. (He had previously attended home births with midwives and doulas, but had stopped because of pressure from the medical board.) The obstetric society of Rio de Janeiro immediately denounced him (even though he was no longer attending home births) and called for resignation of his license. Brazilian women responded to that challenge to Dr. Kuhn and to home birth with a country-wide march on Saturday and Sunday June 16-17, 2012 that saw over 5000 women, husbands, partners, and children parading in the streets of 31 Brazilian cities wearing T-shirts and carrying signs and placards supporting home birth—the initial, powerful, ritual step of a social movement that will continue to grow.

To recap and further summarize, these Brazilian holistic obs, including our interviewee Jorge Kuhn, accomplished their paradigm shifts: (1) by reading and learning and accepting the scientific evidence in favor of normal birth on an intellectual level; then (2) by giving up, one by one, the rituals that enact the technocratic paradigm of birth, thereby experiencing the joy and fulfillment of attending normal, physiologic births; (3) by developing new rituals of personal engagement with their clients that enabled them

Figure 10.1. March for Home Birth in Rio de Janeiro, July 17, 2012. Photo by Maira Fernandez

to complete the paradigm shift from technocratic to holistic practice. In their cases, intellectual engagement with the scientific evidence led to giving up technocratic rituals, leading to emotional engagement with the happy results thereby achieved, leading to further reading and deeper intellectual penetration into the holistic paradigm, further implementation of its tenets through the development of alternative rituals of engagement with their clients, an ultimate full paradigm shift, and a resultant "truing" of their new ideology with their new experiences. As they lowered the number of interventions they performed, including massively lowering their cesarean rates (most of them have CS rates between 7% and 15%), they achieved better and better birth outcomes—healthy babies, happy and fulfilled mothers, and happy and fulfilled obstetricians. They changed their practices by first giving up traditional obstetric rituals (like episiotomy and fundal pressure) in accordance with the scientific evidence, then changing their ideology, and then enacting their new ideology through new rituals that support the normal physiology of birth.

Herb Kelleher and Southwest Airlines: The Intentional Creation of a Consciously Alternative Corporate Culture

In *Nuts! Southwest Airlines' Crazy Recipe for Business and Personal Success,* authors Kevin and Jackie Frieberg begin with the original vision for the creation of Southwest Airlines, which was co-written on a cocktail napkin by founder and first CEO Herb Kelleher and one of his law clients, Texas businessman Rollin King. The authors continue with a description of a corporate culture built on the values of having fun via providing excellent and dependable service from city to city in inner-city, smaller airports that would get people closer to where they wanted to go. According to Wikipedia,

> During his tenure as CEO of Southwest, Kelleher's colorful personality created a corporate culture which made Southwest employees well-known for taking themselves lightly—often singing in-flight announcements to the tune of popular theme songs—but their jobs seriously. Southwest has never had an in-flight fatality. Southwest is consistently named among the top five Most Admired Corporations in America in *Fortune* magazine's annual poll. Fortune has also called him "perhaps the best CEO in America."

Prospective Southwest employees were encouraged to write extraordinarily creative letters of application that fully demonstrated their sense of humor—a basic requirement for SWA flight attendants. Robbie well recalls her first flight on Southwest many years ago—attendants hidden in the overhead bins popped out announcing that "the bins are full—of us!" and the announcement during takeoff noting that smoking was available on the outside "wing lounges" where the air was cool and the wind blew free! While insisting on an intense work ethic, Kelleher also insisted on making that ethic fun to instantiate. At the annual Southwest Airlines (highly ritualized) conventions, Kelleher was famous for cracking hysterical jokes and stating that he trusted his employees so much that he was willing to entrust his body and his life to them—and then ritually enacting that trust by literally jumping off the stage into the waiting arms of the dozens of employees who caught him and carried him to safety. Chapters in *Nuts!* include titles and subtitles such as: "Hire for Attitude, Train for Skills," "Kill the Bureaucracy," "Be Creative, Color Outside the Lines," "Honor Those You Love," "Make Work Fun," "Customers Come Second, and Still Get Great Service," "Employees Come First: Great Service Begins at Home." These captions show us that Kelleher created his corporation in defiance of traditional corporate norms that focus on serving the customer and not on the wellbeing of employees, choosing instead to create and enact alternative norms focused on enhancing the wellbeing of employees in the belief that the happier the employee, the happier the customer he or she serves. (For a full description of the rituals that Kelleher and his colleagues created to enact their corporate values on keeping fares low, taking people where they want to go, and opening the skies to the democratic value of "availability to all," read *Nuts!*)

We must note that it now appears that Southwest Airlines has mostly abandoned this original and very successful model. Today we (and our reviewers) find that flying SWA is like flying almost any other airline. The playfulness seems to have disappeared—perhaps it has disappeared from the corporate SWA culture as well. It is often the case that originally innovative models lose that original energy over time and turn into typical corporate models that are just about providing efficient service and making money via the sort of efficiency-based rituals that pervade business practice. Ritual spontaneity morphs into ritual bureaucracy as the cultural core values change—a very old and ongoing story.

SUMMARY: RITUAL, CULTURAL PRESERVATION, AND SOCIAL CHANGE

Through explicit enactment of a culture's belief system, ritual works both to preserve and to transmit that belief system, and so becomes an important force in the preservation of the status quo in any society. Thus one usually finds that those in power in a given social group have unique control over ritual performances. They utilize ritual's tremendous power to reinforce both their own importance and the importance of the belief and value system that sustains them in their positions.

Yet the power of ritual is even more strongly manifested in people's habitual choices to behave in the ritualized ways they have been socialized into since early childhood. Laws and explicit rules in every society may officially dictate appropriate behavior, *yet most people behave appropriately most of the time because of their ritualized socialization* to stop at stop signs and red lights, to hold the door open for the one who comes behind you, to obey the laws most of the time. When cultural behavior changes dramatically and official laws and rules cease to match or mirror those changes, those laws and rules usually get changed. When they do not, social resistance movements (such as labor union strikes) often manifest to work for the needed changes, unless that society is totalitarian and does not allow social resistance and change. Yet as we have seen in this chapter, even totalitarian societies can be overthrown by massive social resistance in the form of huge public rallies and other collective rituals. When those don't work, as they did not in Libya and have not to date in Syria, all-out internal warfare can become the agent of social change. (Of course, it's better to effect such change through collective ritual than through war—if only those in power would listen to the messages those rituals are sending them!)

Again, as we have seen in this chapter, ritual, with all of its insistence on continuity and order, can paradoxically be an important factor not only in individual transformation but also in social change. New belief and value systems are most effectively spread through new rituals designed to enact and transmit them. Even if a ritual is being performed for the very first time, its stylistic similarities with other rituals make it feel tradition-like, thus giving entirely new belief systems the feel and flavor of being strongly entrenched and sanctioned by ancient tradition. Moreover, entrenched belief and value systems are most effectively altered through alterations in the rituals that enact them, just as a change in beliefs can lead to changes in ritual practice, as the "good guy and girl" obstetricians of Brazil exemplify. As they change their ritual practices around birth, their students will also incorporate those changes. Indeed, ritual represents one of society's greatest potentials for the kind of revitalization that comes from internal growth and change in response to changing circumstances.

Suggested Reading

Davis-Floyd, Robbie, Lesley Barclay, Betty-Anne Daviss, and Jan Trittten (2009) *Birth Models That Work*. Berkeley: University of California Press.

Rappaport, Roy A. (1984) *Pigs for the Ancestors* (2nd edition). New Haven, CT: Yale University Press.

Turner, Victor and E.M. Bruner (Eds.) (1986) *The Anthropology of Experience*. Urbana: University of Illinois Press.

Wallace, Anthony F. C. (1956) "Revitalization Movements." *American Anthropologist* 58: 264-81.

Chapter 11

DESIGNING RITUALS

Jerusalem. Religious Syncretism as Adaptive Ritual Strategy. Implicit vs. Explicit Ideologies and Their Enactment in Ritual. The Intentional Creation of Personal Rituals: Two Memorial Services, Two Weddings, and One Birthday Party. Ray Robertson Designs a Puberty Rite. Pink and Ruby Tents for Adolescent Girls. Charlie's Personal Tantric Rituals. Prayer Practice among Evangelical Christians. Designing Personal Rituals: Healing and Danger. Summary: Designing Personal Rituals–Failure and Success.

JERUSALEM

A few years ago, Robbie had the good fortune to be invited to give talks in Israel. She was simply stunned by Jerusalem. Because she was raised as a Presbyterian Christian, the name itself already had powerful symbolic connotations for her. Actually being there was far more powerful. Robbie found herself standing at the intersection of three of the world's great global religions—in historical order, Judaism, Christianity, and Islam. There she experienced both religious history and religious tolerance (and gender division). At the Wailing Wall (aka the Western Wall)—the most sacred site in Judaism—she witnessed hundreds of Jews, segregated by gender (because of the influence of the Orthodox Jews who insist on gender segregation), standing and praying in front of what to Robbie appeared to be just a huge stone wall, kissing its stones, and slipping paper notes containing prayers into the crevices between those stones. The Wall is a symbol and its historical context is the meaning of the symbol—that wall represents all that is left of the sacred second Jewish Temple (the first was built by Solomon in 957 BCE and destroyed by the Babylonians in 586 BCE). The second

Temple was constructed in 516 BCE and destroyed by the Romans in 70 CE; the Wall is the foundation on top of which the Temple was built. The worshippers in front of the Wall were symbolically honoring the Temple—the most powerful symbol of Judaism itself—which now exists only in their historical cultural memory. (Numerous shops in the Jewish Quarter of Old Jerusalem displayed small wooden mockups of what the Temple might have looked like.) Less than a mile away, hundreds of Muslims were at the same time worshipping in the shrine called the Dome of the Rock (which was built between 689 and 691 AD on the site where the Temple used to stand). This shrine is a holy Islamic site because the prophet Mohammed, founder of Islam, is believed to have ascended into heaven, accompanied by the Angel Gabriel, from the Rock of Moriah, which lies inside that shrine and which many Jews believe to be the ancient location of the Holy of Holies (the inner sanctum of the Temple), and also the site where Abraham prepared to sacrifice his son Isaac at God's command, then stopped because God changed that command.

And within a ten-minute walk, Robbie was in the Church of the Holy Sepulcher, where Jesus Christ is believed to have been crucified and buried (in the sepulcher that is now inside the church). She had expected it to be as beautiful as the huge cathedrals of Europe, yet it was not—it was a rough-hewn hodgepodge of large spaces and pigeonholes, first constructed by Crusaders, then damaged and reconstructed many times by various groups across the centuries. The Greek Orthodox, Eastern Orthodox, Armenian Apostolic, Roman Catholic, Coptic Orthodox, Ethiopian Orthodox, and Syrian Orthodox have their very own spaces inside the Church, carefully delineated from each other (down to who cleans which part of the continuous floors), containing their very own altars where priests robed in differing raiments prayed. And yet, as Robbie was told by her guide, two Muslim families have for around 700 years held the keys to this sacred Christian church, because the vying Christian sects could not agree on which one should hold those keys.

These three major religions hold Jerusalem sacred, and each religion claims to be the only valid and true one, as does each competing sect within each religion. From a logical, rational perspective, they can't all be right! Yet each claims to be right and true. And (for the first time in the history of Jerusalem) they all manage to peacefully co-exist within the same square mile.¹⁵ Here once again we tap into what we said in preceding chapters about the truing function of myth. If a myth—a creation, origin, or explanatory story—sticks close enough to lived reality, it can shape that reality into a viable belief system to which its followers can adhere, each believing that their way is the right and true way, each living within the reality that their belief system expresses and performing the rituals that enact and vivify that belief system. The fact that they allow others to do the same without trying to harm them exhibits at least a Stage 2, ethnocentric tolerance (explained in Chapter 9 on the 4 Stages of Cognition). Insofar as each and every religion and belief system facilitates its adherents to live in the world with a sense that their lives have value, meaning, and purpose, and to show them that the world they live in "makes sense"—then that religion or belief system successfully "trues" its adherents to the world they live in.

We recognize the tautology of this argument—it is inherently circular—and in that circularity our argument mimics the "cycles of meaning" to which most members of most cultures adhere. You believe, and when the world you live in appears to confirm that belief (as it usually does), then you believe ever more deeply, and you consistently enact and perform the rituals that express that belief and that continue to deepen it.

But what happens when your beliefs and the myths, paradigms, and rituals that encode and express those beliefs no longer "true" you to your lived reality? When that reality changes so profoundly that your belief system no longer can explain what you experience around you, make it make sense, enable you to live within it on its terms, and the rituals no longer work for you? As we have seen in this book (most especially in the preceding chapter), the death of its rituals can mean the death of a culture, whereas adaptive changes in its rituals can work to "true" that culture to its new reality.

---

15. It must be noted that the relatively "peaceful" coexistence we are describing here is enabled by the strict rules and regulations of the Israeli government and practically and carefully managed via the continuous presence of police forces, and is sometimes disrupted by political conflict. The Temple Mount area is a highly-charged site that has long been the focus of political struggles not only between Jews and Muslims but also among various Jewish sects. Yet for now, peace prevails.

RELIGIOUS SYNCRETISM AS ADAPTIVE RITUAL STRATEGY

The religious syncretism that characterizes the Christianity of many indigenous peoples is a case in point. Don Lucio's huge altar, like that of his friend Don Julio (see Chapter 7 on ritual frames), contained both Catholic icons and pagan artifacts. Don Lucio could tell you one moment that the sudden weather change was due to the displeasure of the mountain spirits, and in the next moment instruct you to pray to a particular Catholic saint! When anthropologist Evon Vogt lived with the Chamula of Highland Chiapas, he often saw their shamans kneeling on the mountainside in front of large wooden crosses festooned with evergreen boughs. Most observers would assume that they were praying to the risen Christ, when in fact those crosses were believed by the shamans to constitute portals (at the intersection of the bars) through which the mountain spirits could manifest themselves and become available to hear the prayers and petitions of the shamans, assisted in doing so by the living evergreen boughs (which "vivified" the cross—brought it to life), and at the same time, to represent the risen Christ (Vogt 1976). This sort of religious syncretism has enabled indigenous peoples around the globe to appear to be good practicing Christians while at the same time maintaining (vivifying, revitalizing, and transmitting) some of their ancient traditions, values, and beliefs. Once again, the human brain can be plastic, fluid. It can encompass various explanations of reality and meld them together through the performance of ritual. Or, the brain can become concrete, rigid, its neural networks entrained to one and only one view of reality by the consistent performance of inflexible rituals that enact that one view.

IMPLICIT VS. EXPLICIT IDEOLOGIES AND THEIR ENACTMENT IN RITUAL

We find it striking that *clearly articulated belief systems can make do with soft and fuzzy rituals, while belief systems that are not clearly articulated often require very clear rituals.* For example, the technocratic model of birth and health care that we described in Chapter 3 (on the cognitive matrix of ritual) is *not* clearly articulated. Professors of obstetrics do not say to their students that "the body is a machine, the female body is a defective machine, and therefore we need to correct its defects through

Figure 11.1. The altar decorated bi-annually by Don Lucio and his followers in a grotto in the side of the volcano Iztaccihuatl in central Mexico, early 1990s. Photo by Robbie Davis-Floyd.

massive technological interventions in birth." The ideology is not verbally expressed; rather, it is actively performed and transmitted through the rituals of hospital birth and implicitly encoded in the official textbooks. Take for example the following quotation from *Williams Obstetrics,* the most widely used American textbook for obstetricians:

> The uterus is a muscular organ that is covered, partially, by peritoneum, or serosa. The cavity is lined by the endometrium. During pregnancy, the uterus serves for reception, implantation, and nutrition of the conceptus, which it then expels during labor......Birth is the complete expulsion or extraction from the mother of a fetus irrespective of whether the umbilical cord has been cut or the umbilical cord is still attached. (Cunningham et al., *Williams Obstetrics* 1989:877)

Then contrast that quotation with the following one:

> We value pregnancy and birth as personal, intimate, internal, sexual, and social events to be shared in the environment and with the attendants a woman chooses. We value the oneness of mother and child, an inseparable and interdependent whole. (Midwives Alliance of North America (MANA) Statement of Core Values and Ethics 1994:1-2).

The quotation from *Williams Obstetrics* seems to be simply "scientific"—yet without saying so, it implicitly expresses the technocratic ideology of the body as machine, whereas the MANA statement explicitly expresses a holistic ideology of birth.

While the technocratic model of birth is taught implicitly through its texts and through the rituals of hospital birth, the home birth/midwifery model is explicitly written down in many articles and books, explicitly taught in childbirth education classes, and explicitly articulated by home birth midwives, doulas, birth activists, and mothers. They *have* to be explicit about their model and their belief system around birth because it is alternative, counter-hegemonic, not recognized by society-at-large. (To recap, this midwifery model holds that the female body is a healthy organism; birth is a normal physiological, psychological, and social experience that should be facilitated by midwives and lived by mothers; and that women can birth under their own power without any need for interventions in the vast majority of cases.) The more oppressed a given culture or sub-culture, the more explicitly its members will tend to develop and articulate their own counter-cultural belief system. This explicit model is enacted in rituals, yet those rituals can be soft and fuzzy—as we mentioned previously, lighting candles or a fire and "throwing your fears into it," chanting and praying, etc. In contrast, implicit models like the technocratic paradigm of birth have to be massively enacted in ritual so that the students being imbued in that model will "get it" without being explicitly told what "it" is.

Quesalid and Implicit vs. Explicit Rituals

Quesalid was a Kwakiutl shaman who became a shaman because he didn't believe in shamanism and wanted to learn more about it so that he could confirm his skepticism (Whitehead 2000). He studied under senior Kwakiutl shamans, learning techniques like "sucking the illness out" of a person and then manifesting what he had "sucked out" by showing a bloody piece of blob (which he had previously tucked into his pocket). To his surprise, most of the ill people for whom he performed this "healing" ritual actually got well! He ultimately came to recognize the psychological effects of this sort of ritual performance and continued his shamanic work, to great cultural acclaim. He never believed that he was actually sucking anything out of anyone, but he did come to believe, through lived experience, that if his patient *believed* that his or her illness had been sucked out, that belief could help them to heal—what we in contemporary times would call "the power of visualization" (which we described in Chapter 8 on ritual as performance). The belief system Quesalid was taught by other shamans was explicit, and the people he treated believed in that explicit belief system. So he implied through his healing performances that the ritual would work. And since it usually did, he eventually came to value implicit ritual performance that utilized, to great effect, the core beliefs of the explicit belief system. Ritual can work both ways! You can first believe in the "belief system" and so experience the "truth" of ritual through performing the rituals that enact that belief system. Or you can believe in nothing, as Quesalid initially did, then perhaps gain a different sort of belief through the performance of rituals when you perceive that those rituals do in fact produce results. As we have previously stated, ritual is inherently paradoxical.

THE INTENTIONAL CREATION OF PERSONAL RITUALS: TWO MEMORIAL SERVICES, TWO WEDDINGS, AND ONE BIRTHDAY PARTY

Thus far in this book we have mostly spoken about ritual as a social and cultural enactment of values and beliefs. But ritual also has the ability to enact extremely individual and personal beliefs, and here we home in on that ability, using as examples the Memorial Service that Robbie and her family members created to honor Peyton shortly after she died (an extremely successful ritual), a second Memorial Service that Robbie planned on her own one year later that went all wrong in the end (a failed ritual), and the extremely successful ritual wedding of Chris and Lisa.

Peyton's Memorial Service/Birthday Party: A Conscious Ritual Enactment of Personal Beliefs and Values That Worked (written by Robbie)

Our family called it a "Memorial Service" because we hated the word "funeral." More than mourning her death, we wanted to celebrate her life. Within a day of her death (Sept. 12, 2000), it had become apparent to us all that the event *had* to happen on her 21st birthday, Sept. 16. It would be the birthday party she never got to have, plus some! Our friends—our massive support system—flew into action. At first we thought we would hold her Birthday Party/Memorial in her father's condo where she had already planned to celebrate her birthday with her Austin friends. Quickly, it became apparent that the condo was far too small. "OK," I said on the phone, "Let's do it at my house." Within minutes the answer came back (from Peyton's dad Robert Floyd), "You don't understand how many people are going to come—we need a bigger venue!" Our dear friend Robert Smith found Umlauf Sculpture Garden, a gorgeous outdoor site that would both honor Peyton's love of nature and accommodate the 400+ people who were by then expected to attend.

Once we agreed on the site, it came down to constructing the program—how should this Memorial Service proceed? Peyton was highly spiritual yet belonged to no organized religion, so obviously, if we really wanted to honor her and who she was, no minister or preacher could preside. Clearly, we needed a Master of Ceremonies. In the car after visiting

Umlauf Garden (the day after my return home from Roanoke, where the accident had happened), Robert and I got into a discussion/argument over who should take on that role. I thought that he should, but he said that he couldn't, that he would break down. Then I said that I would, but he said, "No, you will break down too." I protested that I was a professional public speaker and would not break down—and then our 16-year-old son Jason, from the back seat, said, "I'll do it. I can do it!" And we both stopped in astonishment, thought about it for one second, and agreed. Jason would take on the ritual role of Master of Ceremonies.

We also agreed that into this Memorial Service we would put all the money we had been saving for Peyton's ongoing university tuition, her college graduation party, her eventual (we hoped) wedding, the baby showers—now none of those events would ever happen. So we decided to throw all our "Peyton savings" into this one event—this massive celebration of Peyton's life. It would be a party beyond all parties! Since P had just graduated from the Natural Gourmet Cookery School in New York, obviously the catered dinner we were planning would use the menu she had cooked for her graduation (she had sent it to us as a booklet, complete with recipes for each dish and photos—our caterer found it a huge challenge, yet he succeeded—the food was beyond delicious!). Since she loved Texas wildflowers, obviously our florist should decorate Umlauf Gardens with the most beautiful Texas wildflowers he could find. And because carrot cake was her favorite dessert, obviously we should celebrate her 21st birthday with a huge carrot cake.

Two days before the Memorial Service (that is, two days after she died—this had to happen fast!), all of Peyton's closest girlfriends came to my home to help me unpack her luggage (which I had fetched from the wrecked car in Roanoke) in order to select the clothes her body should be dressed in for the viewing. (Viewing the dead corpse is a tradition for many Americans, a way to really get that the person is dead, a chance to say goodbye. That tradition makes millions of dollars per year for the funeral industry (see Mitford 1998), yet we tend to cling to it because we really want to see them just that one more time.) Together, we unpacked the bags I had brought back from the wrecked Big Blue and organized them into piles—long pants here, shorts there, dresses here, long-sleeved shirts, short-sleeved shirts, vests, etc. Then I asked her friends, "OK, so what should we dress her in?" Her best friend Corrie pulled out a beautiful gray embroidered long vest, and said, "This!" After that it was easy—long gray pants to match the vest, a gray long-sleeved T-shirt to go under the vest (her arms were so broken and bruised that I didn't want anyone to see them). And then, what else should go into the casket to be cremated with her? Her toe shoes, of course—she was such an amazing dancer. Her Natural Gourmet chef's hat. A T-shirt from Broadway Dance, where she was training in NYC to dance on Broadway. A dolphin figurine, to symbolize the seven summers she spent dancing in the ocean with wild dolphins off of Key West with Captain Victoria Impallomini. And here is the ritual program we created in a blur of hurry, along with my annotated comments in brackets:

MEMORIAL SERVICE AND 21ST BIRTHDAY CELEBRATION
FOR
PEYTON ELIZABETH FLOYD

September 16, 2000

6:00   Arrival. Please sign the guest book.

6:30   Jason Floyd, Master of Ceremonies, initiates the service. Speakers:

- Jason Floyd [who, wearing a Hawaiian shirt and beach trunks in honor of her love of the ocean, told hysterically funny stories about P]
- Adam Lyons [one of P's two best friends, who spoke about their climbing adventures in Utah's Zion National Park where, he said, "I was the happiest I have ever been in my life…ready to forget the past and put off the future in order to live in the present, in her presence on Angel's Landing."]
- Robbie Davis-Floyd [I told everyone about Peyton's hopes and dreams and how hard she worked to achieve them, and how one night I found her crying, not because she was sad, but because "Mom, there isn't enough time in a 24-hour day to do all I want to do! I wish we lived on a planet with 26-hour days!!"]
- Corrie MacClaggan [Peyton's other best friend, who spoke of Peyton's intense love of food and cooking—mussels and sauce, yuummm!]
- Robert Floyd [with Kara, the young and injured driver of Big Blue—we collectively recited the Lord's Prayer for Kara's healing and recovery].

6:50   Music and Spiritual Celebration

>   - Rocky McAshan [my cousin, who sang, in his operatic voice, "The Impossible Dream"]
>   - Brian Hudson [One of P's dearest friends, who sang a beautiful lullabye he had written for her before she died, entitled "Sweet Dreams"]

7:00   Intermission. Peyton's family understands that many present have other commitments this evening and may need to depart at this time.

7:15   Reconvene for testimonials and 'Peyton Stories' until everyone who wishes to has spoken [and so many people did speak, telling such wonderful P Stories!]

8:15   Service ends and dinner and refreshments are served. Peyton's dance videos are showing in the Learning Center; photos and albums are also on display there. This is the time for last visits with Peyton. [When I was called to attend the lighting of the candles on the birthday cake, I told the caterers to STOP and hold it for a little while, and then I took my sweet time to walk around the beautiful gardens to note how friends and relatives had clustered to eat and to talk about Peyton—forever engraved in my memory are the shining candles and my equally shining relatives and friends. I had learned not to simply ride the ritual train, but to *stop it* for a little while, so that I could simply bask in the moment to drink in from the ritual every single thing it could give me. Peyton's death was far too sudden; I did not want this precious and powerful ritual to stop me suddenly in any way, and I succeeded in achieving that very important goal.]

9:00   We light the candles on the cake and sing "Happy Birthday" and *Las Mananitas* to Peyton for her 21st birthday. [Everyone participated!]

9:10   The family closes the casket and the pallbearers carry it out. [We made a spontaneous ritual of that too—my godson Hank gathered the male pallbearers and me in a circle, and asked us to call in every ancestor and historical figure whom we thought should grace this occasion with their presence—he started with Susan B. Anthony and we went on from there!]

Pallbearers: Jason Floyd, Adam Lyons, Brian Hudson, her friend and roommate Jeff from NYC, KC Leinnen, Martin Cvejanovich, Hank Lee Star, Robert Floyd.

*** Stay and speak with Peyton's friends and family *** [which lots of people did for a very long time, even after the hearse took her casket away. I vividly remember my son Jason standing in the middle of a huge group hug given to him by his many friends who were there. There was never any rush—we took our needed time—I had learned that lesson in the hospital where I spent almost all day with P's body—bathing her, loving her—it was so incredibly valuable and important to me that nobody rushed me, so I worked hard to make absolutely sure that nobody would rush this Birthday Party. And nobody did. Oh, you know, we *can* control *some* things in life!]

It was the best party ever!—as any and all of the 400+ people who attended will attest to this day. The success of this ritual event—meaning that it succeeded in celebrating Peyton's life, honoring her multiple contributions to the world and the people she touched, and completely acknowledging who she was—carried us for a good while, and helped us in the long term to survive the pain of her death. In terms of this book, this ritual celebration worked at a Stage 4 level: it did not enact any specific religious or cultural beliefs, as most "funerals" do—it simply enacted our personal valuations of Peyton and the globally humanistic life that she lived. (She was always and ever the defender of the abused—she was both renowned and respected in all the schools she attended for openly "jumping the case" of anyone who abused or belittled anyone else. Always fearless in the cause of justice and the right, she called the bullies on their bullying and made them stop! She believed, in a Stage 4, globally humanistic way, that everyone has rights to personal dignity and respectful treatment, and she enacted those beliefs on a daily basis—that's a small part of why she was so loved by so many.)

Peyton's Second Memorial Service: A Ritual That Failed

One year later, I planned a second Memorial Service for Peyton on what would have been her 22nd birthday, in the hope that it would carry me through my ongoing grief for some months as the first one had so successfully done, and be cathartic as well for others. And it should have worked—it almost worked—yet for me this very carefully planned ritual utterly failed in the end. I had rented a school auditorium for the event. I recruited some of Peyton's best friends to sing songs and tell stories about her. Some of her dance teachers even came out of retirement to perform a dance they had created in her honor, to the song "Sweet Dreams" that her friend Brian had written as a lullaby for Peyton—such a beautiful dance. We showed some of her dance videos—she was a dream on screen!

This 2nd Memorial Service for Peyton was a major performance, yet there was no dress rehearsal, so we got the timing all wrong. Some of the people who came on stage to speak about Peyton talked for way too long. There were problems with the visual and sound effects, causing further delays. It dragged, and lots of people, including my beloved cousins who had come from Houston, left far before the end. And at that end, which I had planned to be cathartic, absolutely everything went wrong. By then, those remaining had gathered, according to my plan, into a circle around the auditorium, holding hands. I had printed a program that included words to circle songs that we all were to sing together, but the sound system went crazy and the music was too loud for anyone to hear anyone else. I regret to this day that I didn't stop everything at that point and get the sound manager to fix the system before we carried on. And I understand that I was carried, at that point, by the ritual train—even I, who had designed the ritual, could not bring myself to stop it in order to make it better! So we sang the songs in our circle, yet nobody could hear anybody else singing, and instead of the closure I was hoping for and expecting, everyone just kind of drifted off in disarray.

I was devastated, and all the more so because this long-planned ritual happened just a few days after 9/11, when the Twin Towers fell and so many people died. So its failure, in combination with that terrible attack, and other very bad things that happened to me in the preceding and ensuing days (on top, of course, of Peyton's death one year before), led to my having a massive nervous breakdown that led into a deep depression, which took me many, many months to recover from. Ritual can carry you, but if it fails, it can also majorly screw you up! All I can say is remember ice-skater Debi Thomas, whom we mentioned earlier, and be very, very careful in how you choose to employ ritual and work hard to get it right. And if you see it going wrong, *stop everything and fix the problem*! If you don't, given that your emotions and those of everyone participating will probably already be massively engaged, the ritual will *not* carry you through and you will suffer more as a result. (For a fascinating analysis of the multiple ways in which ritual can go wrong, see Grimes 1996b.)

A Wedding That Worked: Chris and Lisa

Actually, there were two weddings—Chris and Lisa got married twice, because their respective grandparents lived in different states (California and Pennsylvania) and were unable to travel. Yet we will describe these two weddings as if they were one because of their structural similarities (and to save space). The guests are gathered in a beautiful outdoor setting that enacts and displays the couple's love of nature. White chairs are set up in formation in front of a huge table—the wedding altar. Instead of bridesmaids and groomsmen, each family member proceeds down the aisle holding a flower, which he or she places in a large, water-filled vase on the table/altar, ultimately creating a huge bouquet that symbolized, as Chris and Lisa later explained (ritual interpretation, this time by its designers) the creation of the extended family to which they both were about to belong. The family members take their seats on rows in front of the altar, facing the wedding audience—a further manifestation of family solidarity. In overt rejection of traditional norms, nobody is to give anybody "away." Lisa and Chris walk the aisle individually, put their own flowers into the now-almost-overflowing vase (it was a large Irish family!), and turn to face each other with deep smiles. And then, they each turn to face the "audience" and tell their individual stories of how they had met and how, when, and why they fell in love. And they tell moving stories about how their present family members and friends had affected their lives and how they were enriched by those relationships. And then they turn toward their minister—a family friend in both cases—and recite vows to each other that they had written themselves. The following receptions, which included full dinners, were enlivened by singing, guitar playing, and dancing—all performed by friends and family and by Chris and Lisa themselves.

In terms of our book, these wedding rituals enacted and vivified Chris and Lisa's personal values on their relationship, their families, and their friends. Both weddings "worked" as rituals, meaning that all participants, including Chris and Lisa, left with feelings of satisfaction and transformation—family and friendship ties were expressed and thus deepened by the rituals, as was their love for each other, which continues in their happy marriage to this day. The rituals they personally created and carried out worked for them and for their participants. And of course, as we have seen, rituals do not always work, but that doesn't mean that we shouldn't try! Because when they do work, they can be positively transforming, in very good ways.

Weddings and Funerals: Lessons from Personal Rituals

Our friend and colleague Betty Sue Flowers, author of the Foreword to this book, notes here (personal communication 2012):

> I've never been to a wedding that didn't work, because the spirit is usually one of shared happiness for the couple. But I've been to many funerals that didn't work, usually because the master of ceremonies (the minister) didn't know the deceased and "went through the motions" of the ritual—thus not matching the feelings of those present. I think there's a key point here that hasn't been mentioned yet and that is that a public ritual must embody the feelings of those present. A wedding almost always is a happy occasion; but a funeral/memorial service is far more variegated depending on the different extents to which people are mourning for the deceased and how they remember him/her. What made Robbie's Memorial Celebration for Peyton so powerful (I was there, so I know!) is that it was so beautifully done that people joined in a similar feeling in the end (here "not rushing" was important so that people took the time to reach the same shared feeling).

Rima's "Sensational at Sixty" Surprise Birthday Ritual

We follow Betty-Sue's astute observation with an example of another ritual that joined people in a similar shared feeling at the end. When Robbie's best friend Rima Star turned 60, Robbie decided not only to throw Rima a huge party, but also to design a ritual that would hold psychological and spiritual significance for her. Robbie knew Rima quite well enough to understand her core values on breath, spirit, healing, natural childbirth in water, dolphins and consciousness—and dance as a form of art, self-expression, and exercise. So Robbie did her best to create a ritual that would display and enact those core values. She enrolled the assistance of a women's support group that she and Rima had both been participating in since 1993, called "The Wild Women Tea Party," and of Rima's three grown children Mela, Orien and Hank. All of this planning and the number of people invited were kept a secret from Rima.

Robbie took advantage of her big circular driveway deep in the woods to place signposts at measured intervals around the circle marking each decade of Rima's life (ages birth-10, 10-20, 20-30, and so on, up to 50-60). At each signpost stood one of Rima's children or Wild Women friends, who facilitated the ritual by asking these questions: *What was most memorable during this decade? What did you learn? What are you grateful for?* If someone felt that Rima was leaving out significant experiences, they would shout them out and she would respond. When she received an ovation for that decade she could move on to the next decade station. Many times she would blush, take a deep breath and share experiences of profound pain, meaning or exhilaration. Her former husband was another surprise—a guest Rima had not expected to see. When she got to the decade of their marriage, she suddenly experienced and expressed a deep sense of loving forgiveness towards him. Everyone, including her ex, was moved. After their reconnection at the party, they began to spend time together every now and then, and remained close friends until his death (Star 2016). Rima later noted that the ritual helped to open her heart and make that forgiveness and their ensuing friendship possible. (Robbie of course was delighted at this unexpected outcome of her ritual design.)

At the end of the circle, Robbie asked the entire group of 60 plus people to form two lines with their arms raised to touch the hands of the person on the other side, symbolically creating a birth canal (a gentle gauntlet) through which Rima was to move slowly, receiving kisses and embraces from the friends on each side to help "birth" her into her new, *sensational* (her choice of term), sixties. Emerging from the birth canal, Rima was carried by two male friends into a throne-like chair in Robbie's living room that had been decorated especially for her and placed in the center of the room. As Robbie settled a sparkling rhinestone tiara upon Rima's head, she dramatically intoned, "By the power invested in me as your best friend, I hereby crown you Rima, Sensational at Sixty, Queen of Breathwork, Waterbirth, Dolphins, and the Dance!" to much applause and acclaim.

Next, Rima's friends were invited to step forward and say anything loving and affirmative they wanted to say to Rima—this was a very beautiful part of the ritual, as some had written lovely poems, had chosen special readings, or simply spoke from their hearts about what Rima meant to them and all they had learned from her. The formal, orchestrated part of the ritual ended, of course, with a huge birthday cake and 61 candles ("one to grow on") and everyone singing "Happy Birthday" as a slow chant in three-part harmony! With impeccable timing, precisely as the song ended our chef Alan gleefully announced that dinner was served, and the formality of the ritual gave way to the casual, fun and meaningful (ritualized) feasting and toasting that characterize any good birthday party anywhere.

For Rima, this ritual was a huge success in that it helped her achieve her personal goal of having a positive attitude about entering her 7th decade of life. When Robbie first proposed the idea of this birthday party, Rima had responded, with a puzzled look, "But who will come?" Thus this ritual and its surrounding party was also for Rima a strong manifestation of how very many dear friends and relations she has and the many ways in which they value their relationship to her. For Robbie and all others present, this ritual succeeded in clearly demonstrating their love to Rima and their understanding of her values on healing, presence, consciousness, and life as an ongoing lesson. It made each of us feel good to help her feel good; we were very happy to turn the power of ritual to that worthwhile end, and to internalize the message that one can indeed be "sensational at sixty"—an empowering notion for us all.

RAY ROBERTSON DESIGNS A PUBERTY RITE

As we saw back in Chapter 8, many rites of passage around the globe involve a recognition of puberty and sexual maturity and are designed to help young people accomplish that transition in socially appropriate ways. How youths are prepared for adulthood varies from society to society. You see, many societies do not recognize the extended childhood phase that we call "adolescence," which may last from around 13 years of age to 20 or even 25 years of age (Benedict 1950). And in modern technocratic society, there may not be anything like a transformative ritual marking puberty or the beginning of "adolescence" or adulthood.

One of Charlie's old friends, Raymond Robertson, is an anthropologically trained social worker in Canada who recognized a great need for a consciously designed rite of passage for kids 12-14 years of age who were participating in a Unitarian Universalist church school program in which Ray was involved. (We met Ray when he and Charlie confronted Darth Vader back in Chapter 2.) So Ray decided to experiment with consciously designing a rite of passage for the kids, basing his design on his studies in anthropology, especially the writings of Victor Turner. He began by preparing them for this ritual during the several months prior to the event—thus mimicking the periods of "bush school" type preparation that many children in indigenous societies undergo before their coming of age ceremonies. Ray writes:

> The students learned about symbology. They were asked to submit a written statement of what their childhood had meant to them. We kept our requirements for this statement deliberately vague and open-ended to encourage personalization. The students were asked to choose a private, secret name for themselves, different from their birth name. These new names were then printed on name tags. The students also used plaster gauze wrap to make a mask—a cast of their own faces—which they then decorated as they wished. Finally, the students were asked to write their own personal summary of their religious views.
>
> On the night of the ritual, the students were dropped off by their parents. They were greeted by two of the adult leaders who told the parents, "Say goodbye to your child, you will never see her/him again" because their expected ritual transformation was planned and designed to transform them from children to adolescents. When all the students were gathered, the leaders then donned robes and masks, entered the room where the students were waiting, and placed a robe over each student, all of whom had a name tag with their birth name on it. They were blindfolded and led as a group through the building by a circuitous route, to a room where they were to wait in silence, keeping vigil.
>
> One by one they were taken to another room where they were asked, "What do you seek?" They responded as previously coached, "Light!" Their blindfold was removed and they found they were in a candle-lit room facing a table which held the four symbols of the Tarot's minor arcana: pentacle, sword, cup and wand. They were asked for their statement of childhood, and told, "I now take your childhood from you," and the statement was placed in a box.
>
> Students were asked for their birth name. When they responded, the leader replied, "That was your name as a child, I take it from you now." Their name tag was removed and burned. They were then instructed, "Look into the mirror." A curtain above the table was drawn briefly aside, and the student saw an empty frame through which they could see a table, arranged identically to the table on their side of the curtain. This created

the illusion that they were looking into a mirror that had no reflection. (Several of the students gave a visible start in reaction.) The curtain was then replaced.

The leader said to the student, "You have no image, you have no name, you are no longer a child, but not yet an adolescent. What remains? Think on this when you have left this place. For now, we need a name by which to call you. I give you the name you have chosen for yourself." A name tag with that name was placed on the student's robe. "We need a way to recognize you, therefore wear this." Their mask was placed on their face. "Go now, and think on what has happened here, and speak to no one." Their blindfold was then replaced and they were led back to keep vigil.

When all the students had gone through this part of the ceremony, they were gathered together and their blindfolds were removed. They were told that they had a test to pass before they could be recognized as adolescents, to witness their beliefs to the group. They were then asked to state their personal beliefs regarding the existence of a deity, life after death, and what constitutes a moral life. (It is interesting that several adults had questioned whether this was too difficult a task to expect of people this age, yet every student rose admirably to the task.)

When all had done so, they were told that they had passed the test and were accepted into our community as adolescents. They were instructed not to reveal what had taken place to any younger person (but could share as much as they liked with their parents). All were gathered outside where they fed their statements of childhood into a small fire. They then removed their robes and masks, and shared a communal meal.

After a sleepover, all students attended the church service the next morning. The students had chosen the music for the service, mostly by contemporary artists whose music spoke to them. They were presented to the congregation as our newest adolescents, came masked to the dais, removed their masks, and placed them at the front of the dais. The students were welcomed by the community with applause, ending the ceremony on a note of celebration. (Raymond Robertson, personal communication, 2012)

As fascinating as this purposely designed ritual is, Ray's reasoning behind the symbolism is even more interesting. Again, in his own words:

> This ceremony is a way of externalizing and concretizing the transition from one stage of life, childhood, to another, adolescence. This transition is known to be problematic for many young people, because their culture does not normally prepare them for what is expected of them. A common parental lament is that teens often seem stuck in childhood, and "don't act their age." The process of removing and destroying markers of childhood symbolizes that this stage of their life is over, and the time has come to let go and adopt a new self-concept. The process of replacing these markers with self-chosen aspects of identity symbolizes the process of individuation. The message is to make one's own choices, and take responsibility for one's self-concept, identity, and beliefs. As such, this ritual performs a function similar to psychodrama. In making this transition from childhood to adolescence ceremonial, the transition, rather than being open-ended and indefinite, is compressed into a single night. In much the same way, cultures that ritualize the transition from childhood to adulthood might be said to compress adolescence into a confined period of weeks or months, rather than a prolonged period of seven or (increasingly) more years. (Raymond Robertson, personal communication 2012)

This kind of ritual works, when it does work, by linking up the universal mimetic properties of ritual (see Chapter 5 on ritual drivers, where "mimesis" is explained) with the very real processes involved in the development of consciousness. It can be argued (indeed, has been argued—see Muuss 1975) that the failure of modern societies to ritually underscore and symbolically manipulate the puberty crisis in young people is responsible, in part at least, for the chaos so many young people experience during their teen years—what the great psychologist G. Stanley Hall once called the *Sturm und Drang* (German for "storm and stress") of adolescence. Such societies leave their young people in a kind of identity limbo where they are vulnerable to peer pressure, role uncertainty, and dependence upon family even as they reject/rebel against many of their family-assigned roles and ties. Consciously designed rituals like the one that Robertson created can empower young people to make the transition from childhood to adolescence in full awareness of the meaning of this transition, thereby enabling them to reconcile its inherent paradoxes and to move into their new social status in conscious and healthy ways.

Such consciously designed rituals will be especially important to young girls experiencing their menarche—a much more dramatic transition to adolescence and later adulthood than boys experience. Boys entering adolescence grow facial hair and experience the lowering of their voices, all major biological transitions. Girls entering adolescence experience breast development and bleeding when they first get their "periods." When girls receive little or no information from their parents about the biological processes they are undergoing, they can become massively confused, and can experience a major sense of shame for the "messiness" of bleeding and sometimes unwelcome sexualized comments about their budding breasts (or their odor) from their male or female peers. Rituals that honor and appropriately channel these biological transitions can be of enormous help to adolescents by endowing their physical changes with deep cultural meaning, as the following section will describe.

OUR PINK AND RUBY TENTS FOR ADOLESCENT GIRLS

written by Jeanna Lurie

Several years ago, my dear friend Jennifer Penick started leading Red Tent evenings in our community in Silicon Valley, California. These monthly circles offer women the opportunity to connect with one another and reflect on their lives in an intimate, supportive, and celebrative setting. It was important to Jennifer to create a space for women, not just to connect socially, but to gather on an emotional and spiritual level as well. She felt that was the environment described in Anita Diamant's famous book *The Red Tent,* and never considered calling her circles anything else. Like the environment in the book, Red Tents include women of all generations, from menarche on. The age range so far has included young girls of 11 years to women in their 70s.

During a Red Tent two years ago, during which we reflected on our experience of our first menstruations, it occurred to me how valuable it would be to have this same discussion in the company of my daughter, who was 10 at the time. With Jennifer's support, just a few months later "Pink Tents" for girls ages 9 to 13 with their mothers and "Ruby Tents" for teen girls were born. The colors—variations of the red color palette (re menstrual blood) —came to mind automatically and stuck. Pink had a soft connotation that seemed to match the younger set and ruby gave a feeling of sparkle, flashiness, and sass that fit teens. The groups have been open to the public and Pink Tents in particular are always full, with about 12 mother/daughter pairs. Because teens are at a stage in which they are finding themselves and appropriately seeking autonomy from their families of origin, it felt natural to not include their mothers. Ruby Tents average about six girls—while there is great interest, teens have very busy schedules and we are finally just settling into a time that seems to work. Each circle is a separate event, so while many of the girls have attended regularly, each month the mixture of attendees has been slightly different. Everyone is invited to wear pink or red and bring food to share.

Similar to Mother Blessing circles used to honor new mothers in our community (which I'm sure may have been part of what inspired Jennifer), all Red Tents, Ruby Tents, and Pink Tents include the string ritual in which each woman shares her name and the names of her female relatives while wrapping a string around her wrist, then passing it to her neighbor to do the same. This ritual literally connects the women in the circle. After the string makes it around the entire circle, it is cut and tied around the wrist as a reminder of our connection to and support of each other. Usually, pink string is used at Pink Tents and at Ruby Tents we use a sparkly red.

Although I researched before we started to see what similar rituals others had created and to get ideas for our new group, our ritual was developed for the most part through my own experience participating in Mother Blessings and Jennifer's Red Tents, a bit of creativity, and trial and error. Our first Pink Tent combined both education and storytelling. We started with an activity to diagram the female anatomy, and then discussed the mechanics of the menstrual cycle. The mothers in the group shared their stories of their first periods—what it was like, what they wished they had known. I also brought in examples of menstrual products, from reusable cloth products and menstrual cups to the typical disposable pads and tampons, and each girl received samples from a couple of different menstrual product companies. And throughout the circle we indulged in "goodies"

—strawberries, chocolate, brownies, tea. Our first circle was quite long, but all of the girls who participated had a great time and couldn't wait to return.

In the following months, our topics came to include other "girl stuff" (bras, shaving, make-up...), relationships, and finally reproduction. Every circle opened with a simple meditation using the breath to fully "arrive," and included time at the end for anonymous questions written on scraps of paper, then read aloud and discussed within the group. While the mothers and I all wanted to make sure our daughters received factual information, we put just as much emphasis on their feelings, curiosities, and the need to simply be witnessed in this stage of their lives. Depending on the topic, we used a number of creative activities to explore thoughts and ideas. For example, in our second circle, the girls used magazines to create collages representing what it meant to them to be female. Most circles included poems or readings, and sometimes Jennifer, who has a beautiful voice, led us in song or played her harmonium.

The first few Ruby Tents followed the same topics as the Pink Tents: menstruation, relationships, reproduction, but since the participants were older and more experienced, and I was the only adult in the circle, I left the activities a bit more open-ended. We always started with a simple opening meditation, and passed the string around acknowledging the women in our lineage, but mostly our time together consisted of a juicy discussion on the evening's topic. Often we strayed from the subject—I felt it was important for the girls to "own" their circle and have the time to talk about what was most important to them. Sometimes they brought poems or readings to share—once, one of the girls performed a long poem she had written and memorized.

After our first four months, we had a party and invited any girl who had attended a Pink or Ruby Tent and her mother to join us. At this party we shared food and an amazing storyteller, who entertained us with stories starring empowered women. It was a special celebration just before the winter holidays to wrap up the first installment of these unique circles.

In the New Year, we took a slightly different approach to the Pink Tent based on the most successful elements of the previous circles. It was clear that the girls attending had mothers who were giving them a fair amount of factual information. What the girls needed more than a clinical sort of education was the opportunity for self-expression, to share their stories and hear others, and to ask questions in a safe space. Our topics changed from concrete subjects like menarche and reproduction, softening into topics like boundaries, authenticity, and finding one's passion. Interestingly, the concrete clinical issues often come up within the context of open-ended topics, and when they do, everyone is able to relate to the clinical information more deeply. No longer abstract, it can be applied to real-life situations they are likely to encounter or perhaps have already encountered on some level. The girls love the opportunity to ask anonymous questions. These mostly request advice regarding situations with other kids at school. The irony is that these questions never stay anonymous: "Um….that question was mine…and …what happened was…" This speaks to the comfort the girls feel within the intimacy of the group.

The Ruby Tents continued with the support of Zoe Beaman, a faithful member of the circle who decided to form a school-sponsored club. Like any school club, they meet on a regular basis during lunchtime. This has helped teens new to the ritual to understand what to expect and get them committed to attending the actual Ruby Tent circles off-campus. At our most recent gathering, I gave them a short, simple writing exercise to reflect on a topic and all were very willing to share what had come up for them. The topic was "Yes, no, maybe so," exploring how and why we set boundaries. I asked, "Can you think of a time when you agreed to do something that you didn't really want to do? Or you had an opportunity that you turned down and later regretted? How did it make you feel?" The girls took a few minutes to jot down thoughts, words, or pictures, which quickly turned into a discussion. The energy of the younger Pink Tent girls has demanded that I take a more active role as facilitator. With the Ruby Tent teens, I merely need to give them a topic and hold the space.

Pink Tents can be personalized to honor a girl experiencing her first menarche, as we did with my daughter Jeannessa last fall. For Jeannessa's special circle, it was up to her to decide whom to invite. It was important that every woman in the circle was someone with whom she felt a special connection. My extrovert daughter had quite the guest list including her grandmothers, aunts and cousin, friends of all ages and a number of girls and their mothers from our monthly Pink Tent. All were asked to wear red or pink.

With my guidance, Jeannessa chose the activities for her celebration with inspiration from each of the menarche circles that were held in honor of Zoe and her sister Isobel a few years prior. (Jeannessa had been too young at the time to attend with me, but the older girls were included on Jeannessa's special guest list.) Jeannessa's circle was held in our backyard on a September evening. A special chair draped with pretty tapestries was reserved at the head of the circle for her. In the center of the circle was a small altar with trinkets symbolizing fertility or the feminine and three candles: pink for the girls who had not yet started to bleed, red for those that have a monthly cycle, and plum for the elders who had experienced menopause. As each guest came into the backyard, they were smudged with a stick of burning sage. After everyone was settled in the circle, the candles were lit and we opened with a short guided meditation focused on the breath. A dark pink string that matched the dress Jeannessa chose especially for this occasion was passed around as everyone acknowledged their children, mothers, and grandmothers. About two thirds of the way around the circle, we ran out of string! Luckily, I had the Ruby Tent string on hand and we were able to tie it on and continue the string ritual. Nothing happens by accident! It was a perfect symbol of Jeannessa growing out of the "pink" stage and into "ruby."

Next, everyone in the circle had the opportunity to say how they knew Jeannessa, and to share any poems, readings, or special gifts they had brought for her. It was touching how much thought everyone put into the mementos they brought! I too had gifts for her: a box I made with a red fabric lid for her to store any strings or tokens from Red Tents (which she was now able to attend since she had gotten her period), Ruby Tents, or Pink Tents and a matching journal that we can use to communicate on issues that may be a little awkward face to face. (While teens who go to Ruby Tents can obviously attend Red Tents (and occasionally they do), it's clear that it is more comfortable for them to be in the company of other teens. It's "their" circle.)

Then it was Jeannessa's turn to acknowledge each person in the circle. She walked around, stopping to tell each person what she meant to her. She carried a basket filled with pink, red, and plum tea light candles, every person taking one that corresponded to her own stage of life—pink for not yet bleeding, red for bleeding, plum for post-menopausal. I then brushed Jeannessa's hair and massaged her feet and hands with lotion as a reminder that she is nurtured by the women in her circle and to continue to nurture herself. We then closed the circle by acknowledging the four directions, and Jennifer led us in song.

Afterwards we celebrated with a wonderful spread of food—Jeannessa's favorites that happened to be red or pink: pomegranate juice, strawberries, shrimp cocktail, raviolis with meat sauce, and an antipasto platter my mother prepared as she always does for special family gatherings.

For years Jeannessa knew that there would be a celebration in honor of her first menarche, and so she looked forward to menstruation. At the Pink Tent, most of the girls have expressed enthusiasm and positivity as they look forward to getting their first periods. Mothers are certain their daughters are gaining insight that they probably would not have found without the circles. Providing pre-teen and teenage girls the space to celebrate being female and seeing how much it has positively impacted their lives thrills me! I feel blessed and honored to connect with girls and their mothers through our Pink and Ruby Tents.

Robbie can only add here that she would have been thrilled to participate in Pink and Ruby Tents as a young girl and then teenager. Like so many middle-class parents in many countries whose children were born in the 1950s and 1960s, Robbie's parents found themselves simply unable to talk to her about her biological transitions. Her first period found her alarmed and scared—she ran to her mother, who simply handed her a book explaining the biology of menstruation, and a box of Kotex. The book was instructive and helpful—it did answer her concrete questions with specific information, yet gave her no context for the *knowledge and spiritual understanding* that she would have delighted in at the time. She would have loved to be imbued with the power of the Pink and Ruby Tent rituals, and she was deeply grateful that her daughter Peyton did receive this kind of ritual initiation into young womanhood via her then-mentor

Captain Victoria Impallomeni in Key West, Florida, on the beach with a fire and the wild dolphins nearby.

CHARLIE'S PERSONAL TANTRIC RITUALS

As we mentioned earlier, Charlie spent years as a Buddhist monk studying Tibetan Tantric-style meditation. What "Tantric" means is way too complicated, abstruse, and confusing to get into here. Moreover, it is beside the point. What is important here is that Tantrism in all of its forms engendered ritual practices that offer some of the richest examples of mimetic symbolism found in the world today. Meditation upon symbols is older than Buddhism. Most of the meditation techniques the Buddha reputedly taught were borrowed from earlier traditions. In those traditions, simple objects like bowls of water, clay circles, fire, mandalas, etc. were used as foci for intense concentration. These meditations were frequently embedded within more complex rituals such as *pujas*—rituals of worship within the Hindu and Buddhist traditions. Tantric practices continue in that vein, but often use more complex and elaborate symbols and rituals, performed repetitively until their intended meanings arise in an alternative SOC. Tantric practitioners have developed complex meditations embedded within *pujas* (or *sadhanas*) involving the visualization (often with the aid of a precise description, a picture or a painting) of a "deity" or spiritual being, often shown in sexual union and dancing in flames. Access to the instructions for each type of meditation practice is via what is called by Tibetans a *wangkur* (or simply a *wang*; an initiation or "empowerment") during which the teacher (lama) will enact the ritual practices and meditations, presumably transforming him or herself into the appropriate deity and bestowing sublime blessings on the initiate. The *wang* stands as an official permission for the initiate to perform the meditation practices associated with that particular deity (e.g., *Mahakala, Demchog, Dorje Palmo,* and so forth).

By practicing these rituals in a group or individually—especially practicing the appropriate visualizations—the practitioner is in essence creating the possibility of inter-state mimesis and the evocation of profound experiences and insights that are in fact the intent of the rituals. These visualizations (indeed any visualization carried out with persistence and concentration) can result in symbolic penetration into the unconscious mind, and the stimulation of archetypal structures that, when they become activated, may result in the arising of feelings, sensory experiences and insights—thus such practices are called *arising yogas*. Charlie attended scores of *wangs* over many years, but only practiced a few of them diligently (Laughlin 1994; Laughlin, McManus and Webber 1984). Each deity is associated with a series of visualizations and reciting of mantras literally hundreds of thousands of times, a process that can take months to complete. Once a practitioner has learned the essential methodology of Tantric meditation, he or she can easily adapt those methods and form new configurations.

An Aside: "Tantra" in the West

If you are like most westerners, you will likely associate "Tantra" or "Tantric" with exotic ways for making love/having sex. When Western explorers first discovered temples full of art exhibiting the Tantric symbolism of male and female forms in various sexual postures, they were shocked and made the natural but erroneous assumption that Tantric practitioners must be profligate hedonists who only had sex on their minds. Only later did more careful explorers discover that Tantric sexual iconography was intended as an aid to visualization meditations—manipulating archetypal symbols that had more to do with unifying consciousness than having coitus. Very few Tantric practitioners used actual sexual liaisons in their meditation work, and only those who had reached a very advanced state of proficiency were allowed to practice Tantric sex. But by the time the true meaning of the iconography was understood, the previous interpretation had become widespread in the West, leading of course to a systematic misunderstanding of Eastern Tantric practices, and to all kinds of "Tantric" sex programs propagated through books, tapes and workshops. Totally lost have been both the meditational importance of true Tantric practice and the accompanying sexual abstinence required of all but the most advanced practitioners.

Nevertheless, thousands of people do practice "Tantric sex" in the West, and do ritualize their encounters so as to evoke special, even extraordinary, experiences. So here we provide an example of ritualized "Tantric" sexuality as practiced in the contemporary American West:

> Deeply and passionately in love, a woman and a man (the man had been trained in Tantra, the woman had not, yet she was

receptive), spent time in a hot tub together somewhere in Northern California. And when they began to make love, the experience for both of them melted into not only ongoing ecstasy but also a profound sense of timelessness. With their bodies fused together through total symbolic and physical penetration, they sat on the edge of the hot tub without moving, for what could have been hours for all they knew or cared, experiencing an ongoing orgasm so intense that it seemed to grow from deep inside their fusion and eventually expanded until they experienced oneness not only with each other, but also with all that was around them, and then, as the mighty orgasm continued, with the heavens and stars above.

The couple who told us this story experienced this fusion as life-transforming and as an affirmation of the Tantric declaration that during sex, the participants' energy fields are united and they can then experience a sense of "cosmic consciousness." According to Wikipedia (2012):

> Tantric texts specify that sex has three distinct and separate purposes—procreation, pleasure, and liberation. Those seeking liberation eschew frictional orgasm for a higher form of ecstasy, as the couple participating in the ritual lock in a static embrace. The sexual act itself balances energies coursing within the *pranic ida* and *pingala* channels in the subtle bodies of both participants. The *sushumna nadi* is awakened and *kundalini* rises upwards within it. This eventually culminates in *samadhi*, wherein the respective individual personalities and identities of each of the participants are completely dissolved in a unity of "cosmic consciousness." Tantrics understand these acts on multiple levels. The male and female participants are conjoined physically, and represent *Shiva* and *Shakti*, the male and female principles. Beyond the physical, a subtle fusion of *Shiva* and *Shakti* energies takes place, resulting in a united energy field. On an individual level, each participant experiences a fusion of one's own *Shiva* and *Shakti* energies.

Tantric Dreamwork

Returning to the non-sexual yet equally fascinating realm of dreams, we note here that Charlie was early-on drawn to the Tibetan Buddhist practice of *dream yoga* (*mi-lam*; see Laughlin 2011:Chap. 13 for a detailed description). Dream yoga amounts to the application of Tantric meditation methods to retain and enhance awareness during dreaming. The specific intention of Buddhist dream yoga is to retain awareness across warps and throughout all SOCs, and to come to realize that each and every one of them is an illusion produced by the mind for its own consumption. Furthermore, once one has learned the simple properties underlying the various yogas (regardless of tradition, by the way), one can begin to manufacture yogic rituals for oneself. When Charlie began working on "incubating" (ritualizing the process of falling asleep) his dreams, he used all the usual techniques in vogue at the time (Garfield 1974). And he learned that the only things necessary to increase dream recall were to develop an intense interest in his dreams and to put a tablet of paper and a pen next to his bed and write down every scrap of dream that he could recall immediately after waking. It was as though his unconscious "got it" that ego-Charlie had become interested in dreams, and the unconscious obliged by upping his nightly dose of conscious dreams. He also drank half a glass of water before falling asleep and finished the glass of water upon waking—a common practice among dream enthusiasts to help ritualize the process of going to sleep and waking up. He would fall asleep focusing upon an intention to become more aware of his dreams, or upon a problem he wished to solve with the help of the "depths." Charlie found that all of these ritualized pre-sleep practices had a positive effect, and deepened his conscious involvement in his dream life.

Then, at age 40 or thereabouts, Charlie was introduced to Tibetan dream yoga. The Tibetan methods essentially changed Charlie's ritual practice to a more active concentration during the process of falling asleep. He began his nightly practice by going to bed before he was actually tired. He then focused his attention inwards, first visualizing a neon red English letter 'A' at the base of his throat (Tibetans use their letter corresponding to the "ah" sound in the "throat chakra"), and later simplified this image to a pea-sized red bubble (Tibetan: *Tig Le*). At the same time he chanted "ahhhhhh" softly in his throat. Ritualizing his going-to-bed rituals and using these simple techniques, Charlie found that he could enter sleep onset—what psychologists call the hypnagogic state—in an alert, energized and focused state of awareness, and eventually found that the hypnagogic (usually lasting only a few seconds in normal sleep onset) began to stretch out into minutes of intense kaleidoscopic imagery, which began as a kind of gorgeous two-dimensional slide show, but then deepened into dynamic, four-dimensional experiences (time being the fourth dimension). In addition, his dreaming became more vivid and even lucid—that is, he could remain aware that he was dreaming while still in the dream.

But Charlie remained frustrated because he would eventually become tired and lose consciousness. Heretofore he had carried out these ritual practices while lying flat on his back in bed. He realized that he was struggling against a lifetime's conditioning to lose consciousness when he laid down, so he decided to remain sitting-up in half-lotus posture, meditating his way into sleep onset. This worked to some extent in prolonging the hypnagogic and even entering deep lucid dreaming, but again, the conditioning was too strong and he would wake up after a while lying flat-out on the rug. He even tried the Tibetan trick of using a wide strap around his legs and torso to maintain proper posture, to no avail. He would still wake up lying on his side.

Charlie finally decided to make it impossible to lie down during the night. He built a box out of plywood approximately four feet square and higher than his shoulders when sitting in half-lotus posture (see Figure 11.2). He lined the bottom and sides of the box with foam pads thick enough that it made the inside comfortable. He left the corner of the box in front of him open, as the two sides that would have met to form

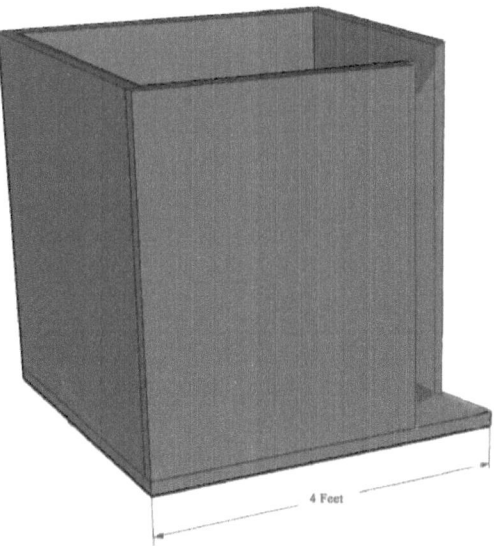

Figure 11.2. Charlie's sleeping box. Four feet on a side and higher than his shoulders with foam padding and an opening for getting in to reach various materials.

the corner extended only half the length of the side of the bottom. This configuration left a corner for his back and two angles on each side for his knees, and an opening in front to enter the box and to place objects (water, tablet and pen, rosary, etc.) within easy reach on the floor. He slept sitting up in this box for many months, and although he never succeeded in remaining conscious throughout the night, he spent much of his sleep in lucid dreaming, wafting in and out of the waking and dream states and recording experiences on the note pad as he could.

Charlie's dreams during the sleeping box phase of his practice were a mixture of the chthonic and the sublime. Many were dark and disturbing, and some downright frightening. Charlie's Buddhist studies came in handy once again, and he built into his sleep-ritual practice another Tibetan method. He visualized his dream-ego as a particular fierce "deity" he had been assigned by one of his teachers. The figure was that of his *yidam*, or personal protector, and was called Mahamaya, the Great Sorcerer, who is depicted in Tibetan paintings (*thangka*) as a huge light blue figure dancing in flames with four multicolored heads, each with a mouth with fangs and two red eyes and a "third eye" just for good measure, two sets of arms with hands holding various implements for dealing with scary apparitions, clothed in a tiger skin and wearing a necklace of human skulls. After some practice Charlie was able to assume this dream body at will, and this practice alone transformed encounters with the unconscious to a less terrifying tone.

Experiences had while dreaming often informed Charlie of the real meaning behind some of the meditative rituals he had been taught to do while awake—hence, these practices took on an inter-state mimetic quality (in which one SOC influences or shapes another via continuity through the warp; see Chapter 5 on ritual drivers and mimesis/imitation). One of the "foundation" rituals in Tibetan Buddhism is to complete 100,000 repetitions of deep prostrations to the guru—for the more sophisticated student, the "guru" represents the goal of perfect enlightenment (see Pabongka Rinpoche 2006). This practice is accomplished while standing before an altar, or while visualizing the guru, and then moving from a standing posture to a position of total prostration, repeated over and over, hour after hour. Charlie was well into this practice when he had a lucid dream while in his sleeping box, in which he was starting a prostration before a colorful altar at the end of his in-breath and by the time he had reached the end of the out-breath and completed the prostration, his dream body had exploded and his consciousness expanded into a vast, infinite void, accompanied by intense ecstasy. When he awoke, it was with the certain understanding that if one were to do a prostration properly, only one repetition would do the trick to evoke the transcendental mind state toward which the ritual is pointing. This experience points to the ability to shift one's state of conscious from egoistic to universalistic with an act of will, an ability greatly prized in Buddhist psychology.

PRAYER PRACTICE AMONG EVANGELICAL CHRISTIANS

The practice of arising yoga (meditation on an object such as a mandala, flower, bowl of water, etc., which may produce a spiritually significant experience) is thousands of years old within Eastern meditation traditions. We have seen how Charlie (like countless other yoga practitioners) manipulated the principles of mimetic ritual and concentration to evoke experiences that then became the meaning, for him, of the symbols used in the rituals. This process completed a spiritual cycle of meaning for Charlie—a process that continues to unfold in his dreams and other SOCs up to the present day.

What is very interesting is that some practitioners in Western Christian spiritual traditions have stumbled across more or less the same principles in order to ground their spiritual life in the direct experience of the sublime. Anthropologist Tanya Luhrmann (2012) has done ethnographic fieldwork on American evangelical Christians, specifically members of a sect known as The Vineyard. It is very important to members of The Vineyard, and of course to many other evangelical Christians (Rose 1988), that a personal relationship be established with God. But just how is this personal relationship to be established? The answer is "through prayer." As Luhrmann (2012:133) says:

> ...all the faith practices involve prayer. They are, in fact, prayer practices. The central point of the renewalist evangelical church—on Sunday mornings, in the small house groups, in the endless numbers of books people read, and in the lyrics of the music they play—is that one should build a personal relationship with God through prayer. No instruction is made more plainly or more emphatically. Prayer is understood as the only way to create a relationship with God and indeed the only way to reach God at all.

As her hosts told Luhrmann, most people require training in order to pray properly and effectively. Some people are better at it than others, and some enjoy praying while others do not. Moreover, there is an awareness that part of the training is to interpret signs, images and insights in the "right" way. As people become more proficient at prayer, the clearer and more detailed their imagery becomes. As one of her informants noted, "Depending on the prayers and depending on what's going on, the images that I see [in prayer] are very real and lucid" (ibid:135). Luhrmann's informants made it clear to her that praying is a *technique* (see Chapter 6 on ritual techniques and technologies)—a set of ritual procedures that must be learned and that operate to invite or evoke the presence of the divine within the individual consciousness.

Prayer practice involves working with (concentrating upon) images—indeed, is essentially a meditation upon imagery. One of Luhrmann's informants worked with the images of flowers, and the more adept she became, the less control she (her waking ego) had over the images, and the more lucid and revealing they became. In other words, images "came alive," as well as ideas, and were interpreted by her as communication with God (ibid:134). The more she meditated, the clearer and more complex her imagery became, and the more she experienced "flow" (see Chapter 7 on ritual framing, which facilitates flow) and openness to the depths. Moreover, these practices and their results were transpersonal, for over time they had changed "how her mind worked." She spoke of her prayer practices as the "technical" aspect [read ritual] of praying—setting things up so that the voice of God could get through to her. In addition, she believed that when she was praying for someone else, her technical practice of prayer opened a conduit for the Holy Spirit to reach the target of the prayer.

Another of Luhrmann's informants carried out a number of other ritualized practices, some of them drivers (Chapter 5). When he began his practice he would first read scripture and then pray for an hour at a time in a closet on his knees (ibid:141). He later used fasting and praying in a rural field. He eventually was able to enter into a profound state of rest and openness. Later still he found that imagery popped up spontaneously, sometimes of people he knew, for whom he would then pray. His experience was that God eventually talked to him a few times. Still other informants told Luhrmann they had gone on retreats or "Holy Weekends" that resulted in out-of-body and transpersonal experiences, profound bliss states ("electricity in the body"), speaking in tongues, and the physical presence of God. Once again, the results of ritual practices may have a profound and transformative impact upon practitioners.

DESIGNING PERSONAL RITUALS: HEALING AND DANGER

It is very unlikely that people who are designing a ritual for themselves or a group will, with the exception of high-tech artifacts, discover a ritual element that has not been found in rituals already extant in other cultures and used for thousands of years. As in the case of prayer practice among evangelical Christians, the age-old principle of "arising yoga" may be re-discovered over and over again when people find ritual methods for evoking spiritually poignant experiences. Readers who have followed our discussions closely will recognize many other features described in the above rituals, including designating a special (holy, sacred) ritual frame—a Church, school auditorium, retreat center, closet, sleeping box, quiet field out in nature, space around an altar, etc.—and making the occasion even more special/ritualistic through clothing and iconography, etc. Various nervous system drivers may be used, including singing, dancing, fasting, chanting, drama, etc. (as we explain in Chapter 5 on ritual drivers).

When a personal transformation is intended, symbols that may potentiate yet undeveloped aspects of the psyche can be employed. A case in point is Ray Robertson's use of the "hoodwinking" technique with his students, which involved leading the initiates around blindfolded and then pulling off their blindfolds so they could see a prepared scene—in Ray's case, a faux mirror. When Charlie was initiated into the Shingon-shū sect of Japanese Buddhism, he and his fellow initiates were led in a serpentine line all around the temple, blindfolded and chanting a Buddhist mantrum ("mantra" is the plural of "mantrum," like the much more common "data" and "datum"). At one point, Charlie's blindfold was whipped off so that he could see a beautiful altar and painting of one of the Buddhist deities, and then he was re-blindfolded and led on to the end of the course. Blindfolding as a ritual practice can be found among many religions and has been used for centuries in rituals because it works. It especially works if it is associated with a visualization practice in which the initiate's mind returns to the image he or she saw during the "hoodwinking" —hoodwinking being an ancient technique for ritually controlling what an intitiate sees.

Visualization practices occur in many traditions. The object of the practice is to construct what is called an *eidetic image*—that is, a clear, vivid, stable image of some object before the mind's eye, and then concentrate upon it. In ancient Hindu and Buddhist yoga work, an image might be stimulated by a real external object that one may visually scan, then close the eyes and retain the internal (eidetic) image and then concentrate upon the image, perhaps while repeating a mantrum or prayer associated with that image. As we saw above, the Buddhist meditation tradition calls this kind of practice an "arising yoga," thus named because if one meditates intensely enough and long enough, the eidetic image will "come alive" and take on a life of its own. The key to understanding this practice is to realize that for every eidetic image one can construct before the mind, there are associated experiences that may eventually arise because of concentrating upon that image (Laughlin, McManus and d'Aquili 1990:199; Laughlin, McManus and Webber 1984). The experiences that arise are rarely logically connected to the eidetic image, but they are predictable to those who have already become adept. The really important thing to realize here (as we have already emphasized) is that *there is no such thing as an experience that is interpretable in one and only one way.* For example, one of Luhrman's evangelical Christian informants heard an internal voice in her dream that "...startled her awake. *Read James,* the voice said, and she knew it was God" (Luhrmann 2012:138). Charlie had a similar experience which he published in his book *Communing with the Gods* (2011:191). He wrote:

> After what was perhaps the most intense and transformative meditation retreat of my life, which lasted for months, I had a uniquely profound dream. I dreamed that I was standing hand in hand with my child self under a fiery arch that had morphed from two enormous serpents that had arisen on each side of us and touched their heads above us. I was lucid and watching the scene from a position behind the fiery portal and my dream selves, so I could see they were located on a vast plain upon which stood the ruins of a city. I knew in the dream that I was looking at the transformation of myself after the realizations of the past retreat. I was beginning to awaken from the dream and was in a hypnopompic state [the state at the end of sleep and just prior to waking] when a fiery golden chariot being drawn by huge golden horses appeared out of an intense, almost blinding golden light, and a deep, booming voice called out, "Read Ezekiel!" This image could not have lasted more than a few seconds, but I awoke knowing that I had not (and indeed have never since) experienced a dream like that.

In reflection, Charlie understood that the dream might have drawn on a childhood memory of material presented to him in Bible school (he was raised a Methodist), although at the time of the dream he could not recall what the Book of Ezekiel was about. He quickly acquired a Bible, read the passages indicated, and was astounded to find that the section in question began with a visitation by a fiery chariot and outlined instructions from God about building a new city over the ashes of the old city. But the difference between Charlie's interpretation of the experience and that of Luhrmann's informant is that Charlie is a Buddhist, not a Christian, and moreover is very much a Jungian in his interpretation of dream material. So what for Luhrmann's informant was God talking to her was for Charlie a message from his unconscious depicting transformations happening at the time in his psyche. He further understood how any theist could well interpret his dream as a message from God.

If you have followed our earlier discussions, you will appreciate the importance of lodging ritual within either a myth/ritual or a paradigm/ritual context. That is, in order for ritual to do its work appropriately, *it must be lodged within a cycle of meaning*. The Buddhist and Christian contexts of Charlie's and Luhrmann's informants respective experiences are quite different. Each has an explanatory framework that allows the integration of the experience within a distinct world view. If no such cycle of meaning is available to a practitioner, they must either find one or build one themselves. It is quite possible to construct a *personal mythology*, a process that integrates one's own experiences into a coherent story line (see Feinstein 1990; Feinstein and Krippner 2009 [1988]). After all, somebody, or somebodies, had to originally invent all cycles of meaning. Why not invent one's own? Many people do, with varying degrees of success.

Robbie for example built her own cycle of meaning out of Peyton's death. Forced by her desperate need to find meaning in her daughter's apparently random death in a random car wreck, and led by the rituals she, her family, and Peyton's friends constructed to memorialize Peyton's life and her many contributions to the lives of others, Robbie formulated the only meaning/interpretation she could—namely, that Peyton's death had something to do with her multiple contributions to life while she lived. Perhaps, Robbie thought then and hopes now, Peyton had already accomplished her purpose in life and God was calling her home to rest, and then to send her spirit to help others in spirit form or maybe in another incarnation? Questions with no answers—yet we have to ask, we always ask, "Why did this horrible thing happen? Where is the meaning, the sense of it—does it, can it, make any kind of sense?" The rituals that Robbie and her family and friends performed around and about Peyton's death and life, the successful ones and even the failed one, gave Robbie a very clear sense of her daughter's many accomplishments at such a young age—she did so much for so many—maybe she was simply done with her work on this planet.

When Peyton appeared to Robbie in a dream three weeks after her death, Robbie was full of questions: "Why did you die? Why did you have to die?" And Peyton said, "Mom, it was my time, it was just my time!" And Robbie asked, "Where are you now, what are you doing now?" And with a huge smile, and spreading her arms out wide, Peyton answered, "Mom, I am everywhere, I live everywhere!" Robbie then asked, ""But how am I to live without you—and your dad and your brother? How can we live without you?" She grinned, and said "Mom, I will take care of you all, and I live right here inside you" and, touching Robbie's heart with a glowing finger, she said, "Mom, it's just like ET—I live right here, inside your heart!"

At the same time as we note that Robbie's EMDR experience at Sierra Tucson led her younger, formerly frozen self to find Peyton in Robbie's heart (see Chapter 8), we have to ask (as Robbie did in Chapter 6), did Peyton's spirit really come to Robbie during that dream, or did Robbie dream Peyton to get the answers Robbie needed from her own psyche, her own unconscious mind? And we collectively answer now that it doesn't matter, because the effect is the same. Robbie got the answer she needed to help her make sense of and thus reconcile, over time, to her daughter's death. Whether that answer came from Peyton's spirit or from Robbie's psyche, it helped Robbie to find the meaning she sought. And that is precisely what rituals and the myths and paradigms they enact do for their participants, when they work.

Yet we must be cautious here, for people suffering from various psychopathologies quite commonly invent a cycle of meaning for themselves that is far from wholesome, far from integrative, and far from peaceful. The rituals that individuals create for themselves, along with the stories those rituals enact, can help to true them to their sociocultural reality or can lead them into an individually constructed reality that may or may not help to true them to the world they live in. Fiction novelists like C.S. Lewis and J.R.R. Tolkien can construct whole worlds (Narnia and Middle Earth), along with their mythological constructs (and their ensuing ritual enactments), in their minds and write them down in ways that make their readers choose to "suspend disbelief" and live in those worlds while they are reading those books or watching the movies made from those books. Yet when the (healthy) readers close the book, they return to their own lifeworlds, which are generally aligned, "trued," to the belief systems and worldviews of their larger societies. Such readers (like Robbie) might *wish* to live in Tolkien's Middle Earth during King Aragorn's long and happy reign, and might go there in fantasy or in wishful dreams, yet always know upon waking that it was only a dream. Those suffering certain psychopathologies, in contrast, cannot distinguish between their fantasy worlds and their socio-cultural context, so the rituals they individually construct only lead them further into their imagined realities. A powerful example is detailed in Joanne Greenberg's *I Never Promised You a Rose Garden* (1964, written under the pen name Hannah Green), in which she describes the schizophrenia that led her to invent for herself the imagined world of Yr, whose gods over time became tyrannical dictators who controlled her each and every word and action. (Again, please see Grimes 1996b; Hüsken 2007 for a detailed discussion of the many ways in which rituals can fail or malfunction.)

SUMMARY: DESIGNING PERSONAL RITUALS – FAILURE AND SUCCESS

We began this chapter on "Designing Rituals" with a discussion of Jerusalem and its multiple symbolic implications for the followers of three major world religions—Judaism, Christianity, and Islam. We recognized that each and every enduring belief system manages successfully to true its adherents to their conceptual world through their lived reality as expressed in ritual. And then we asked, what happens when your beliefs and the myths, paradigms, and rituals that encode and express those beliefs no longer "true" you to your lived reality?

We answered that question through a discussion of religious syncretism as adaptive ritual strategy, explaining how peoples whose reality changes dramatically can combine traditional rituals with new ones that combine old and new beliefs in successful, synthetic, and syncretic forms. In our discussion of explicit vs. implicit ideologies, we explained that implicit ideologies (like the technocratic model of birth) need explicit enactment in ritual to enact and transmit those ideologies and their underlying values and beliefs, while explicit ideologies (like those of homebirthers) can make do with soft and fuzzy rituals because their countercultural belief and value systems are so explicitly detailed in their writings and communications.

We used the example of the Kwakiutl shaman Quesalid to show how a practitioner who did not initially believe in his ritual practice came to understand that it worked psychologically if not physically—his physical presentation to his clients of the bloody glob he supposedly sucked out of their bodies enabled them symbolically to believe that they were healed. Thus we noted that ritual is inherently paradoxical: you can first believe in the "belief system" and so experience the "truth" of ritual through performing the rituals that enact that belief system—or you can believe in nothing, as Quesalid initially did, then gain a different sort of belief when you perceive that the rituals you perform do in fact produce results.

We described the intentional creation of personal ritual through the examples of two memorial services (one worked, the other failed) and one wedding (held twice), illustrating the happy consequences of successful rituals as well as the potentially dire consequences when ritual fails. We followed up with detailed descriptions of an intentionally designed puberty rite that worked for the adolescents who participated in it, of the Pink and Ruby Tents designed to help adolescent girls and teens find meaning in their biological and cultural transitions, of Charlie's personal Tantric rituals that worked well to deepen his understanding of himself and the cosmos he lives in, and of the correlating prayer rituals that some evangelical Christians design for themselves or within their prayer groups, which affirm and reaffirm their close relationship to God as they perceive and experience "Him."

We noted, quite emphatically, that in order for ritual to do its work appropriately, *it must be lodged within a cycle of meaning*—which can be created by the society in question, or by the individual. We also noted, equally emphatically, that people suffering from various psychopathologies quite commonly invent a cycle of meaning for themselves that is far from wholesome, far from integrative, and far from peaceful. We conclude by once again stating that ritual, even when individually designed, can be powerful and should be employed with consciousness and caution.

Suggested Reading

Feinstein, David and Stanley Krippner (2009[1988]) *Personal Mythology: Using Ritual, Dreams, and Imagination to Discover Your Inner Story*. Fulton, CA: Energy Psychology Press.

Grimes, Ronald L. (2002) *Deeply into the Bone: Re-Inventing Rites of Passage.* Berkeley, CA: University of California Press.

Further reading on how to create effective rituals (from recent "New Age" books):

Beck, Reee and Sydney Barbara Metrick (2009) *The Art of Ritual: Creating and Performing Ceremonies for Growth and Change.* Berkeley, CA: The Aproyphile Press.

Farmer, Steven D. (2002) *Sacred Ceremony: How to Create Ceremonies for Healing, Transitions, and Celebrations.* Hay House.

Zell-Ravenheart, Oberon and Morning Glory Zell-Ravenheart (2006) *Creating Circles & Ceremonies: Rituals for All Seasons and Reasons.* Prompton Plains, NJ: New Page Books.

(And see the Appendix to this book, "How To Create and Perform an Effective Stage 4 Ritual")

Chapter 12

CONCLUSION: THE POWER OF RITUAL

Chapter Summaries. Parting Remarks.

Ritual is a form of repetitive and communicative behavior that humans and animals share. As such, ritual is deeply embedded in our evolutionary past. Leaving aside the question of whether or not animals have "culture" in the sense that humans do, a *human* ritual is a patterned, repetitive, and symbolic enactment of a cultural (or individual) belief or value. More simply put, ritual enacts cultural (or individual) beliefs and values. Although seemingly easy to define, and even recognize when we see or perform one, ritual is far from simple in its structure, psychological and cultural contexts, and emotional and cognitive elements. The previous chapters of this book explored the many facets of ritual and isolated the aspects that account for ritual's power, efficacy and endurance through time.

CHAPTER SUMMARIES

In the introductory chapter we detailed the "anatomy of ritual"—the core characteristics that enable ritual it to do its work in the world, primarily in the human brain. To repeat, with a bit of elaboration, the core characteristics that constitute the anatomy of ritual include:

1. the neuro-endocrine basis of ritual behaviors as coordination and communication systems that first developed in animals
2. the use of symbols to convey a ritual's messages
3. a cognitive matrix (belief system) from which ritual emerges, and which rituals are designed to enact, express, and transmit
4. rhythm, repetition and redundancy: ritual drivers
5. the use of tools, techniques, and technologies to accomplish ritual's multiple goals

6. the framing of ritual performances
7. the order and formality that separates ritual from everyday life, identifying it *as ritual*
8. the sense of inviolability and inevitability that rituals can generate
9. the acting, stylization, and staging that often give ritual its elements of high drama, the fact that it is *performed* and that it often intensifies toward a climax.

Rituals are above all a means of communication. In Chapter 2 we saw that rituals use symbols to convey the messages that the group seeks to send into the individual human brain—a process we called "symbolic penetration." We described the three (core, emotional, and cortical) levels of neural processing and how ritual engages all three levels. We discussed "core symbols," describing their primary characteristics:

1. **Core symbols are pervasive** in most domains of life, involving both the sacred and the everyday.
2. **Core symbols may be archetypal in origin**, deriving from and representing the deep levels of the human psyche.
3. **Core symbols often link individual identity with that of one's social group** by displaying group membership in culturally recognized ways.
4. **Core symbols lie at the very center of nationalism and work to bind the homeland together** through linking the people to the land and to each other.
5. **Core symbols reveal the hidden forces operating in the world**, often working to evoke an epiphany—that is, the realization of normally hidden forces or the existence of sacred beings, or even of the powers of high-tech diagnostic machines that can make the hidden manifest.
6. **Core symbols are "pregnant with meaning,"** rich in cognitive and emotional associations.
7. **Core symbols are multi-vocal**—they speak with many voices, often penetrating to many layers of meaning. Levels of symbolic meaning range from the most primitive emotional reactions to highly elaborate intellectual understandings of the symbols and their interrelations. Much of the power of symbols derives from the ways in which they simultaneously evoke interacting meanings at all these levels.

We then described how hard anthropologists often have to work to understand a culture's core symbols, their meanings and interpretations, and their very palpable effects on cultures and individuals, providing examples from (1) Charlie's fieldwork with the So and the "gray goop" they ritually painted on their bodies to, as Charlie eventually figured out, protect themselves from evil spirits; (2) the warnings Michael Winkelman received from the messenger mice, which he was able to interpret from his long years of experience with studying shamanic practice; (3) the experiences of Charlie and his friend upon meeting a facsimile of Darth Vader in a hotel hall during a science fiction convention; (4) the successful efforts of Old Naro's lineage members to appease her disturbed spirit through the performance of appropriate rituals; (5) a debate among midwives over what was the most appropriate gift to give to their annual honoree—a kettle, or a pressure cooker?—both of which were powerfully symbolic of the midwives' varying worldviews.

We concluded Chapter 2 on symbolism in ritual by re-noting that symbols can penetrate individual consciousness and evoke strong emotional reactions in accordance with the system of beliefs they express. Core cultural symbols like a national flag or the Christian cross encapsulate essential elements of a culture, subculture, or religion, link individual identity with that of a group, and manifest hidden elements of the natural and cultural worlds.

In Chapter 3, "The Cognitive Matrix of Ritual," we explained that rituals are not arbitrary—they always emerge from a "cognitive matrix" —a system of meaning and belief that rituals are designed to express, enact, and transmit. We described myths and paradigms, what they are, how they differ (a myth tells an origin or creation story, a paradigm consists of a set of tenets that encode a specific belief system without making it into an actual story), and how rituals enact and thus transmit myths and paradigms and the value and belief systems they entail. We used the Navajo creation myth of Changing Woman and "dream incubation" as examples of the "cycle of meaning" that each and every culture develops to explain the origins of and give meaning to their lifeworld. For paradigms and the cycles of meaning they create, we described as examples the old and new paradigms of business and the technocratic, humanistic, and holistic paradigms of birth and health care. We noted, very importantly, the partial relationship between myth and historical reality, stating that from an anthropological viewpoint, the story of Adam and Eve being cast out of the Garden is a metaphorical way of addressing and explaining the transition from hunting and gathering to agriculture. We provided another example of how myth incorporates this historical transition from the Huichol of Nothern Mexico, who had to abandon their historical traditions of hunting and gathering as they fled north to escape the Spanish invasion. They settled down in the Sierra Madre mountains to become agriculturalists. We described the new worldview they developed—one that incorporated their ancient traditions with their contemporary reality, combining the deer they formerly hunted, the peyote they used to stay in touch with alternative realities, and the maize they currently grow into one, unified, worldview that both informs and illuminates their contemporary lifeworld.

We described the "cognitive imperative" to understand our lifeworlds, and how indigenous psychologies can over time organize individual experience, collective social life, consciousness, agency, social hierarchy, and the physical and supernatural worlds into one coherent system of meaning that is then enacted and perpetuated through collective rituals. We also described *expressive culture* and *collective consciousness*, noting through examples from Australian aborigines that the reality expressed in myth is not merely the figment of somebody's imagination, *but is reality itself imagined*. In other words, *through their myths, people collectively imagine reality, and then they live in the collective reality they have imagined*. And we noted that mythic images, operating as metaphors, can work to trigger the growth of neurocognitive structures in the brain. There are no human cultures without myths and the rituals that enact them—these are cultural universals. So we went on to provide examples from contemporary technocratic societies, including the "myth of technological transcendence" —the notion that through technology, we will ultimately transcend the limitations of nature, which enables us to sleep at night because this myth insists that the problems we have generated with technology will not lead to doom for humanity, but *will be solved with more technology*.

We concluded Chapter 3 by noting that human beings universally seek to understand local events by referencing a more global worldview. This quest for meaning is met in part by the myth/paradigm-ritual complex and the integration of individual processes within biologically based patterns of knowing. Myths and paradigms can provide a system linking the archetypal features of human nature and capacities for knowing with culturally and personally specific systems of development and expression. These mythic or paradigmatic systems provide socially shared representations of personal and external realities. Ritual integrates archetypal psychology and cultural influences within a single frame of action. This interaction between the universal and the local has the very great advantage of patterning personal knowledge and behavior to the immediate circumstances of the environment, while retaining a cosmic outlook within which social responses may remain "real." The tension between archetypal and local ways of knowing can be resolved, at least to some extent, by the concerted, meaningful activity of ritual performance.

In Chapter 4, we looked at the nature of belief systems, showing that such systems are only partial pictures of larger realities, yet they serve to "true" those pictures—to make them reflect enough of reality to ensure that the cultures that create and live through them will be able to function effectively in the world. Belief systems can vary enormously across cultures. We examined the roles of these systems among "sensate," "idealistic," and "ideational" cultures and how the members of these different cultural types enact their beliefs and values through ritual, as well as how they manipulate myths and paradigms, and the rituals that enact them, to accommodate themselves to cultural and environmental change.

The need to know about and to understand the world is a human universal. Knowledge and understanding are first and foremost adaptive strategies that have been evolutionarily selected for over hundreds of thousands of years. If our systems of knowledge—our cultures—were not adaptively accurate enough for us to survive—sufficiently "trued" to the world we live in, we would simply die off as a species. (We re-note here that hundreds if not thousands of indigenous and other types of cultures have already died off when their conceptual systems and the rituals that enacted those belief systems could no longer true them to the realities of their changing environments.) The rituals we perform enable us to express and enact the understandings of the world that we develop, at the moment and over time. The role of ritual in truing knowledge and understanding is fundamental to revitalizing the paradigm or cosmology of the culture. Yet there is always the possibility of truing going wrong. Thus, as we explained, the worldview of a group must be kept more or less current—more or less trued—with the daily experience of people on the ground. Otherwise ritual fails in its primordial function, imposing the enactment of a world-as-we-want-to-force-it-to-be instead of an enactment of the world-as-is.

Continuing our analysis of the "anatomy of ritual," in Chapter 5 we described ritual "drivers"—sensory stimuli such as drumming, chanting, singing, dancing, and even electronic fetal monitoring—that work to entrain the human central nervous system with the structure of the ritual and the sense of "flow" that ritual structure can produce. We described states of consciousness (SOCs) and warps of consciousness (WOCs) and how ritual can generate altered states of consciousness by manipulating the warps between them through creating "portals." We also described the differences between monophasic and polyphasic cultures and the roles of ritual in each. We have seen that the range of rhythmic and repetitive stimuli through which rituals act on the human body and consciousness are many and varied—yet they all in one way or another operate upon the human nervous system. The enactment of rituals can "drive," or control, states of consciousness among its participants. Taking this approach to the anatomy of ritual, we are able to uncover the source of much of ritual's power, and to answer the question, "Why are ritual drivers so compelling?"

In Chapter 6, we investigated in even greater detail the ritual techniques and technologies that make ritual so efficacious. We have seen that ritual is technique, and most rituals are also technologized—we experience rituals not just through activity and symbols but also through physical objects and the manipulation of the causation lying behind events. We took the question "What is technology?" as fundamental to our understanding of ritual. How do some technologies serve as implements of ritual practice, and how on earth did the manipulation of a pair of sandals lead the African diviner to find the purloined pots? Of course no discussion of ritual technologies would be complete without examining magic. We asked what is "spooky causation," and how can ritual serve as a vehicle for "divine inspiration" and "psychic power"? Moreover, how is it possible that ancient techniques embedded in ritual manifest and operate effectively in the contemporary high-tech and virtual worlds?

Because ritual is so often instrumental, it influences our experience and understanding of the world. Modern rituals often involve high technology, and thus express the changes in a society's technology just as they enact changes in its members' core values. Modern electronics have made "virtual" rituals possible. Contemporary video games provide an outlet for both conscious and unconscious feelings and behavioral inclinations while at the same time conditioning players to an underlying set of rules of virtual behavior. The games make certain virtual technologies available to the player and exclude other technologies, all the while limiting what players can do with these objects and what actions they can take while utilizing them.

We proceeded in Chapter 7 to explore how rituals are always "framed"—set apart from ordinary reality. Framing, order, and a sense of formality are primary characteristics of ritual that are essential to its efficacy. Ritual spaces and places are typically culturally acknowledged. People respect these spaces, even if they are casual passers-by. Most often, buildings and other structures designed to create ritual spaces generate this cultural acknowledgement. Yet, as previously mentioned, invisible lines of energy can nonetheless be felt both by participants and observers, who can define these spaces and places even when architecture does not do it for them. Shrines and altars created in individual homes can demarcate ritual spaces that constitute the focusing of energy on family religion, beliefs and values, cherished memories, and individual and family accomplishments. A memorial or cemetery plot may offer people a place where they feel connected to their deceased loved ones. The frame may be more mental than physical, as in the case of prayer or meditation. The mind seeks an inner space where the "decks are cleared" and one may contemplate without distraction.

In Chapter 8, we turned to the performative aspects of ritual. We examined how ritual healing can work through the sensory manipulation of repetitive and symbolic stimuli embedded in the ritual. We explained the excitation and relaxation nervous systems and described how ritual can cause them both to discharge simultaneously, producing a strong sense of flow and sometimes even ecstasy—which underscores for the participant the efficacy of the ritual process, which in turn advances a belief in the healing system. We pointed out ritual mechanisms for generating emotion and belief, including ritual performance, extrinsic and intrinsic drivers, charisma, beauty, mandalas of perception, ritual socialization, collective effervescence, and ritual drama. We looked at rites of passage and religious conversions, and showed how "raw" individual experiences can be (and almost always are) interpreted in cultural and religious terms to give them socially-shared meaning. These ritual aspects—the rhythmic repetition, evocative style, and precise manipulation of symbols and sensory stimuli—enable collective rituals to focus the emotions of participants on intensifying the ritual's underlying message. We repeat here that *belief tends to follow emotion*. Ritual generates intense emotions, even ecstasy, and intense emotion, in turn, generates belief.

Following our discussion of the role played by emotion in generating and intensifying belief, we turned in Chapter 9 to the more cognitive aspects of ritual. We defined two basic types of thinking—concrete and fluid—and four stages of cognition. We more or less equated those four stages to the anthropological categories of naïve realism/fundamentalism/fanaticism (Stage 1); ethnocentrism (Stage 2); cultural relativism (Stage 3); and global humanism (Stage 4). Within Stage 1 thinking, we analyzed the differences between naïve realism (not knowing any other way), fundamentalism (knowing that there are other ways of thinking and believing, yet truly believing that your way is the only right way), and fanaticism (believing so much in the rightness of your way that you also believe that all other ways, most especially those most opposed to yours, should be eliminated if they cannot be assimilated). We have shown that positive ethnocentrism simply results in a culture's celebration of itself and in attempts on its members' parts to preserve and perpetuate that culture, while negative ethnocentrism can result in one group trying to persecute, enslave, impoverish, or eliminate other groups (especially when those groups occupy the same geographical territory).

In the course of discussing the cognitive aspects of ritual, we emphasized the weakness of cultural relativism—simply acknowledging the right of every culture to exist and to have its own lifeworld and lifeways can result in tolerating behaviors like wife-beating and torture as morally acceptable because they are accepted within the parameters of that culture. We also examined how global humanism evinces Stage 4 thinking: the ongoing effort to find that elusive "higher ethical ground" that ensures universal rights to all human beings, and how these rights play out within a global system. Ritual is utilized to enact, display, and transmit the beliefs and values held by Stage 1, 2, 3, and 4 thinkers, as well as to *stand between cognition and chaos* by stabilizing every level of thinking at Stage 1 in times of crisis and distress, in order to keep individuals from regressing into Substage—"losing it." We noted that fluid thinking is a type of cognition that readily deals with diversity and change. In a multicultural and constantly changing society like ours, fluid thinking is far more adaptive than rigid naïve realist, fundamentalist, or fanatical (Stage 1) or ethnocentric (Stage 2) thinking. We showed that even fluid thinkers can be reduced to lower cognitive levels by daily stress overload or major disasters, and how the conscious performance of ritual can help them find "cognitive anchors" to keep them from regressing into Substage and "get a grip" on their new reality, giving them time, space, and the energy needed to grow the new neural networks they will need to cope with the distressing challenges they face.

As we saw in Chapter 10, most rituals have a built-in conservative effect. Ritual works both to preserve and to transmit its associated belief system, and so becomes an important force in the preservation of the status quo in any society. Thus one usually finds that those in power in a given social group have unique control over ritual performances. They utilize ritual's tremendous power to reinforce both their own importance and the importance of the belief and value system that sustains them in their positions. Laws and explicit rules in every society may officially dictate appropriate behavior, yet most people behave appropriately most of the time because of their ritualized socialization. When cultural behavior changes dramatically and official laws and rules cease to match or mirror those changes, those laws and rules usually get changed. When they do not, social resistance movements often arise to effect needed changes, unless that society is totalitarian and does not allow social resistance and change.

Ritual, with all of its insistence on continuity and order, can paradoxically be an important factor not only in individual transformation but also in social change. New belief and value systems are most effectively spread through new rituals designed to enact and transmit them. Even if a ritual is being performed for the very first time, its stylistic similarities with other rituals make it feel tradition-like, thus giving entirely new belief systems the feel and flavor of being strongly entrenched and sanctioned by ancient tradition. Moreover, entrenched belief and value systems are most effectively altered through alterations in the rituals that enact them. Indeed, ritual represents one of society's greatest potentials for the kind of revitalization that comes from internal growth and change in response to changing circumstances.

Having thoroughly discussed the aspects of ritual that collectively impart such great power to it, we felt it appropriate to end our analysis with a reflection on the process of creating and using ritual. In Chapter 11 we noted that each and every enduring belief system manages successfully to true its adherents to their conceptual world through their lived reality as expressed in ritual. We then questioned what happens when your beliefs and the myths, paradigms, and rituals that encode and express those beliefs no longer "true" you to your lived reality? We explored that question by examining religious syncretism as an adaptive ritual strategy, explaining how peoples whose reality changes dramatically can combine traditional rituals with new ones that combine old and new beliefs in successful, synthetic, and syncretic forms. In our discussion of explicit vs. implicit ideologies, we explained that implicit ideologies (like the technocratic model of birth) need explicit enactment in ritual to reflect and transmit those ideologies and their underlying values and beliefs, while explicit ideologies (like those of homebirthers) can make do with soft and fuzzy rituals because their countercultural belief and value systems are so explicitly detailed in their writings and communications. We explained that ritual is inherently paradoxical: you can first believe in the "belief system" and so experience the "truth" of ritual through performing the rituals that enact that belief system—or you can be quite skeptical, then gain a different sort of belief when you perceive that the rituals you perform do in fact produce results.

We showed that intentional creation of a personal or social ritual may or may not be successful. We noted that in order for ritual to do its work appropriately, it must be lodged within a cycle of meaning—which can be created by the society in question, or by the individual. We also noted that people suffering from various psychopathologies quite commonly invent a cycle of meaning for themselves that is dysfunctional. We conclude by once again stating that ritual, even when individually designed, can be powerful and should be employed with consciousness and caution.

PARTING REMARKS

We humans are social primates. Inherent in being a social primate is that we learn to get things done by participating in rituals. We are so thoroughly ritual practitioners that it is nearly impossible to imagine a society or stable group (family, school, corporation, state) that does not have its rituals. You can now appreciate why anthropologists are immediately faced with rituals when they go to live within a culture that is alien to them. And you can understand why people all over the planet have cleaved to ritual solutions to identity formation, to modulating states of consciousness, to transmitting knowledge from generation to generation, to regulating resources, to buffering themselves against change, enhancing courage, transforming identity and effecting healing. Ritual still plays many of these roles in modern society, but much of its power still goes untapped—kind of ritual by default. For example, because we don't officially ritualize puberty for our youths, it gets ritualized by default by cultural institutions not specifically designed for this purpose such as schools, sports, gangs, and the medical system. Participation in everyday rituals, whether secular (football game, school class or program, voting) or religious (Sunday school, the Mass, meditation group), is so automatic that most people never reflect upon why they perform rituals, how the rituals work, or why they seem to be so powerful in evoking emotional experiences. Now that you have traveled with us through this long and hopefully edifying journey through the anthropology of ritual, you will find that you are much more able to isolate and identify the various elements of rituals that produce whatever effects they have on you and your fellow participants.

Not only that, but this journey may have placed you in the position of questioning whether or not you really want to participate in this or that ritual. You will certainly be aware of how rituals can be used to manipulate your feelings, perceptions, thoughts, decisions, and behaviors. After working your way through this book, you have likely become a more enlightened participant in your society, able to decide, as a consumer, whether to "get into it" with this ritual, and "back off" from that ritual. Furthermore, when need be, you have at hand the knowledge to design and carry out your own ritual (see Appendix), and then step back and evaluate the ritual's efficacy—understanding why it worked the way it did, and perhaps what should be changed, added, or eliminated in order to make it more effective. You may even find yourself in the position of teaching about ritual to others (Bell 2007; Grimes 2013). You will not only be able to describe rituals in different contexts, but also to isolate the various elements that go into building a ritual—its anatomy, its constituent actions, relations to ideology and to direct experience.

You can now appreciate the extent to which rituals facilitate daily living—engendering belief, concretizing that belief, maintaining religious vitality, enhancing courage, effecting healing, initiating individuals into new social groups or new ways of being, preserving the status quo in a given society, and, paradoxically, effecting social change. You can also see how rituals may be used for your own self-discovery and transformation. This may be as simple as building in a morning run, an hour of yoga, a period of foreign language learning, eating four small meals instead of three big ones, or progressive relaxation. Or, the transformative ritual you find or create for yourself may entail working with the depths of your psychic being—perhaps discovering your inner spiritual nature thorough phenomenological exercises like Jungian "active imagination," dream work, prayer, insight meditation, or guided visualization.

We repeat once again that ritual is a powerful didactic and socializing tool. To grasp its inner workings is to have a choice as to whether to accept the beliefs and values transmitted through the rituals that permeate our daily lives—as well as to be able to harness the power of ritual to enact beliefs and reinforce behaviors that we consciously choose. And we add here that such a choice is becoming increasingly important in our contemporary globalized world, where all of us confront conditions of rapid social, technological, and environmental change. If we make the right choices for our collective and individual human future, we can consciously use ritual to reflect, express, and enact those choices and the new belief and value systems such choices will inevitably entail, and thereby transmit those new worldviews to future generations.

Appendix

HOW TO CREATE AND PERFORM AN EFFECTIVE STAGE 4 RITUAL: THINGS TO REMEMBER AND INCLUDE

(This Appendix is a check-list based on all that we say about ritual in this book. It won't make full sense to you unless you actually read the book!)

Be clear about the beliefs and values you want to enact. Make sure that those who will be performing the ritual with you either share these beliefs and values, or wish to share them.

Choose meaningful symbols. If the ritual is new, explain the symbols before you begin the ritual—by engaging the intellect in advance, you increase the chances of an emotional response.

Hold the center. People often feel silly performing rituals, especially new ones. Several people, or only one, who can hold the center for the group can create a sense of specialness (even sacredness) and acceptance that everyone eventually can feel if the ritual works.

Tell the participants in advance, especially if they are new to ritual, *"If you feel ridiculous, let the feeling wash over you and pass away."*

Once it is established, don't break the ritual frame. If it gets broken, re-establish it as quickly as possible. (Remember that what generates "flow" is a narrowed, focused cognitive field.) If your ritual is being performed in a circle of people holding hands, make sure that everyone understands that if they need to leave the circle, they should depart silently and engage the hands they were holding with those next to them in the circle.

Evoke mystery when appropriate—use semi-darkness, flickering candles, etc. —for their neurological opening effect.

Allow for spontaneity and playfulness. There is a certain quality of playfulness in ritual that does not break, but strengthens, the frame. Laughter and lightness alternating with seriousness can make the ritual more powerful by making the energy come in waves that can build in intensity.

Ritual drivers include: drumming, chanting, singing, dancing, mantric meditation, privations, ordeals, hazing/physical challenges, isolation, sensory deprivation, and others. *Treat them with respect!*

Utilize the power of repetition. To generate a lot of energy and a strongly special or sacred atmosphere, the drumming and/or chanting/singing should go on for a long time. The more repetitive the rhythm, the more powerful the neural entrainment.

If you are including songs in your ritual, make sure there is someone with a strong voice who knows the songs to be sung or chanted, and so can "hold the center" for the songs.

Keep the songs short, so they can be easily learned without need of paper (or put them up on Powerpoint), and sing them at least four times. That's really important—it takes at least four repetitions of the songs for everyone to learn them, sing them properly, and figure out appropriate harmony. But don't sing them more than four times—that can get boring! (Chants are a different matter—they can go on for hours.)

Provide a strong opening that clearly establishes the frame, and a definite closure at the end—a cementing song, or prayer, or "so be it," "Amen!" "We love you all!" or the Wiccan "Let the circle be open yet unbroken!" Clear closure holds the integrity of the frame until it is intentionally dropped, and allows participants to leave with a feeling of completeness.

Be aware of ritual's power for transformation, and be responsible in its use!

Author Biographies

Robbie Davis-Floyd Ph.D., Senior Research Fellow, Dept. of Anthropology, University of Texas Austin and Fellow of the Society for Applied Anthropology, is a cultural and medical anthropologist specializing in interpretive and symbolic anthropology, ritual studies, and the anthropology of reproduction. After 25 years of teaching anthropology at the University of Texas Austin, Trinity University in San Antonio, Texas, Rice University in Houston, and Case Western Reserve University in Cleveland, Ohio, where she served as Flora Stone Mather Visiting Professor, she currently works as an international speaker and researcher. She is author of over 80 articles and of *Birth as an American Rite of Passage* (1992, 2004); coauthor of *From Doctor to Healer: The Transformative Journey* (1998); and lead editor of 10 collections, including *Childbirth and Authoritative Knowledge: Cross-Cultural Perspectives* (1997); *Intuition: The Inside Story* (1997); *Cyborg Babies: From Techno-Sex to Techno-Tots* (1998); and *Mainstreaming Midwives: The Politics of Change* (2006). Her most recent collection is *Birth Models That Work* (2009), which highlights optimal models of birth care around the world. Her research on global trends and transformations in childbirth, obstetrics, and midwifery is ongoing—her current research project studies the paradigm shifts of holistic obstetricians in Brazil. *Birth Models That Work, Volume II: Birth on the Global Frontier,* co-edited with Betty-Anne Daviss, is in process. This present book, *The Power of Ritual* carries her longstanding work on ritual, begun in her first book, to full fruition. Robbie speaks frequently at national and international childbirth, obstetrical, and midwifery conferences around the world and offers workshops and talks on "The Power of Ritual." She currently serves as Editor for the *International MotherBaby Childbirth Initiative (IMBCI): 10 Steps to Optimal Maternity Care* (www.imbci.org), Board Member of the International MotherBaby Childbirth Organization (IMBCO), Senior Advisor to the Council on Anthropology and Reproduction, and Associate Editor of *Medical Anthropology Quarterly*. Her email is davis-floyd@austin.utexas.edu.

Charles D. Laughlin Ph.D. completed his graduate work in the Department of Anthropology, University of Oregon, in 1972. He taught university courses in anthropology and religion for over 30 years, first at the

State University of New York at Oswego, and then at Carleton University in Ottawa, Ontario, Canada, as Full Professor. He is now Emeritus Professor at Carleton. He carried out ethnographic fieldwork among the So (Tepeth) people of Northeastern Uganda, Tibetan Buddhist lamas in Nepal, Chinese Buddhists in Southeast Asia and the Navajo Indians of the American southwest. He is one of the first neuroanthropologists; he completed a postdoctoral fellowship at the Institute of Neurological Sciences, University of Pennsylvania. He has authored and co-authored over 100 articles and book chapters, and has co-authored *Biogenetic Structuralism* (1974), *Extinction and Survival in Human Populations* (1978), *The Spectrum of Ritual* (1979), and *Brain, Symbol and Experience: Toward a Neurophenomenology of Human Consciousness* (1990), all published by Columbia University Press. He is considered to be one of the leading authorities on the evolution and operation of human ritual. His empirical research has been mainly concerned with how the ritual process can evoke extraordinary states of consciousness. Charlie spent seven years as a Tibetan Tantric Buddhist monk, and learned procedures for altering his state of consciousness by way of mimetic rituals. He has recently authored *Communing with the Gods: Consciousness, Culture and the Dreaming Brain* (2011), which explores the anthropology of dreaming and recounts his experiences as a practitioner of Tibetan dream yoga. His theoretical work has focused upon how the brain produces experience, and how cultures impact that process. He founded and edited the *Neuroanthropology Network Newsletter*. He is one of the early founders of the sub-field called transpersonal anthropology and was the second editor of *Anthropology of Consciousness*, the journal of the Society for the Anthropology of Consciousness (SAC). He is now one of the editors of the journal *Time & Mind* published by Berg, as well as a contributing editor of the *International Journal of Transpersonal Studies*. He may be reached at cdlaughlin@gmail.com.

References

Ackerman, Robert (2002) *The Myth and Ritual School: J. G. Frazer and the Cambridge Ritualists.* New York: Routledge.

Adler, Margot (1988) *Drawing Down the Moon: Witches, Druids, Goddess-Worshippers, and other Pagans in America Today* (2nd edition). Boston: Beacon Press.

Aizenstat, Stephen and Robert Bosnak (Eds.) (2009) *Imagination and Medicine: The Future of Healing in an Age of Neuroscience.* New Orleans, LA: Spring Journal Books.

Alcorta, Candace, and Richard Sosis (2005) "Ritual, Emotion, and Sacred Symbols. The Evolution of Religion as an Adaptive Complex." *Human Nature* 16: 323-359.

Andresen, Jensine (Ed.) (2001) *Religion In Mind: Cognitive Perspectives On Religious Belief, Ritual, and Experience.* Cambridge: Cambridge University Press.

Argüelles, J.A. and M. Argüelles (1972) *Mandala.* Berkeley: Shambhala.

Assmann, Jan (2011) *Cultural Memory and Early Civilization: Writing, Remembrance, and Political Imagination.* Cambridge: Cambridge University Press.

Atkinson, Quentin D. and Harvey Whitehouse (2011) "The Cultural Morphospace of Ritual Form: Examining Modes of Religiosity Cross-Culturally." *Evolution and Human Behavior* 32(1): 50-62.

Atran, Scot (1990) *Cognitive Foundations of Natural History: Towards an Anthropology of Science.* Cambridge: Cambridge University Press.

Atran, Scott (2002) *In Gods We Trust: The Evolutionary Landscape of Religion.* Oxford: Oxford University Press.

Atran, Scott and Joseph Henrich (2010) "The Evolution of Religion: How Cognitive By-Products, Adaptive Learning Heuristics, Ritual Displays, and Group Competition Generate Deep Commitments to Prosocial Religions." *Biological Theory* 5: 18-30.

Atran, Scott and Ara Norenzayan (2004) "Religion's Evolutionary Landscape: Counterintuition, Commitment, Compassion, Communion." *Behavioral and Brain Sciences* 27(6): 713-730.

Barrett, Justin L. (2000) "Exploring the Natural Foundations of Religion." *Trends in Cognitive Sciences* 4: 29-34.

Barrett, Justin L. and E. Thomas Lawson (2001) "Ritual Intuitions: Cognitive Contributions to Judgments of Ritual Efficacy." *Journal of Cognition and Culture* 1(2): 183-201.

Beidelman, T.O. (1973) Review of Colin M. Turnbull, *The Mountain People. Africa* 43(2): 170-1.

Bell, Catherine (1992) *Ritual Theory, Ritual Practice.* Oxford: Oxford University Press.

Bell, Catherine (1997) *Ritual: Perspectives and Dimensions.* Oxford: Oxford University Press.

Bell, Catherine M. (Ed.) (2007) *Teaching Ritual.* Oxford: Oxford University Press.

Bell, Catherine (2008) "Embodiment." In Jens Kreinath, Jan Snoek, and Michael Stausberg (Eds.), *Theorizing Rituals. Issues, Topics, Approaches, Concepts.* Leiden: Brill, pp. 533-543.

Benedetti, Fabrizio (2008) *Placebo Effects: Understanding the Mechanisms in Health and Disease.* Oxford: Oxford University Press.

Benedict, Ruth (1950) "Continuities and Discontinuities in Cultural Conditioning." In W.E. Martin and C.B. Stendler (Eds.), *Readings in Child Development.* New York: Harcourt Brace.

Berlin, Brent (1992) *Ethnobiological Classification: Principles of Categorization of Plants and Animals in Traditional Societies.* Princeton, NJ: Princeton University Press.

Biesele, Megan (Ed.) (2009) *Ju/hoan Folktales: Transcriptions and English Translations: A Literacy Primer by and for Youth and Adults of the Ju/hoan Community.* Victoria, BC: Trafford Publishers.

Blackmore, Susan (2003) "The Evolution of Meme Machines." In A. Meneghetti et al. (Eds.), *Ontopsychology and Memetics.* Rome: Psicologica Editrice, pp. 233-240.

Blanchard, K. (1986) "Play as Adaptation: The Work-Play Dichotomy Revisited." In B. Mergen (Ed.), *Cultural Dimensions of Play, Games, and Sport.* Champaign, IL: Human Kinetics Pubs.

Bloch, Maurice (2004) "Ritual and Deference." In Harvey Whitehouse and James Laidlaw (Eds.), *Ritual and Memory: Toward a Comparative Anthropology of Religion.* Vol. 6. Rowman Altamira, p. 65.

Bohm, David (1980) *Wholeness and the Implicate Order.* Boston: Routledge and Egan Paul.

Bonner, J. T. (1980) *The Evolution of Culture in Animals.* Princeton, NJ: Princeton University Press.

Bourguignon, Erika and T. L. Evascu (1977) "Altered States of Consciousness within a General Evolutionary Perspective: A Holocultural Analysis." *Behavior Science Research* 12(3): 197-216.

Boyer, Pascal (1993) *Cognitive Aspects of Religious Symbolism.* Cambridge: Cambridge University Press.

Boyer, Pascal (1994) *The Naturalness of Religious Ideas: A Cognitive Theory of Religion.* Berkeley, CA: University of California Press.

Boyer, Pascal (1996a) "Cognitive Limits To Conceptual Relativity: The Limiting-Case of Religious Ontologies." In John Joseph Gumperz and Stephen C. Levinson (Eds.), *Rethinking Linguistic Relativity. Studies in the Social and Cultural Foundations of Language*, No. 17. Cambridge: Cambridge University Press, pp. 203-231.

Boyer, Pascal (1996b) "What Makes Anthropomorphism Natural: Intuitive Ontology and Cultural Representations." *Journal of the Royal Anthropological Institute* 2(1): 83-97.

Brown, S. (2000) "The 'Musilanguage' Model of Music." In N. Wallin, B. Merker and S. Brown (Eds.), *The Origins of Music.* Cambridge: MIT Press.

Campbell, Joseph (1986) *The Inner Reaches of Outer Space: Metaphor as Myth and as Religion.* New York: Harper.

Campbell, Joseph, with Bill Moyers (1988) *The Power of Myth*, edited by Betty Sue Flowers. New York: Doubleday

Cantril, H. (1960) *Morning Notes of Adelbert Ames.* New Brunswick, NJ: Rutgers University Press.

Cassirer, Ernst (1955) *The Philosophy of Symbolic Forms.* Vol. 2, *Mythical Thought.* New Haven, CT: Yale University Press.

Cassirer, Ernst (1957) *The Philosophy of Symbolic Forms.* Vol. 3: *The Phenomenology of Knowledge.* New Haven, CT: Yale University Press.

Chagnon, Napoleon (1982) *Yanamamo: The Fierce People* (2nd edition). New York: Holt, Rinehart & Winston.

Chapple, Eliot D. (1970) *Culture and Biological Man: Explorations in Behavioral Anthropology.* New York: Holt, Rinehart and Winston.

Chapple, Eliot D. and Carleton S. Coon (1942) *Principles of Anthropology.* New York: Holt, Rinehart and Winston.

Cheyney, Melissa (2011) "Reinscribing the Birthing Body: Homebirth as Ritual Performance." *Medical Anthropology Quarterly* 25(4): 519-542.

Chick, Garry (2008) "Altruism in Animal Play and Human Ritual." *World Cultures* (eJournal) 16(2).

Corbin, Henry (1969) *Alone With The Alone: Creative Imagination in the Sufism of Ibn 'Arabi.* Princeton, NJ: Princeton University Press.

Cove, John J. (1987) *Shattered Images: Dialogues and Meditations on Tsimshian Narratives.* Ottawa, Canada: Carleton University Press.

Csikszentmihalyi, Mihaly (1975) *Beyond Boredom and Anxiety: Experiencing Flow in Work and Play.* San Francisco: Jossey-Bass.

Damasio, Antonio (1999) *The Feeling of What Happens: Body and Emotion in the Making of Consciousness.* New York: Harcourt.

D'Aquili, Eugene G., Charles D. Laughlin & John McManus (Eds.) (1979) *The Spectrum of Ritual.* New York: Columbia University Press.

D'Aquili, Eugene G. and Andrew B. Newberg (1998) "The Neuropsychological Basis of Religions, or Why God Won't Go Away." *Zygon* 33(2): 187–201.

Davis-Floyd, Robbie (1987a) "The Technological Model of Birth." In *Folklore and Feminism,* Special Issue of the *Journal of American Folklore* 100 (398): 93-109.

Davis-Floyd, Robbie (1987b) "Obstetric Training as a Rite of Passage." In Robert Hahn (Ed.), *Obstetrics in the United States: Woman, Physician, and Society,* Special Issue of the *Medical Anthropology Quarterly* 1(3): 288-318.

Davis-Floyd, Robbie (1988) "Birth as an American Rite of Passage." In Karen Michaelson (Ed.), *Childbirth in America: Anthropological Perspectives.* Beacon Hill, MA: Bergin and Garvey Publishers, pp. 153-172.

Davis-Floyd, Robbie (1990) "The Role of American Obstetrics in the Resolution of Cultural Anomaly." *Social Science and Medicine* 31(2):175-189.

Davis-Floyd, Robbie (1991) "Ritual in the Hospital: Giving Birth the American Way." In Phillip Whitten and David E. K. Hunter (Eds.), *Anthropology: Contemporary Perspectives* (6th edition). Whitten and Hunter, Boston: Little, Brown and Co., pp. 275-285.

Davis-Floyd, Robbie (1994) "The Technocratic Body: American Childbirth as Cultural Expression." *Social Science and Medicine* 38(8):1125-1140.

Davis-Floyd, Robbie (2001) "The Technocratic, Humanistic, and Holistic Models of Birth." *International Journal of Gynecology & Obstetrics* 75, Supplement No. 1, pp. S5-S23.

Davis-Floyd, Robbie (2002) *"Knowing*: A Story of Two Births." Unpublished article, available at www.davis-floyd.com.

Davis-Floyd, Robbie (2003) "Windows in Space/Time: A Personal Perspective on Birth and Death." *Birth: Issues in Perinatal Care* 30(4): 272-277.

Davis-Floyd, Robbie (2004[1992]) *Birth as an American Rite of Passage.* Berkeley: University of California Press.

Davis-Floyd, Robbie, Lesley Barclay, Betty-Anne Daviss, and Jan Tritten (Eds.) (2009) *Birth Models That Work.* Berkeley: University of California Press.

Davis-Floyd, Robbie and Melissa Cheyney (2009) "Birth and the Big Bad Wolf: An Evolutionary Perspective." In Heleine Selin and P. Stone (Eds.), *Childbirth across Cultures.* Dordrecht, The Netherlands: Springer Science, pp. 1-22.

Davis-Floyd, Robbie and Kenneth J. Cox (1999) "Oral History Interview with Guy Thibodaux, rocket scientist." Full text available at www.davis-floyd.com.

Davis-Floyd, Robbie and Kenneth J. Cox (1999) "Joint Oral History Interview with Guy Thibodaux, rocket scientist, Max Faget, father of spacecraft design, and Paul Purser, former manager, Langley Research Center." Available at www.davis-floyd.com.

Davis-Floyd, Robbie, Kenneth J. Cox, and Frank White (2012) *Space Stories: Oral Histories from the Pioneers of the American Space Program.* Kindle E-Book.

Davis-Floyd, Robbie and Elizabeth Davis (1996) "Intuition as Authoritative Knowledge in Midwifery and Home Birth." In Robbie Davis-Floyd and Carolyn Sargent (Eds.), *The Social Production of Authoritative Knowledge about Childbirth*, a special issue of *Medical Anthropology Quarterly* 10(2): 237-269.

Davis-Floyd, Robbie and Christine Barbara Johnson (2006) *Mainstreaming Midwives: The Politics of Change*. New Brunswick, NJ: Rutgers University Press.

Davis-Floyd, Robbie and Gloria St. John (1998) *From Doctor to Healer: The Transformative Journey*. New Brunswick, NJ: Rutgers University Press.

Deacon, Terrence W. (1997) *The Symbolic Species: The Co-Evolution of Language and the Brain*. New York: W.W. Norton.

Deliège, Robert (2004) *Lévi-Strauss Today: An Introduction to Structural Anthropology*. Oxford: Berg.

De Lomnitz, Larissa Adler, Rodrigo Salazar Elena, and Ilya Adler (2010) *Symbolism and Ritual in a One-party Regime: Unveiling Mexico's Political Culture*. Tucson, AZ: University of Arizona Press.

de Waal, Frans and Frans Lantings (1997) *Bonobo: The Forgotten Ape*. Berkeley: University of California Press.

Devereux, Paul (1992) *Symbolic Landscapes*. Somerset, England: Gothic Image Publications.

Devereux, Paul (1996) *Re-Visioning the Earth*. New York: Simon & Schuster.

Devereux, Paul (2008) *The Long Trip: A Prehistory of Psychedelia*. Brisbane: Daily Grail.

Devereux, Paul (2010) *Sacred Geography: Deciphering Hidden Codes in the Landscape*. London: Octopus.

Diamond, Jared (2005) *Collapse: How Societies Choose to Fail or Succeed*. New York: Viking/Penguin.

Dilthey, Wilhelm (1977) *Dilthey: Selected Writings*. H. P. Rickman (ed and trans). Cambridge: Cambridge University Press.

Dissanayake, Ellen (1992) *Homo Aestheticus: Where Art Comes From and Why*. Seattle: University of Washington Press.

Donald, Merlin (2001) *A Mind So Rare: The Evolution of Human Consciousness*. WW Norton & Company.

Dossey, Larry (1993) *Healing Words: The Power of Prayer and the Practice of Medicine*. San Francisco: Harper.

Driver, Thomas F. (1991) *The Magic of Ritual: Our Need for Liberating Rites That Transform Our Lives and Our Communities*. San Francisco: Harper.

Driver, Thomas F. (2006) *Liberating Rites: Understanding the Transformative Power of Ritual*. North Charleston, SC: Booksurge.

Dulaney, S. and A. Fiske (1994) "Cultural Rituals and Obsessive-Compulsive Disorder: Is there a Common Psychological Mechanism?" *Ethos* 22: 243-83.

Durkheim, Emile. (1995[1912]) *The Elementary Forms of Religious Life* (translation by Karen E. Fields). New York: The Free Press.

Ehrenreich, Barbara and Deirdre English (1973) *Witches, Midwives, and Nurses: A History of Women Healers*. Old Westbury, New York: The Feminist Press.

Eisenberg, David M., Ronald C. Kessler, Cindy Foster, Francis E. Norlock, David R. Calkins, and Thomas L. Del Banco (1993) "Unconventional Medicine in the United States: Prevalence, Costs, and Patterns of Use." *New England Journal of Medicine* 328:246-252.

Eliade, Mircea (1963) *Myth and Reality*. New York: Harper and Row.

Eppler, Martin J. and Jeanne Mengis (2004) "Side-Effects of the E-Society: The Causes of Information Overload and Possible Countermeasures." *IADIS International Conference e-Society*, Avila, Spain, pp. 1119-1124.

Faiola, Thomas John (2002) "The Relationships Among Religious Orientation, Conceptual Systems, and Values." ETD Collection for Fordham University. Paper AAI3040394. http://fordham.bepress.com/dissertations/AAI3040394

Fauconnier, G. and M. Turner (2002) *The Way We Think: Conceptual Blending and the Mind's Hidden Complexities*. New York: Basic Books.

Feather, John (2008) *The Information Society: A Study of Continuity and Change* (5th edition). London: Facet Publishing.

Feinstein, David (1990) "The Dream as a Window on Your Evolving Mythology." In Stanley Krippner (Ed.), *Dreamtime and Dreamwork*. Los Angeles: Tarcher, pp. 21-33.

Feinstein, David and Stanley Krippner, (2009[1988]) *Personal Mythology: Using Ritual, Dreams, and Imagination to Discover Your Inner Story*. Fulton, CA: Energy Psychology Press.

Festinger, Leon, Henry W. Riecken, and Stanley Schachter (1956) *When Prophecy Fails: A Social and Psychological Study of a Modern Group that Predicted the Destruction of the World*. University of Minnesota Press (reissued 2008 by Pinter & Martin).

Fiske, Alan and Nick Haslam (1997) "Is Obsessive-Compulsive Disorder a Pathology of the Human Disposition to Perform Socially Meaningful Rituals? Evidence of Similar Content." *Journal of Nervous and Mental Disease* 185(4): 211-222.

Freeman, W. (2000) "A Neurobiological Role of Music in Social Bonding." In N. Wallin, B. Merker and S. Brown (Eds.), *The Origins of Music*. Cambridge: MIT Press, pp. 411-424.

Frieberg, Kevin and Jackie Freiburg (1996) *Nuts! Southwest Airlines' Crazy Recipe for Business and Personal Success*. New York: Bard Press.

Galanter, Mark (1989) *Cults: Faith, Healing, and Conversion*. Oxford: Oxford University Press.

Garfield, Patricia (1974) *Creative Dreaming*. New York: Simon and Schuster.

Garrels, Scott R. (Ed.) (2011) *Mimesis and Science: Empirical Research on Imitation and the Mimetic Theory of Culture and Religion*. East Lansing, MI: Michigan State University Press.

Geertz, Clifford (1973) *The Interpretation of Cultures: Selected Essays by Clifford Geertz*. New York: Basic Books.

Geertz, Clifford (1983) *Local Knowledge*. New York: Basic Books.

Geissmann, T. (2000) "Gibbon Songs and Human Music from an Evolutionary Perspective." In N. Wallin, B. Merker and S. Brown (Eds.), *The Origins of Music*. Cambridge: MIT Press, pp. 103–23.

Gell, Alfred (1992) "The Technology of Enchantment and the Enchantment of Technology." In J. Coote and A. Sheldon (Eds.), *Anthropology, Art and Aesthetics*. Oxford: Clarendon, pp. 40–66.

Gell, Alfred (1998) *Art and Agency: An Anthropological Theory*. Oxford: Clarendon.

Gellhorn, Ernst (1967) *Principles of Autonomic-Somatic Integration*. Minneapolis: University of Minnesota Press.

George, Marianne (1988) *A Wosak Maraluon! The Barok Pidik of Hidden Power, and the Ritual Imaging of Intent and Meaning*. Unpublished doctoral dissertation, University of Virginia.

Georges, Eugenia and Robbie Davis-Floyd (2016) "Humanistic Obstetricians in Brazil: A Revolution in Maternity Care." In Lenore Manderson, Elizabeth Cartwright, and Anita Hardon (Eds.), *The Routledge Handbook of Medical Anthropology*. New York: Routledge.

Giacobini, Giacomo (2007) "Richness and Diversity of Burial Rituals in the Upper Paleolithic." *Diogenes* 54(2): 19-39.

Gluckman, Max (2006[1965]) *Politics, Law and Ritual in Tribal Society*. Piscataway, NJ: Aldine Transaction.

Goethals, Gregor (2003) "Myth and Ritual in Cyberspace" In Jolyon Mitchell & Sophia Marriage (Eds.), *Mediating Religion: Conversations in Media, Religion and Culture.* New York: T&T Clark, pp. 257-269.

Goffman, Erving (1959) *The Presentation of Self in Everyday Life.* University of Edinburgh Social Sciences Research Centre. Anchor Books edition.

Goffman, Erving (1961) *Asylums: Essays on the Social Situation of Mental Patients and Other Inmates.* New York: Anchor Books.

Goffman, Erving and Joel Best (2005) *Interaction Ritual: Essays in Face to Face Behavior.* Chicago: Aldine Transaction.

Gould, Steven J. (1991) "Exaptation: A Crucial Tool for an Evolutionary Psychology." *Journal of Social Issues* 47: 43-65.

Greenberg, Joanne (pen name Hannah Green) (1964) *I Never Promised You a Rose Garden.* St. Martin's Paperback.

Greene, Brian (2003[1999]) *The Elegant Universe: Superstrings, Hidden Dimensions, and the Quest for the Ultimate Theory.* New York: W. W. Norton.

Greene, Brian (2004) *The Fabric of the Cosmos: Space, Time, and the Texture of Reality.* New York: Vintage Books.

Greene, Brian (2011) *The Hidden Reality: Parallel Universes and the Deep Laws of the Cosmos.* New York: Vintage Books.

Griaule, Marcel (1965) *Conversations with Ogotemmeli.* London: Oxford University Press.

Grimes, Ronald L. (1990) *Ritual Criticism: Case Studies in Its Practice, Essays on Its Theory.* Columbia, SC: University of South Carolina Press.

Grimes, Ronald L. (1996a) "Introduction." In Ronald L. Grimes (Ed.), *Readings in Ritual Studies.* Upper Saddle River NJ: Prentice Hall, pp. xiii-xvi.

Grimes, Ronald L. (1996b) "Ritual Criticism and Infelicitous Performances." In Ronald L. Grimes (Ed.), *Readings in Ritual Studies.* Upper Saddle River NJ: Prentice Hall, pp. 279-292.

Grimes, Ronald L. (Ed.) (1996c) *Readings in Ritual Studies.* New York: Prentice Hall.

Grimes, Ronald L. (2002) *Deeply into the Bone: Re-Inventing Rites of Passage.* Berkeley, CA: University of California Press.

Grimes, Ronald L. (2003a) "Ritual Theory and the Environment." *The Sociological Review* 51(s2): 31-45.

Grimes, Ronald (2003b) "Ritual and Performance." *Religion and American Cultures: An Encyclopedia of Traditions, Diversity, and Popular Expressions* 2: 515-528.

Grimes, Ronald L. (2007) "Ritual, Performance, and the Sequestering of Sacred Space." *Discourse in Ritual Studies* 14: 149.

Grimes, Ronald L. (2008) "Performance." In Jens Kreinath, Jan Snoek, and Michael Stausberg (Eds.), *Theorizing Rituals: Issues, Topics, Approaches, Concepts.* Leiden: Brill, pp. 379-394.

Grimes, Ronald L. (2014) *The Craft of Ritual Studies.* Oxford: Oxford University Press.

Grimes, Ronald L., Ute Husken, Udo Simon, and Eric Venbrux (Eds.) (2011) *Ritual, Media, and Conflict.* Oxford: Oxford University Press.

Hallowell, A. Irving (2002) "Ojibwa Ontology, Behavior, and World View." In Graham Harvey (Ed.), *Readings in Indigenous Religions.* New York: Continuum, pp. 17-49.

Handelman, Don (1998) *Models and Mirrors: Towards an Anthropology of Public Events.* New York: Berghahn.

Handelman, Don (2004) "Re-Framing Ritual." In Jens Kreinath, Constance Hartung and Annette Descher (Eds.), *The Dynamics of Changing Rituals: The Transformation of Religious*

Rituals within their Social and Cultural Context. New York: Peter Lang, pp. 9-20.

Handelman, Don and David Shulman (1997) *God Inside Out: Śiva's Game of Dice.* Oxford University Press.

Harkin, Michael E. (Ed.) (2007) *Reassessing Revitalization Movements: Perspectives from North America and the Pacific Islands.* Lincoln, NE: University of Nebraska Press.

Harley, George W. (1950) *Masks as Agents of Social Control in Northeast Liberia* (Papers of the Peabody Museum of Archaeology and Ethnography, Harvard University, Vol. 32, no. 2). Cambridge, MA: Peabody Museum.

Harner, Michael J. (1990[1980]) *The Way of the Shaman.* New York: HarperOne.

Hart, Mickey (1990) *Drumming at the Edge of Magic.* New York: Harper Collins.

Harvey, Oscar Jewell, David E. Hunt, and Harold M. Schroder (1961) *Conceptual Systems and Personality Organization.* New York: Wiley.

Hass, Robyn and Robbie Davis-Floyd (Eds.) (2016) *Surviving the Death of an Ex: Managing the Grief That No One Talks About.* Praeclarus Press.

Heelas, Paul and Andrew Lock (Eds.) (1981) *Indigenous Psychologies: The Anthropology of the Self.* London: Academic Press.

Heidegger, Martin (1977) "The Question Concerning Technology." In *Basic Writings.* D. Krell, translator. New York: Harper and Row.

Heilpern, John (1999) *Conference of the Birds: The Story of Peter Brook in Africa.* London: Routledge.

Heine, Bernd (1985) "The Mountain People: Some Notes on the Ik of North-Eastern Uganda." *Africa: Journal of the International African Institute,* Vol. 55, No. 1, pp. 3–16.

Hellige, Joseph B. (1993) *Hemispheric Asymmetry: What's Right and What's Left.* Boston: Harvard University Press.

Hicks, David (Ed.) (2010) *Ritual and Belief: Readings in the Anthropology of Religion.* New York: Rowman & Littlefield.

Hill, Anne (1998) "Children of Metis—Beyond Zeus the Creator: Paganism and the Possibilities for Embodied Cyborg Childraising." In Robbie Davis-Floyd and Joseph Dumit (Eds.), *Cyborg Babies: From Techno-Sex to Techno-Tots.* New York: Routledge, pp. 330-344.

Hillerbrand, Hans J. (2009) *The Protestant Reformation: Revised Edition.* New York: Harper Perennial.

Hobsbawm, Eric and Terence Ranger (1992) *The Invention of Tradition.* Cambridge: Cambridge University Press.

Hocart, A. M. (1915) "Psychology and Ethnology." *Folklore* 26:115-137; reprinted in Rodney Needham (Ed.), *Imagination and Proof: Selected Essays of A.M. Hocart.* Tucson AZ: University of Arizona Press, pp. 35-50 (1987).

Hocart, A. M. (1916) "The Common Sense of Myth." *American Anthropologist* 18(3): 307-318.

Holmberg, David (2000) "Derision, Exorcism, and the Ritual Production of Power." *American Ethnologist* 27(4): 927-949.

Huizinga, Johan (1996[1919]) *The Autumn of the Middle Ages.* Chicago: University of Chicago Press.

Humphrey, Caroline, and James Laidlaw (1994) *The Archetypal Actions of Ritual: A Theory of Ritual Illustrated by the Jain Rite of Worship.* Oxford: Clarendon Press.

Hunt, Terry and Carl Lipo (2011) *The Statues That Walked: Unraveling the Mystery of Easter Island.* New York: Simon and Schuster.

Hüsken, Ute (Ed.) (2007) *When Rituals Go Wrong: Mistakes, Failure and the Dynamics of*

Ritual. Leiden: Brill.

Ievers-Landis, Carolyn E., et al. (2006) "Cognitive Social Maturity, Life Change Events, and Health Risk Behaviors Among Adolescents: Development of a Structural Equation Model." *Journal of Clinical Psychology in Medical Settings* 13(2): 107-116.

Ihde, Don (1990) *Technology and the Lifeworld: From Garden to Earth*. Bloomington: Indiana University Press.

Ihde, Don (1991) *Instrumental Realism*. Bloomington: Indiana University Press

Ihde, Don (1993) *Philosophy of Technology: An Introduction*. New York: Paragon House.

Iteanu, André (2004) "Partial Discontinuity: The Mark of Ritual." *Social Analysis* 48(2): 98-116.

Jackson, Michael (1982) *Allegories of the Wilderness*. Bloomington: Indiana University Press.

Jahn, Robert G. and Brenda J. Dunne (1987) *Margins of Reality: The Role of Consciousness in the Physical World*. New York: Harcourt Brace Jovanovich.

Jahn, Robert G. and Brenda J. Dunne (2011) *Consciousness and the Source of Reality*. Princeton, NJ: ICRL Press.

Jones, Ricardo Herbert (2005) *Memórias de um Homem de Vidro Reminiscências de um Obstetra Humanista*. Encadernação: Brochura.

Jones, Ricardo Herbert (2012) *Entre as Orelhas: Histórias de Parto*. Porto Alegre, Brazil: Ricardo Herbert Jones.

Jorgensen, Dan (1980) "What's in a Name: The Meaning of Nothingness in Telefolmin." *Ethos* 8(4): 349-366.

Jorgensen, Joseph G. (1972) *The Sun Dance Religion*. Chicago: University of Chicago Press.

Jorgensen, Joseph G. (1983) "Comparative Traditional Economics and Ecological Adaptations." In A. Ortiz (Ed.), *Southwest Handbook on North American Indians* 10: 684-710. Washington, DC: Smithsonian Institute.

Jung, Carl G. (1964) *Man and His Symbols*. New York: Doubleday.

Jung, Carl G. (1969) *Mandala Symbolism*. Princeton, NJ: Princeton University Press.

Kapferer, Bruce (2004) "Ritual Dynamics and Virtual Practice: Beyond Representation And Meaning." *Social Analysis* 48(1): 35-54.

Katz, Richard (1982) *Boiling Energy: Community Healing Among the Kalahari Kung*. Cambridge, MA: Harvard University Press.

Katz, Richard, Megan Biesele, and Verna St. Denis (1997) *Healing Makes Our Hearts Happy: Spirituality and Cultural Transformation among the Kalahari Ju|'hoansi*. Rochester VT: Inner Traditions.

Kay, Jonathan (2011) *Among the Truthers: A Journey through America's Growing Conspiracist Underground*. New York: HarperCollins.

Kehoe, Alice Beck (2007) *The Ghost Dance: Ethnohistory and Revitalization* (2nd edition). Long Grove, IL: Waveland Press.

Kingwatsiaq, Novaliinga, and Kumaarjuk Pii (2003) "Healing the Body and the Soul Through Visualization: A Technique Used By the Community Healing Team of Cape Dorset, Nunavut." *Arctic Anthropology* 40(2): 90-92.

Kipling, Rudyard (2009) *Just So Stories*. Oxford: Oxford University Press.

Klingberg, Torkel (2008). *The Overflowing Brain: Information Overload and the Limits of Working Memory*. Oxford: Oxford University Press.

Kohlberg, L. (1981) *The Philosophy of Moral Development: Moral Stages and the Idea of Justice*. Vol. I. New York: Harper and Row.

Kosslyn, Stephen M. (1994) *Image and Brain: The Resolution of the Imagery Debate*. Cambridge, MA: MIT Press.

Kuhn, Thomas S. (2012) *The Structure of Scientific Revolutions* (4th edition). Chicago: University of Chicago Press.

Laderman, Carol (1991) *Taming the Wind of Desire: Psychology, Medicine and Aesthetics in Malay Shamanistic Performance.* Berkeley: University of California Press.

Lakoff, George and Mark Johnson (1980) *Metaphors We Live By.* Chicago: University of Chicago Press.

Laland, Kevin N. and Bennett G. Galef (Eds.) (2009) *The Question of Animal Culture.* Cambridge, MA: Harvard University Press.

Lalich, Janja (2004) *Bounded Choice: True Believers and Charismatic Cults.* Berkeley: University of California Press.

Laughlin, Charles D. (1974) "Deprivation and Reciprocity." *Man* 9: 360-396.

Laughlin, Charles D. (1991) "Pre- and Perinatal Brain Development and Enculturation: A Biogenetic Structural Approach." *Human Nature* 2(3): 171-213.

Laughlin, Charles D. (1994) "Psychic Energy and Transpersonal Experience: A Biogenetic Structural Account of the Tibetan Dumo Practice." In David E. Young and Jean-Guy Goulet (Eds.), *Being Changed by Cross-Cultural Encounters.* Peterborough, Ontario: Broadview Press, pp. 99-134.

Laughlin, Charles D. (2001) "Mandalas, Nixies, Goddesses, and Succubi: A Transpersonal Anthropologist Looks at the Anima." *International Journal of Transpersonal Studies* 20:33-52.

Laughlin, Charles D. (2011) *Communing with the Gods: Consciousness, Culture and the Dreaming Brain.* Brisbane: Daily Grail.

Laughlin, Charles D. and Ivan A. Brady (1978) *Extinction and Survival in Human Populations.* New York: Columbia University Press.

Laughlin, Charles D. and Eugene G. d'Aquili (1974) *Biogenetic Structuralism.* New York: Columbia University Press.

Laughlin, Charles D. and Elizabeth R. Laughlin (1974) "Kenisan: Economic and Social Ramifications of the Ghost Cult Among the So of North-eastern Uganda." *Africa* 42(1): 9-20.

Laughlin, Charles D., John McManus and Eugene G. d'Aquili (1990) *Brain, Symbol and Experience: Toward a Neurophenomenology of Consciousness.* New York: Columbia University Press.

Laughlin, Charles D., John McManus, Robert A. Rubinstein and Jon Shearer (1986) "The Ritual Control of Experience." In Norman K. Denzin (Ed.), *Studies in Symbolic Interaction* (Part A). Greenwich, CT: JAI Press.

Laughlin, Charles D., John McManus and Mark Webber (1984) "Neurognosis, Individuation, and Tibetan Arising Yoga Practice." *Phoenix: The Journal of Transpersonal Anthropology* 8(1/2): 91-106.

Laughlin, Charles D. and C. Jason Throop (1999) "Emotion: A View from Biogenetic Structuralism." In A.L. Hinton (Ed.), *Biocultural Approaches to the Emotions.* Cambridge: Cambridge University Press, pp. 329-363.

Laughlin, Charles D. and C. Jason Throop (2001) "Imagination and Reality: On the Relations Between Myth, Consciousness, and the Quantum Sea." *Zygon* 36(4): 709-736.

Laughlin, Charles D. and C. Jason Throop (2006) "Cultural Neurophenomenology: Integrating Experience, Culture and Reality Through Fisher Information." *Culture & Psychology* 12(3): 305-337.

Laughlin, Charles D. and C. Jason Throop (2008) "Continuity, Causation and Cyclicity: A Cultural Neurophenomenology of Time-Consciousness." *Time & Mind* 1(2): 159-186.

Laughlin, Charles D. and C. Jason Throop (2009) "Husserlian Meditations and Anthropological

Reflections: Toward a Cultural Neurophenomenology of Experience and Reality." *Anthropology of Consciousness* 20(2): 130-170.

Lee, Hyeonseo, with David John (2015) *The Girl with Seven Names: A North Korean Defector's Story*. London: William Collins.

Léveillé, Jean (2007) *Birds in Love*. New York: MBI Publishing Company.

Levinson, Stephen C. and N. J. Enfield (Eds.) (2006) *Roots Of Human Sociality: Culture, Cognition and Interaction*. Oxford, UK: Berg.

Levinson, Stephen C., and Judith Holler (2014) "The Origin of Human Multi-Modal Communication." *Philosophical Transactions of the Royal Society B: Biological Sciences* 369(1651): 20130302.

Levi-Strauss, Claude (1966) "The Culinary Triangle." *Partisan Review* 33: 586-595.

Ludwig, Arnold M (2002) *King of the Mountain: The Nature of Political Leadership*. Lexington, KY: The University Press of Kentucky.

Luhrmann, T. M. (2012) *When God Talks Back: Understanding the American Evangelical Relationship with God*. New York: Knopf.

Lewis-Williams, David J. and David G. Pearce (2004) *San Spirituality: Roots, Expression, and Social Consequences*. New York: Rowman Altamira.

MacDonald, George F., John Cove, Charles D. Laughlin and John McManus (1988) "Mirrors, Portals and Multiple Realities." *Zygon* 24(1): 39-63.

Math, Suresh Bada et al. (2006) "Tsunami: Psychosocial Aspects of Andaman and Nicobar Islands: Assessments and Intervention in the Early Phase." *International Review of Psychiatry* 18(3): 233-239.

McCauley, Robert N. and E. Thomas Lawson (2002) *Bringing Ritual to Mind: Psychological Foundations of Cultural Forms*. Cambridge: Cambridge University Press.

McManus, John (1979) "Ritual and Human Social Cognition." In Eugene G. d'Aquili, Charles D. Laughlin and John McManus (Eds.), *The Spectrum of Ritual*. New York: Columbia University Press, pp. 216-248.

McNeley, James K. (1981) *Holy Wind in Navajo Philosophy*. Tucson AR: University of Arizona Press.

Mead, George Herbert (1934) *Mind, Self and Society*. Chicago: University of Chicago Press.

Mead, Margaret (1979) *Culture and Commitment*. New York: Natural History Press.

Mead, Margaret (1989[1955]) *Cultural Patterns and Technical Change*. New York: Mentor.

Merker, B. (2000) "Synchronous Chorusing and Human Origins." In N. Wallin, B. Merker and S. Brown (Eds.), *The Origins of Music*. Cambridge: MIT Press, pp. 315-327.

Merker, B. (2009) "Ritual Foundations of Human Uniqueness." In S. Malloch and C. Trevarthen (Eds.), *Communicative Musicality: Exploring The Basis Of Human Companionship*. Oxford: Oxford University Press, pp. 45-60.

Metcalf, Peter and Richard Huntington (1991) *Celebrations of Death: The Anthropology of Mortuary Ritual* (2nd edition). Cambridge: Cambridge University Press.

Meyerhoff, Barbara (1974) *Peyote Hunt: The Sacred Journey of the Huichol Indians*. Ithaca, NY: Cornell University Press.

Miller, G. A. (2003) "The Cognitive Revolution: A Historical Perspective." *Trends in Cognitive Sciences* 7: 141-144.

Mitford, Jessica (1998[1963]) *The American Way of Death*. New York: Simon and Schuster.

Moerman, Daniel E. (2002a) "Deconstructing the Placebo Effect and Finding the Meaning Response." *Annals of Internal Medicine* 136(6): 471-476.

Moerman, Daniel E. (2002b) *Meaning, Medicine, and the "Placebo Effect."* Cambridge:

Cambridge University Press.

Molino, J. (2000) "Toward an Evolutionary Theory of Music." In N. Wallin, B. Merker and S. Brown (Eds.), *The Origins of Music*. Cambridge: MIT Press, pp. 165–76.

Murphy, G. Ronald (1979) "A Ceremonial Ritual: The Mass." In Eugene G. D'Aquili, Charles D. Laughlin, and John McManus (Eds.), *The Spectrum of Ritual*. New York: Columbia University Press, pp. 318-341.

Murphy, G. Ronald (2002) *The Owl, The Raven, and the Dove: The Religious Meaning of the Grimms' Magic Fairy Tales*. Oxford: Oxford University Press.

Muuss, Rolf E. (1975) *Theories of Adolescence* (3rd Edition). New York: Random House.

Nash, June (1979) *We Eat the Mines and the Mines Eat Us: Dependency and Exploitation in Bolivian Tin Mines*. New York: Columbia University Press.

Nash, June (1992) *"I spent my life in the mines": The Story of Juan Rojas, Bolivian Tin Miner*. New York: Columbia University Press.

Norbeck, Edward (1979) "Rites of Reversal of North American Indians as Forms of Play." In Edword Norbeck and Claire R. Farrer (Eds.), *Forms of Play of Native North Americans*. New York: West Publishing, pp. 51-66.

Pabongka Rinpoche (2006) *Liberation in the Palm of Your Hand: A Concise Discourse on the Path to Enlightenment* (2nd edition). Essex: Wisdom Books.

Pagels, Elaine (1989) *The Gnostic Gospels*. New York: Vintage.

Paul, Russill (2004) *The Yoga of Sound: Healing & Enlightenment Through the Sacred Practice of Mantra*. New York: New World Library.

Pozas, Ricardo (1962) *Juan the Chamula: An Ethnological Recreation of the Life of a Mexican Indian* (translated by Lysander Kemp). Berkeley: University of California Press.

Puthoff, Harold (1990) "The Energetic Vacuum: Implications for Energy Research." *Speculations in Science and Technology* 13(4): 247.

Puthoff, Harold E. and Russell Targ (1976) "A Perceptual Channel for Information Transfer over Kilometer Distances: Historical Perspective and Recent Research." *Proceedings of the IEEE* 64(3): 329-354.

Quayle, Ethel and Max Taylor (2003) *Child Pornography: An Internet Crime*. New York: Routledge.

Radin, Dean I. (1997) *The Conscious Universe: The Scientific Truth of Psychic Phenomena*. New York: Harper.

Rapoport, J. and A. Fiske (1998) "The New Biology of Obsessive-Compulsive Disorder: Implications for Evolutionary Psychology." *Perspectives in Biology and Medicine* 41(2): 159-175.

Rappaport, Roy A. (1984) *Pigs for the Ancestors* (2nd edition). New Haven, CT: Yale University Press.

Rappaport, Roy A. (1999) *Ritual and Religion in the Making of Humanity*. Cambridge: Cambridge University Press.

Reagan, Albert B. (1904) "The Moccasin Game." *Proceedings of the Indiana Academy of Science* 14: 289-292.

Reichel-Dolmatoff, G. (1971) *Amazonian Cosmos*. Chicago: University of Chicago Press.

Reisberg, Daniel and Paula Hertel (2004) *Memory and Emotion*. Oxford: Oxford University Press.

Rest, James, D. Narvaez, M. Bebeau, and S. Thoma (1999) *Postconventional Moral Thinking: A Neo-Kohlbergian Approach*. Mahwah, NJ: Lawrence Erlbaum Associates.

Ricoeur, Paul (1990) *Time and Narrative* (Volume 1). Chicago: University of Chicago Press.

Ricoeur, Paul (1991) *From Text to Action*. Evanston: Northwestern University Press.

Ridington, Robin and Jillian Ridington (2006) *When You Sing It Now, Just Like New: First Nations Poetics, Voices and Representations*. Lincoln, NE: University of Nebraska Press.

Rock, Adam J., Einar B. Thorsteinsson, and Patrizio E. Tressoldi (2014) "A Meta-Analysis of Anomalous Information Reception by Mediums: Assessing the Forced-Choice Design in Mediumship Research, 2000-2014." In Stanley Krippner, Adam J. Rock, H. L. Friedman and Nancy L. Zingrone (Eds.), *Advances in Parapsychological Research* Vol. 10. Jefferson NC: McFarland.

Rose, Susan D. (1988) *Keeping Them Out of the Hands of Satan: Evangelical Schooling in America*. New York: Routledge.

Rothenbuhler, Eric W. (2006) *Ritual Communication: From Everyday Conversation to Mediated Ceremony*. New York: Sage.

Rowlands, Mark (2006) *Body Language: Representing in Action*. Cambridge, MA: MIT Press.

Rubinstein, Robert A., Charles D. Laughlin and John McManus (1984) *Science as Cognitive Process*. Philadelphia: University of Pennsylvania Press.

Rudgley, Richard (1993) *Essential Substances: A Cultural History of Intoxicants in Society*. New York: Kodansha International.

Sahlins, Marshall (1963) "Poor Man, Rich Man, Big Man, Chief: Political Types in Melanesia and Polynesia." *Comparative Studies in Society and History* 5(3): 285-303.

Salzen, E. (2010) "Whatever Happened To Ethology? The Case For the Fixed Action Pattern in Psychology." *History and Philosophy of Psychology* 12(2): 63-78

Sax, William S. (2010) "Ritual and the Problem of Efficacy." In William S. Sax, Johannes Quack and Jan Weinhold (Eds.), *The Problem of Ritual Efficacy*. Oxford: Oxford University Press, pp. 3-16.

Schechner, Richard (1982) "Collective Reflexivity: Restoration of Behavior." In Jay Ruby (Ed.), *A Crack in the Mirror: Reflexive Perspectives in Anthropology*. Philadelphia: University of Pennsylvania Press, pp. 39-81.

Schechner, Richard (1986) "Magnitudes of Performance." In Victor Turner and E.M. Bruner (Eds.), *The Anthropology of Experience*. Urbana: University of Illinois Press, pp. 344-369.

Schechner, Richard (1993) *The Future of Ritual: Writings on Culture and Performance*. Washington, D.C.: Psychology Press.

Schechner, Richard (2011) *Between Theater and Anthropology*. Philadelphia: University of Pennsylvania Press.

Schieffelin, Edward L. (1985) "Performance and the Cultural Construction of Reality." *American Ethnologist* 12(4): 707-724.

Schroder, H. M. (1971) "Conceptual Complexity and Personality Organization." In H.M. Schroder and P. Suefeld (Eds.), *Personality Theory and Information Processing*. New York: Ronald Press.

Schroder, H.M., M. Driver and S. Streufert (1967) *Human Information Processing*. New York: Holt, Rinehart and Winston.

Schultes, R.E. and A. Hofmann (1980) *Plants of the Gods: Origins of Hallucinogenic Use*. London: Hutchinson.

Seligman, Martin and J. Hager (1972) *Biological Boundaries of Learning*. New York: Appleton-Century-Crofts.

Selleri, Franco (1988) *Quantum Mechanics Versus Local Realism: The Einstein-Podolsky-Rosen Paradox*. New York: Plenum Press.

Selye, Hans (1974) *Stress Without Distress*. Toronto: McClelland and Stewart.

Senft, Gunter and Ellen B. Basso (Eds.) (2009) *Ritual Communication*. Oxford: Berg.

Sharp, Lauristan (1952) "Steel Axes for Stone Age Australians." *Human Organization* 11(2): 17-22.

Sherman, D. George, and Hedy B. Sherman (1990) *Rice, Rupees and Ritual: Economy and Society Among the Samosian Batak of Sumatra*. Stanford, CA: Stanford University Press.

Sias, Shari M., Glenn W. Lambie, and Victoria A. Foster (2006) "Conceptual and Moral Development of Substance Abuse Counselors: Implications for Training." *Journal of Addictions & Offender Counseling* 26(2): 99-110.

Simonton, O. C., S. Simonton and J. Creighton (1978) *Getting Well Again*. Los Angeles: Tarcher.

Smith, Margaret (1993) *Ritual Abuse: What It Is, Why It Happens, and How to Help*. San Francisco: Harper.

Smith, W. John (1979) "Ritual and the Ethology of Communicating." In Eugene G. D'Aquili, Charles D. Laughlin, and John McManus (Eds.), *The Spectrum of Ritual*. New York: Columbia University Press, pp. 51-79.

Smith, W. John (1990) "Animal Communication and the Study of Cognition." In Peter Marler and Carolyn A. Ristau (Eds.), *Cognitive Ethology: Essays in Honor of Donald R. Griffin*. Washington D.C.: Psychology Press, p. 209.

Snoek, Jan (2006) "Defining 'Rituals.'" In Jens Kreinath, Jan Snoek, and Michael Strausberg (Eds.), *Theorizing Rituals: Issues, Topics, Approaches, Concepts*. Leiden: Brill, pp. 3-14.

Snoek, Jan (2014) "Masonic Rituals of Initiation." In Henrik Bogdan, and Jan Snoek (Eds.), *Handbook of Freemasonry*. New York: Brill, p. 321.

Sorokin, P. A. (1957) *Social and Cultural Dynamics*. Boston: Porter Sargent.

Sorokin, P. A. (1962) *Society, Culture, and Personality*. New York: Cooper Square Publishers.

Southard, D. and Andrew Miracle (1993) "Rhythmicity, Ritual, and Motor Performance: A Study of Free Throw Shooting in Basketball." *Research Quarterly for Exercise and Sport* 64(3): 284-90.

Spiro, Melford E. (1953) "Ifaluk Ghosts: An Anthropological Inquiry into Learning and Perception." *Journal of Abnormal and Social Psychology* 48: 376-382.

Spomer, Ron (1996) *The Rut: The Spectacular Fall Ritual of North American Horned and Antlered Animals*. Willow Creek Press.

Stall, Fritz (1989) *Rules Without Meaning. Ritual, Mantras and the Human Sciences*. New York: Peter Lang.

Star, Rima (2016) "Love Lives On." In Hass, Robyn and Robbie Davis-Floyd (Eds.), *Surviving the Death of Your Ex: Managing the Grief No One Talks About*. Praeclarus Press, ch. 12.

Stewart, Pamela, and Andrew Strathern (2014) *Ritual: Key Concepts in Religion*. London: Blooksbury.

Strathern, Andrew (1971) *The Rope of Moka: Big-Men and Ceremonial Exchange in Mount Hagen, New Guinea*. Cambridge: Cambridge University Press.

Strathern, Andrew (1979) *Ongka: A Self Account by a New Guinea Big-Man*. Duckworth, London.

Sumegi, Angela (2008) *Dreamworlds of Shamanism and Tibetan Buddhism*. Albany: State University of New York Press.

Tainter, Joseph A. (2006) *The Collapse of Complex Societies* (15th printed ed.). UK: Cambridge University Press. pp. 17–19, 210.

Tambiah, S. J. (1979) "A Performative Approach to Ritual." *Proceedings of the British Academy London* 65: 113-169.

Tannen, Deborah (2005) *Conversational Style: Analyzing Talk Among Friends*. Oxford: Oxford University Press.

Targ, Russell, and Harold Puthoff (1977) *Mind-Reach*. New York: Delacorte Press.

Taylor, Diana (2003) *The Archive and the Repertoire: Performing Cultural Memory in the*

Americas. Durham, NC: Duke University Press.

Tedlock, Barbara (2005) *The Woman in the Shaman's Body: Reclaiming the Feminine in Religion and Medicine*. New York: Bantam Books.

TenHouten, Warren D. (2005) *Time and Society*. Albany NY: State University of New York Press.

Trakhtenberg, Ephraim C. (2008) "The Effects of Guided Imagery on the Immune System: A Critical Review." *International Journal of Neuroscience* 118(6): 839-855.

Trinkaus, Erik (1983) *The Shanidar Neanderthals*. New York: Academic Press

Trompf, C. W. (Ed.) (1990) *Cargo Cults and Millenarian Movements: Transoceanic Comparisons of New Religious Movements*. Berlin: Mouton De Gruyter.

Turnbull, Colin M. (1962) *The Forest People. A Study of the Pygmies of the Congo*. New York: Simon and Schuster.

Turnbull, Colin M. (1972) *The Mountain People*. New York: Simon & Schuster.

Turnbull, Colin M. (1978) "Rethinking the Ik: A Functional Non-Social System." In Charles D. Laughlin, Jr., Ivan A. Brady (ed.): *Extinction and Survival in Human Populations*. New York: Columbia University Press. pp. 49–75.

Turnbull, Colin M. (1983) *The Human Cycle*. New York: Simon and Schuster.

Turner, Edith (1996) *The Hands Feel It: Healing and Spirit Presence Among a Northern Alaskan People*. DeKalb, IL: Northern Illinois University Press.

Turner, Victor (1969) *The Ritual Process: Structure and Anti-Structure*. Chicago: Aldine.

Turner, Victor (1974) *Dramas, Fields, and Metaphors: Symbolic Action in Human Society*. Ithaca: Cornell University Press.

Turner, Victor (1979) *Process, Performance and Pilgrimage*. New Delhi: Concept Publishing House.

Turner, Victor (1982) *From Ritual to Theatre*. New York: Performing Arts Journal Publications.

Turner, Victor (1987) "Betwixt and Between: The Liminal Period in Rites of Passage." In Louise Carus Mahdi, Steven Foster and Meredith Little (Eds.), *Betwixt and Between: Patterns of Masculine and Feminine Initiation*. Chicago: Open Court, pp. 5-22.

Turner, Victor (1990) "Are There Universals of Performance in Myth, Ritual, and Drama?" In Richard Schechner and Willa Appel (Eds.), *By Means of Performance: Intercultural Studies of Theatre and Ritual*. New York: Cambridge University Press, pp. 8-18.

Turner, Victor and E.M. Bruner (Eds.) (1986) *The Anthropology of Experience*. Urbana: University of Illinois Press.

Turner, Victor and Richard Schechner (1988) *The Anthropology of Performance*. New York: Paj Publications.

Vogt, Evon Z. (1976) *Tortillas for the Gods: A Symbolic Analysis of Zinacateco Rituals*. Cambridge: Harvard University Press.

Wagner, Rachel (2012) *Godwired: Religion, Ritual, and Virtual Reality*. New York: Routledge.

Walker, Iain and Heather J. Smith (2001) *Relative Deprivation: Specification, Development, and Integration*. Cambridge: Cambridge University Press.

Wallace, Anthony F. C. (1956a) "Tornado in Worcester: An Exploratory Study of Individual and Community Behavior in an Extreme Situation." Publication 392, *National Academy of Sciences-National Research Council*, Washington, D.C.

Wallace, Anthony F. C. (1956b) "Revitalization Movements." *American Anthropologist* 58: 264-81.

Wallace, Anthony F. C. (1957) "Mazeway Disintegration: The Individual's Perception of Socio-Cultural Disorganization." *Human Organization* 16: 23-27.

Wallace, Anthony F. C. (1966) *Religion: An Anthropological View*. New York: Random House.

Wallace, Anthony F. C. (1969) *The Death and Rebirth of the Seneca*. New York: Random House.

Wallis, Wilson D. (1996) *Heyoka: Lakota Rites of Reversal*. Kendall Park, NJ: Lakota Books.

Weil, Andrew and Martin Rossman (2006) *Self-Healing with Guided Imagery*. New York: Sounds True.

Weiner, James (1988) *The Heart of the Pearl Shell: The Mythological Dimension of Foi Sociality*. Berkeley: University of California Press.

Whitehead, Alfred North (1978) *Process and Reality: An Essay in Cosmology* (the corrected edition ed. by D.R. Griffin and D.W. Sherburne). New York: The Free Press.

Whitehead, Harry (2000) "The Hunt for Quesalid: Tracking Levi-Strauss' Shaman." *Anthropology and Medicine* 7(2): 149-168.

Whitehouse, Harvey (2000) *Arguments and Icons: Divergent Modes of Religiosity*. Oxford University Press.

Whitehouse, Harvey (2001) "Transmissive Frequency, Ritual, and Exegesis." *Journal of Cognition and Culture* 1(2): 167-181.

Whitehouse, Harvey (2004) *Modes of Religiosity: A Cognitive Theory of Religious Transmission*. New York: Rowman Altamira.

Whitehouse, Harvey (2005) "Emotion, Memory and Religious Rituals: An Assessment of Two Theories." In Milton, Kay and Maruška Svašek (Eds.), *Mixed Emotions: Anthropological Studies of Feeling*. Oxford: Berg.

Whitehouse, Harvey (2007) "Towards an Integration of Ethnography, History, and the Cognitive Science of Religion." In Harvey Whitehouse and James Laidlaw (Eds.), *Religion, Anthropology, and Cognitive Science*. Durham, NC: Carolina Academic Press, pp. 247-274.

Whitehouse, Harvey (2008a) "Cognitive Evolution and Religion: Cognition and Religious Evolution." *Issues in Ethnology and Anthropology* 3(3): 35-47.

Whitehouse, Harvey (2008b) "Transmission." In Jens Kreinath, Jan Snoek, and Michael Stausberg (Eds.), *Theorizing Rituals: Issues, Topics, Approaches, Concepts*. Leiden: Brill, pp. 657-669.

Wilcken, Patrick (2010) *Claude Lévi-Strauss: The Poet in the Laboratory*. New York: Penguin.

Young-Laughlin, Judi and Charles D. Laughlin (1988) "How Masks Work." *Journal of Ritual Studies* 2(1): 59-86.

Zuckerman, Phil (2008) *Society Without God: What the Least Religious Nations Can Tell Us About Contentment*. New York: NYU Press.

Index

Abrahams, Roger 251
Adler, Margot 1
affective semantics 129-130
Aleorta, Candace 17
altered states of consciousness (ASCs)
    see consciousness
Alvarez, Yin 217
Ames, Adelbert 107
Among the Truthers (Kay) 269
André, Father 257
Archetypal Actions of Ritual, The
    (Humphrey, Laidlaw) 17
archetype xlii, 54, 104, 237
    archetypal cosmology 102-119, 121
    defined 54
    "innate releasing mechanisms" 104
    king 237
    potentiating 104
Art of Grieving Gracefully, The (Davis-Floyd) 289n
ASC
    see consciousness
Atran, Scott 15-17
Australian Aboriginal societies 110, 178, 300

belief
    see ritual
Biesele, Megan 314
big-man systems 301-303
biogenetic structuralism xl-xliv, 101n, 384
Biogenetic Structuralism (Laughlin, d'Aquili) xl, xli
Biological Boundaries of Learning (Seligman, Hager) 19
birth, birthing, childbirth, rebirthing xxxi-xliv, 4, 6, 8, 26, 57, 83, 87, 92-97, 101, 133-141, 165-171, 277, 300-322, 332, 342, 378
Blackmore, Susan 13
Birth as an American Rite of Passage (Davis-Floyd) xxxvii, 9, 139, 206, 383

Bloch, Maurice 20
Bohm, David 112
Boiling Energy: Community Healing among the Kalahari !Kung (Katz) 133
Bolivian tin miners 26, 205-208, 219
Bonobo: The Forgotten Ape (de Waal, Lantings) 33
Boyer, Pascal 19-20, 23, 144
Brady, Ivan 289, 297
brain xxxiii, xxxix, xl-xlii, 5
    adaptation 286
    animal brains 32-33
    "blank slate" 101
    brain functions 5, 34, 41,
    brain structures (organization) xxi, xxxix, xli, 24, 33, 37, 50, 51, 108, 233
    corpus callosum 33, 39, 136
    core xxi, 37, 38, 41, 224
    cortical xxi, 23, 37, 39-40, 48
    development xxiv, 48-49, 103, 108
    emotional brain xxi, 37, 38, 41, 52
    evolution xviii, 13, 17, 37, 39-41, 100, 285
    excitation and relaxation systems 234-236, 260, 375
    frontal cortex 34, 38, 40
    gyrus and sulcus 39
    hemispheres, left and right 33-37, 39-42, 49, 136, 230, 238
    integration (three levels of function) 41-43
    neocortex 39-42, 52, 61, 107
    neural network xxvi, xxvii, 33, 48, 50-51, 164-165, 268, 270, 280, 286, 289. 294, 330, 376
    neuroendocrine system 146-147, 150, 151, 189
    "organ of exaptation" 103
    plasticity, neuroplasticity, synaptic plasticity xxix, 49, 103, 293, 330
    prefrontal cortex (PFC) 40-41, 51

preparedness to learn 20, 110, 158
ritualizing 170, 285
sex and 38, 235
symbolic function xxix, xli, 32
synapse, synaptic 49-51
transformation of brain-state 152, 156, 171, 279
truing the 100-106
visual cortex 34, 147
Brain, Symbol and Experience (Laughlin, McManus, d'Aquili) xli, xliv, 384
Brook, Peter 196
Buckley, William F. 275

Camp Cimarroncita 213
Campbell, Joseph xvii, 83-84, 100, 104
Camping, Harold 221
cargo cult xxi, 309
Carroll, Lewis 153
Cassirer, Ernst 56
Castro, Fidel 239
causation 87, 103, 113, 174, 181, 191, 374
    backwards 178
    causation-at-a-distance 178, 180
    magical 175, 178-180
    "spooky" 26, 181-185, 374
ceremony, ceremonial
    see ritual
Chagnon, Napoleon 144
Chekhov, Anton 15
Childbirth across Cultures (Selin, Stone) 300n
cognition, cognitive xxiii, 16, 44, 47-53, 77, 81, 84, 86, 101, 116, 128, 131, 164, 215, 254, 259, 264, 279, 292
    brain and 19-20, 40-42
    adaptation 5-7
    anchor 279-282, 289, 294
    binary opposition 119
    binding xlii
    categories 279
    complexity 263-264, 288, 293
    concrete thinking 27, 263, 265-276, 292
    evolution xxvi, 7, 17, 129
    functions 39, 146, 214
    fluid thinking 27, 265-293, 376
    four stages of 27, 107, 265-285, 292, 376
    imperative xxii, 25, 72, 82

information overload 282
inverted U-curve 284
linguistics 32
"local knowledge" 63
map 89
matrix 24, 70-73, 119, 138, 161, 174, 237, 264
neurocognitive operator 85
regression xxii, 291
simplification 264, 296
substage xxiii. xxix, 279, 282-283, 287-297, 376
transformation 252, 254
science 17, 20
stages of xxviii, 263-293, 329
theory of ritual 19
truing
    see truing
universal structures xi, 19, 23, 32
Collapse: How Societies Choose to Fail or Succeed (Diamond) 296
collective consciousness
    see consciousness
Collier, John Jr. 199
communication 5, 15, 96, 249, 254, 284
    and art 130
    animal 31
    coordination and communication systems 24
    miscommunication 124, 311
    nonverbal 6, 38, 42
    ritual as 6, 10, 14, 38, 127, 202, 263, 283
    symbols and 32, 41-42, 46, 50, 53
Communing with the Gods: Consciousness, Culture, and the Dreaming Brain (Laughlin) xliii, 77, 140, 362
consciousness 43, 46, 73, 82, 101, 142, 145-146, 346
    and adaptation 142-143
    and archetypes 105
    and intuition 107
    and myth 99
    and reality 144, 225
    and ritual 50, 70, 127, 132, 250
    altered states of consciousness (ASCs) xxi, 7, 26, 62, 77, 113, 121, 133, 136-137, 140-144, 215, 235, 243, 255-256, 354, 358

INDEX 403

brain and 128, 145
collective consciousness xxii, 73, 83-84, 99
collective effervescence 241-243
cosmic 355
flow xxiv, 26, 131, 148, 214-216, 234-235, 287, 360, 374, 381
near-death experience 244
numinosity 216
psychic power 26, 175, 178, 374
self-consciousness 131, 140
state of consciousness (SOC) xxi, xxiv, xxv, xxiii, xli, 23, 25, 39, 42, 127, 128-131, 139-157, 214-216, 305, 343
store-consciousness (*alaya-vijnana*) 113
stream of 143
time 106
warp of consciousness (WOC, warp) xxx, 128-131, 140, 146, 156, 374
coordination, internal and external 164-166
Corbin, Henry 77
core symbol
see symbol
cosmology xxii, xxxiv, 7, 59, 72, 74, 81, 83, 88, 220, 307, 373
and consciousness 113
and ritual xxxvii
and cycle of meaning 83, 241
and myth 72
archetypal 102-106, 110, 119-121, 151-156, 179
Dogon 78
worldview 72
Cove, John 73, 154, 307
Cox, Kenneth J. 124
Csikszentmihalyi, Mihaly 214
cults
see religion
cultural relativism
see culture
cultural universal
see culture
culture, cultural
and environmental adaptation 80, 110-115, 296

animal 33
conservation and change of 298-299
corporate 123-124
"culture-bearer" 308
ethnocentrism xxiii, 27, 144, 270-272, 274-293, 376
ethos 129
expressive xxiii, 82, 372
historical status quo 27, 300-303
idealistic, ideational and sensate xxiv, 108-111
"invented tradition" xxiv, 71, 306
memory (mnemonics) 299-301
monastic xliii, 134
monophasic and polyphasic xxvi, 25, 142-146, 151-158, 174, 374
relativism xxii, 27, 272-276, 293, 376
standardized interpretations 117
subculture 8, 102
universal(s) xxii, xl, 1, 2, 14-23, 54, 84-85, 101, 104, 109, 119, 185, 245, 247, 346, 372-376
cycle of meaning xxii, 20, 25, 73-74, 77, 80-87, 90, 103-104, 116-121, 150-156, 185, 220-221, 244, 296, 300, 306-307, 311, 359, 363-366
axis of instantiation 117, 121
axis of interpretation 117
defined 73

Dane-zaa, Northern Athapaskan people (aka Beaver Indians) 311
D'Aquili, Eugene G. xl
Darth Vader 64
Das Rheingold (Wagner) 148
Davis, Walter Gray 201
Davis-Floyd, Robbie E. xvii, xli, 9, 25, 57. 83, 85, 92, 101, 110, 152, 167, 168, 179, 194, 195, 198, 206, 208, 209-211, 216, 220, 233, 240, 299, 317-325, 334, 339, 341
biography xxxi-xxxvii, 383
personal experiences 36, 42, 66, 113-115, 122-124, 130-131,137-138, 139-142, 182-185, 200-203, 213-214, 227-232, 242-244,

256-260, 280-281, 289, 327, 363
Der Ring des Nibelungen (Wagner) 147
Die Walkure (Wagner) 148
development
   see brain
Devereux, Paul 55, 197
Diamond, Jared 296
Dilthey, Wilhelm 60
Dissanayake, Ellen 245
distress
   see stress
divine 113, 145, 155, 165, 172, 179, 247, 249, 360
   blessing 152, 176
   divination 25, 163, 174-180, 186-187, 191, 374
   explanation 80
   inspiration 26, 177-178
   propitiation 203
Dogon 78
Don Julio 199, 330
Don Lucio 194, 212, 330
drama
   see ritual
dream(s), dreaming xl, 34, 47, 50, 77, 110-111, 118, 128-129, 130, 131, 142, 146, 165, 175, 178, 184, 209, 216, 238, 241, 280, 312, 362-363, 364, 365
   brain and 35
   dream incubation 25, 28, 134, 241, 291, 312
   Dreamtime (Australian Aborigine) 83, 110, 178
   imagery 34, 144
   lucid xlii
   Tantric dreamwork 140, 143, 153-156, 355-359
Dossey, Larry 179
driver, ritual
   see ritual
Driver, Tom 7
Drumming at the Edge of Magic (Hart) 132
Durkheim, Emile 83, 241

Easter Island 297
ecological adaptation 297
eidetic image xxiii, 361-362

"Einstein, Podolsky, Rosen effect" (EPR) 182
Eisenhower, President Dwight 275
electronic fetal monitoring (EFM) xxvii, 57, 135, 138-139, 373
Elegant Universe, The (Greene)
entrain, entrainment xxiii, xxiv, 24, 48-49, 51, 62, 129, 131-132, 200, 215, 218, 235-237, 254, 277, 305, 330, 374, 382
ethnocentrism
   see culture
exaptation xxiii, 102-103
eustress
   see stress
evil 59, 67, 238
   quintessence of 64-65
   spirits 162, 371
expressive culture
   see culture
Extinction and Survival in Human Populations (Laughlin, Brady) 297

Fabric of the Cosmos, The (Greene) 113
fanatic, fanaticism xxiii, 27, 266-293, 376
Feather, John 291
fixed action pattern xxiii, 5-6, 9
flow, experience of
   see consciousness
Flowers, Betty Sue 78, 109, 286, 341
Floyd, Jason Phillip xxxv, 130-131, 201, 202, 227, 256, 280-281, 335-338
Floyd, Peyton Elizabeth xxiv, xxxiv-xxxvii, 130, 141, 152, 184-185, 201, 257, 352
   altar 280
   death of xxiv, 227-232, 244, 289, 363-364
   memorial service for xxxv-xxxvii, 334-339
Forest People, The (Turnbull) xxxix
frame, framing 17, 150, 166, 193-194, 197
   breaking 198, 209-211, 212
   physical and non-physical 195-196
   "power of" 198

ritual 194, 196-198, 199, 232, 245
  also see ritual
Freiberg, Kevin and Jackie 322
From Doctor to Healer: The Transformative Journey (Davis-Floyd, St. John) 92
fundamentalism, fundamentalist xxiv, 27, 109, 113, 236, 264, 266-293, 376

Galanter, Mark 255
Gandhi, Mohandas (Mahatma) 239
Gaskin, Ina May 66
Geertz, Clifford 32, 58, 63
Gell, Alfred 188
Georges, Nia 208, 318
Ghost Dance 222, 310-311
Girl with Seven Names: A North Korean Defector's Story, The (Lee) 304
global humanism xxiv, 27, 273-276
Gluckman, Max 291
Goer, Henci 206
"Good Guys and Girls" of Brazil 317-322
Gould, Stephen J. 102
great kettle debate 66-67
Greene, Brian 113, 155
Griaule, Marcel 78
Grimes, Ronald 7, 13, 21-23

Handelman, Don 193
Handsome Lake, Seneca Indian prophet 212
Harner, Michael 137
Hart, Mickey 132
hazing
  see ritual
healing
  see ritual
Healing Makes Our Hearts Happy: Spirituality and Cultural Transformation among the Kalahari Ju|'hoansi (Katz, Biesele, St. Denis) 133
Healing Words (Dossey) 179, 191
Heaven's Gate cult 220
Heelas, Paul 82
Heidegger, Martin 166
Hidden Reality, The (Greene)

Hitler, Adolf 237-239, 264-265, 304
Hocart, A. M. 70
holistic model 94
Holy Wind in Navajo Philosophy (McNeley) 87
Huichol people of Mexico 80
humanistic model 94
Humphrey, Caroline 17-19, 20
Huntington, Richard 70

I Never Promised You a Rose Garden (Green, aka Greenberg) 365
idealistic culture
  see culture
ideational culture
  see culture
ideology xxiv, xxx, 54, 61, 244, 266, 318, 322, 332, 379
  implicit and explicit 330-333
Ik people of Uganda 80
imitation 13, 129, 358
  adaptation and 13
  inter-state mimesis 130
  mimesis 129-131, 358
In Gods We Trust (Atran) 99
indigenous psychology
  see psychology
initial structure xxv, 101-102
Inner Reaches of Outer Space: Metaphor as Myth and as Religion (Campbell) 83
intention movements xxv, 5
intuition xxxix, 39, 42, 63, 72, 100-124, 145, 175, 180, 185, 210, 249
Iroquois people 55

Jerusalem 227-330
Jorgensen, Dan 105
Jorgensen, Joseph 295
Juan the Chamula 226, 232-233, 254
Jung, Carl G. 54, 110
"just-so story" xxv, 43, 105

Karuk Indians of California 81
Katz, Richard 133
Kay, Jonathan 269
Keech, Marian 222
Kelleher, Herb 28, 322-324
Kennedy, President John F. 121-122

King, Martin Luther 237
King, Robert J. 299
King, Rodney 275
Kitzinger, Sheila 215
Kuhn, Jorge 321
Kuhn, Thomas 91
!Kung (aka Ju|'hoansi) trance dance 133, 235, 313

Laderman, Carol 113
Laidlaw, James 13, 17-19, 20
Laughlin, Charles D. xxxi, 11, 19, 22, 23, 44, 47, 64, 65, 66, 74, 76, 77, 89, 104, 110, 113, 140, 149, 184, 195, 199, 213, 240, 242, 244, 289, 297, 343
   biography xxxix-xliv, 383-384
   personal experiences 58-60, 153-156, 162-164, 226, 238, 287, 343, 353-359, 361-363
Lee, Hyeonseo 304
Levi-Strauss, Claude 32, 90
Lewis, C. S. 153
Leyva, Daniel 217
lifeworld xxv, 72, 80, 81, 90, 121, 164-172, 177, 178, 189, 220, 261, 283, 365, 371, 372, 376
   defined 72
   instrumental 174-175
limen (liminal) xxv, 152-153, 252
   defined 22
Limon, José 243
Lock, Andrew 82
Luhrmann, Tanya 359
Lurie, Jeanna 347-352
Luther, Martin 301, 310

Malinowski, Bronislaw 204
mandala
   see symbol
matrix, cognitive
   see cognition
McAuliffe, Christa 124
McGraw, Frank "Tug" 149
   "sweet spot in time" 148
McManus, John xli, 267
McNeley, James 87
Mead, George Herbert 165
Mead, Margaret 307

medicine, Western 135, 233-234
   holistic or alternative health care 111
   medical spectrum 94
meditation xxiii, xxvii, xxviii, xli-xliv, 128-135, 149, 152-156. 171, 178, 187, 234, 255, 259. 287, 349-351, 353-360, 362, 375, 378-379, 382
   mantra 132
   see also Tantra
Mescalero Apache of New Mexico 212
messenger mice 60, 371
Metcalf, Peter 70
midwife, midwifery xxxii, 4, 66-67, 96, 208, 210, 229, 277, 305, 320, 383
Modes of Religiosity (Whitehouse) 20
monophasic culture
   see culture
Moon, Reverend Sun Myung 255
Morningstar, Sandra 210
mnemonics xxvi, 135, 299-300
Murphy, Father Ronald 240
myth, mythology xxii, xxiv, xxvi, 8, 13, 25, 43, 50, 54-55, 62, 64, 69-96, 101-119, 120, 129, 147, 150, 173, 241, 276, 282, 290, 296, 298, 300, 304, 307, 311, 314, 329, 363, 364
   and ritual school, Cambridge 69
   changeling 102
   grail quest 105
   hero 84
   imaginatio 77
   multi-vocality
      see symbol
   myth/paradigm ritual complex 81-90, 282, 290, 296
   mythopoeic 237
   of technological transcendence 85
   "personal mythology" 12, 363

naïve realist xxvi, 266, 269, 271-274, 294, 376
Naro's grave 25, 65-66, 371
Nash, June 205, 219
Native American Church 43
Naturalness of Religious Ideas, The

(Boyer) 19
Navajo xliii, 25, 74-76, 77, 84, 104, 105, 112-113, 134, 134-135, 172-173, 195, 241, 311, 371, 384
  cosmology 25, 75, 88, 247
  Great Seal 248
  hogan 173
  hozho (beauty) xliii
  indigenous psychology 84
  kinaalda ceremony 86-90
  myth 25, 74-76, 114-115
  symbolism 53-54
Needham, Rodney 136
neurognosis 101n
Norse settlers in Greenland 296
Nuts! Southwest Airlines' Crazy Recipe for Business and Personal Success (Friebergs) 322

Ongka's Big Moka: The Kawelka of Papua, New Guinea (episode of Granada Television's *Disappearing World*) 302n
Owl, the Raven, and the Dove, The: The Religious Meaning of the Grimms' Magic Fairy Tales (Murphy) 240

Paiute Prophet 222, 310-311
paradigm(s) xxvi, 13, 25, 68, 70-71, 78, 90-96, 101, 116-119, 121, 291, 298, 300, 304,307, 317-318, 319, 320-321, 333, 363,
penetration
  see symbol
"personal space" 5
plasticity, neural
  see synaptic plasticity
plot, plotting xxvii, 40, 43-44, 90, 131, 148, 150-154, 158, 203, 218, 375
polyphasic culture
  see culture
poro secret society, West Africa 176
portal(s), portalling xxvii, 25, 32, 83, 137-138, 151-156, 194-196, 247, 250, 262, 374
  device 152
praxis xxvii, xxix, 165, 166

Prentice, Tracey 89n
Princeton Engineering Anomalies Research (PEAR) labs 180
Process and Reality (Whitehead)
psychology, psychological 1, 2, 7, 8, 27, 37, 57, 127, 141, 153, 170, 188-189, 195-196, 205, 206, 217, 227, 229, 252, 264, 269, 270, 293, 332, 341, 356, 366, 369
  animal perception 197
  animal play 214
  brain and 51
  catharsis 43
  development 158
  evolutionary 17
  indigenous (local) psychology xxv, 81-82, 84
  Piagetian 108
  post-traumatic stress disorder (PTSD) 85
  seasonal affective disorder (SAD) 146
  transformation 27, 264
psychotherapy xxxi, 134, 227, 227
Puthoff, Harold E. 112

quantum physics 112, 182-185
Quesalid (a Kwakiutl shaman) 333, 366

Rappaport, Roy 14-15, 316-317
Readings in Ritual Studies (Grimes) 13
Red Tent, The (Diamant) 347
Redfield, Robert 131
religion xxiii, xxix, xxxii, xli, 3, 8, 9, 13-16, 19, 21, 27, 53, 64, 69, 73, 78-83, 86. 114, 119-121, 132, 144, 162, 179, 185, 200, 211-212, 222, 249-250, 255, 260, 267, 273, 274, 285, 308, 310-311, 327-329, 334, 361
  conversion xxxiv, 27, 242-243, 250-260, 375
  cults 71, 132, 220, 258, 262
  evangelical Christian 221, 359-360, 362, 366
  fundamentalism 27, 266, 276
  millenarian movement 222
  modes of religiosity 20

supernatural beings (agents) 16
syncretism xxix, 330, 365, 377
Tantra xlii, 21, 117, 153, 178, 353-359, 366, 384
Re-Visioning the Earth (Devereux) 55
revitalization 16, 118-121, 377
   revitalization movement xxvii, 28, 320-325
rhythmo-affective semantics xxvii, 129
Ricoeur, Paul 62, 148n
Ridington, Robin and Jillian 311
Riefenstahl, Leni 264
rite of intensification
   see ritual
rite of passage
   see ritual
rite of reversal
   see ritual
ritual
   anatomy of 24
   and adaptation 13, 17, 42, 49
   and ecstasy 148, 157, 216, 235-236, 355, 358
   animal 1-2, 4-7, 11, 13, 129, 235, 369
   anthropology of 14, 145
   as performance 3, 15, 18, 21, 21-23, 26, 51, 54, 57, 70, 73, 82, 86, 100, 116, 124, 127, 130, 147-149, 185, 195, 205, 208, 214-218, 220, 225, 236-239, 242, 244, 249, 276, 285-286, 294, 297, 300-301, 315, 318, 330, 339
   beauty and xliii, 76, 203, 244-249, 375
   belief and 3, 9, 10, 12-17, 69-77, 81, 89, 95, 108, 114, 127, 161, 175, 185, 203, 205, 208, 214, 219-223, 225-226, 233-237, 240-244, 250-256, 259-260, 263, 276, 282, 284-286, 297-301, 306-308, 310, 315, 318, 329-334, 345-346, 365-366
   "belief follows emotion" 225
   birthday party 334-338, 343
   bridges cognitive levels 50
   ceremony, ceremonial xli, 58, 65, 70-71, 75, 80, 86-101, 117, 120-121, 157, 164, 172-173, 189, 194, 205, 209, 211-214, 226, 236, 245-248, 278, 281, 286, 291, 299, 302-310, 334, 344-346
   clown 290-291
   commitment 18
   control of states of consciousness xliii, 13, 146-150, 217
   definition of 3, 6, 9-11
   designing xxxv, 4, Appendix
   disruption of 211
   divination, diviner 25-26, 162-163, 174-175, 177, 186-187, 206, 374
   drama, dramaturgy as xxiii, xliv, 8, 22, 36, 71, 73, 78, 82, 86, 130, 147-148, 161, 189, 227, 236-237, 249-250, 260, 346, 361, 375
   driver xxviii, 24, 127-158, 161, 165, 171, 222, 225, 242, 257, 259, 308, 360, 361, 369
   "orchestra of drivers" 147
   emotion and xxxiii, 17-18, 21, 22, 35-57, 62, 71, 81-82, 101, 117, 130-131, 141, 157, 214, 227, 234-236, 240-242, 249, 251, 254, 322
   evolution of 13, 17, 19, 129-130, 158, 226, 281, 369
   exorcism xl
   failure of 25, 28, 138, 219-223
   "foreplay" as 38
   frame, framing
      see frame
   funeral(s) 2, 35, 189, 190, 225, 245, 251, 289, 334-335, 338, 341
   hazing xxiv, 43, 132, 135, 252, 255, 288, 382
   healing xxxiii, xliii, 3, 8, 10, 27, 51-53, 55, 130, 133-135, 165, 172, 179, 186, 216, 226-233, 247, 281, 333
   "hoodwinking" 361
   implements of 25, 185-189, 358, 374
   instrumentality and 162, 169, 181, 185, 187
   intensification 16, 190, 194, 236, 249, 261, 308

intentional use of xxxiii, 136, 217
labs as 57
ludic dimension of 26, 212-214
memorial service xxxv, 228, 334
mystery plays 15
mythic enactment 86
obstetrical xxxii, 207-208, 318
of stabilization 281-282
paradigmatic enactment 90-91
personal 12, 341, 361-365
placebo and 53
power (efficacy) of xxxiv, xliii, xliv, 4, 9, 17, 43, 48, 50, 73, 131, 175, 179-181, 199, 205, 207
prayer as 2, 10, 12, 56, 140, 179, 195-196, 200, 205, 226, 245, 249, 281, 327, 330, 359-360, 362, 366, 375
puberty rite 8, 54, 87-88, 89, 140, 165, 172, 176, 251, 254, 343, 366
"random event generator" 177
rite of passage xxvii, xliii, 8, 153, 172, 250-253, 288, 343
rite of reversal xxvii, 290
ritual order 216
ritual train 26, 124, 207, 208-211, 320, 337, 339
ritualize, ritualization 11
"shadow side" of 43
shrines and alters 26, 199, 375
socialization and 6
spectrum of 11
theories of xli, 3, 19-23
the "work" of religion 86
transition 8
virtual 189-190
warp control and 139-142
wedding 2, 35, 189, 190, 201-211, 251, 281, 334, 340, 366
Ritual: Perspectives and Dimensions (Bell) 13
Ritual and Belief (Hick) 13
ritual driver
   see ritual
Robbie's Short Stories: Vignettes of My Magical Life (Davis-Floyd) 143n
Robertson, Raymond 64, 343-347, 361
Sahlins, Marshal 301

Sax, William 4
Schechner, Richard 21-22
Secular Ritual (Moore, Myerhoff) 203
sensate culture
   see culture
Sexual Life of Savages, The (Malinowski) 204
shaman, shamanism xxviii, xxxiii, 3, 20, 32, 59, 60-64, 78, 104, 105, 113, 129, 131, 134-136, 145, 187-188, 226-227, 291, 307, 330, 333, 366, 371
   and altered states of consciousness 3, 62, 137, 152
   animal helpers 138
   animal imagery 61
   healing and 51, 130
   masters of ritual 236
   mirror 154-155
   soul loss and 229, 232-233
Sharp, Lauriston 168
Sioux people of the American plains 120
Smith, Robert 334
So (aka Tepes, Tepeth) people, Karamoja District, Uganda xxxix, 2, 47, 58-60, 76, 162-164
Society without God (Zuckerman) 19
Sorokin, Pitirim 109
Sosis, Richard 17, 144
space program, the (NASA) 25, 119-124
   Challenger disaster 123
Spectrum of Ritual, The (d'Aquili, Laughlin, McManus) xli, 11
Spiro, Mel 16
St. Augustine 273
St. John, Gloria 92
Staal, Frits 23, 127
stages of cognition (thought)
   see cognition
Star, Rima 341
state of consciousness (SOC)
   see consciousness
Stein, Gertrude 215
strange-making 253
stress xxiii, 8, 27, 52, 85, 92, 134, 142, 174, 214, 267, 279-293, 308, 320
   distress xxiii, 95, 171, 207, 282,

293, 308, 317, 320, 346, 376
eustress xxiii, 282-293
Structure of Scientific Revolutions, The (Kuhn) 91
substage
   see cognition
Sun Dance, the 25, 43, 120-121, 134-135, 140, 158, 291, 309
Surviving the Death of Your Ex: Managing the Grief That No One Talks About (Hass, Davis-Floyd) 289n
symbol(s), symbolic 10-12, 14, 35
   action 40
   animal as 165
   animal use of 32
   are "brain talk" 32-37
   behavior 10
   "community of cells" 49
   core 53-60
   defined 31, 44
   evoking and fulfilling meaning 46
   evolution of 32
   expressive penetration 47
   function xli
   healing 53, 173
   interpretation of 24, 33, 63-67, 166
   inversion xxix, 252, 255
   mandala 152, 153-155, 173, 187, 245, 247-250, 260, 353, 359, 375
   multi-vocality xxvi, 31, 57, 370
   "other-than-human persons" (Hallowell) 144
   penetration xxvii, 45-53, 56, 146, 150, 152, 156, 255, 370
   plotting and xxvii, 40, 43
   pregnance xxix, 55-56, 165, 172
   process xxix, 31-32, 35, 48, 164-166, 225, 237
   ritual and 31-67, 127, 218, 240, 253-254, 284-286, 304, 353-355
   "send messages" 31
   structure(s) 48
   system 73-75, 78, 80, 87, 89, 99, 105
   technological 166, 170, 188, 202-204, 222, 250, 281
   unconscious meanings of 35
   "vehicles for communication" 32
Symbolic Landscapes (Devereux) 55

symbolic penetration
   see symbol
synaptic plasticity
   see brain

Tantra, Tantric xlii, 117, 179, 353-357, 366
   lama 117, 384
   mandala offering 153
   ritual 21
   sex 354-356
technocracy 53, 124
   from technique to 316
   technocratic model 94
technology, technological xxix, xxxviii, 53-54, 57, 86, 161-190
   animal tool use 170
   "art as agency" (Gell) 188
   artifacts of knowledge 171
   imperative xxx, 167
   innovation 124
   "myth of technological transcendence" 85, 90, 372
   "random event generator" 177
   ritual 139, 205, 232
   "technology of enchantment." 188
Tedlock, Barbara 113
Telefolmin people of the South Pacific 105-106
text(s) 62-63, 355
Theorizing Rituals: Issues, Topics, Approaches, Concepts (Kreinath, Snoek, Strausberg) 13
theory of ritual
   see ritual
thin and thick description xxx, 58-59
Thomas, Debi 217
Through the Looking-Glass (Carroll) 153
Tibetan xlii, 17, 104, 117, 134-135, 140, 142-143, 153, 155, 178, 187, 353, 355-358, 384
Triumph des Willens (*Triumph of the Will*) (Riefenstahl) 264
Trobriand Islanders 26, 188, 204-208
true, truing xxx, 58, 322
   and adaptation 100
   brain and 100-106
   culture and 108-111
   myth and 112, 116, 314, 329, 373
   of cognition 100, 106

ritual and 99-101, 119
Tukano Indians of the Amazon basin 152
Turnbull, Colin xl, 81
Turner, Victor 21-23, 63, 214, 252, 343
Tzotzil people of Highland Chiapas
    (Southern Mexico) 226-227

vacuum, physics of the 111-115, 214
Van Gennep, Arnold 251
Vogt, Evon 330

Wagner, Richard 147-148
Wallace, Anthony F. C. 16, 86, 118,
    162-163, 288, 308
Warner, Roy 70, 253
warp of consciousness (WOCs, warps)
    see consciousness
Way of the Shaman, The (Harner) 137
Whitehead, Alfred North xxxix
Whitehouse, Harvey 20-21, 23
Wholeness and the Implicate Order
    (Bohm) 112
Williams Obstetrics (Cunningham et al.)
    332
Wilson, Jack (Paiute Indian prophet,
    aka Wovoka) 223
Winkelman, Michael 4, 60-62, 371
witches, witchcraft 66-67, 102, 290
Witches, Midwives, and Nurses
    (Ehrenreich, English) 66
worldview
    see cosmology

Yahey, Charlie 311-314
Yanomamo Indians of Venezuela and
    Brazil 144

Zuckerman, Phil 19

www.ingramcontent.com/pod-product-compliance
Lightning Source LLC
Chambersburg PA
CBHW030103010526
44116CB00005B/82